Michael Bentine is p[...] founder member of [...] successful star of ra[...] recent years he has devoted more and more time to writing. His other books include *The Condor and the Cross, Templar, The Door Marked Summer* and *Open Your Mind*.

C000246992

Also by Michael Bentine

OPEN YOUR MIND

and published by Corgi Books

THE RELUCTANT JESTER

Michael Bentine

CORGI BOOKS

THE RELUCTANT JESTER
A CORGI BOOK 0 552 13653 0

Originally published in Great Britain by Bantam Press,
a division of Transworld Publishers Ltd

PRINTING HISTORY
Bantam Press edition published 1992
Corgi edition published 1993

Set in 10pt Linotype Plantin by
Chippendale Type Ltd, Otley, West Yorkshire.

Corgi Books are published by Transworld Publishers Ltd,
61–63 Uxbridge Road, Ealing, London W5 5SA, in Australia by
Transworld Publishers (Australia) Pty. Ltd, 15–25 Helles Avenue,
Moorebank, NSW 2170, and in New Zealand by Transworld
Publishers (NZ) Ltd, 3 William Pickering Drive, Albany, Auckland.

Made and printed in Great Britain by
Cox & Wyman Ltd, Reading, Berks.

To all my children, my grandchildren
and my great-grandchildren for
whom the adventure is still to come

NOTE

To write my life story and remain true to its content, parts of this book inevitably must refer to some incidents in my previous autobiography, *The Long Banana Skin*, now out of print.

I have lived seventeen eventful years since writing that first book. Inevitably, I have reassessed the key events of my life and describe them in greater depth. I have also remembered many other strange things that happened to me during those years.

Since 1975, my life has taken many more traumatic turns, most of them dipping into bathos on the way. These wildly varying events have convinced me that I was right to meet the twentieth century head on and to overcome my reluctance to view it through the eyes of a jester.

My sense of humour, which many times has saved my reason from tottering over the edge of the abyss, was inherited from my mother and sharpened by my brother. For which I thank them both with all my heart.

MB
November 1991

CONTENTS

Introduction

The Makings

My father, Adan (later Adam) Bentin, came from Peru and my mother, Florence Dawkins, came from Essex. Neither Mother nor her family had ever met a Peruvian and none of them had the vaguest idea where Peru was located. Pop might just as well have come from another planet. In fact, I am often asked, 'Where is Peruvia?'

My grandfather, Don Antonio Bentin Palamerra, was a silver miner. For eight years he was also Vice-President of the Republic and at his death was President-elect. He was a vital man, compassionate and sensitive and gifted with remarkable foresight. He had become a politician because he could not tolerate the rampant exploitation of the Peruvian Indians. He was acutely shy and had an almost pathological distaste for interrupting the interminable sittings of the Peruvian Senate in order to relieve himself. He kept a carriage and a fast horse waiting outside, specifically to race him back home to urinate.

This unnecessary strain on his bladder eventually caused his death from kidney failure at the age of fifty-five. Adan's mother had died shortly after he was born, and on his father's death, when he was four, he was looked after with great affection by his half-brother, Ricardo, Don Antonio's eldest son.

Adan dearly loved Ricardo, who often took him on visits to the family silver mines at Cerro de Pasco, high up in the Andes. One terrifying experience that Adan remembered with great clarity happened to them when he was about six years old.

Owing to a sudden worsening of the weather, Ricardo decided to spend the night in an old adobe hut in the mountains. To comfort his frightened little brother, Ricardo cuddled him to sleep in the same rickety bed.

During the night the storm cleared. Adan had slept soundly in his brother's arms, but he woke at sunrise. A slight sound had disturbed him and his eye was caught by a gleam of light reflected on something metallic. This seemed to be coming out of the wall near Ricardo's head. The little boy watched the twinkling point of light grow larger. Suddenly he realized that the blade of a machete was silently working its way through the mud-brick wall.

He sensed that he must not make a noise. Quietly shaking his brother awake, he pointed at the machete. The long knife had cut right through the wall and the hand holding it was circling as if searching for Ricardo's head. Ricardo grabbed his Colt revolver and shot the hand clean off. With a dreadful scream, the would-be assassin staggered off down the mountain.

On a previous occasion Adan had come close to death from shots fired by a drink-crazed sniper who had secreted himself behind a chimney on the roof of the family residence in Lima, a two-storey house built four-square round a central patio.

Unnoticed, four-year-old Adan had toddled out into the centre of the patio and the sniper's first shot missed him by inches. Before the man could fire again Adan's nurse, twelve-year-old Angelica, rushed out and threw herself on top of the little boy. The next shot wounded her, luckily not fatally, and before the sniper could fire a third time, Ricardo appeared and settled the matter with two shots from his revolver.

Don Antonio had seen that Peru badly needed well-educated leaders, and had decreed that five of his sons would be educated in Europe, in different countries so that each could master a contrasting academic discipline: engineering, law, science, medicine and the arts. Ricardo stayed in Peru to run the family silver mines. Arturo went to Heidelberg, Hernan to Madrid, José to the Sorbonne in Paris and Carlos to Milan.

In 1899 when Adan was thirteen, Ricardo, with a heavy heart, sent his youngest brother to England in accordance with Don Antonio's wish that he should study engineering there.

To get to England my father had first to cross the malaria-infested isthmus of Panama. Travellers crossed the isthmus on mule-back or were rushed through in a train, with every window and door close-netted against the mosquitoes which had killed half the men working on the Panama Canal. The Americans finally opened that important waterway in 1914.

At that time Adan had no knowledge of English, but he did have a natural gift for mathematics, a prerequisite for an engineering student. His guardian in Britain was Mrs Southery, a family friend who, after years in Peru, kept a large boarding house for foreign students in Holland Road, London. She became Adan's surrogate mother and he loved her dearly, always referring to her as 'Granny'.

Life was tough for a foreign schoolboy in Victorian England, but Adan (who for convenience changed the spelling of his name to Adam) learned the secret of living at peace within the chauvinist ethos of the time. He decided to be better at sport than his British schoolmates were, and succeeded.

Mrs Southery, a small Welsh lady, was a widow twice over and her son by her first marriage, William Hope-Jones, became Adam's closest friend. Adam's home life with the Southery family was further brightened by the presence of the twenty or so foreign students who boarded with them. This cheerful bunch of youngsters came from all over the world and picked up each other's languages with ease, although Granny insisted that they all spoke English in her presence.

Adam first went to Forest School near Epping and then the London School of Electromagnetism, where his mathematical ability came into its own.

While my father was turning into an anglophile, my mother was growing up in Westcliff, part of London's traditional playground, Southend-on-Sea.

Whereas my father's ancestral background could scarcely have been more exotic, with his family's mixed lineage of Spanish Conquistadors and Inca nobility, my mother's family tree went back to the kin of Daw, which is about as Anglo-Saxon as you can get.

When James Dawkins, my English grandfather, married Minnie, who was of Dutch descent, it caused quite a stir in the xenophobic Dawkins family. Little did they know that the younger daughter of that union would marry a Peruvian.

Grandfather Dawkins worked for the Southend Water Board. I believe he was the engineer who designed and built the local reservoirs, which still supply the towns of Leigh, Westcliff and Southend.

Florence, my mother, had four older siblings, James, Frank, Arthur, and Mary, all of whom she adored. Florence was a baby when her mother died, and she later came to regard her sister Mary as her surrogate mother.

According to my mother, life in Westcliff was prosaic and conventional, seasonally enlivened by the hordes of London cockneys who used to stream down in their thousands to neighbouring Southend to enjoy the Easter and summer breaks.

Mother often reminisced about her early days when the world was, supposedly, a more innocent place. 'But it wasn't all innocence and complacent middle-class morality,' she would chuckle. 'Your great aunt Nellie, a formidable woman, was a captain in the Salvation Army, and when I was old enough she took me with her on her forays into the Limehouse area of the London docks.

'It was a perilous part of London where the police

went around in twos, often accompanied by specially trained dogs. Murder was a frequent occurrence, and the Chinese population, who made up the bulk of Limehouse citizens, were involved in "Tong" wars fought between hatchet-wielding assassins from rival secret societies.

'Missionary work in Limehouse and the London docks was scary but Auntie Nellie, though she was small and slight, would stand no nonsense from anyone. She used to take me with her into every rough riverside pub, dive and doss-house, wherever she felt the Lord had work for her to do. But in all the time Auntie and I spent there, I never heard a man swear in our presence, and we were always treated with courtesy and consideration. There's no doubt about it. The Sally Army was genuinely loved in that poverty-stricken part of London.'

Ma also told me she used to keep half a brick in her handbag, just in case.

By 1910, when Adam graduated, with distinction, in electrical, mechanical and civil engineering, he had also acquired a number of years' experience of practical engineering, working in the locomotive sheds at Darlington and building large dynamos in Scotland.

When his four brothers had graduated from their various universities in Europe, they had returned home to Peru. But Adam, on receiving a substantial part of his inheritance, stayed in England and, somewhat surprisingly, in 1912 set himself up as a farmer in Devonshire.

His hobby was breeding show-jumpers and he was so successful at show-jumping that, riding Daisy, his favourite pony, he won most of the prizes at the local agricultural shows. News of these feats reached the Peruvian Ambassador, a family friend, who approached him to represent Peru at the next Olympic Games.

But Adam had other plans, too time-consuming to allow him to be diverted by sporting interests. He had become bored with farming and was now deeply interested in the mathematical and light-weight engineering problems of the infant science of aeronautics. Furthermore, he had built and flown successfully a number of large model aeroplanes.

During the course of these experiments he had become acquainted with a number of like-minded engineers, such as A.V. Roe, Tommy Sopwith, Geoffrey de Havilland, and T.M. Dunné, all of whom later became famous pioneers of aviation. Most of these enthusiastic young engineers and scientists were associated with the Royal Aeronautical Establishment of Farnborough and, by 1913, Adam, whose ideas were new and practical, was invited to visit this pioneering centre. From the moment he set foot on the premises, Adam realized that aeronautical engineering was his true *métier*.

Florence Dawkins, meanwhile, had fallen in love with the boy next door and they had got engaged. Then one day the world went mad. In June 1914 the Archduke Franz Ferdinand of Austria-Hungary and the Archduchess Sophie were assassinated in Sarajevo. Suddenly Europe was on the brink of war.

War was declared on 14 August 1914. Florence's fiancé, like so many young Britishers, immediately volunteered for the army and, before they could get married, left with the British Expeditionary Force for the Western Front, promising Florence that before Christmas he would return for their wedding. Tragically, he was soon reported 'Killed in action'.

Florence was heart-broken and her sister Mary wisely kept her busy, sending her up to London to help look after the children of some friends, whose father was away at the Front.

At the outbreak of the war Adam, being an electrical engineer, volunteered for the Royal Corps of Signals and was turned down flat. 'We can't have foreign nationals, especially non-Europeans, in the British army.'

He volunteered a second time, on this occasion for service in the Royal Flying Corps, and got the same treatment from the RFC recruiting board. However, a sensible young officer on the interviewing panel realized the real potential of my father's qualifications, took him aside and advised him to contribute his aeronautical engineering skills to the war effort.

Adam thought about it and decided that the young airman was right. He immediately sold his farm and his horses and moved up to London, getting himself a job as an aeronautical engineer and designer with the Vickers-Supermarine Aircraft Company, a new firm which specialized in building seaplanes and flying-boats for the Royal Navy.

In 1915, my father who was tone-deaf, and who was by no means the world's best businessman, was conned by a 'friend' into financing a music-school. In fact this turned out to be the best investment of his life for by sheer chance Miss Florence Dawkins happened to visit the school with a girl-friend.

Adam was strongly attracted to her and soon, despite his shyness, was courting the pretty English girl. Mother had finally come to terms with the death of her girlhood sweetheart. She was flattered and intrigued by her ardent Peruvian admirer, and she soon found herself attracted by his kindness, thoughtful generosity and quick intellect. In 1915 they were married at Marylebone Register Office.

For many wartime couples there was no honeymoon. My parents' consisted of a couple of days in a small hotel near London. From then on, Adam was busy dashing from Hythe in Hampshire, where the Supermarine works were located, to Felixstowe in Suffolk where the Short Brothers Company was building flying-boats and seaplanes. It may seem strange that my father was employed by two rival aircraft companies at the same time, but his talents had singled him out to be one of the small group of aeronautical engineers who had the necessary qualifications to become members of the newly-formed AID, Aeronautical Inspection Department. This was based at Farnborough and was solely concerned with aircraft safety, at a time when many young pilots were being killed by pushing their flimsy machines beyond their structural capabilities.

One of Adam's inventions was prompted by his inability to distinguish pitch in music. At that time the tension of rigging wires on the flimsy flying machines largely determined how safe they were. If the wires were too tight, they would over-stress the aircraft and cause them to break up during aerobatics. If they were too loose, the wings and other flying surfaces would sag and distort under the severe stresses of dog-fighting, with the same disastrous results.

The textbook test to determine the state of the rigging wires was by 'twanging' them and then tightening or loosening them in tune with the pitch of special tuning-forks supplied by the AID. My father recognized the National Anthem only when people stood up, and was unable to use the tuning-fork method of tensioning the wires. He therefore invented a gadget which he called the 'tensometer'. It was simple and effective, and the test rig was immediately adopted by the AID.

Seventy years after my father invented this important instrument and gave it, without securing patent rights, to the AID, the Royal Aeronautical Establishment presented me with a tensometer in a beautifully fitted case made for me by the young Farnborough apprentices. It is a treasured possession.

My brother Tony, named after our grandfather Don Antonio, was born in 1916, and gave my parents great joy. Although my father was being employed in a very responsible job dealing with secret aircraft development, as an alien – neutral or otherwise – he had to report to the local police station wherever he was working, and he worked in a number of different locations.

Food was a problem, especially as the family never lived long enough in any one place to get established and in wartime, even with rationing, knowing the right people determined how much you got. My mother told me a story that illustrates this.

My father and mother enjoyed their tea. Ma always said

that without tea the British would have lost both world wars. By 1916, tea was in short supply. Every grocer saw to it that his regular customers got what there was, but Ma was at a disadvantage because of the family's frequent moves.

One grocer, where my mother shopped for a time, told her that there was no tea available. Ma was about to pay for the rest of her meagre groceries when a large woman swept into the shop.

'I'll take my two pounds of tea now, Mr Brown,' the woman said imperiously.

Mother was furious. 'In that case, you won't need my order,' she said, bursting into tears and rushing out of the shop. As she was crossing the road a van drew up beside her. On its side were the words 'London Tea Company'.

The driver of the van asked what was the matter. Ma needed a bit of sympathy, so she told him.

'Don't worry, dear,' said the kindly cockney, 'I can let you have some. How about a couple of pounds of Darjeeling?'

My mother kissed him. What is more, the London Tea Company sent her two pounds of their excellent tea every other week for the rest of the war.

Slowly the Great War dragged on, killing millions and leaving a ghastly flotsam and jetsam of dreadfully wounded men and women in its wake. From sheer exhaustion hostilities finally ceased on 11 November 1918. The complacent world of the Victorian and Edwardian eras was so changed as to be unrecognizable. History only needed the vengeful Versailles Treaty to set the stage for the Second World War.

In 1920 my father was approached by the Peruvian government to come back and build the republic its new air force. He accepted and, with the blessing of his employers, he, my mother and four-year-old brother set off for Peru aboard the SS *Ortega*.

My mother, whose cheerful and outgoing personality made her extremely popular among passengers and crew alike, was able to relax in luxury and, what was much harder to do, she made my father relax as well and shed his usual shyness. They both enjoyed themselves while Tony, who was the only child aboard, was pampered by everybody.

Their arrival in Peru was epic, the entire family — around sixty of them — having turned up on the docks at Callao to welcome them. But then our Peruvian family seemed to think that my father had won the war single-handed.

Tony was another smash-hit and, to make their triumph complete, my parents had brought with them a tiny Shetland pony as a gift to the horse-loving Bentins.

For Ma it was another world. 'I had never seen anything like it. The contrast between Westcliff and Lima was unimaginable. I promptly started a migraine.'

My poor mother had suffered from these crippling sick-headaches from the time she was a girl. These attacks were so severe that at one time during the war the local doctor suspected my father of poisoning her.

The whole Bentin family had taken Ma and Tony to their ample bosoms and gave them the time of their lives. Moreover, Pop had been invited to join the board of the Bentin family business, and it now looked as though they would stay in Peru, but other events intervened.

First there was a revolution, with much shooting in the streets. This changed the government overnight and put an end to the plans for my father to build the Peruvian air force. Secondly, there was a bad earthquake which terrified my mother, who had no idea what they would be like. She once told me it sounded as though she was being run down by an express train. Thirdly, my mother was shocked by the enormous difference between the rich and the poor in South America. There was virtually no middle class. Either you were a *mestizo*, of mixed Spanish and Inca blood, like my family, and were rich and lived in a mansion on one of the broad *avenidas*, surrounded by servants. Or you were pure Indian and so poverty-stricken that you lived in a flimsy match-board shack or mud hut and slowly starved to death.

What finally persuaded them to return to England was the discovery that Ma was pregnant. In my mother's mind that meant only one thing: boy or girl, the coming child must be born British. So, after a year of the loving Bentin family embrace, my father, mother, brother and myself, by now kicking away inside Ma, set sail for England aboard the SS *Orcoma*.

Five months later I was born an Aquarian at Tusmore Lodge, Watford, Hertfordshire, early on a cold January morning in 1922. I was a fortnight late in hatching and my delivery was hastened by my mother taking large doses of raspberry tea, a traditional Dawkins remedy. Ma was a long time in labour, and as I finally emerged I bawled long and lustily. When the physicians smacked my small bottom I must have sensed that here was my first, inverted, head-on collision with the twentieth century. And, to this day, I am addicted to raspberries.

Chapter One

'Folkestone is Marvellous for Asthma'

By 1923 there was a crisis in my father's life. He had been suffering increasingly from bronchial asthma since the end of the war. It now began to affect him badly, forcing him to stop work. A specialist recommended an immediate move from Watford to the bracing air of the south coast of England.

'Folkestone, high up on its chalk cliffs, is marvellous for asthma.' The specialist exuded confidence, as though he knew what he was talking about. My father promptly sold up and we all moved to that Channel port. The doctor was right. Folkestone was marvellous for asthma. It nearly killed my father, when the Channel breezes gave him severe attacks three days a week. However, the family resources were so strained by the expensive move from Watford that we could not afford to move anywhere else. Mercifully, my father slowly became acclimatized to the ozone-rich air of the Straits of Dover, and the asthma attacks tailed off to a more bearable once a month.

At the start of our residence in Folkestone, we lived in rented accommodation at Elysée Mansions in Westbourne Gardens. The household consisted of Ma, Pop, Tony, me, Betty the cook and Nanny Ockenden.

When it came to the arrival of the Bentins, the people of this stuffy seaside resort made the prejudiced Southenders seem almost liberal. Folkestonians ranked South America with Africa and other dark continents. They could hardly believe my father was white. However, my parents had just enough income to be classified as 'retired gentlefolk' and my mother, who had a wicked sense of humour, dropped hints that Pop was descended from the 'famous Spanish Conquistadors'. That made him 'Spanish nobility' in the eyes of the super-snobs of Folkestone.

Consequently, we were given a position 'above the salt' in the resort's 'society', and Ma was allowed to join the bridge club, where she consistently won, owing to her outstanding ability as a player. This cemented her growing popularity, and the club members vied with each other to be her partner.

So that my mother could play bridge practically every afternoon, and thereby enhance the family income, Nanny Ockenden was engaged to look after me and my brother, who was at a local school.

I claim to remember Elysée Mansions from the age of four. I have a clear image of a tall, yellow-and-red-striped brick block of terraced Victorian buildings, of which we occupied the middle slice. This memory is vividly imprinted on my mind, because it was there that I had a tonsillectomy performed on me by a doctor who must have been drinking, because he not only gouged out my swollen tonsils but ripped out half my naso-pharynx as well. Even today, throat specialists look at the damage and wonder how anyone could have made such a mess of a simple tonsillectomy.

This unnecessarily brutal operation was carried out on the kitchen table, which had been well scrubbed and draped with a clean sheet for the occasion. The anaesthetic was administered by my sniffing it from a bottle through a two-pronged device in the rubber stopper. Anaesthesia was then maintained by more chloroform being dripped on to a gauze-covered tea-strainer held over my mouth and nose. The memory of its sickly-sweet smell remains with me. In fairness to my parents, who watched anxiously, this was not blatant child-abuse but a common surgical practice among general practitioners of that unenlightened era.

The shock of that savage operation caused me to lose my speech and I stammered badly from then on until I was cured by a speech-trainer at Eton. I was sixteen years old before I spoke normally.

My next medical memory was a year later when, by some superhuman feat of childish strength, I toppled a massive stone jardinière which landed on my feet, crushing them badly. That hurt even more than the tonsillectomy and I was carried home screaming. Once again, that filthy-smelling anaesthetic was used to knock me out, while the same inept, and probably half-pissed, doctor sewed up and splinted my damaged toes, leaving me with what my mother called 'cheap feet'.

When I was five we had just moved to a house in Bouverie Road West when I suffered severe stomach pains after eating some blackcurrant-flavoured pastilles. My parents brought in a new family doctor who was efficient, sober, and a welcome change for me until he probed my small unsuspecting rectum with a rubber-covered finger, and correctly diagnosed appendicitis.

The previous summer, my brother had been hit in the stomach by a cricket-ball and, after suffering similar severe pains in the abdomen, had been attended by the alcoholic doctor, who had diagnosed indigestion and pre-scribed castor-oil. The result was a burst appendix. My poor brother was rushed to the local nursing home, where it was discovered he had acute peritonitis. Just in time, an emergency operation was performed which saved his life, but while in care he caught a cross-infection of scarlet fever and was immediately shunted off to the Folkestone isolation hospital. This left him weak as a new-born puppy and required weeks of convalescence.

Because of this near-tragedy, my parents were not taking any chances with me and an immediate appen-dectomy was carried out in the same nursing home. By now, I was quite a veteran when it came to the gauze-covered tea-strainer method of administering anaesthetic and, once again, that nauseating smell stifled me into unconsciousness. By the time I woke up, I had developed a cross-infection of whooping-cough and promptly broke all my stitches. It took me weeks to get back into the swing of things.

Meanwhile, news had arrived from Peru of the death of the head of the family, Uncle Ricardo. Pop had been expecting this because Ricardo suffered from even worse asthma than Pop, and in addition was grossly overweight. Pop often told me that Uncle Ricardo, a massively built man, could lift a mule on his back, but he never explained why he should need to do so. Sadly, Uncle's mule-lifting days were over.

The good news was that, under the terms of Uncle Ricardo's will, my father had inherited a further share of my grandfather's estate. This meant that we could move to a bigger house. At this point, Ma had an inspiration. 'Why don't we *build* a house? We know an excellent architect, Seton Dahl. I'm sure he will design us a lovely home.'

Mother had met this gifted man at her bridge club. He was an outstanding architect, who later designed and built the revolutionary Leas Cliff Hall, which still juts out from Folkestone's tall cliff, securely anchored by huge reinforced-concrete cantilevers set deeply into the rock-face.

Dahl liked my mother for her skill at contract bridge and frequently dropped in for a game. He also admired my father for his engineering skills. He agreed to design and build us a house. It was called Belen, after the family house in Lima, and was sited next to a large playing-field belonging to a girls' school. It proved to be a happy home for us all. It was a spacious, white, Georgian-style house full of light, its upper storey set with large dormer windows, and it featured a nursery which ran the whole length of the attic.

We lived there contentedly for several years, but Ma had become hooked on house-building and when some-one made her an offer for Belen that she could not refuse, Seton Dahl designed us another charming white-stuccoed home, this time in the Dutch style with overhanging slate tiles, its wide windows flanked by louvred shutters. Pop called the new house Rimac, after the river that flows through Lima.

It was sited at the end of Pelham Gardens, on top of Sandgate Hill. Like Belen, Rimac also was built near playing-fields, but this time our new home overlooked the Channel. It was a delightful spot, enjoying a semi-rural aspect. However, as it was in such a favoured spot other people soon followed Mother's lead and built houses round us. Eventually, that splendid view was blocked, except from the dormer windows of the big attic nursery. Here I enjoyed hours gazing out at the distant ships as they passed majestically on their lawful occasions up and down the Channel. I was so fond of Rimac, with its well-proportioned, spacious rooms that, years later when I got married and had children of my own, I contemplated buying it.

In the twenties and thirties, Folkestone was at its most elegant, prosperous best. The harbour itself was little more than a long, tall grey-stone mole, with a fishing port at its landward end and a small inner basin which dried out at low tide. Therefore, the port was only partly responsible for the town's prosperity. It certainly could not compete as a Channel terminal with its rival, Dover.

The latter port, which lies seven miles further east, boasted a far bigger harbour, protected from the savage Channel gales by a massive outer breakwater. Consequently, Dover carried the bulk of the cross-Channel traffic.

This ancient Cinque Port also had the advantage of large, well-equipped docks and, in wartime, was an important naval base, controlling the entrance to the Channel with its batteries of long-range heavy artillery. The town's strategic importance was obvious, but it never prospered in peacetime as it did in war.

In complete contrast, Folkestone relied for its peacetime prosperity on its reputation as a seaside resort for the well-to-do. It was also a retirement centre for the elderly, especially for ex-army, navy and air force officers and their families. It enjoyed an outstanding position. Sweeping south from the foot of the lush, green-mantled North Downs, Folkestone spread out in a series of broad avenues lined with tall chestnut trees, until it perched high up in the bracing air on top of the Leas, a well-groomed grassy plateau which runs for nearly two miles along the summit of its rocky escarpment.

Below these tall cliffs lie a narrow strip of pine woods, some plantations of wind-sculpted bushes, a winding promenade surmounted by hundreds of small bathing-chalets, and the stony beaches themselves, with their miles of shifting pebbles, kept in place by dozens of dividing breakwaters.

In the twenties and thirties, Folkestone, which stretches over four miles from east to west, was class-consciously divided into the east cliff, covered with rows of small working-class two-up two-down terraced houses, and the west end of the town with its fine shops, imposing hotels, tall mansions and large family homes. At the western end of the Leas, which is marked by a Napoleonic-period Martello Tower, the town plunges down a steep hill towards the small, less fashionable fishing village of Sandgate.

Today Folkestone has a forlorn look, a once-wealthy Victorian matron fallen on hard times. Most of the great houses and many of the luxurious Edwardian hotels have been sub-divided into small holiday apartments and bed-sitting rooms, while the fine old shops are long since gone, their place taken by cut-price supermarkets. Mercifully, the repellent class-conscious snobbery has gone as well, for the town has become heavily commercialized in its new role as the British terminal for the Channel Tunnel.

There has been a heavy price to pay. Folkestone's unique setting between the rolling downs and the sea has been slashed through by the dark ribbon of the M20 motorway to Dover. Even worse, the lovely valley that once graced the western approach to the town has been ripped apart to accommodate the complex maze of railway-lines and sidings which mark the entrance to the 'Chunnel'.

In the twenties Folkestone bore many scars from its recent wartime role. These were not so apparent on the structure of the town, but they were clear for all to see among its people. The Star and Garter Home for the gravely wounded was filled with tragic human debris. Limbless men, sightless men, the mindless staring of the shellshocked and the racking coughs of the survivors of poison gas, all served to remind us of the price of Empire. Some of these human wrecks were wheeled out once a year to huddle round the Folkestone war memorial at the top of the Road of Remembrance, the steep hill down which these shattered men had marched so proudly only a few years before.

That picture stands out in my mind, because every 11 November, Remembrance Day, we local schoolboys, wearing our red Flanders poppies, walked in long, chattering crocodiles to the top of that hill, to stand in wondering groups round the laurel-wreathed granite Memorial Cross for the obligatory two minutes silence for the glorious dead.

Furthermore, many of my schoolfriends were war-orphans. Others had fathers who had lost an arm or a leg, sometimes both limbs. Often a parent's face was heavily scarred. Some men wore a black patch to hide an empty eye-socket, or they concealed both sightless eyes behind dark glasses. I still recall trying to shake hands with one parent who wore an artificial arm. He bravely made a joke of it, but I never forgot my shocked realization that his hand was made of carved wood.

Considering what they had to endure and the meagre pensions that most of them received for all their sacrifice and suffering, these were warm and friendly men who loved their children. Despite their appalling physical disabilities, many of them still played strenuous games with their young families and friends. To me, that was courage of the highest order. I have seen it equalled but never surpassed.

Taken overall, my life between the wars in Folkestone unfolded without too many surprises. But there were highlights that stand out in my memory. One vivid recollection was of toddling along the Leas, holding my father's hand, waiting for Lindbergh to fly up the Channel at the end of his epic crossing of the Atlantic. At that early age I was firmly convinced that he would wave to me as he passed by in his flying machine. When he failed to show up, having chosen a shorter route to Paris, I burst into tears. I do not think I ever forgave him.

Twice during my boyhood big ships were stranded on the shoreline, driven on to the beaches when they lost their rudders during savage Channel gales. How enormous those vessels seemed to be, with their stranded rust-stained hulls towering high above me like huge beached metal whales.

Then there was the big monoplane that survived a spectacular emergency landing on the narrow strip of beach at Seabrook. After engine failure near the coast, the skilled pilot somehow brought his motorless machine in low over the surf and pancaked the plane on to the perilously narrow stretch of pebble-beach. Rushing up the steep slope in a shower of small stones, the plane came to a screeching halt with its wooden propeller almost touching the solid stone wall of the seafront. I clearly remember my father's words of wonder and admiration at the superb airmanship of the pilot.

Some tragic memories also stand out in my mind. One awful day, thousands of seabirds were covered in crude oil when a tanker skipper pumped out the dregs of his ship's tanks near the coast. Many bird-lovers, in which Folkestone abounded, assisted the coast-guards and the RSPCA in trying to clean the birds' feathers. Detergent had not been invented and almost every seabird died, presenting the shocking spectacle of thousands of stinking black bundles of feathers heaped along a full mile of the Folkestone beaches.

My first encounter with death and human tragedy was while out for a walk along the Leas with Nanny Newman, who joined us after Nanny Ockenden retired. It had been raining and the roads were wet but the sun had broken through, quickly dispersing the earlier mist and cloud. We had just rounded the corner of one of the roads leading off the Leas when a powerful motorcycle combination raced past us. It was ridden by a leather-coated rider in helmet and goggles, with a similarly clad young woman clinging excitedly to him on the pillion. In the open side-car was an older woman with two children cheering him on.

The rider took the sharp corner much too fast and the machine skidded viciously, the tyres shrieking and the passengers all screaming with terror. In an awful instance, while the horrified man desperately fought for control, the heavy three-wheeled motorcycle combination smashed head on into an open-topped charabanc, filled with day-trippers. One moment the scene was full of laughter and excitement and in the next few seconds the road was littered with the broken bodies of the dead and dying, while the air was filled with the screams of the injured. The motorcycle combination was a flattened, twisted wreck, half of it sticking out from under the crumpled front of the bus.

Nanny Newman covered my eyes and ears but she was torn between two responsibilities, whether as a trained nurse to help the victims of the smash or to get me away from the scene as quickly as possible. She was able to do both. Hurrying me back round the corner she met a family friend.

Leaving me with her, Nanny did what she could to help the victims. Many of the local residents rushed out of their houses when they heard the crash and the screams, and immediately set about dealing with the casualties. At least the recent experience of war had been of some use.

At Folkestone we had a broad tidal range. At low tide the beaches stretched far out, revealing rocks covered with limpets, cockles and winkles. As children, we had a wonderful time collecting them. When the tide was in, the surge of the sea reached almost to the foot of the tall seawall which carried the three-mile sweep of the Lower Promenade.

During storms and unbeknown to our parents, my brother and I often played at dodging dense showers of pebbles thrown high by waves thundering against the seawall, raising great towers of green water topped with grey foam. We dodged the pebbles by jumping behind the rows of bathing-cabins which lined the upper side of the promenade, and which were safely perched behind thick, pebble-dash walls. It was a wildly exciting, if dangerous, sport and we thoroughly enjoyed it. But despite the game of wave-dodging, I have always had an irrational fear of tidal waves.

There was the ornate Victorian iron-work pier, complete with a 'hard-hat' diver who, for a small fee, sang 'I'm Forever Blowing Bubbles' while working on the bottom inside his traditional copper helmet and heavy rubberized-canvas diving suit. This only happened during the season, which started at Easter and continued until the middle of September. There was also a one-legged spring-board diver, a war amputee who, for a small donation, dived off a plank set high up on the pavilion at the end of the pier. His meagre takings depended entirely on the generosity of the watching crowd. It seemed to me to be a degrading way for a brave man to make a living.

Great War memorabilia were displayed prominently around the district. Apart from the war memorial, there was a wartime airship hangar, which had once housed Royal Navy 'blimps' used for spotting submerged U-boats sneaking their way through the Straits of Dover. At Hythe, there was a captured German 76-mm field gun and a large British tank. Both these relics of war on the Western Front fascinated me and were the delight of hundreds of other boys in the area, who endlessly played war-games with them.

One of my greatest delights was a visit to the New Romney, Hythe and Dymchurch Railway, which was then being built. This wonderful fifteen-mile-long, passenger-carrying, one-third scale model of a whole railway system has attracted me ever since, at the age of five, I 'helped' the gangs of Irish plate-layers, the 'Gandy Dancers' as they were called, to build that miniature track. It was while giving them my unasked-for assistance that I heard my first Irish phrase, 'Piss off, yer little bastard, or Oi'll break your fockin' arm!' I still have a postcard showing me as a golden-haired little boy solemnly shaking hands with the driver of one of those beautiful trains.

As well as the miniature railway, the whole broad stretch of the Romney Marsh, with its long-walled foreshore and its golden sands, provided me with many wonderful memories.

To some people, especially if they do not know the 'Levels', Romney Marsh is flat and boring. These reeded flatlands stretch well over seventeen miles, from the outskirts of Hythe, running past the famous Hythe School of Musketry, backing Dymchurch, New Romney, Littlestone, Greatstone, Dungeness and Camber, until they come to an end past the Cinque Port of Rye.

The northern border of the Levels is formed by the long chalk escarpment at its back. This is carpeted with rich downland grass, and keeps much of the Marsh free from the savage northeasterly gales, for winter on these flatlands can be fearsome. I know, because as teenagers, a friend and I got lost during a sudden snowstorm that quickly turned into a complete white-out. Luckily we found shelter in an isolated farmhouse, otherwise we surely would have frozen to death.

In summer, the Levels are quite different. Then the water-meadows are liberally sprinkled with clover, cowslips, guelder-roses, cuckoo-flowers, meadowsweet, flag irises, and water violets. Hawthorn, wild cherry, elderberries and sloes abound. The reeded dykes are lined with bulrushes, clattering together as they sway in the wind. Everywhere, dandelion puff-balls shed their seeds, to float on the breeze like tiny paratroopers, carrying the weed all over the marshes. At night, the darkness is alive with the croaking of millions of frogs that live in the maze of water-courses and the bordering Military Canal.

When I was a boy, this whole scene was as near to an Arcadian idyll as I could imagine. This was mainly because there were so few people abroad on the Levels. It still is sparsely populated. But, apart from that one terrifying time in the snowstorm, Romney Marsh has never been a lonely place for me. I always had my imagination to keep me company, and I peopled those winding tracks with Roman legionaries, Saxon serfs, and squires and knights on their way to Rye to cross the Channel in a broad-beamed cog to fight in the Hundred Years War with France. Then, in a flash, I would change the scene and fill the Marsh with wily smugglers and grim revenue men, engaged in the deadly game of hide and seek that has cost so many lives over the centuries.

Folkestone and its countryside provided me with a wonderful childhood background, irrespective of the seasons of the year. At the early stirrings of spring, the endless rows of steel-grey Channel rollers lose their winter crowns of gale-driven spume and flow through the narrow Strait with a gentler rhythm, the waves becoming greener in colour and often half-hidden in a warm, low-lying mist. This is the time when the apple and cherry trees burst into a glory of white and pink blossom, and all too soon shed this rich mantle on to the new spring grass. At the foot of the hills, flocks of unshorn sheep stand guard over their new-born lambs.

Groves sacred to the Great God Pan and shrines to Mithras had been planted by the Roman legions nineteen centuries before our present era, and whispers of their memory still haunted the woods which covered the countryside at the foot of the North and South Downs. Rudyard Kipling called them 'The old things of England'. For me, this mystical countryside was full of them.

Some of my favourite memories are of Christmas time. This was because there was always plenty of dazzling white snow from the downs to the foreshore, and with it came all the delights of winter sports. As yet, skiing was not the sport of the people. Instead, young and old, we tobogganed down the slopes on everything from expensive wooden luges and home-made sleds to tin-trays and the seat of the pants. During that short season of goodwill, Folkestone appeared to change into something better. For a few wonderful days, the old class divisions seemed to melt away. It was a season of laughter and joyous activity, full of happy memories.

One slight drawback was Ma's penchant for making Christmas presents for her friends. She felt that buying a present was not enough. For her, it was the spirit of giving that counted, and the effort you put into it.

From an economic point of view this made sense. We were not well off in the Folkestone sense of the word, but owing to Ma's skilful management of the family funds we enjoyed a reasonable standard of living. That made us extremely fortunate in comparison with many other families during the Depression. But expensive Christmas presents were out of our reach.

So, from the end of August, right up to the week before Christmas, the Bentin family was busily engaged in manufacturing suitable gifts, their form being determined by Mother's whim of the moment.

One year it was 'useful' hearth-brushes, made of short lengths of springy manila rope, cut laboriously from a heavy coil of sub-standard ship's hawser purchased from a local boatyard. These recalcitrant pieces of rope, which seemed to possess a diabolic life of their own, could be forced into a tight loop to form the handle, which was then quickly bound in place with yards of raffia. We next painted them and liberally sprinkled the looped handle with 'gold-dust', leaving the worst job till the last. This consisted of teasing out the rope's ends to form the bristles of the brush. It sounds easy enough to do, but in practice it was the sort of task that His Majesty's prisoners were forced to do. Picking oakum in Dartmoor gaol must have been much the same and probably just as hard on the fingernails.

Unsuspected by us, there was built-in obsolescence in these unusual hearth-brushes. With the heat of the fire the retaining raffia became brittle and broke, releasing the tightly looped manila hawser with a loud bang. If this happened while the brush was held in the hand it inflicted only superficial skin damage, but with one elderly person it precipitated a heart attack, luckily not fatal. On the whole it was not a popular gift, and the obligatory letters acknowledging its receipt had a chilly tone.

The following year we made a floral display using dried poppy-heads on sticks, intended by Ma to brighten the winter of the recipients. These bulbous seed pods were painted in various bright colours and sprinkled with the same 'gold-dust', which seemed to clog every bodily orifice of the unfortunate family member assigned to the task. Only a thorough soaking in the bath removed the clinging gilt particles from the most intimate parts.

These floral displays, like the booby-trapped hearth-brushes, also contained an unexpected self-destruct mechanism. As a result of an odd reaction with the paint, they would suddenly crumble, filling the room with poppy seeds and a fine penetrating dust, with dire results for anyone who suffered from allergies.

But Ma's masterpiece was the matchbox filled with hundreds of non-safety matches. These we tastefully covered in highly inflammable green velour fringed with gold braid, and glued on with volatile rubber solution. The part which turned it into an infernal machine was the finishing touch, a long gold tassel sewn firmly by Ma on to the stout tab which, when pulled, opened the matchbox. If tugged incautiously this could cause the instant ignition of the entire contents of 500 phosphorus matches, with the consequent loss of facial hair of one bearded opener, who until then had been a close family friend.

The next year, when we called to deliver our Christmas offerings, we found few of the intended recipients at home. I suspect they were there, keeping under cover when they saw us coming, ignoring repeated ringing of their door bells, and praying that we would go away with our parcels undelivered.

Perhaps this was just as well, as that year Mother had purchased a quantity of even larger matchboxes, with twice the amount of chemically unstable contents. Appropriately, they were called Lucifer matches. That was also the year when one friend's stately home burst into flames. Arson was suspected, but never proved.

Chapter Two

Peruvian Invasion

The first visit, in 1929, of members of the South American Bentin contingent caused quite a stir in Folkestone.

As Peruvian women of that time never went out alone, my young and extremely attractive first cousin Rosita was properly chaperoned by her mother, Aunt Rosa, Don Ricardo's widow, and her elder brothers, Antonio and Pedro.

This was my first contact with my Peruvian relations and it was an exciting experience. Like all South Americans they loved children, and my brother and I were overwhelmed with their affection and kindness.

Father had not forgotten his Castilian Spanish, and I remember listening with pride and wonder to his rapid exchanges in that musical language, which they all seemed to speak at the same time. They also gesticulated extravagantly while they spoke, for our relations had opened the door to my father's real temperament, normally closed because of his shyness, and now he was every bit as animated and Latin as they were themselves.

Aunt Rosa was small, slim and white-haired, and at first seemed formidably austere, dressed in her widow's black. Her high cheekbones, small features and total composure, except when speaking volubly, were indicative of her Spanish Hidalgo background. So was her pale complexion which, according to my mother, was typical of South American ladies, who spent almost all their time indoors looking after their large families and rarely went out into the sun unless suitably covered with a shawl or mantilla.

Ma told me my aunt wore many petticoats which she used as a kind of personal filing system, her keys being in one layer and her chatelaine in another, while she kept a small pair of scissors in a leather case in a third underskirt.

Aunt Rosa's English was almost non-existent. When speaking to me, it was confined to, 'Kees me, and I geeve you chocolate.' She would give me a warm hug and a dazzling smile, which completely changed her whole personality from withdrawn widowhood to loving aunt. She also spoiled me by slipping me delicious French Marquise de Sévigné chocolates whenever she thought my mother was not looking.

Rosita was eighteen years old, petite and slim like her mother, but totally different in every other way. Whereas Aunt Rosa was reserved and composed, my cousin was animated and excitable, her elfin face alive with sparkling personality and her mouth always on the verge of laughter.

She adored her two brothers, who obviously returned her affection, and the four of them made a wonderfully refreshing change from the normal restraint of our Folkestone friends. My Peruvian family taught me the importance of touch, hugging and embracing us at every opportunity. This was something I had experienced with my mother more than with my father, but in no way was our normal show of family affection on the scale that I enjoyed with my uninhibitedly tactile Peruvian relations. The joyous memory of it remains with me to this day, and I freely bestow that warm *mestizo* embrace on family and friends alike, sometimes to their surprise and even embarrassment.

Antonio and Pedro could not have looked less alike, the former being small and dapper and the latter being taller and more sturdily built. Their features also bore little family resemblance to each other. Antonio looked like his mother and sister, while Pedro's face was larger and his complexion more swarthy, an inheritance from his father. Only in temperament were the brothers similar, both being warm and affectionate, with a parallel enjoyment of life and laughter.

At that time foreign languages were almost unheard in Folkestone, except during the summer invasion by French day-trippers. My relations' animated flow of Castilian Spanish, accompanied by their dramatic gestures as they enthusiastically shopped in the town, stopped many of the locals in their tracks. Had the Martians landed, they could scarcely have made more impact.

The Bentins were accompanied by Pop and Ma on these expeditions, Pop acting as interpreter and Ma as economic adviser. This inhibited my South American family in no way, and their admiring cries of '*Muy bien hecho!*' and '*Ay, que linda!*', meaning 'Very well made!' and 'How beautiful!' rang out as they minutely examined the goods or stopped in wonder at the sight of a pretty blond child.

When the management of the shops realized that they were dealing with wealthy foreigners rather than with French trippers who handled everything and bought practically nothing they were served attentively. This earned the shops a small fortune, because the Peruvian Bentins were taking the opportunity to shop for the entire family in Peru.

One typical South American trait was my aunt's conviction that she should haggle over the price of every purchase. This was normal practice in Peru, and Aunt Rosa found it difficult to accept that this was not the case in Britain.

'What do you mean, Adancito?' she said to my father. 'The shop cannot expect me to pay the price marked on the ticket. Of course we must make them an offer. After all, we are paying cash.'

The purchase in question was a large number of sterling silver articles which Aunt Rosa was buying for various members of the family who were getting married, or being christened, or about to be confirmed, or who otherwise were 'in need' of English silver tea-sets, coffee-pots, serving trays, cigarette boxes, flatware, bonbon dishes, candlesticks and other items.

The bill came to several hundred pounds and my aunt was determined to make an offer which would give her a decent discount. Pop took the manager aside and said, 'My sister-in-law seldom comes to Europe and this is her first visit to England. I'm sure you can explain how different things are over here. I'll translate for you.'

The manager was courtesy itself. 'How much discount is your sister-in-law requiring?' Aunt Rosa remained firm on her figure of 10 per cent.

The manager made some calculations and smiled, 'We will be delighted to give it to you, Señora.'

When my surprised father translated this, his sister-in-law smiled complacently. 'You see, Adancito, if you don't ask, you don't get! Now, what about the *yapa*?'

My father groaned with embarrassment, but explained the new request to the amused manager. 'In Peru, it is also the custom for the shop to give a small added item, gratis, if the purchase warrants it. For example, even if you only buy a few yards of ribbon, the shop throws in a *yapa*, such as a packet of pins.'

The manager was somewhat taken aback. 'I'll see what I can do.' He went into his office. In a few moments he returned with a small silver cream-jug in the shape of a cow. With a courteous bow he handed it to my aunt. 'Señora Bentin, your *yapa*.'

The South American Bentins left the town in triumph, having become the toast of the Lord Mayor's annual ball. This was held at the Grand Hotel, where they were staying, a favourite summer resort of the King of the Belgians. The Bentins' success had been assured when Antonio and Rosita, who were both good dancers and who had consumed just the right amount of champagne, demonstrated a 'real' smouldering South American tango, with Rosita holding a rose between her teeth. No-one there, wildly applauding at this skilled display, had the slightest idea that the gentlest of mickeys was being taken. As far as Folkestone society was concerned that was the authentic way people danced the tango in Peru.

My relations' visit clinched our position in the town's snobby club society. My mother's tongue-in-cheek hints at the bridge club that we were descended from Spanish Conquistadors were now universally accepted. Pop was even asked to join the Folkestone golf club but, having been turned down on a previous occasion by the racist committee, Pop declined the 'honour' and joined the Hythe golf club instead, where he prospered as a golfer, eventually playing off a handicap of four, and winning the coveted Borough of Hythe golf trophy. I still cherish that fine silver replica of a small medieval ship, copied from Hythe's Cinque Ports emblem. It must have been the only time that very British golf trophy was ever won by a Peruvian.

I was delighted to have such loving relations, just as I was very fond of my British family in Westcliff and Southend who were more restrained than my Peruvian relatives but just as loving. It was only when I went to school, aged six, that I began to realize that I was considered to be a dago and would have to live with that 'stigma' for the rest of my life. At least that is how things seemed to be when, in floods of tears, I told my mother that this was what the other little boys were calling me.

Ma was a wise woman. 'But you and your brothers *are* dagoes, and what is more you should be proud of it. Your grandfather was Vice-President of Peru for over eight years, and your uncle Ricardo enjoyed the same honour for twelve years. Both of them were also mayor of Lima, and each of them died President-elect. Now, how many of the other boys can say that about their families?'

I never again felt badly about the name-calling. As far as I am concerned, I am a dago and proud of it.

The real problem at school was the headmaster, a tall, gaunt man of craggy severity who, to the parents, was all rugged charm and bluff British bonhomie, but to his boys was a tyrant of the worst kind. He was racially bigoted and thought nothing of his pupils unless they fitted into his ideal mould of what a young Britisher should be. He cared even less about their schoolboy problems, except when they were exceptionally good at sport, which seemed of paramount importance to him.

That he was an accomplished scholar is undeniable. He was also a fine draughtsman as well as being an excellent actor, who read aloud the classics with great skill, but his unstable temperament was totally unsuited to his chosen career. He was far too short-tempered and physically unrestrained to be given the power to shape the lives of his young pupils. Yet he was so adroit in his handling of the parents that they believed him rather than their sons, putting it down to schoolboy exaggeration when we complained about his sadistic behaviour.

He would stand me, aged seven, either alone or with another boy who had offended him, on our chairs. Then he would slap the backs of our bare legs with a bamboo ruler while intoning a kind of ritual in the grating voice we all dreaded, 'You're a lazy, idle little boy. That's what you are, a lazy, idle little boy.'

With my appalling stammer, I found it very difficult to answer his insistent questions, even when I knew the answers. He sensed this and would wait cruelly until I was about to speak and then deliberately interrupt me with that demonic ritual. It was an act of pure malice. Along with the few of us who survived the war, I have never forgotten him.

That was when I learnt to weep silently, because any loud protestations only made matters worse. My brother had the same bitter experiences. I remember that a small Jewish boy also became the object of sadistic attention. He was a bright and withdrawn lad who became a good friend. His life must have been hellish.

Those six years of fear and frustration under this man's tyranny caused me to experience the only resentment I ever felt towards my mother and father. But in fairness to Pop and Ma, nearly all the boys at that unhappy place had the same problem with their parents.

It was only when he went too far with one tough lad, whose even tougher father was a bookmaker and could not have cared less about any scandal, that the power of this cruel and unbalanced man was finally curbed.

Meanwhile, an event occurred in our family that changed the course of all our lives. My father had been asked to drive a family friend to a spiritualist meeting which was being held in a bungalow near the aerodrome at Hawkinge. Presiding over this unusual gathering was the widow of an RAF pilot who had been killed in a crash near the airfield a few years before.

Pop, being a shy man, was reluctant to go but Mother was insistent. The small bungalow was crowded with women, which made my father even more uncomfortable. Accordingly, he fitted himself inconspicuously into a corner at the back of the room.

The spiritualist meeting opened with a short prayer, and a hymn was sung in which my tone-deaf father wisely declined to join. Then a large lady, the visiting medium from Canterbury, gave personal messages to some of the women, none of which meant anything to anyone else present, least of all to Pop.

Quite unexpectedly, she sought out my father sitting in the shadows at the back of the room. 'I feel I want to come to you sir.'

As Pop was the only male, this was of some interest to the twenty or so women present. Several of them turned round to look at him.

'Do you know the name Bolton, sir? There is a young lady in the spirit world who is telling me this. She says you know the name Bolton.'

My father squirmed with embarrassment. 'I'm sorry, I'm afraid I don't know anyone of that name.'

'The young lady is saying that Bolton is not her name.

It is the name of a town. Does that ring a bell, sir?'

'I'm afraid not. I don't remember ever having been to a town called Bolton.'

The medium was unabashed. 'The young lady is saying that she wants to thank you for what you did for her, in Bolton, many years ago when you were a young man.'

'I am very sorry,' Pop said firmly, 'but I don't know what the young lady is talking about.'

The medium still persisted. 'The young woman is getting very excited. She tells me that this will convince you. Her message is about a theatre in Bolton. Are you a "theatrical", sir?'

'No, madam. I am an engineer.'

The medium seemed puzzled. 'Well, sir, the spirit world is showing me the stage of a theatre. The young lady says that you will know what she is talking about, because there is an *auction* being held on the stage. Do you understand what she is saying?'

'My God!' my father whispered, then said in a firmer voice, 'Yes, I *do* remember. It was all such a long time ago, I just couldn't place the message at first. I'm sorry I took so long to understand the message. Thank you.'

By now the medium was beaming. 'No, sir. It is *you* the young lady wishes to thank. She is so excited. She says you were very kind to her, and that she is so happy that, through her message, you will now become very interested in our spiritualist movement. She says, "God bless you!" '

When he got home, Pop gathered us all together and told us what had happened. My mother was surprised because Pop had never before mentioned his theatrical adventure. I believe he had never told anyone else about it except Granny Southery.

What made the whole thing so convincing to my father was that no-one at the meeting could have known of the strange circumstances, twenty-seven years before, when he had arranged the auction of the costumes and props of a failed touring company in Bolton and had given one of the actresses money to keep going.

From that moment our lives changed. Until then I had received a conventional Church of England upbringing, with prayers at assembly in the morning and an occasional visit to the local church. I was soon surrounded by all the trappings of a full investigation into the mysterious world of the supernormal, as it was then called.

My father considered it very important that h.; sons should participate in this psychic research as part of our education, and he used both Tony and myself as guinea-pigs. This may seem to have been an ill-considered move on my father's part but my father never did anything without a great deal of thought, and he had reached this decision only after long deliberation, and consultation with my mother.

He later told me that he instinctively realized that these researches were going to be impossible to repeat, because they would deal with living beings who are naturally in a constant stage of change, and he wanted us to witness the experiments.

Both my brother and I were willing subjects, with a healthy curiosity and total trust in Pop's ability to handle any problems.

It soon became obvious to us, even me, that genuine mediumship resulting in paranormal phenomena cannot be turned on and off like a tap. Its validity seems to depend largely on the state of mind of the medium at the time and partly on the circumstances in which the research is undertaken. In the case of my father's investigations, the most effective results were obtained in the friendly atmosphere of our own home, where the medium under test felt comfortable and relaxed.

Sometimes it happened spontaneously, and on other occasions, even when the circumstances appeared to be ideal, nothing whatsoever would happen. This did not necessarily mean that the medium was a fake, for in many cases we had previously had excellent results with the same person.

My father was not trying to prove, or disprove, the

existence of extrasensory powers. As a scientist, he was observing the phenomena closely, making careful records of each incident and evaluating them at his leisure. Moreover, he was not alone in these researches. My mother's down-to-earth and perceptive nature was invaluable to him. Her wit always maintained the balance between the mystical and the practical. It was not easy for Ma, for most of her bridge-club 'friends' disapproved, and some even deserted her when they found out that the Bentin family was 'dabbling in the occult'. But a number of her real friends, who themselves had experienced similar inexplicable phenomena, kept in touch and took a keen interest in what we were doing.

During his research Pop met a number of other valid investigators with whom he shared his findings. Among them was Air Marshal Sir Hugh Dowding, who told me many years later, when he generously allowed me to interview him for the BBC, that he was convinced he had been 'guided' throughout his life, and especially during the Battle of Britain.

Slowly and with infinite care, my father built up a small team of dependable colleagues whose qualifications and integrity matched his own. These included two retired friends who were members of the Inner Magic Circle, the organization of professional and amateur stage-magicians. Major Webster and Arthur Condy both possessed outstanding sleight of hand and their extensive knowledge of how theatrical illusions were performed ideally suited them for the detection and exposure of fraudulent mediums, of whom, sadly, there were plenty, whether as a result of deliberate charlatanry or self-delusion.

We examined every known facet of the supernormal, including table-turning, Ouija board, the use of the up-turned glass, crystal-gazing, palmistry, tarot, automatic-writing, and physical mediumship such as telekinesis, levitation and materialization. This was in addition to clairvoyance, clairaudience and psychometry.

In other words, my family and our colleagues investigated any and every form of known physical or predictive mental paranormal phenomena, no matter how strange the manifestations might be. We concluded a phenomenon was genuine only after we were convinced it could not be explained by the accepted tenets of physical science.

I have often been asked whether these excursions into the realms of the supernatural had any harmful effects on me, either then or in later life. In my case it was the reverse, and I believe this applied to my brother as well. Up to this time I had been nervous of the dark and suffered from the usual childish fear of ghosts, ghouls, haunted graveyards and other archetypal monsters of the unconscious mind. But in the security of our own home, with the reassuring presence of my parents, elder brother, and occasionally family friends, all of whom I could trust, why should I have felt nervous? Rather, I felt a sense of wonder at the genuine paranormal phenomena and I discovered a growing ability to separate the real from the fraudulent mediums.

This new viewpoint on life and death, and my close involvement with my parents' researches, also gave me sufficient strength to endure the 'psychic attacks', by which I also mean psychological attacks perpetrated against me and my schoolfriends by that demoniacal headmaster.

Those early days of research were filled with marvels. Several of the lesser-known mediums were downright charlatans and others were self-deluded, but a surprising number of the mediums we tested were believed to be genuine, even by my parents' exacting standards. Furthermore, the predictive information they gave us was accurate way above the mathematical laws of chance. This was an important criterion for my mathematician father.

This is the sort of prophetic message we received: 'There will be another Great War seven years from now. [This was in 1932.] It will once again start in Germany and last for many years, but it will be quite unlike the last war. There will be a different sort of fighting, and the whole world will be involved. Completely new kinds of aeroplanes and other amazing weapons you have not dreamed of will play an important part in the course of the war. This country will have to fight hard for survival, and it will suffer great hardship. It will be bombed heavily, with many dead and wounded in our cities. But we will win in the end. As a family, you will all survive. You will suffer and endure hardship, but none of you here will be killed or wounded.'

Among the most convincing predictive evidence we received in the mid-thirties was some that concerned my parents and both of us boys. In 1938, my father and mother were told that they soon would leave Folkestone and settle in London, a most unlikely eventuality. Yet, by 1940, my parents were forced to leave the coast.

About the same time my brother was told that he would do well as an artist, but that drawing and painting would not be his final profession, which would be in business. The latter part of that prediction seemed as unlikely as the thought of our parents leaving their home in Folkestone. But that is precisely what happened to Tony, who gave up painting after the war and went into advertising.

Two different mediums told me, in 1935 and 1936, that my ambition to be a Royal Air Force pilot would never be fulfilled, but that I would be involved with the RAF, in wartime, in another capacity. One medium told me that I would have considerable success in a theatrical career. In 1934, when that prediction was made, I could hardly speak because of my appalling stammer, yet that medium proved to be absolutely correct.

When our regular sittings at home became a part of my life, my mind slowly opened to the infinite horizons of creative thinking, a door through which I have passed many times, with great rewards. I cannot remember more exciting or more rewarding times than these. They spanned my emergence from boyhood and youth to early manhood, when I entered the tough world of show

49

business, and later experienced horrific events during my wartime service with the RAF. Had I not been so carefully prepared to deal with the esoteric side of life, and so painstakingly conditioned by both parents to cope with the sort of extreme emergencies that I eventually had to face, I do not believe I would have survived. From a frightened, inarticulate little boy, I grew into a resourceful person, capable of sensing the onset of many normally unforeseeable dangers.

Chapter Three

Into the Fourth Dimension

My parents chose table-turning as their main method of paranormal communication. This was because it required none of the paraphernalia of the other methods then in use. There were other reasons for selecting this technique. For instance, their objection to using tarot cards, which constantly needed shuffling and laying out in patterns, was that the results had to be interpreted, a skill that required years of study and application. They mistrusted Ouija boards and the use of the upturned glass, both of which needed a smooth surface covered with letters and numbers over which to move and spell out their messages. Moreover, my parents believed that, like crystal-gazing, these techniques positively invited self-deception and, in the case of the crystal, self-induced hallucination as well.

Neither my father nor my mother attempted to develop automatic-writing, whereby the pen or pencil in the hand of the writer becomes the instrument of another intelligence. This form of mediumship also tends to over-encourage the intervention of the unconscious mind of the writer, sometimes leading to obsession and subsequent possession. However, my parents did investigate several mediums who were automatic-writers, one of whom was outstanding.

They both considered palmistry, and sand-scrying – the individual interpretation of patterns in sand – to be a means of focusing the medium's innate art of clairvoyance or clairaudience. Once again they felt that these methods were too easily affected by the unconscious mind and wishful thinking. My father could never accept astrologers as being engaged in a scientific practice, but he freely acknowledged that they too seemed to be practising an art, with varying degrees of success.

Another reason my parents chose table-turning was that many other forms of paranormal phenomena required the employment of an experienced professional medium in order to obtain valid results, and this was beyond their means. Table-turning had been employed by many investigators since about 1850, and generally had been found to be effective. Nevertheless, unless carefully observed and strictly regulated, this system can also become an easy route to the unconscious mind. This drawback is lessened when more than two people are involved in the table-sitting, as several individuals are unlikely to coincide with their wishful thinking.

A practical consideration determined their choice. The table, when not being used for paranormal purposes, could stand unnoticed in the room. In other words, both Ma and Pop wanted to be as discreet as possible in their unusual researches.

A suitable table was obtained by my father, whose hobby was cabinet-making and antique furniture restoration. He found it in a Folkestone bric-à-brac shop, a solid, round piece of Victorian craftsmanship, under three feet in diameter, made of solid mahogany. Its top was inlaid with a floral marquetry pattern, and was supported on a single, sturdy pillar. It was very stable, and proved to be ideal for its purpose, heavy enough to need considerable force to lift it, move it, or rock it off-balance. Therefore, any surreptitious attempt to do so during an experimental session would be obvious to the other sitters because of the amount of effort required.

The procedure for table-turning was for those sitting round it, usually three to four people, to place their fingers lightly on top of the table, thereby exerting as little pressure as possible on its surface so that it could move with the minimum of friction under their finger-tips. During our table-sittings, this meant anything from a strong rocking movement to a pronounced circling motion, with our fingers sliding lightly over the surface of the table, showing that no significant force was being exerted, and only the lightest of contacts was being maintained. To all of us, this implied that some form of electrical force was in operation when the table was being moved.

On several occasions there was complete levitation of that weighty piece of furniture. It was raised several inches above the floor, and it *moved* about the room. We had to leave our seats and move with it, for once the light contact of our fingers on its surface was discontinued the table became inert.

These phenomena took place in our sitting-room in Wellfield, the final house that we built and lived in at Folkestone. At these sittings everything was clearly visible, even in the reduced light we used in summer when we drew the curtains, or by the cheerful firelight when we held our sittings in winter. I have also experienced paranormal phenomena of this kind when the lights were on, but I noticed that such sittings were of short duration and that after them we were very tired. Apparently, a low level of light is conducive to better and longer-lasting results.

Before anyone cries 'Fraud!', let me point out that sensitive photographic material also requires a low level of light to develop, print and fix. Just as one does in photography, we also used red light for certain paranormal phenomena. At no time could fraud, or unconscious self-delusion, have remained undetected for very long in our home. We all knew each other far too well for that to happen. I was a witness to nearly all these phenomena and I can testify to their authenticity.

The object of the exercise was to communicate messages between a paranormal source and the sitters involved. The technique employed was simplicity itself, if somewhat tedious. It involved a basic code, which consisted of the table rocking out the letters of the alphabet in order to spell out the messages. One rock would be given for A, two for B, three for C and so forth.

If a question was addressed to the entity or intelligence who was communicating, the answer was either spelled out or, if a simple 'Yes' or 'No' was required, three definite rocks of the table were given for 'Yes' and a single emphatic rock for 'No'. There was seldom any confusion between a single rock spelling out the letter A and a negative answer to a direct question. It only required common sense to sort out.

As the regular sitters consisted of my parents, my brother and myself or, when Tony was away at Eton, just the three of us with sometimes a trusted colleague, fraud could be eliminated. Self-delusion, though harder to detect, requires certain parameters before it can manifest, the most obvious one being a conscious or unconscious desire to communicate with the dead, for they were supposedly the source of these messages. When the object of the operation was to investigate rather than to communicate, self-delusion was unlikely.

The content of the messages received, most of which were personal and concerned the sitters alone, proved to be extremely accurate. This was very much the case when they were long-range predictions concerning the things that would happen to each of us in the years ahead. Because of their accuracy, they were most helpful to all of us.

Whatever the source, the phenomena I saw, heard, sensed and felt during most of these sittings remain beyond any explanation so far offered to me by sceptics who were not present at the proceedings. Certain factors appeared to play an important part:

(1) I invariably felt a distinct drop in room temperature immediately before the manifestations. This was so pronounced as to cause me to shiver, not with apprehension but with cold.

(2) I often smelt the odour of ozone. Being the resident

of a seaside town, I was familiar with this aroma. But I do not remember detecting it inside the house, except during this type of phenomenon.

(3) I also felt the presence of static electricity. This part of the phenomena was quite unmistakable because, like my mother, I had thick curly hair which tended to be dry, and both Ma and I found that during the sittings our hair became unmanageable, sometimes even standing up on end. In addition to this, if we passed our hands lightly over our heads we could hear a faint crackling sound. In the reduced light we could see tiny blue sparks, like a real electrical discharge, coming from the same source. It was like standing close to a small electrostatic generator.

(4) Before the table started to move, I distinctly felt a surge of cold air, like an intense draught. This started at my feet and circled upwards with a rapid swirling motion round the pillar of the table, rising until it seemed to reach my lap. Then the table would start to come alive.

(5) The only other factor that accompanied these phenomena was that, as soon as the seance commenced, my mother and I would both start to yawn uncontrollably, but this would cease as soon as the table started to move.

Most of these strange manifestations were felt by each of us at these table-sittings. I have no explanation for their occurrence, but my father thought they were caused, especially the yawning, by physical, i.e. electro-chemical, energy being drawn from each of us and then being utilized to operate the table.

Mumbo-jumbo? I do not think so. None of us would have spent so many years on these experiments had not the results been so dramatic and so effective in altering our viewpoint on the power of the human mind. Nevertheless, there were various factors which finally convinced me that we were dealing with intelligences other than our own unconscious minds. Absurd though it might seem, the table displayed different characteristics as each new intelligence manifested and took control of it, just as a wooden marionette takes on a distinct personality of its own, when manipulated by a skilled puppeteer.

That active Victorian table seemed to be able to convey affection, enthusiasm, impatience and even annoyance bordering on anger during the course of the many sittings held in our home. As the source of each message purported to change, so the table itself appeared to alter its behaviour, as did the pace, rhythm and style of its rocking while the information was being spelled out. Years later, when I was being taught Intelligence techniques in the RAF, I learnt that the identity of the operator of a Morse-code key can easily be detected by the distinct individuality in rhythm, style and pace of his or her transmitting style. In fact on a number of occasions during the war, false information was quickly detected by the subtle change in the Morse-key sending technique. Radio experts realized the signals were being transmitted by an enemy agent, who had taken over the operation of one of our clandestine radio-sets.

I cannot find an explanation for the constant change in the *way* that the information was imparted to us, and can only assume that the table was being manipulated by different intelligences at different times and that none of them was being generated by us. In other words, I am convinced that this form of phenomenon was genuine.

I was about eleven years old when my mother took me to see a woman medium who specialized in automatic-writing. She lived in a small bungalow set back from the main road and overlooking the sea. She was a homely body, plump and bustling, with a cheerful, down-to-earth personality, and she chatted away to us with a flow of trivia, while all the time she wrote busily.

Sometimes she used her right hand, sometimes her left, and occasionally she wrote with both hands simultaneously, and in completely different handwriting, using a supply of previously sharpened pencils which she constantly changed. The documents were written in literate English and were full of detailed information. My father told me that their style was excellent, as though they were the products of accomplished academic minds.

Pop had several sittings with the lady, who also produced manuscripts in French and in perfect German, languages with which my father was familiar. These documents were rapidly written with both hands simultaneously and contained political and literary commentaries in the first language, and complex mathematical equations and scientific dissertations in the second.

Both my parents were certain that the documents could not possibly be the products of the medium's conscious or unconscious mind. However, we often were confronted by phoneys and fakes, as well as by numbers of self-deluded folk who were quite certain that they possessed supernormal power.

Over the course of those pre-war years, we attended seances where 'entities' who purported to be spirits of historical figures clamoured for our attention. Favourite among these unconvincing manifestations, which my mother called 'The Regulars', were those who announced themselves as Napoleon Bonaparte, Bismarck, and Queen Victoria who, on one memorable occasion, introduced herself as 'Victoria Vagina'.

The Napoleons could neither speak nor understand French, the Bismarcks spoke no German, and the Queen Victorias sounded less regal than our splendid cleaning-lady. It was depressing, and even more so when the other sitters present swallowed it hook, line and sinker.

When these communications purported to originate from such unlikely sources as Socrates, Plato, Julius Caesar, Sir Isaac Newton, Abraham Lincoln, Gladstone and Disraeli, their content was unbelievably trite, even to a youngster like me. They were full of 'thees' and 'thous', misquoted biblical references, and weighty pronouncements, such as, 'You, my children, in your blind ignorance that you call science, cannot know the bliss and the marvels that surround us here in the summerland. Here, we can talk to Goethe, Beethoven, Michelangelo,

Leonardo da Vinci, and other famous spirits of the departed. Recently I was talking to Pythagoras, etc., etc.'

Stimulating stuff! I often wondered what they talked about.

The best of the genuine mediums were well-known psychics such as Mrs Helen Hughes, a small, modest woman who invariably gave us definitive and accurate evidence. Names were always correct, details of the person's past life were exact, and the content of the messages was verifiable and, if predictive, would happen precisely as the medium described the future circumstance.

I witnessed exceptional demonstrations of clairvoyance, clairaudience, and psychometry by other convincingly genuine mediums. In psychometry the medium picks up information and vivid subjective impressions by handling articles such as watches, wallets, spectacle-cases, letters, and other personal items belonging to those present at the sittings or to people who are not there at the time. Later, my father became adept at psychometry.

The undeniable evidence from genuine mediums, received and evaluated over a lifetime, has led me to make definitive statements about my involvement with the paranormal. To quote my father, as closely as I can remember, 'The paranormal is not just the province of cranks, imbeciles, the over-credulous and the unbalanced. The little-understood paranormal abilities are a valid and valuable part of our heritage, and they are possessed in varying degrees by most children. To ignore the possibility of the existence of these subtle forces as an integral part of the phenomenal power of the human mind is to exhibit bigotry of the worst kind. It is the sure sign of a closed mind.'

Closed minds were all too prevalent at that time and I certainly did not discuss our researches at school. Being a dago was quite enough to cope with, without being thought of as a raving lunatic as well.

In a way I led two separate lives. One was that of a tyrannized schoolboy impatiently waiting to go to Eton, where my godfather, William Hope-Jones, would be my house tutor. The other was that of a co-researcher into the paranormal alongside my father and mother and their colleagues. It certainly was an unusual situation to be in!

Chapter Four

Etonians Don't Cry

In my last term at my preparatory school, after six years of misery there, my parents finally realized what an obnoxious man my headmaster was. It was his own fault. He had predicted to them that I would not pass the Common Entrance exam, which was mandatory before entry to Eton and other British public schools. 'I'm afraid Michael hasn't got a chance of passing. He just doesn't seem to be able to apply himself to his work. I can't think why, because heaven knows we've tried hard enough.'

'I can't accept that,' my mother said, bristling. 'Michael has always been quick to study when anything interests him.'

The headmaster immediately changed his tactics. 'Of course, we will be sorry to lose such a nice lad. But he has problems which we haven't been able to resolve.'

'We're certainly going to do something about his stammer as soon as he settles down at Eton,' said my mother, her worst suspicions now aroused. She told me later she had felt sick when she realized the truth. The headmaster's rugged forthrightness now had a hollow ring to it. For a few unguarded seconds he had allowed that clever façade to slip. In the event, I passed the Common Entrance with ease. I could not have been more relieved.

During my last year at prep school, our Peruvian cousins once again descended on us. It was a joyous event, but this time only my cousins Antonio and Pedro came. The object of their visit, apart from being re-united with their gringo relations, was to leave Pedro in Folkestone to improve his English.

They arrived by cross-Channel ferry with Antonio's car, a silver Bentley built as an open four-seater tourer. My parents were on the dock to welcome them and help them pass through Customs. Ma was horrified when Antonio presented her with a giant-size bottle of eau-de-Cologne.

'It's sweet of you, my dear,' she remonstrated, 'but I'm afraid it will cost you a fortune in duty.'

Antonio waved aside her protests, 'My dear Aunt Florencia, I am only too happy to pay the Customs.' But when Antonio parked the car in our garage and lifted the back seat, my mother nearly fainted at the sight of the wines, spirits and liqueurs stacked in the compartment below.

It was not that my cousins were dishonest, far from it. This, apparently, was the way South Americans be-haved when dealing with their own Customs and Excise. Being freedom-loving people they considered the high level of Customs duty to be an imposition on their basic rights. This it often was, as the funds obtained were usually misapplied, with the money ending up in the Customs officers' pocket. To my Peruvian family it was a game. If you got caught, you paid!

My first term, or 'half', at Eton College was filled with wonder and relief: wonder at the experience of moving into a 500-year-old school, with 1,200 other boys, and relief that my previous persecution was over.

I was separated from the home I loved, but I was happy because, like my father before me, I was surrounded by the warmth of the Southery/Hope-Jones family. My tutor, William Hope-Jones, and his wife had a large family con-sisting of three sons and two daughters. All of them were bright, intelligent and affectionate. In addition, there was dear, gentle Granny Southery, who now lived with them.

Although he always treated me impartially as one of the

boys in his House, Uncle Billy, whom I always referred to as 'M'tutor', invited me to join in his family activities as often as he could without showing overt favouritism.

The Hope-Joneses were unique. The entire family, whose intellectual level was far above mine, had their own version of such games as charades and consequences. They played them in a number of languages, without any trace of intellectual snobbery. Few families could have played these games as they did, in French, Spanish, German, and even Latin and Greek. Yet, somehow, they never made me feel left out.

When their family games involved their extraordinary mathematical ability I found myself floundering. With skill and ease they would take numbers; square them; cube them; calculate their logarithms, square roots, cube roots, and sundry other mathematical properties. They would also make magic squares out of them, which M'tutor explained to me was a favourite pastime of Benjamin Franklin. All this they did out of their heads, only putting pencil to paper to construct the 'magic squares'. They also played 'blindfold chess', M'tutor taking on his whole family simultaneously. Above all, with their wild enthusiasm they made everything seem great fun.

One summer day, M'tutor, who had been a Cambridge rowing blue, was coaching his house-eight crew as they sped over the surface of the Thames. He was shouting into a megaphone while pedalling his ex-Post Office bicycle, vintage 1900, along the towpath when he rode straight into the Thames. In a trice, he was out of the river and back in the saddle. Dripping wet but still shouting instructions into the megaphone, he raced away as fast as his long legs could pedal. The crew had seen it happen and were laughing like hyenas but, to their credit, they never missed a stroke.

William Hope-Jones's eccentricity was an integral part of the Etonian scene. For instance, the way he recorded his comments on our report cards was highly idiosyncratic. If you did well he drew a little smiling angel with wings and a halo, and with twelve buttons on its robe. 'One for each of the Apostles,' he explained solemnly.

If you did exceptionally well, only the feet of the angel showed at the top of the report. 'He has ascended,' he would say.

If you were doing badly, you got a robed figure with the same number of buttons, but drawn in red ink, with horns on its head. If you did really badly, you got the lower half of the red devil, upside down, with only the feet showing at the bottom of the report. 'He has descended,' M'tutor would shake his head sadly.

Most of the other Eton 'beaks', as we referred to the masters, were eccentric to some degree, some outstandingly so, but M'tutor was far and away the most memorable.

One housemaster, A.C. Beasley-Robinson, left Eton after the war to become a Dominican monk, Brother Paul. He was a keen Scoutmaster and a fanatical motor enthusiast. He kept two beautiful yellow Railton cars, open tourers, which he crammed with Scouts and drove with great verve and dash, earning the nickname of the 'Yellow Peril'. Beasley-Robinson was, like all the other beaks, an accomplished scholar and a good teacher. Perhaps his eccentricity was a form of defence against the constant mental onslaught of some 1,200 boys.

Twenty years after I left Eton, I was driving my small family to a holiday near Sandbanks in Dorset. Stuck in the sand beside the road was one of those unmistakable yellow Railton tourers. It was being pushed by a crowd of Scouts, encouraged by the shouts of the driver, a slim, energetic, elderly monk wearing a beret. It was Beasley-Robinson. I stopped my car, leapt out and ran over to help. Brother Paul instantly recognized me, despite the many years since our last meeting and the fact that I was sporting a thick moustache and beard.

'Give us a hand, Bentin, there's a good chap!' he shouted with a broad grin.

'Right, sir,' I said, touching the brim of my hat, an

instinctive return to the Etonian practice of 'capping a beak' by giving them a brief salute as they passed by. I put my shoulder against the car and heaved with the Scouts. It began to move. The cheering boys leapt aboard, and off they drove in a cloud of sand. Beasley-Robinson waved to me and yelled, 'Nice to see you again, boy. Don't make it so long next time!'

Brother Paul had shown no surprise at meeting me. Presumably to this deeply religious man everything was ordained; therefore why remark on it?

A.E. Conybeare, the Lower Master, head of the Lower School, which was made up of the younger boys, thirteen to fifteen years old, was another unusual character. His tall, gaunt figure always seemed to be in a hurry. I can still picture him, muttering to himself as he swept along the streets, his long legs striding from classroom to chapel and back to other classrooms.

Unlike most other beaks, Mr Conybeare always wore a mortar-board, tipped forward as though to prevent it from blowing off. His threadbare gown, which streamed behind him in the draught of his rapid progress, completed this odd illusion of determined haste. The prominent features of his high-cheekboned, ascetic face seemed to be eternally mobile, changing from a benevolent smile to a ferocious grimace as he spoke. This was purely a nervous habit, as Mr Conybeare had in fact an equable temperament, but to a nervous new boy like me, it was alarming on first encounter.

E.L. Churchill, an elderly savant known throughout the school as 'Jelly', was no doubt an excellent academic, but he would have been far more effective as a teacher had we been able to understand what he was saying. His lisping speech was a mixture of splutter and gurgle, as he constantly swallowed his wise words in a shower of saliva. This was caused by his woeful lack of teeth. Understandably, he was impatient with us.

Another prize eccentric was H.K. Marsden, known universally as 'Bloody Bill'. An exceptionally tall man of great mathematical ability, he seemed to loom above his pupils. With his long, drooping black moustache, he had an air of contained fury. His piercing dark eyes glowed beneath shaggy brows as he stood with his hands deep in his trouser pockets, constantly moving them as though perpetually playing with his balls. We called it 'pocket billiards'. Actually, he suffered badly from arthritis and, rather than rubbing his painful hands in the spartan chill of our winter classrooms, he thrust them deep into his pockets to keep them warm and mobile.

I remember my first class, or 'division', with this forbidding man. As this was our initiatory division with Bloody Bill, he needed to know our names. When he came to me, he asked brusquely, 'Name, boy?'

I was speechless, dreading a repetition of my grim experiences with my former headmaster. Though I struggled, not a single word came out.

H.K. Marsden immediately switched his attention to the rest of the class. 'What is this boy's name?'

'Benskin,' one boy replied.

'Bending,' another volunteered.

This released a flood of names. Cries of 'Berkin', 'Belting', 'Bonking', and other odd versions of my name filled the classroom. Bloody Bill held up a commanding hand. There was immediate silence.

'Bentin!' I finally got the name out in an explosion of sound.

The great man spoke quietly, 'Odd name. Odd boy. *But*, while he is in my division, no-one will make fun of either.'

From then on, I liked and respected Bloody Bill.

Life at Eton was a perpetual whirl of activity. Here is a typical day in my life as an Etonian:

Early school was at 7.30, spring, summer, autumn and winter. During the latter season, this meant going to school in the pitch dark.

We were all boarders, and rose at 6.30. After a quick 'lick and a promise', we had a steaming hot cup of cocoa poured from huge enamel jugs, swallowed a biscuit and rushed off for our first division. We returned for breakfast at 8.30. This was a substantial affair of piping hot porridge in winter and cornflakes during the rest of the year, followed by egg and bacon or sausage or bubble-and-squeak, and as much toast as we wanted. All this had to be consumed at high speed, as by nine we had to be in chapel, unless a boy was either Catholic or Jewish.

This daily service in College Chapel or Lower Chapel, depending upon your position in the school, lasted for half an hour. It consisted of prayers, a short lesson taken from the Bible, the singing of a psalm by the choir and the lusty singing of everyone of a rousing hymn. This I thoroughly enjoyed as, like others, I often sang words of my own composition, which fortunately were inaudible in the melodious bellowing that passed for schoolboy singing.

We then quickly dispersed to our various divisions, of which we normally had two consecutive one-hour sessions. We dashed back to our Houses for a mid-morning cup of cocoa, or lemonade in summer, and another fortifying biscuit. This was a ten-minute break before joining our individual Classical tutors who supervised our revisions and with whom we also wrote Latin verse. My tutor was Philip Snow, an even-tempered, patient man with terminal dandruff of the eyebrows, whose genuine enthusiasm for the Classics inspired my own growing affection for them.

This late-morning session finished at one o'clock, although you could leave earlier if you had finished your work. We then had about three-quarters of an hour before lunch. I presume this lull in our scholastic dash was intended to keep the school 'sock' shops, as the tuck-shops were called, solvent and in profit, for by this time we were all extremely hungry. My appalling stammer forced me to order in writing any snack I intermittently could afford out of my weekly three shillings and sixpence pocket-money.

Lunch was filling and the food, though basic and predictable, was good and well-cooked. William Hope-Jones, unlike some housemasters, never skimped on feeding his boys, which was one reason why his finances were always strained to their limit, and why he had no nest-egg when he retired. Other housemasters were not so generous to their boys.

No matter what the season, the afternoon was devoted to sport. This lasted for two hours and presented a broad choice, apart from the house matches which were obligatory. During the autumn term only, when it was the time for 'training', it was decreed that we must run for one hour or play Eton-fives, racquets or squash for the same length of time.

The house matches included the Field Game, an odd hybrid sport, unique to Eton, involving much footwork, savage tackling and physical mayhem without actually handling the ball, as in rugby football. We all played Field Game in winter and, being lightly built, I loathed it as I kept getting hurt. This happened during the 'ram', a part of the game when a closely packed line of heavy boys charged their opponents, who were standing in the goal-mouth in a wedge formation behind the ball, the object being to ram the ball past them into the net. Usually I was the idiot selected to stand behind the ball on the receiving end of the ram. I lost count of the number of times I was winded, sometimes to the point of unconsciousness. It was not my favourite game.

We played rugby football in the spring term, and enjoyed cricket or rowing, which were called 'dry bobbing' and 'wet bobbing', during the summer. For me it was cricket, because the choice of whether a boy played cricket or rowed depended entirely on his ability to pass the stringent swimming test. This was held for all new boys at Cuckoo Weir, a sluggish backwater of the Thames into which you dived from a high, grassy slope called the Acropolis. You had to prove you could tread water for one minute even in the cold, polluted water of the weir-stream, while wearing a singlet, shorts and plimsolls, and with both arms above your head. I failed miserably and became a cricketer.

I enjoyed cricket, especially as I was already an able spin-bowler, a skill taught me in our back garden by my father and brother, both of whom were fine cricketers.

When the daily routine of sport was over, we dashed back and changed into our formal school clothes, ready for our last division of the day. In those days, our everyday clothing consisted of short Eton jackets, if we were five feet tall or less, which we wore with overlapping wide white collars and black ties. When we were taller, we progressed to tails, worn with an ordinary white collar and a narrow white bow tie tucked in under it.

I spent my first half in jackets and finished my time at Eton in tails. With this formal outfit we all wore the obligatory black silk topper, inside which we kept ice-cream in summer, and pet frogs and other indispensable schoolboy items in winter. One boy even kept a small tortoise in that useful container until one day he absentmindedly took off his topper to the Headmaster, who was the only beak to whom you removed your headgear. I remember he got beaten for cruelty to animals when the suddenly exposed tortoise fell to the pavement.

The final division lasted an hour and a half. We then returned to our Houses for tea and toast. Lower boys, as 'House-fags' – a term I never use in America – first had to provide toast or cook sausages for senior members of the House, called the 'Library', before eating their own bread and jam.

Fagging, the traditional Lower School practice of being at the beck and call of the 'Library' or Upper Schoolboys in each House, interrupted my studies and often intruded on what little leisure time I had. I objected to its excessive use and many other boys felt the same.

We did our 'extra work', as we called our weekly prep, till suppertime, which was at seven, and rounded off our demanding day by continuing our studies until lights out came at nine, by which time we were all exhausted and slept like proverbial logs.

On Sundays, we rose at eight, breakfasted and went to Matins in Chapel at nine. After that we had the rest of the morning free till lunchtime, apart from the obligatory 'Absences', the roll-calls we all had to attend morning and evening, seven days a week, in order to make sure none of us had done a bunk. From time to time a few boys did just that, probably because they could not stand the tough school routine.

After Sunday lunch of roast beef, Yorkshire pudding and two vegetables, we went for long walks, or alternatively pursued a wide spectrum of hobbies, until Evensong, the second Chapel service of the day.

Perhaps the entire rugged, demanding routine was designed to exhaust the boys so that we had little time or energy left to experiment with sex. Our monastic life was a real problem for boys emerging into puberty, which some Etonians overcame by practising a mild form of homosexuality, playing with each other until they achieved mutual sexual release. A very few others practised sodomy. If caught, those boys were instantly expelled.

M'tutor was well aware of this and gave each one of us a straightforward and explicit talk on the subject of schoolboy sex and its dangers. Although I had learned something of the facts of life from my brother, I was still naïve and what M'tutor told me helped me to understand what was happening to me, physiologically and psychologically. I realized I was growing up.

I personally was not propositioned by another boy for these purposes during my entire time at Eton, and my own experience, probably, was like that of most of the other 1,200 boys who were my contemporaries. The whole legend of Eton buggery has been grossly exaggerated, mainly by people who were not at the school.

If the beaks generally were remarkable, so were many of the boys. I was at school with Patrick Macnee who, in the sixties, became an international star with his portrayal of John Steed in the TV series *The Avengers*. Other contemporaries of mine were Humphrey Lyttelton, the jazz trumpeter, Ludovic Kennedy, the TV presenter and author, who played drums in the school jazz band, and Simon Phipps, who became Bishop of Lincoln, and was an excellent actor in school plays.

As none of them was in my House, and both Ludovic Kennedy and Humphrey Lyttelton were slightly older than I was, I did not know any of them at school other than by sight. But each had a very definite style about him, singling him out from the others.

For example, during his adventurous time at Eton, Pat Macnee, who was the son of a race-horse trainer, was reputed to have swum the Thames in order to place bets for himself and his friends with the bookmakers at the Windsor Races. Years later, I tackled him about this rumour.

'Rubbish,' he grinned lazily, 'that was much too energetic for me. I crossed Windsor bridge just like everyone else, and *then* slipped on to the race course to make the bets. I did all right too.'

There were boys at Eton from many parts of the world. For instance, in my brother's day there were two Siamese princes, both of whom later became racing motorists. There were also British aristocrats. The Lascelles boys, who were members of the British royal family, were my contemporaries, along with a number of dukes, earls, viscounts, barons and a whole mass of honourables.

Sounds repellently snobbish, doesn't it? And in rare cases it was, but on the whole there was a surprising lack of snobbery at Eton, probably because princes, dukes, earls, viscounts or commoners, such as my brother and me, all had to buckle down to the school's strict discipline and had to take an active part in those rough, tough, knock-down-and-drag-out games and sports. Furthermore, each and every one of us got beaten at some time during our school careers, although my brother and I both believe that this last indignity was an unnecessary and degrading practice for both the beaten and the beater.

M'tutor also disapproved of corporal punishment. I don't think he ever laid a cane on any boy in his House, although he was forced by the school rules to leave some latitude in the administering of beating to the Head of House and to members of the 'Library'. Other house masters were not so restrained.

Our whole ethos at Eton was angled towards the 'nobility of self-sacrifice'. We were told, 'It is better to be a good loser than a bad winner,' whatever that means. Looking back, I realize that our whole education was based on the tradition that the Battle of Waterloo was won on the playing-fields of Eton. In other words: we were being conditioned for imperial war.

Chapter Five

Love at First Sight

Coming home for the Christmas holidays after that first half at Eton was like seeing Folkestone through a different person's eyes. For a start the buildings along the route back to our house seemed much smaller. I had been away for only three and a half months, yet I sensed a definite change all around me. Then I realized I was the one who had changed.

Ma and Pop were exactly as I remembered them and both were as delighted as I was to be together again. My happiness was complete when Tony came down from the Royal College of Art in Kensington, where he was a student. So, for Christmas at least, we were a whole family.

Family has always meant a great deal to me. It was my secure base, my place of the heart. To my surprise I discovered this was not the case with some boys at Eton. Many of them came from colonial homes in the Dominions. These could be as far away as New Zealand and Australia. There was no way they could get back home by ship during school holidays which lasted a few weeks, and commercial flying was still in the embryo stage. There were air services to Africa and even as far as India, but this meant many stops to refuel the big Imperial Airways multi-engined biplanes and flying-boats. I believe some of these flights took over fourteen days to get to Peshawar in north-west India.

These unfortunate boys had to spend Christmas in Britain with relations or stay with guardians, as my father had done. Even the ones who did fly to Africa and India only saw their families during the summer holidays. These lasted for over two months, but the long flights both ways consumed a large part of it. Alternatively, they sometimes met their families in Britain when their parents came home on leave. Having heard some of my friends at Eton crying when they found themselves in this predicament, I can appreciate what a miserable arrangement this could be. Their tutor's House had become their substitute home, with their close friends as their surrogate family.

There were a number of boys whose parents were divorced or who had a single parent owing to a death in the family, so in many cases the holidays did not offer the same source of happiness as our close-knit home life gave my brother and me.

Like most fourteen-year-olds, I had grown considerably in those three months away from home. My voice had broken, so presumably my balls had dropped at the onset of puberty. I was by no means a basso-profundo, but whenever I managed to control my stammer my voice had a baritone ring to it.

My mother immediately sensed I was taking notice of girls, in particular our new dentist's daughter, whose family had just moved into a house across the road. This lovely girl was an only child and a year younger than me. She was tall for her age, with short, wind-tossed blond hair framing fine, regular features. The small, lightly freckled face made an entrancing setting for her large, gentle eyes. Strangely, I cannot remember their colour, only their innocence and the mesmeric effect they had on me.

Her slim body was not yet fully budded, and her long, slender legs gave her the look of a young faun. Since the morning I first saw her, I have never doubted that there is such a thing as love at first sight.

Owing to my stammer, which a speech-trainer at Eton

was helping me to master, over a year had passed before I managed to speak to her, and then only because her father had just given me dental treatment. Maybe the injection I had received temporarily numbed my shyness. To my amazement, she seemed just as eager to talk to me.

Our first walk together was a revelation. It was thrilling just to hold hands. We did not talk much, because she, too, was shy and I was still struggling with my newly found speech. But there was little need for words; being together was enough. I still remember the sound of her laughter.

During that long summer we covered miles of the rolling downlands, running to exhaustion with our much-loved dogs, who also sensed the delight of our idyll. It was innocence itself: a gentle affair of laughter and young love. At last I had found someone who sensed the same magic abroad in the land, someone special to share the caress of tingling sea-breezes and catch the whispers of rustling trees in ancient woods.

Our first kisses were unskilled, a brief contact of tensely closed lips and trembling bodies, but gradually these grew into a marvel of natural blending.

Day after day we lay on the downs, artlessly cuddled together among the rippling waves of summer grass, and lazily scanning the sweeping panorama of that beautiful valley till it melted into the mists on the distant horizon of the shimmering Channel. This was the simple mystery of young love as yet untouched by passion.

Our summer idyll abruptly ended when her father decided to move to a new dental practice in Devon, and we were torn apart. It was heart-rending. Letters, no matter how tender, are no substitute for physical presence; the intense longing was just as real as it would have been for mature adults.

It was just as well we parted. With hindsight I have no doubt we eventually would have become lovers and, in our sexual innocence, I would have fathered her child. In those days, in that hide-bound, merciless town, it would have been a needless tragedy.

After the war, by sheer accident, we met again on a summer's day. We found that none of the magic had faded during the intervening years, even with the trauma of war. Once again, for a few delightful hours, we recaptured the innocence of that gentle time when memory was young. That sunny afternoon, despite a mutual longing, we both sensed that sexual love would have broken the spell of the idyll. It was purely a sentimental decision to leave things as they were. I am sure we were right. We had one more brief encounter. We met by chance in a London bookshop, and she introduced me to her handsome fiancé. I never saw her again.

During the school holidays I had rejoined my parents in their paranormal research. Those absorbing sessions helped me to fill the emptiness she left behind.

Throughout those long years of research into the paranormal, our balance as a family and our normality in day-to-day living was largely determined by Ma's common sense. She would not let things get out of hand, and she never once lost her invaluable sense of humour. Ma wisely insisted that we should spend part of the summer holidays with our family at Westcliff and Southend. Their outgoing and cheerful personalities did much to keep our mental balance from tipping too far into the esoteric aspects of life.

I chuckle when I remember Uncle Jim and his way with words. He was an even-tempered man, with a natural merriment that sprang from his unjaundiced view of the world. Where others saw only badness or downright evil, Uncle Jim would find some redeeming feature. Then, through the alchemy of his wit, he would show us another, funny side to a bad deed which, miraculously, took the sting out of it.

It truly was a marvellous gift, which was apparent also in my mother. Both of them said they had inherited it from their father, James Dawkins, whom Ma now firmly believed was one of the guiding influences in our researches.

My Dawkins relatives were the happiest, healthiest, and most mentally stable of families.

It was always a great joy for us to meet up with one another for two hilarious weeks every year from my earliest childhood right up to the start of the war. During those magical summer days, we youngsters seemed to be in a continuous whirl of excited activity, full of laughter. We were busily engaged in kite-flying on windy Shoeburyness, dashing up and down Southend's lengthy pier, and generally rushing around the Essex country-side in a breathless ecstasy of effort. We did not need expensive toys and budget-breaking gadgetry to have a marvellous time. We made the kites ourselves, the pier-master was a friend of Uncle Jim, so that pastime was free, and the only wear and tear was on the soles of our sandals, which in those days were cheap to replace. They were wonderful times, and are among my treasured store of happiest memories.

Pop, with his knowledge of aerodynamics, was a wizard at constructing kites and successful model aeroplanes which flew for at least a minute, though they were only powered by rubber bands. 'Tubby', a particularly success-ful monoplane, with a four-foot wingspan, consistently flew much longer, surviving numerous collisions with trees and other obstacles in the course of its soaring flights.

My father would spend much of his time in the winter, when I was at school, building these models to have them ready for when I came home. Sometimes I was so impatient to fly them that I could not wait for an ideal day. This sometimes resulted in a crashed model which required hours to reconstruct, but Pop never re-proached me for my impatience and cheerfully repaired them for the next suitable day.

I often wonder if I thanked him enough for all his efforts, but console myself with the thought that he en-joyed them as much as we did.

Pop stopped designing model aircraft after I showed

him an article in an American modelling magazine which had the design for an eighteen-inch wingspan solid balsa-wood glider. This extremely light, pulpy wood came from South America and my father was familiar with it from his boyhood. While I was away at Eton he made half a dozen of these cheap, easily constructed gliders. When I came home for the summer holidays we went to try them out at the foot of Caesar's Camp, the big, green hill that dominates the downs behind Folkestone.

As they were 'chuck gliders' we launched them by hand. The results were amazing. Each one of those gliders sailed up into the sky like soaring gulls. Round and round they circled in the warm air currents as they climbed up alongside the steep hill till they vanished out of sight high over its summit. One of them set off on its own towards the town, rising the whole time as though it was attempting to cross the Channel. It vanished into the heat mist on the horizon.

Within twenty minutes there was no sign of any of them. We could hardly believe it. Every one of those simple models was a champion glider, ideally suited to the local conditions.

Pop took off his cap and threw it on the grass. 'Those damn gliders are better than anything I can design. That's the last time I ever build one of those complex models. From now on you can make these little ones yourself.'

However, Pop did build one more glider but this time it was full-size.

That same summer, Lyons, the London-based catering firm, sponsored an exhibition of sail-planing, which took place on the east cliff at Folkestone. This was a new sport which had caught on in Austria and Germany but was quite new to our shores. In Nazi Germany, as we now thought of it, this sport was enthusiastically pursued with a strong ulterior motive.

Be that as it may, that summer, Magasuppe, a Romanian sail-plane pilot, and Kronfeld, a German airman who was not sympathetic to the Nazi cause, demonstrated with breath-catching brilliance the beauty and grace of flying gliders.

In front of a huge crowd lining the high ground of the east cliff and the downs, these two skilful airmen flew for hours in the full-lift generated by the on-shore winds blowing through the Straits of Dover. All the while, loudspeakers on the top of a large Lyons van blared out 'The Stein Song', a popular German ditty of the day, interspersed with announcements extolling the skill of the pilots and the virtues of Lyons Tea.

I can still picture the two gliders as vividly as on that morning when I fell deeply in love with the sport of motorless flight. Pop was equally entranced and promptly joined the newly formed Channel Gliding Club, volunteering to help them build their first glider, which the other enthusiastic members had already purchased in kit form.

While Kronfeld and Magasuppe were demonstrating their machines, a British team had been industriously assembling their aircraft, which was called the Scud. This was much smaller than the other sail-planes and, whereas they were both beautifully proportioned, even the most patriotic Britisher could see that the Scud was an ugly duckling. Stumpy, with a rhomboid fuselage, the little glider sat poised to leap into the air at the top of the steep slope.

Like the others, she was to be 'bungy-launched'. This was an exciting part of the display, when two teams of strong young men lined up in front of the plane and grasped the ends of two lengths of thick rubber shock-cord covered with cotton, rather like the elastic 'octopus' cords used today to secure luggage on the roof-racks of cars. This primitive device, with the middle of the cord attached to a quick-release hook set in the nose of the glider, looked like a gigantic catapult, which is precisely what it was.

Four heavy young men at the rear of the glider hung on to a short piece of rope secured to another hook built into the tail-skid of the Scud.

The two forward teams spread out on either side of the glider, taking up their positions a short way down the slope, while the rearward team dug their heels into the turf and leaned back to take the coming strain.

The leader of the Scud team, who was standing safely to one side, shouted the single command, 'Walk!' The two widespread lines of catapulters started gingerly down the slope, the thick shock-cord visibly tightening as they did so.

At the appropriate moment, the team leader shouted, 'Run!' The forward teams broke into a fast shuffle, which accelerated with the steepness of the slope. The shock cord was now much thinner as it stretched tight and was thrumming with the tension. The rearward team clung desperately to the rope attached to the tail-hook.

Then came the final command: 'Release!'

The result was pure farce. The forward team fell flat on their faces, and the rearward group collapsed on their backs. The Scud, with the pilot tense at the controls, rushed down the slope.

'Why doesn't he pull back on the stick and get airborne?' muttered Pop in amazement.

The bewildered airman was doing so, but nothing was happening apart from the machine hurtling ever faster down the steep incline.

'Jesus Christ,' shouted someone, 'he's going to crash!'

In front of our eyes, the chunky little glider bounced drunkenly over the low bank at the bottom of the hill, skidded wildly across the road in front of two cars whose drivers braked just in time, smashed through a fence in a shower of splinters, shedding its wings on the way, shot across the front garden of a terraced cottage and, mercifully, came to rest only a couple of feet away from a jutting bay-window.

Despite urgent pleas coming from the public-address system on the Lyons van begging us to remain where we were, everyone rushed down the hill, either to help rescue the pilot or to gawk ghoulishly at the wreckage.

Incredibly, apart from his pride, the pilot was unhurt. He was hauled out of the wreck, gesticulating wildly and furiously angry.

Apparently, in their eagerness to get the British sailplane ready to show our prowess to the 'bloody foreigners', who had given such a magnificent display of airmanship, the Scud team had rigged the elevator-controls upside down and the wrong way round. The result was that the harder the pilot pulled back on the control-column to raise the elevator and lift the machine off the ground, the more the crossed wires lowered the control-surfaces and kept the Scud firmly earthbound.

The Channel Gliding Club profited by their colleague's mistake and eagerly accepted my father's offer to help build and rig their own new glider. This machine, called a Zogling or Dagling, made the Scud look positively graceful. It was described in the plans as a 'primary' glider, and that is precisely what it was.

It consisted of an open, flat, skeleton frame, like a roof-truss, made out of spruce and ash. This served as the fuselage, at the front end of which there was a short reinforced skid bolted to its base. The aluminium bucket seat for the pilot was perched on top of the skid, and located just forward of the broad, blunt-ended wings. These were bolted to the top of the fuselage frame and braced with wires fanning out from a triangular wooden king-post, which projected above the centre section of the wing.

The tail section was equally basic and was attached to the end of the fuselage frame by more bolts and more wires. The whole machine was braced with so many rigging-wires that it looked like a large winged bird-cage.

During its assembly, one of the club members, who fancied himself as an expert, started to explain to my father how to use the special rigging device with which they would determine the tension of the wires. 'It's called a tensometer,' he explained loftily.

'So I believe,' said Pop, 'I invented it.'

Six months later, the glider was ready for flight testing. Despite my mother's protests, Pop volunteered for the job. The club was only too happy to hand over that vital task to someone who knew what he was doing.

The excited Bentin family assembled on the downs to watch the test flight. First, Pop inspected every inch of the aircraft before settling himself into the bucket seat, his hand on the control-column and his feet on the rudder-bar which projected either side of the narrow skid. The pilot sat in the open, completely unprotected.

He was securely strapped in with a Sutton harness, although nothing would prevent him from falling off the machine if the seat-retaining bolts sheered. Pop had further strengthened them to make sure this would not happen. He tested his controls, looking back at the stabilizer to see that the elevators and rudder were moving correctly, and sideways under the wings to check that the ailerons were correctly connected and free to operate.

Pop then turned his cap the wrong way round, so the peak was at the back, pulled down his goggles and nodded to the team leader. Once again, we watched the forward bungy teams take up their launch positions down the slope, gripping the two lengths of rubber shock-cord. The rear team clung manfully on to the rope fixed to the second hook underneath the tail. It was just like the preliminaries for the launch of the Scud. We all prayed the results would be different.

'Walk!' shouted the leader. Down the slope trudged the catapult team.

'Run!' he yelled. The two forward teams ran downhill and with every stride the tension of the rubber cord increased until we could hear it humming in the breeze.

'Release!'

As the forward and rearward teams fell to the ground, the glider shot forward and rose steeply into the air, far too steeply, threatening a stall. Pop immediately corrected the acute angle of ascent and the machine swooped down, briefly touching the grass slopes before my father gingerly

81

pulled back on the stick to haul the unstable machine into another, and this time less dramatic, climb. A hundred yards further down the slope, Pop came in for a neat landing.

I nearly burst with pride. My father was an intrepid birdman. Ugly or not, the machine had flown.

Pop's appraisal of the 'test hop' was less sanguine. 'She's a cow,' he said. He never flew her again.

Chapter Six

Ways of Making Me Talk

From the start of my first half at Eton, M'tutor had been as concerned as my parents over my failure to conquer my stammer. During the holidays he telephoned Pop to tell him he had found a highly recommended speech-trainer. The specialist's name was Harry Burgess, and he was to change my whole life.

I went up to London to meet Tony, who had taken a day off from the Royal College of Art to take me along to the consultation. Mr Burgess was well over six feet tall. Ma would have described him as 'built for comfort and not for speed'. Large and bulky, in his well-cut Wigmore-Street-specialist outfit of black jacket and matching waistcoat worn over pinstriped trousers, he oozed professional sincerity. When he spoke it was in a beautifully modulated voice to match his visual image.

Mr Burgess chatted with us for a while, his big moon-face perspiring freely. He frequently mopped his brow with an expensive-looking silk handkerchief. All the time he watched my struggle to speak, his deceptively docile eyes missing nothing. He asked me searching questions about my boyhood and listened attentively to my efforts to reply.

Oddly enough, my stammer became easier to control as that mesmeric voice droned on, and I found myself relaxing to a point where my speech was no longer the appalling barrier to which I was accustomed. My brother told me later that it was a minor miracle.

At this point, Mr Burgess rose from his chair and walked round his big mahogany desk till he stood looming over me, his face the picture of benign concern. Suddenly he said accusingly, 'Michael, you *stole* my wallet!'

As I stood there in shocked silence, desperately struggling to declare my innocence, my brother leapt angrily to my defence. 'Rubbish! My brother would never steal anything, sir. Let alone your wallet.'

Mr Burgess smiled placatingly. 'Of course he wouldn't. I just wanted to show you both *why* Michael stammers. I'm sorry I was so brutal about it but it was the only way to demonstrate how your speech-blocking mechanism works. The shock of my ridiculous accusation instantly set up an intolerable stress inside you, and that immediately halted your speech-flow, which until then had been steadily improving.'

The big man smiled warmly. 'We are going to beat that block, Michael. When you get back to Eton I will come and visit Mr Hope-Jones. I am an Old Etonian myself and I have known that marvellous man since I was a boy and he was a junior master. You could not be in better hands. There are three other boys who are suffering the same sort of speech difficulties as yourself. I promise you, Michael, that you *will* speak normally, and when I have finished with your speech-training you can go out and earn your living on the stage.'

Harry Burgess's method of speech-training was quite simple. 'I learnt it in Vienna,' he told the four of us sufferers. 'I first obtained some recordings of famous actors and singers. Then I played these records at their slowest speed and listened carefully to their speech patterns and especially to their breathing. I next made dictaphone records of all the patients we were treating for speech defects, and from them I learnt why they stammered and stuttered.'

He then demonstrated what he had discovered. First he played us the recordings of famous actors. 'As you can hear, they speak with a swing and a rhythm, and a pause, and a run. Their speech pattern is never monotonous. This pronounced variation in their manner of speaking is the essence of the method I am going to teach you. Your own way of speaking is your handicap, because it is too regular, too monotonous. You simply run out of breath, and to start again you have to inhale sharply so as not to interrupt the flow. You are letting the words determine your breathing and it should be the other way round.

'To put it simply: you should only speak when you have sufficient breath to do so. It is rather like when you have been running hard and are out of breath from the effort. You cannot speak normally till you get your breath back. This is one of the reasons why you don't stammer when you sing. I'm sure you all have found that out.'

We nodded.

'Over the years, you have developed an unconscious fear that you will stammer or stutter over certain words, especially the ones that begin with the hard consonants B, D, G, K, etc. But other consonants, such as N, are not as difficult to pronounce, *if* you have sufficient breath to do so. Therefore, we are going to use the easier consonant, N, to overcome the difficulty of pronouncing the difficult ones like D. You simply put the N in front of the D or any other difficult consonant. It will go like this: NDo, NDon't, NCan, NCan't, etc. Now you try it. But, first, you must take in sufficient breath.'

We did so and tried the N before the consonants, with varying degrees of success.

Mr Burgess smiled. 'Not bad for a first show. Now try it again, but this time *vibrate* the N, so that it becomes a Nnnnn sound, before hitting the hard consonants.'

We tried again, with slightly more success. Our large mentor enlarged on his theory. 'Let me give you a simile. Just imagine you are riding a horse in the show-ring and that you are going to jump over some big fences. You all ride, I suppose?'

The four of us nodded.

'Good. Ahead of you, you see a big fence coming up. So you rein in your horse to steady him for the jump, and then let him go at the fence. When you land on the other side, you again pick up the stride of your horse, from where it left off in order to make the jump. It's much the same action as running in a race over the hurdles, except that, in hurdling, you take the jump in your stride.

'We will now try the word Dog. That's a difficult one for most stammerers to say. This time, imagine that the fence coming up is the letter D.'

We all duly vibrated the Nnnnnn and then jumped the letter D. Some of us did not make it. I was one of them. Mr Burgess was patience itself as he explained where we had gone wrong. He was a wonderful teacher.

'You mustn't stop the Nnnnn sound *just* as you make the jump. You must *follow through* with it, right up to where you come down hard on the word Dog.'

This we did, and, blissfully, it worked! We all said 'NnnnnnDog' with great clarity.

Our teacher continued, 'Of course, vowels are difficult, as well. A, E, I, O, U can be dealt with in much the same way, but as they are vowels we don't need N in front to start them off. Take in a breath and vibrate the sound of Aaaaa in that same rising tone before hitting a word starting with A, such as Arm.

'You vibrate Eeeee in the same way, before hitting a word like Egg, and Iiiii before saying Ink, and so on and so forth, with each vowel. Now try the word Arm.'

We did so, and it worked beautifully.

By the fourth lesson we were getting on well with individual words, no matter how hard they once had been for us.

'Next, we are going to learn a speech,' our teacher announced. 'My short speech incorporates all the worst hurdles and fences that a stammerer can meet during the course of a conversation. It isn't much of a speech, as speeches go. But I guarantee that after you have mastered it, and spoken it many times without a hitch in the manner that I have taught you, you will all have gone a long way to beating your stammer.'

It went like this. 'NnnnnLadies and NnnnnGentlemen. Aaaall people in the world are Nnnnncrying for help. NnnnnThey expect the Nnnnnhelp from the Nnnnn-Heavens, the EeeeeEarth, Nnnnnfrom Nnnnnfriends, Nnnnnrelations and Nnnnnfamily. NnnnThey all Nnnnn-forget that . . . etc.'

For me, the test came when I ordered my first snack from Rowlands, the 'sock' shop, where until then I had only shyly tendered a small piece of paper on which I had written, 'a banana, please' or the name of some other gap-filling snack. The boys milling round the counter had become accustomed to this.

This time I stood in the doorway, summoning up my adrenalin before making my move. My speech was short, loud and dramatic. Using the Burgess method of a swing, and a rhythm, and a pause, and a run, I said, 'NnnnnMay I have aaaaa NnnnnFish-cake, NnnnnPlease?'

Total silence fell as the other boys spun round with their mouths open. The dumb had spoken! The effect was spoiled when the elderly lady behind the counter said, 'Of course you can have a fish-cake, dear. Would you like cod or tinned salmon?'

The others waited tensely for me to make my next move. Nothing happened. I had not rehearsed that bit. I paused, drew out my small notebook and wrote one word 'Cod'. As I handed it to the motherly lady the buzz of conversation renewed. At least I had won half my battle.

I lived off those fish-cake snacks for about a month before I mastered the even more dramatic demand, 'Nnnnnn-Bangers and NnnnnnMash, NnnnnPlease!'

Every time I entered the shop the other boys greeted me with joyful cries of 'It's Benters! Come on, what's it going to be? NnnnnFish-cakes or NnnnnnBangers and NnnnnMash?' Thank God I had a well-developed sense of humour. Otherwise it would have been hell.

The miracle of speech took some time to become fully

apparent. Slowly my stammer improved, though it was still full of Nnnnns, Aaaaahs, Eeeehs, Iiiiis and so on, while the strange variations in rhythm and cadence were almost musical. Despite all this, I managed to convey whatever I wished to communicate.

Moreover, as I became more adept in the use of this technique, the Nnnnn and Aaaaa prefixes became unconscious, and therefore were silently expressed. My speech was hesitant but almost normal. Along with this improvement, I was also learning to control my acute shyness. I could now answer questions in class orally, instead of having to write down every word. It also meant that, at last, I could speak to girls instead of just gawping at them longingly, and I finally summoned up the courage to speak to the dentist's golden-haired daughter.

It also opened another door for me. I became interested in amateur theatricals. Wellfield Road, where we lived, had been filling up rapidly with new buildings. Once more, it seemed that wherever Ma took the lead, others followed. Among the new neighbours was a family with four boys, Michael, Peter, David and Paul Tomlinson. The whole family loved amateur theatricals, especially David, who later became a well-known actor. We became good friends as well as neighbours. Tony was contemporary with Michael and Peter, while David, Paul and I formed a junior gang, of which David, being three years older, was the leader.

After I started to speak without stammering too badly, David persuaded Paul and me to join him in writing and performing a play. This tale of adventure and mystery was performed in the large drawing-room of the Tomlinsons' house, before an audience of our joint families and friends. I remember we called this melodramatic offering *Dope* and that the 'jewels', consisting of Mrs Tomlinson's cultured pearls, were cunningly 'hidden' in a large vegetable-marrow which lay prominently displayed on the table, centre-stage.

David, who played both the leading roles of the villain

and the chief of Scotland Yard, wore a bald-wig for one part and a moustache for the other, but he got so excited with his first-night nerves that he forgot to remove his wig when changing parts, which further confused our enthusiastic audience, who were finding the tortured plot hard enough to follow as it was.

That play was my first adventure into the world of the 'theatre' and, for that matter, the same applied to David. It is strange that we both made a career in show business.

By this time, the Spanish Civil War had broken out and, contrary to popular belief, 99 per cent of Eton was on the side of the Republicans and not the Falangists. Being half South American, and strongly influenced by the newsreels of the time, I was more than ready to embark from Folkestone harbour, aged fifteen, to join the International Brigade in Spain. However, my father, who somehow had got wind of this secret plan which a few of my Etonian friends had cooked up, put a temporary end to that idea with some wise words.

'Michael, you will only be a liability to the Republicans. I know you can shoot; after all, I taught you. I also agree with you that Fascism is evil. You are right that there are plenty of youngsters fighting for the same cause in Spain. But it is my fault that your Spanish is nearly non-existent and therefore you won't be able to follow orders as a Spanish soldier.

'Believe me when I say that your war and your brother's war will come soon. It will also be fought against the evil of Fascism. Take my advice, stay here and learn as much as you can. Then, when your turn comes, you will be able to fight that much better and be that much more effective. Have no doubt about it. We will soon be fighting for *our* lives and *our* freedom.'

Even I, with my propaganda-fired pigheadedness, could see the wisdom of what Pop was telling me.

As far as my lack of Spanish was concerned, Pop was right in blaming himself. Tony and I had started Spanish lessons with Pop when I was about five years old, but

Tony wanted to devote himself to his drawing and his cricket and so he devised a plan to halt the Spanish lessons.

He knew that Pop was sensitive about being bald and took me aside. 'Here is a super Spanish phrase to tell Pop: *El profesor no tiene pelo.*' It means, although I did not know it at the time, 'The professor has no hair.'

I rehearsed the phrase until I got it right, and then proudly approached my father. Tugging Pop's plus-fours to gain his full attention, I loudly proclaimed, '*El profesor no tiene pelo.*'

Pop sensed that something had gone wrong somewhere, and mistakenly believed that neither of us wanted to learn Spanish. Later, he blamed himself for being vain, which he was not, but undoubtedly he was sensitive about his baldness.

On one occasion I was playing golf with him, a privilege I had enjoyed under his patient tuition from the age of six. Pop had recently started to rub raw paraffin on his bald head, an odd practice engendered by one of our visiting Peruvian cousins who told him that this would ensure a strong growth of new hair.

At the fifth hole, the other player said, 'It's a peculiar thing, Adam. This morning, ever since we started playing, I keep smelling oil-lamps.' Pop abandoned the paraffin treatment forthwith.

It was after a game of golf that Pop and Tony were nearly killed in a car crash. Their lives were saved because of a definitive warning given during a table-sitting held a short time before.

The message, which purported to come from Grandfather Dawkins, was simple and clear-cut. 'Adam, if you see a ball of blue light in front of your car, *stop immediately*! This is very important.' The message was so unexpected and so dramatic that it stayed in our minds.

Tony and Pop had finished a game of golf, which had been delayed by bad weather. My father then drove Tony to his evening class at the Folkestone Art School, where he was preparing for his entrance exam to the Royal College of Art. The local art school was part of the Folkestone Museum, which was situated at the bottom of a steep hill. At the top of the slope was a cross-roads, which had recently been fitted with the new-fangled traffic lights.

My father was the safest of drivers, but that night he was in a hurry. As they approached the lights at the top of the hill Pop could see that they had just turned green. At the same time a small ball of brilliant blue light appeared directly in front of them hovering over the bonnet of the car. They both shouted, 'The blue light!'

Pop braked sharply and the car skidded to a halt on the wet road, just short of the traffic lights. At that exact moment, another car jumped the red light at his intersection and hurtled over the cross-roads. Pop said later, 'At the speed that idiot was driving, we would all have been killed.'

Make of it what you will, that is precisely what happened.

In 1936 Rudyard Kipling died and was interred in Poets' Corner in Westminster Abbey. He had been in eclipse ever since the First World War, when his genuine love of the British ethos had been deliberately misread by interested parties as an incitement to make imperial war.

However, at Eton during the thirties, there was a welcome revival of interest in his work, especially in the stories written for his own children: *The Jungle Book*, *Just So Stories*, *Puck of Pook's Hill*, and *Rewards and Fairies*, all of which were great favourites with M'tutor. I have re-read them many times and I wish I had a fraction of Kipling's skill at the art of story-telling. Certainly, his books were very much a part of my life, and for the only prize I ever won at Eton I chose his *Humorous Tales*.

Kipling's death was overshadowed by the death of George V but I, at fourteen, felt the loss of the writer far more deeply than the passing of the monarch.

The royal funeral was manipulated skilfully into a

91

national 'gloom-fest' that far exceeded anything I had ever seen before. Everything immovable in and around Windsor and Eton was draped in black crêpe, every flag flew at half-mast, while large numbers of people who could not possibly have known the king personally walked around wearing black ties and arm-bands, their demeanour suitably grave and their voices hushed.

Throughout the land there was genuine affection for the royal family, especially in the town of Windsor, but a lot of this display of grief was sheer hypocrisy. To commemorate his passing with such enormously expensive pomp and circumstance in the middle of the Depression, with the sad spectacle of hunger-marchers converging on London, was inappropriate to say the least. Great numbers of miners, ship-builders, steel workers, craftsmen and labourers, as well as white-collar workers had no prospect of employment, and many of their families were in a state of semi-starvation on the shameful pittance of the dole.

One group of unemployed men, mainly miners from County Durham and Yorkshire, came to spend a day with us at Eton, where they had been invited by the boys. They were a warm and friendly lot and, once the initial shy formalities were over, we got along well, playing a lively game of soccer with no quarter given on either side, followed by a huge tea, and rounding off the day by showing our new-found friends round the ancient school buildings. Their pinched faces showed the hardship they were enduring, and we felt for them, but that day was a worthwhile occasion for us all, filled with laughter and comradeship.

One of the miners endeared himself to us by describing Eton as 'the most expensive bloody slum I ever saw!'

Traditionally, Eton schoolboys provided the final guard of honour for the funeral of the dead monarch, lining the inner courtyard of Windsor Castle from the second archway and gates right up to the steps of St George's Chapel. Half the school was wearing the usual black tails or jackets, with mourning arm-bands, and the rest of us, who formed the Officers' Training Corps, wore Eton's distinctive rust-coloured uniforms, capped, belted, putteed and shiny-booted, and bearing the 1914 pattern short-model Lee-Enfield magazine rifles.

The sound of the muffled drums in the courtyard below and the music of the *Dead March in Saul* played by the massed bands of the Guards regiments counterpointed the measured tramp of the slow-marching military and naval personnel who preceded the cortège. They consisted of a small detachment of gauntleted, dismounted Life-Guards in their shining helmets, long blue-grey greatcoats buttoned right up to the neck over their dress uniforms, with their swords carried reversed under their arms. They were followed by the Royal Navy's guard of honour, slow-marching with the distinctive swaying gait of seagoing servicemen. Their hands gripped the long white trail-ropes attached to the heavy gun-carriage upon which rested the unadorned oak coffin containing the body of the dead king.

Behind the gun-carriage marched his four sons, the Prince of Wales, the Duke of York, the Duke of Gloucester, and the Duke of Kent, each wearing his buttoned-up greatcoat over the uniform of his respective service, with their swords reversed at their sides.

The princes were followed by a riderless horse, led by a Horse-Guards groom. This was the dead king's charger, with the royal cavalry sabre reversed in its saddle-sheath and the late king's riding-boots reversed in the stirrups.

Next came female members of the bereaved royal family. Queen Mary with the princesses and duchesses were in closed carriages, their mourning clothes and pale, veiled faces dimly glimpsed through their coach windows.

After them came the long procession of visiting foreign royalty, among whom were King Haakon of Norway, King Leopold of the Belgians, King Zog of Albania, King

Carol of Romania, and world leaders from practically every country on earth.

It was an unforgettable sight, isolated details of which I can still call vividly to mind. But the thing that impressed me the most was the sheer austerity of the plain oak coffin on the gun-carriage. I was surprised the royal coffin was so short. But then George V was not a tall man.

In complete contrast to all this royal pomp, I met a man in Dover who was to have a profound effect on all our lives. His name was Eddie Partridge and he was a grocer. For me, he was the archetypal proprietor of the little shop on the corner. Eddie's corner store, in Ma's words, sold everything from a needle to an anchor. Whenever I opened his shop door to the sound of a tinkling bell I felt that I had walked straight into the nineteenth century.

Eddie exactly matched the image created by his shop. He was small and compactly built. My mother said he had a typical sailor's face, open, cheerful and alert, with no guile. His positive attitude to life had overcome many obstacles, not the least being that he was almost illiterate, having had to leave school and go to work while still a small boy.

His whole life had been hard work, which was why he understood the people he served so well, and why he had such compassion for the desperate predicament of the unemployed. Eddie was not a religious man in the conventional sense but, like my father and mother, he had an abiding faith in the existence of a higher power, which he believed could be contacted if only we opened our minds in the right way.

Certainly, Eddie Partridge was an extraordinary medium, and my parents 'sat' with Eddie and his equally lovable wife Biny from the mid-thirties to September 1940, when they were forced to leave Folkestone.

During that time, as my father said, 'we were witnesses to miracles,' and Pop never exaggerated. 'During these sittings, your mother and I witnessed telekinesis, materialization, levitation and other remarkable physical phenomena, as well as receiving first-class evidence with an accurate, predictive content that later proved to be a hundred per cent correct.'

Eddie also had exceptional ability as a healer, which my father witnessed when he unexpectedly dropped into the shop for a chat about a coming seance. This was how Pop described it to me:

'While we were talking, the door opened and into the shop rushed a young girl of about fourteen. She was hysterical and crying pitifully.

' "Uncle Eddie," she sobbed, "I'm going to jump off the cliff. Look at me, I can't go on like this."

'The poor lass was suffering from a dreadful case of acne. She would have been such a pretty girl but her whole face was covered in ugly spots, some of them suppurating. Eddie took her in his arms and cuddled her.

' "Don't you worry, dear," he said. "Go home and have a lie down, and when you wake up have a nice cuppa tea. I promise you, love, you will be all right."

'As he spoke, Eddie passed his hands over the girl's face, without touching the skin. The girl had stopped crying and, after giving Eddie a grateful hug, she left quietly.

' "Poor love," Eddie said. "She's an only child, and her dad's dead. But she'll be all right. I was worried for her, 'cos I know she meant that bit about chucking herself off the cliffs."

'About an hour later, the shop door burst open and in rushed the same girl. Only she wasn't the same.

' "Look at me, Uncle Eddie, look at me! You were right, I'm pretty again."

'Believe me, Michael, her face was radiant, shining with happiness. But, what was still more remarkable, *there wasn't a mark on her skin*. No spots, no redness. No sign whatsoever of that appalling acne.'

Eddie Partridge had healed many other local people, some of whom my father was able to interview. They were all sensible, down-to-earth folk; some of them had known Eddie for many years. There was not one word of doubt expressed by any of them when they were referring to this extraordinary man.

Chapter Seven

Our Family Airline

My parents had suffered a severe financial set-back and were finding the fees at Eton a burden. During the holidays I realized this and suggested leaving. M'tutor was upset. He believed I could win a place at a university and offered to board me for nothing so that my parents would have to pay only the tuition fees. Pop, quite rightly, would not hear of it. Moreover, my parents were also helping to support my brother at the Royal College of Art. So, with regret at leaving the splendid Hope-Joneses and my friends at Eton, at the end of the following term I came home to Folkestone.

I still had a burning ambition to become a pilot in the Royal Air Force. I was seventeen and there seemed no reason why I should not join the RAF when I reached my eighteenth birthday. In the meantime, to fill in the long months before I came to that magical age, I enrolled in the Folkestone council's educational scheme, studying drawing, learning to handle a typewriter, and trying to master shorthand, as I thought these skills would be useful. This further education at the town's technical college and the local art school cost a fraction of the fees at Eton so, as I was living at home, there was no great financial burden on my parents.

I spent a lot of my free time that year haunting Lympne airfield, which was within an easy bike-ride. The aerodrome was perched on top of the hills overlooking

Romney Marsh, and I spent hours there absorbing the ethos of flight. At the same time, cousin Antonio arrived from Peru. Like me, he was determined to learn to fly.

That private airfield had long fascinated me. The Cinque Ports Aero Club was one of the oldest in Britain and many famous flyers used it, especially during the two big events of the flying year, the Folkestone air races and the Lympne air show.

In September 1938 we enjoyed the last peacetime Lympne air show, with competitors from all over the continent joining in the open day. There was a fine display of aerobatics by French Caudron and Dewoitine monoplane fighters of the Armée de L'Air, and some disciplined three-plane formation flying by RAF Gauntlet biplane fighters from Hawkinge. This was followed by a single Gauntlet performing the 'Bunt', a spectacular outside loop, with the aircraft diving past the vertical.

The spectacular feat had been heralded by the announcer over the public-address system, 'This is one of the most dangerous stunts ever performed by a standard British fighter, and the Gauntlet has had to be specially braced to take the violent stresses involved.'

After the aircraft had regained its normal flying position, the large crowd at the airfield burst into applause. During the stunt I noticed the German team, who were equipped with Bucker Jungmeister biplanes, lovely taut little aerobatic machines, smiling confidently at each other. We were soon to know why.

Their three-man pilot team from the Richthofen squadron took off and climbed in tight formation. At their chosen altitude they winged over, to dive down low above our heads, sweeping upwards in a soaring chandelle. They levelled off at the top of their climb and then, still in impeccable formation, the three Jungmeisters dived effortlessly beyond the vertical and performed the same outside loop over which the announcer had waxed so lyrical when it was performed by the RAF pilot. There was a gasp from the crowd as they did so, *twice*.

We were stunned by this brilliant display of airmanship. Only scattered applause greeted this double feat. Obviously the crowd was thinking along much the same lines as me: if the Germans are so good, what chance have our pilots got against them?

That last Lympne air show finished with a friendly air race over the old Folkestone–Lympne course, in which the French pilot, flying his Caudron monoplane, came in an easy first.

Cousin Antonio obtained his private pilot's licence, bought a de Havilland Tiger Moth, shipped it to Peru and returned to Lima to await its arrival. It was trucked up to Lima from the docks at Callao, and the large packing cases were stored in the hangar at the airport. Unfortunately, there was no-one at the airfield qualified to put the light plane together. However, the Fates have a strange way of working and, shortly after the Tiger Moth's arrival, an American, who had flown by stages all the way from Texas, landed his single-engined monoplane at Lima airport.

Over six feet four inches in height, this tall Texan was known as John 'Slim' Faucett. He was a fully qualified aeroplane mechanic who had taught himself to fly. The Stinson Reliant monoplane which he flew to Lima had been re-built by him when he purchased it cheaply after a bad crash in the United States.

Antonio had heard about him and his exploits and arranged to meet him. Slim Faucett towered above my cousin who stood, like my father, about five feet five inches in his socks. Their first conversation went something like this:

'Welcome to Lima, Mr Faucett. My name is Antonio Bentin. I understand you are a first-class aero-mechanic.'

'I am,' admitted the Texan modestly. 'Anything I can do for you, *Señor*?'

'I've got a British Tiger Moth here, still in its packing cases. Can you put it together for me?'

'Sure can,' replied the tall slim man, 'but it'll cost you.'

'Of course. How much, Mr Faucett?'

'An airline.'

'A what?'

'An airline, *Señor*. I flew down to South America to start an airline. Looks like I'm stuck here for a spell, having spent my last cent on fuel. This seems as good a place as any, and Peru sure could use a private air service. This country's almost as big as Texas. You help me to build my airline and I'll put your little plane together. Is it a deal?'

Antonio was a shrewd assessor of human nature, and knew an honest man when he saw one. He made up his mind quickly. 'It's a deal, Mr Faucett.' My cousin extended his right hand. It almost vanished inside the grinning American's big leathery palm.

'Call me Slim, Antonio.'

Their successful partnership and close friendship lasted until Slim Faucett's death, some thirty years later.

When they started their airline, it consisted solely of Slim's Stinson Reliant, which was capable of carrying the pilot and four passengers. It grew until it boasted a whole fleet of propeller-driven multi-engined Douglas airliners. Aereas Lineas Aviaçion Faucett finally flew into the jet age with Boeing 727s and British Aircraft Corporation's BAC-111s. After Slim Faucett's death, Antonio carried on alone, retiring when he reached the age of seventy-five.

At about the same time as Antonio was founding an airline, the Peruvian Bentin family decided to go into the brewing business as well. Pop was beaming when he got the news. 'The Bentins are buying the Backus & Johnson Brewery in Lima,' he announced. 'That means they will be safe during any revolution.'

'I don't follow you, darling,' said my mother.

'It's simple. During a revolution in a hot climate, you can shoot the President, blow up the generals and even take pot-shots at the Cardinal. But nobody ever shoots the master-brewer or destroys the brewery, especially when it is also the distillery for our national drink, Pisco. No booze, no revolution.'

Pisco is a raw white brandy, the Peruvian version of the Mexican fire-water. In Pisco Sour it is mixed with lime and lemon juice, white of egg, crushed ice and a touch of gum-arabic. There is a rumour that some Peruvians add gunpowder. That is not true, but although Pisco Sour tastes like harmless lemonade it has the kick of a mule.

My Peruvian family sent various cousins, such as Elias Bentin, to Germany to learn to brew fine lagers, and they have been in the same business ever since. I have drunk our Crystal lager in Peru and found it excellent, but I seldom touch Pisco. The name should be sufficient warning.

My parents had always been animal lovers and we had a succession of dogs and cats. At one time we enjoyed the company of six Scotties and five cats who lived in a constant stage of armed truce but never attacked one another.

We also had an alcoholic parrot, a West African Quaker parrakeet. It nearly died from pneumonia after it got out of its cage and fought a knock-down-drag-out battle with one of the cats, losing all its chest feathers in the fight. On the advice of the vet, Ma wrapped the bird in medicated wool to keep its chest warm, and dosed it liberally with brandy and water. This gave the parrakeet a taste for alcohol and it got upset if it did not get its daily tipple.

When it first arrived, the parrakeet was untouchable, until one day it got its foot caught in the wires which converged at the top of the cage. Pop immediately put his hand inside the cage and released its trapped foot, then, forgetting how vicious the bird could be, he took it out to examine its injuries. Polly promptly climbed up Pop's arm and kissed him gently on the mouth, crooning its thanks. From that moment on, Pop, and *only* Pop, could do whatever he liked with that bird. My brother once tried the same tactics as my father. At first all went well. The parrakeet climbed on to his shoulder and snuggled against his head. It then neatly punched a hole in his right ear like a ticket collector.

When we settled in at Wellfield, my parents built a large aviary at the bottom of our garden. Pop specialized in breeding roller and border canaries and had over a hundred of these beautiful songbirds in one end of the long wooden building. Ma bred some two hundred multi-coloured budgerigars in the other, larger half of the aviary. Apart from the stacks of roomy cages, both parts of the building were equipped with big flight-aviaries, so that the birds got plenty of exercise.

A further wooden section was equipped with yet another flight-aviary. This one contained exotic birds, such as South American parrotlets, pink masks, and other beautiful tropical specimens. These, surprisingly, settled down happily in our changeable climate. Although most of them had been bred in Britain, some came directly from South America and still managed to cope with our appalling weather.

Psittacosis, the parrot-borne disease for which there was no known cure, was the reason why so few breeders of cage-birds were allowed to import parrots from tropical countries where it was known to be endemic. My mother had a special parrot licence, which in those days was harder to obtain than a firearms certificate. She and her friend, the Marquis of Tavistock, were authorities on these rare tropical birds. Ma won many first prizes for her birds at the annual shows at Olympia and the Crystal Palace. We were all proud of that.

Tony and I were very fond of our multiplicity of pets. I particularly loved my dogs. Those wiry, low-bellied Scotties, or West Highland terriers as they are known officially, also won many prizes for my mother, and their brave and friendly personalities captured my heart for ever. When I was home for the holidays, the Scotties were my constant companions. We loved going for long walks, three to a leash in either hand. Once we were clear of traffic I released them, and we would race each other along the crest of the North Downs, their long pink tongues streaming as they scampered over those rolling hills.

It was good to be alive and alone with our God, with His sea-breeze in our faces and His creation all about us. I have known great happiness and great sadness in my life, but I have never been happier than I was on those golden days. If there is continuity of consciousness, as I believe there is, or life after death if you prefer, it would never be complete for me without those wonderful companions and the love and loyalty we shared.

Our long-suffering neighbours were the most tolerant of friends because they never complained about the miasma of animal smells that must have surrounded our home. Moreover, each morning, the dawn-chorus of canaries, budgerigars, tropical birds, barking dogs, miaowing cats, and squawking pet jackdaws must have roused them as early as it did ourselves. I also kept rabbits and guinea-pigs, but they were not audible at a distance.

Throughout those last twelve months of peace, Britain seemed to be under a strange spell. Anyone who was at all sensitive could feel the tension growing like a clock-spring being wound tight. This sense of apprehension was reflected in the newsreels, which all seemed to dwell on the might of the British Navy, the rapid expansion of the Royal Air Force, and the re-arming of our military forces with new weapons. It was as though our leaders were trying to allay public anxiety by showing us how well we were preparing for war. Most of it was a lie. We were anything but ready to call Germany's bluff.

Many youngsters like me knew that this picture of the armed might of Britain was grossly over-optimistic. We knew a lot about British and Allied warships, planes, guns and tanks, and the Germans must have known at least as much as we did. That is why the Nazis invaded Poland when the time was ripe. They knew we were not ready to face them in the field or in the air. Only on the high seas was Hitler unwilling to confront the Royal Navy's fleet of ageing warships with his own modern and more compact Kriegsmarine.

My father sensed that I was disturbed by the increasing tension and took me with him to see Eddie Partridge. It was one of those late-summer evenings that have such a breath-catching beauty.

Eddie closed the shop and asked Pop to drive into the Weald of Kent. Not far from Dover, as the twilight turned to night, we stopped beside a wood. 'This is the place I told you about, Adam,' said Eddie.

He led us to a clearing in the middle of the wood, and signed for us to be still. My father and I stood in silence while our friend moved into the centre of the clearing. A light ground-mist hung low in the bracken, and the thin smoke from a stack of smouldering branches drifted lazily through the clearing. Our friend stood still and let us feel the silence. It was so complete I felt I could reach out and touch it.

As the moon came out from behind a cloud I could see Eddie's face. He was smiling, his face radiant in the silver light. Then he made a sound. I have tried to describe it many times. The nearest I can get is that it sounded half way between a quiet whistle and a whispered word. Its effect was instantaneous. It seemed that every bird and beast, reptile and insect in that wood answered him, with a great shout of welcome. It was as though every owl, nightjar, crow, thrush, starling and hawk, each fox, badger, squirrel, hare, rabbit, stoat and weasel, in fact everything that flew, ran, jumped, scuttled or slithered in that wood joined in a loud cry of greeting to an old and trusted friend.

To me, it was as though Pan himself had entered the wood. I could see tears of joy trickling down Eddie's cheeks. I know I was crying and, behind me, I heard my father sob with wonder. Suddenly I knew that whatever was happening to my world would never alter the course of nature or affect human destiny. This was what it was all about, and everyone and everything on our Earth was part of it.

I have recounted that story many times. It remains one of the outstanding mystical experiences of my life.

In the last days of that long summer I spent a lot of time walking. It was a compulsion, as though I wanted to impress on my mind an indelible memory of all the places I loved, in case I never saw them again. I was strolling along the east Kent cliffs, as usual looking idly out to sea. Suddenly, out of the heat haze over the sea appeared a glowing point of light. It slowly expanded into a great shining silver ball. As this giant sphere emerged from the mist, the shape seemed to alter and elongate. I realized that it was the *Graf Zeppelin*, the giant German airship. My only thought, as the shining colossus sailed majestically across the sky, was how lovely she was.

Years later I discovered that her purpose on that unexpected flight had been to photograph the mysterious antenna arrays recently built on the cliff tops. This was the top-secret system of radiolocation invented by Dr Watson-Watt and his brilliant team, which was destined to give our country the edge in the coming Battle of Britain.

She never again visited our shores. Within three weeks, the Germans invaded Poland.

Chapter Eight

The World Goes Mad

'A state of war exists . . . ' Those understated words were typical of the man who uttered them on that unforgettable morning of 3 September 1939. At the outbreak of hostilities our Prime Minister was still Neville Chamberlain and that simple declaration of war against Nazi Germany has remained in the minds of most people who heard the fateful radio broadcast. Almost immediately after his announcement the air-raid sirens sounded. It was a false alarm, but it was the forerunner of many such warnings. Even today I still feel a chill race up my spine when I hear that all-too-familiar wartime wailing used as a fire-alarm.

Pop had already made some provision against blast damage to our house by taking the two halves of our ping-pong table and placing each piece against the dining-room windows. These thick sheets of plywood were attached in a moment and held in place by heavy bolts.

We also crisscrossed the windows with sticky paper tape, as recommended in the ARP (Air Raid Precautions) manual for further protection from flying glass, and finally covered them with blackout curtains hastily run up by Ma on her sewing machine.

Pop and I joined the local civil defence organization, then called the ARP. We wore overalls, steel helmets and wellington boots and sported armbands with the initials ARP stencilled on them. My brother, who had recently married a fellow art student, volunteered for the army. He was recruited by the Honourable Artillery Company who, although they specialized in anti-aircraft gunnery, still practised Elizabethan pike drill!

There is a truism: 'Every war, at the start, is fought with the weapons of the one before.' In the case of Britain, France and Belgium, who were to bear the brunt of the fighting on the Western Front, this was painfully true. Only Nazi Germany seemed to have concentrated on updating and modernizing its weaponry. Hitler's six-year pre-war policy of 'guns before butter', and his mesmeric influence over the great arms-manufacturers, such as Krupps of Essen, had ensured that the Third Reich was well prepared for battle.

In Britain factories were making guns, tanks and planes as fast as they could, especially the firms of Hawker Aircraft and Vickers-Supermarine, who were turning out Hurricanes and Spitfires. But, by the end of 1939, we still had too few of these precious weapons.

At first, life in wartime Folkestone went on much as before, except that some raving idiot sent two train-loads of London children to homes in and around Folkestone. The only way they could have been brought nearer to Nazi Germany would have been to evacuate them to the continent. The local authorities housed them as best they could but, by 1940, with the threat of an invasion imminent, these kids had to be shunted off to homes less exposed to German attack.

Troop-trains were now starting to arrive at Dover and Folkestone stations for embarkation to France. From nearby Shorncliffe camp, where, as a schoolboy, I had often watched the military parade march past on the King's birthday, battalions of regular servicemen once again tramped down the steep hill of the Road of Remembrance to board the troop-ships waiting alongside the harbour wall.

Knowing that the rosemary-lined road had led to the slaughterhouse of the Western Front in the First World

War, my mother said bitterly, 'Oh, God, will they never learn?' She was badly shaken when she saw those marching men. They must have reminded her poignantly of her girlhood sweetheart, killed in Flanders.

I knew that memories of her dead fiancé still bothered my mother, because I had recently seen her go through an intensely emotional paranormal experience connected with him. Pop, Ma, Tony and I had gone to see a transfiguration medium give a demonstration of his abilities in a large house built in Grimston Avenue. Transfiguration is an eerie form of mediumship when other people's faces seem to superimpose their features over those of the medium in much the same way as a sculptor models a face out of clay. When the phenomenon is genuine, and not a case of a medium pulling faces in dim light, it is one of the most uncanny things I have ever witnessed.

The sitting, at which some thirty people were present, began with a short prayer. The lights were lowered and a red light was switched on. To further illuminate the phenomena, the medium was standing between two luminous slates, placed on either side of his head. The lighting system, though dimmed, was bright enough to give little opportunity for faking.

It was not long before the manifestations started, and various people soon recognized the faces that appeared as members of their families who had passed over.

At one point in the course of the demonstration, the face of a young man, quite unlike that of the medium, materialized over his features. My mother, who was sitting beside me, gave a stifled gasp and put her hand to her mouth. She obviously was deeply shocked. The transfigured face, which was smiling, was looking directly at her. For the first time during that seance, the manifesting entity spoke. It uttered one word: 'Floss'.

My mother burst into tears. This was her nickname, used only by members of her Westcliff family. While Ma sobbed quietly, the transfiguring entity spoke again. This time it was a short series of numbers. They were meaningless to me, but my mother nearly collapsed. Pop, who was sitting further down the room, hurried over when he heard my mother gasp, and now gently led her out of the room. She was weeping as though her heart would break.

Afterwards, when Ma had recovered enough to have a reviving cup of tea, she explained to us what had happened. 'I knew what I was in for when I heard that voice say "Floss". I instantly recognized the face, even though at first the features were not animated. It was more like a mask, yet it was absolutely lifelike. It was the face of my fiancé. The resemblance was uncanny.'

My mother paused. Then she said, quite simply and without emotion, 'When he gave me that number, I was convinced that it was all real. Those were the numbers carved on his headstone in the Imperial War Graves military cemetery. I have seen a photograph of it among row after row of so many others. I just *know* it was him.'

Folkestone was quickly losing its young men as hundreds of local territorials hurried to join their regiments, while others like me were in the process of volunteering. My brother and I were invited to many farewell parties to speed the young volunteers on their way. A few months later many of those young men were taken prisoner, and others died on the beaches at Dunkirk. I went alone to those parties, because Tony was already training with his regiment.

In spite of the miraculous way in which Air Marshal Sir Hugh Dowding had formed, armed and trained Fighter Command for the air defence of Great Britain, there was still a grave shortage of pilots. When I first volunteered for the RAF, I was confident that I would be welcomed with open arms. However, after filling in the forms and passing the physical examination with ease, I was told that the RAF would not accept me. 'We can't have non-Europeans in the Royal Air Force.' Those exact words were uttered by a pompous flight-lieutenant in the administration branch of the service. He certainly was not aircrew and probably knew little or nothing about aircraft. I remember each word with crystal clarity.

Over the subsequent eighteen months I volunteered for the RAF and the Fleet Air Arm on numerous occasions as I moved around the country, hoping for at least one recruiting board to relent, but I always got the same depressing answer.

In the meantime, Pop and I were in the process of becoming effective members of the ARP. Our civil defence drills necessitated a working knowledge of first-aid and ambulance operations. This we acquired in a series of lectures and skilled demonstrations given by members of the local St John Ambulance Brigade.

Along with many others, Pop and I learned the pressure-points of the arteries, how to stop haemorrhaging by using finger-pressure at first and then by applying tourniquets, how to splint broken bones, and how to cover each and every part of the human body with dressings and triangular bandages. We also practised artificial respiration, to be used in cases of drowning, electrocution and any other kind of trauma causing respiratory arrest.

The only remedy we were allowed to give the patient appeared to be cups of hot, sweet tea (except in cases of abdominal wounds). This we did, irrespective of whether the casualty was diabetic or not. This confirmed my mother's theory that we would have lost the First World War if we had not had tea.

Those members of the Folkestone branch of the St John Ambulance Brigade, male and female, young and old, with many retired First World War veterans among them, did a wonderful job in the short time they had before we became operational air-raid wardens and were let loose on the public.

By this time it was spring 1940 and Ma decided it would be a good idea for me to go to Southend to see the family. This was always a treat for me, but now we would not be driving there *en famille*, as was our usual practice. I went alone by train and was delighted to find nearly every member of the family there.

My cousin, John, who was a great favourite of mine not the least because we both loved aeroplanes, had much the same plans as myself. We looked forward to being RAF aircrew cadets together. It was a wonderful holiday until one night the air-raid sirens sounded the alarm. They heralded the first German bombing raid on the Thames Estuary.

It was about midnight. Auntie Mary and Uncle Alf decided that we three would be safer in their hallway. To be honest, I was terrified. As soon as the guns opened up on the German planes droning overhead and I heard the bombs being dropped on Southend, I went into a blue funk. The whole house shook as the explosions seemed to get nearer and nearer.

My aunt cuddled me while Uncle Alf stood over us wearing his newly issued steel helmet, for he was an air-raid warden. 'Don't worry, Michael,' he said in that quiet distinctive way of his. 'Everyone gets upset their first time under fire. It's much the same thing as it was in the trenches in the last lot. I was scared silly by my first taste of a German barrage. Don't worry, son. You'll be fine.'

With those understanding words, my uncle calmed my fears and I winced only when the rustling whistle of a falling bomb came close. But we were lucky. We did not have even a window broken.

By dawn the raiders had flown back to Germany. I was ashamed of myself for my weakness, and I apologized profusely. My aunt and uncle were, as usual, marvellously kind. 'Don't even think about it,' Uncle Alf said. 'I expect we'll have plenty of that sort of thing before this little lot is over. You'll get used to it, Michael.'

Uncle's reference to the war as 'this little lot' put things into perspective. Later on, in the great air-raids on London, I was probably just as scared but, along with millions of others, I had learned not to panic and to judge how near the bombs were falling by their sound. I also learned to avoid falling fragments of shrapnel by dodging into doorways whenever I heard their whistling descent. These pieces of exploding anti-aircraft shell seemed to cause as many casualties as the bombs from the raiders overhead.

When I arrived back in Folkestone, I found that little had changed. So far, the Luftwaffe had only made reconnaissance flights over the town.

In the course of our civil defence operations, we held air-raid exercises. During these we had to wear gas-masks, which were made of somewhat better quality moulded rubber than the cheap civilian issue, which was a very basic affair. We also wore hooded, rubberized-cotton jackets with long rubber gauntlet gloves and waterproof trousers tucked into wellington boots. It was the sort of outfit that, today, would cost a fortune in a sex-shop.

When wearing the gas-mask, we breathed in through the filter element. This filter nearly killed my father because of his asthma, which was not surprising when you consider that the main component of the filter was blue asbestos. We exhaled through a flat rubber valve. I immediately recognized it as an unmodified raspberry blower, which we schoolboys used to buy from novelty shops and through which we blew rude noises. Nothing had changed except that in this wartime application the farting sound was more subdued.

At the side of the mask was a protruding rubber wart, against which you could place the mouthpiece of a telephone. This made you sound like Donald Duck with a bad head cold. With the wheezing sound as you inhaled and the soft raspberry as you exhaled, telephonic communication was difficult. Thank God the Nazis and the Allies both decided not to use gas during the war, even though both sides held huge stocks of it.

After that first air-raid exercise my father had to retire from active duty with the ARP. Dressed in the full anti-gas gear he had rushed out leading his stretcher party, only to return *on* the stretcher a few minutes later. Nothing daunted, Pop immediately volunteered for the LDV, the Local Defence Volunteers, the volunteer force that became known later as Dad's Army.

Almost immediately some busybody pointed out that my father was Peruvian and he was asked to leave. He also had to give up his expensive .22-calibre single-shot target rifle as, under DORA (the Defence of the Realm Act), Pop as a registered alien was no longer considered to be a trustworthy citizen by the local firearms authority. I often wonder who kept that fine precision weapon.

One incident in our civil defence training which has remained forever in my memory occurred on a sunny morning when the phoney war was at its lowest lull, just before the lightning invasion of the Netherlands by the Wehrmacht. I had been detailed with two other volunteers, average age eighteen years, to take our vintage ambulance, which rumour said was a relic of the 1914–1918 war, and carry out an air-raid exercise on the grassy Leas.

The site chosen for this operation was directly opposite the Leas Cliff Hall. The Leas end of Earls Avenue is graced by a life-size bronze statue of William Harvey, the reputed discoverer of the circulation of the blood. The sculpture is mounted on a large granite base. I felt at the time that this was a splendid setting for our first venture into the noble art of healing.

There the three of us stood in our full air-raid gear, tin-hats, anti-gas suits, rubber gauntlets and wellies, waiting for the 'casualties' to arrive. Probably as a result of some misunderstanding in the course of those garbled telephone conversations, they never came.

Nobody took much notice of us, other than to giggle at our bizarre appearance, until it dawned on us that there must have been a hitch. Rather than waste the whole morning, I decided to accost a few people with the object of finding a volunteer. Two or three men and women said they were far too busy but one small, elderly man with the weathered look of a naval officer agreed to help us. I recognized him as a member of my mother's bridge club. I believe he was a retired admiral. He certainly was a most co-operative volunteer.

We first laid a blanket on the grass. Our 'casualty' removed his bowler hat and lay down on the blanket, face up, smiling and confident of our skill.

'I'm going to make you a blast victim, sir,' I said in my best official tones. 'I'll give you a fractured femur and a severed femoral artery.'

As I spoke, I scribbled the description of his supposed injuries on to a large label which I attached to the top button of his waistcoat. I then applied pressure to the top of his femoral artery, which he seemed to enjoy, having been in the Navy for many years. I next applied a loose tourniquet around the top of his thigh, and finally put on two splints, firmly securing them with two triangular bandages.

As a final touch, I wrote, 'Tourniquet applied', and the time '11.30 a.m.' on his forehead with my mother's black eyebrow pencil. This was in accordance with the instructions given to us that the tourniquet was to be loosened every twenty minutes so that the traumatized tissue would not be starved of blood. I felt very professional. I also noted that my colleagues were watching me with undisguised admiration at my efficient and speedy handling of our 'casualty'.

The admiral smiled at me as I straightened up above him.

'Will I be all right?' he asked jokingly.

I grinned and nodded my head vigorously. My 'tin hat' came off, fell like the blunt blade of a guillotine and hit our 'casualty' on his bald head. He went out like a light. I am not a tall man, but a British Second World War steel helmet weighed several pounds and had a heavy welted metal rim. In fact it was often used in hand-to-hand fighting as the last resort of a disarmed combatant. It could deliver a terrible blow.

The three of us stood there, rigid with shock. I recovered first. 'Get him into the ambulance and rush him to the Victoria Hospital,' I hoarsely ordered the others. They hurriedly withdrew one of the folding stretchers and set it up while I hastily examined the suddenly *real* casualty, who was deeply unconscious and breathing stertorously. Obviously I had given my unfortunate victim a hairline fracture of the cranium or, at best, a bad concussion.

I gently applied a dressing to the wound and secured it round his jaw with a bandage, then carefully wiped the black-pencilled message from his forehead and altered the wording on the casualty label to read, 'Fractured skull'.

'Quick, get him on to the stretcher, and for God's sake be careful with him!'

We lifted him and laid him on the stretcher, then gingerly picked it up and tried to get the ancient contraption and its precious burden, head-first, into the ambulance. This antiquated vehicle was equipped with metal channels, into which the steel U-shaped runners of the stretcher were intended to slide.

It seemed to be an unnecessarily tight fit, and no matter how hard we pushed we could not get the stretcher all the way inside the ambulance. The end with the admiral's feet on it stuck out, so that we could not close the rear doors.

I realized why the stretcher had stuck in the runners. Somehow, we had caught the admiral's fingers in the metal channel. I did not dare move him, for I now realized we had probably broken three of his fingers as well.

Then I had an inspiration. I took off my tie and with it I secured the two rear door handles together.

'Get him to the hospital before we kill him,' I shouted, including my colleagues as accessories after the fact. 'I'll phone the casualty department and tell them we're on the way. Don't wait for me. Just get the poor old sod there.'

I rushed to the nearest telephone kiosk, which was some fifty yards up the road, while the eighteen-year-old driver struggled to get the ancient motor started. In so doing, he flooded the carburettor.

I managed to get through to the hospital and breathlessly told the casualty department what had happened, omitting the detail that it was all my fault. I reasoned that the important thing was to get our victim into the hands of people who knew what they were doing and not to start recriminations.

I was sweating like a pig inside my anti-gas gear as I raced back to the ambulance. Before I could reach it, I heard the motor catch and burst into life. The young driver revved it to stop it stalling and crashed home the gears. Surprisingly, the elderly ambulance took off like a rocket. I could see that it was approaching the sharp corner at the top of Earls Avenue much too fast. To my horror, I saw the vehicle lurch over in a skidding turn, with both nearside wheels barely touching the road. Under the stress of centrifugal force my tie broke and the rear doors of the ambulance swung wide open.

Like a torpedo from a destroyer's deck, the stretcher, with the admiral strapped firmly on to it, shot out of the back and crashed, feet first, into William Harvey's statue. I panicked, burst into tears and ran home to get help. As home was a good three miles away, I plead temporary insanity to account for my irrational action.

After I had gasped out my story to my parents, Pop phoned the hospital. The ward sister told him that they had received the admiral and that he was, in their words, 'As well as could be expected.'

After three anxious days and near-sleepless nights, the matron, a firm but kindly soul, let me see my victim. 'Don't stay too long,' she said. 'The shock of seeing you again might kill him.' Then she added with a wry smile, 'He's a tough old bird. Don't worry, your "casualty" will be all right.'

With a sigh of relief, I entered the small private ward. The staunch old sailor was propped up on pillows, his head swathed in a many-tailed bandage. His left arm was in plaster, supported by a metal splint. His legs were raised in plaster splints and were held in traction. He was looking at me between them.

'Hello, sir,' I said brightly. 'Do you remember me?'

That was probably the most unnecessary question I have ever asked.

To my amazement, the old boy, despite all the surgical paraphernalia, was quite cheerful. In fact, when he saw me, he started to chuckle.

'Oh, God!' I muttered to myself. 'Brain damage!'

Mercifully that was not the case. Incredibly, my casualty was seeing the funny side of his predicament. He told me why. 'You see, my boy, that morning my wife said to me, "Go for a nice walk along the Leas. It will do you the world of good."'

I believe that marvellous old man lived for many years, eventually dying peacefully in bed. One thing is certain, I will never forget him. I am sure the feeling was mutual.

Chapter Nine

The Nine-day Miracle

On 10 May 1940 the Germans had invaded Holland and Belgium. Guderian's Panzers had swept on into northern France forcing the French Army and the British Expeditionary Force to retreat towards the coast at Dunkirk. By 28 May, the Wehrmacht had pinned these forces within a narrow perimeter, and Allied troops were desperately dug in around the town and the beaches with their backs to the sea.

Goering's well-trained and battle-hardened Luftwaffe, who had learned their grim trade in Spain and Poland, spread panic and disorder among the Allied troops, many of whom were inexperienced soldiers. Only weeks before, these young men had been civilians, and they were stunned by the terrifying effectiveness of the Luftwaffe's dive-bombers and their first sight of the fast-moving enemy armour.

In Folkestone, we heard the guns and saw the black columns of greasy smoke swirling upwards from the burning French coastal towns as the Allied resistance started to collapse and the Wehrmacht drove towards Calais and Boulogne. British ships carrying more troops, guns and tanks towards the Channel and North Sea ports still in Allied hands were also coming under attack from Goering's dive-bombers.

From the Folkestone cliff tops, I could see these ships in mid-Channel surrounded by the erupting spray of near-misses, while Hurricanes and Spitfires scrambled from Hawkinge and Lympne airfields and roared low overhead to try to intercept the strafing Junkers Ju 87s and 88s. But the German aircraft, with their murderous task already accomplished, were already racing back towards their newly captured French and Belgian airfields.

Norway was a shambles and was being evacuated and, although the Royal Navy sank German destroyers at the port of Narvik, we lost some ships, including *Glorious*, one of our few aircraft carriers. The Dutch had collapsed soon after the razing of the centre of Rotterdam in indiscriminate bombing by Dornier, Junkers and Heinkel medium bombers when thousands of civilians were killed. Most of Belgium was in enemy hands.

Along with many others not actively engaged in fighting the Nazis, I felt utterly frustrated. All this killing and the appalling sight of the great clouds of oily black smoke hanging over Boulogne in the clear summer air had turned a glorious May into a nightmare.

As the battle for northern France reached its climax, the Luftwaffe turned part of its attention to attacking the south-east airfields of the RAF to neutralize the British air opposition. The aerodromes at Manston, near Deal, Hawkinge and Lympne all came under preliminary attacks, probing their ground defences, which were minimal. But these light reconnaissance raids were nothing like the later mass-bombing attacks which almost destroyed our frontline airfields during the coming weeks.

Then came the miracle of the evacuation of Dunkirk. In all the years I had lived in Folkestone, I had never seen the Channel so calm for so long. For nine consecutive days those normally boisterous seas were like a village millpond.

Folkestone, Dover, Deal and Ramsgate were suddenly in the front line. Britain's south-east ports were the bases from which the rescuing ships set out to snatch our army from the beaches and to which they returned over-laden with troops. At the Folkestone end of this operation, the sight was unforgettable.

I saw the men on their arrival. They were exhausted, haggard, hollow-eyed, unshaven and filthy, many of them walking-wounded, and most of them without their weapons. Practically all of them were grey with shock. The Guards, in contrast, somehow had kept their arms, and they still managed to look like effective fighting soldiers. The Guardsmen actually marched off the quay at Folkestone harbour. But then that was what they had been trained to do. Most of the other soldiers were half-trained civilians in uniform. Now, suddenly, they were all veterans, blooded in battle.

We did what we could to help them. Above all, we showed them our heartfelt appreciation of their efforts, welcoming them back from those murderous beaches. But, apart from assisting with bandages and dressings, feeding them and quenching their thirst with hot, sweet tea, helping them to re-kit with essential articles of uniform, and distributing cigarettes and chocolate, what could anyone do in such circumstances?

It was during this time of panic and chaos that I experienced an eerie subjective clairvoyant vision. One summer afternoon I returned home from my civil defence work on the Leas, where I had been standing by with another ambulance team. In the clear air on the cliff top, I had seen more ships, including a hospital-ship clearly marked with a Red Cross, being strafed in mid-Channel by Junkers 87s, the cranked-winged dive-bombers, while, from Lympne and Hawkinge, Spitfires and Hurricanes had roared out over my head to intercept them.

I was standing in the back garden at Wellfield wondering what was going to happen next, when out of the north-west swept a rolling thunder-cloud, barely skimming the tops of the downs. I had never seen anything quite like it, as its huge, seething mass swirled and boiled overhead, racing towards the east.

I was watching its departure in puzzled wonder when my attention was drawn to the clear area of summer sky from which the strange storm-cloud had first appeared. Following it came a large fleet of multi-engined bombers, flying east towards the embattled British forces at Dunkirk.

Formation after formation of the heavy planes swept over my head. As they disappeared from view over Folkestone, I realized that they were all *old* aircraft, machines which were no longer considered to be operational. The thought crossed my mind that we must be scraping the bottom of the barrel to have been forced to muster this large formation of obsolete bombers. Another thing that bothered me was that they were all old *Allied* planes such as Breguets, Latecoères, Amiot, and Potez bombers of the late twenties.

Where were our new Wellingtons and Whitleys, our Hampdens and Blenheims? Surely they were not all committed to the battle? Could this be the only air reserves we had? My mind was racing with these conjectures when a final thought struck me. In all the excitement, I could not recall hearing the roar of their engines and, God knows, they were low enough to have been audible, if not deafening. Furthermore, that strange swirling storm-cloud had been unaccompanied by thunder. What was it all about?

When my parents came home, I asked them what they had seen, and what Pop thought of it all. Both of them looked blankly at me.

'What storm-cloud?' asked my mother.

'What planes?' my father sounded equally puzzled.

I did not pursue the matter further as they were both tired from their welfare work down at the harbour.

Years afterwards, as an intelligence officer in the RAF, I tried to discover what operation those formations had been intended to carry out. All I got was a polite reply that, to the knowledge of the RAF's Operational Records Department, no such mass-formation flight of obsolete Allied bombers had ever taken place. Furthermore, I could find no information, from meteorological records, of such a savage, short-lived storm during the calm, sunny period during which the evacuation from Dunkirk had been accomplished. I have no logical explanation for that extraordinary phenomenon.

As the evacuation struggled on, the Royal Navy, closely supported by Britain's Merchant Navy, was joined by a large fleet of 'little ships'. These ranged in size from the 110-foot Thames sailing-barge *Cambria*, skippered by my friend Bob Roberts, who succeeded in rescuing over fifty soldiers before he was too badly wounded to continue, to Thames pleasure-craft, many of which had never been further downstream than Teddington Lock.

Among this auxiliary fleet of small craft were fishing boats, beach-based lifeboats, an ancient paddle-steamer, *Maid of the Medway*, many small river cruisers and motor-boats. In fact, these flotillas of little ships consisted of any seaworthy vessel, no matter how ancient or diminutive, which would be able to operate in the shoal-waters of the Dunkirk and La Panne beaches. Their task was to ferry the troops, who were standing in lines, up to their chests in the sea, and take them to the larger, deep-draught ships.

It was this unique fleet of little ships which captured the imagination of the free world. The extraordinary feat of bravery and seamanship in rescuing some 340,000 British and Allied troops tended to obscure the fact that the Allies had lost the Battle of France and practically all their war *matériel* which, perforce, they had left behind.

Hitler had won hands down. On 14 June the Germans entered Paris. In those few weeks the Nazis had conquered half of Europe. Now we had to face the Battle of Britain.

Pop and I had volunteered for the Local Defence Volunteers and had been turned down. The fact that most of the officers had known my family for years made no difference. Pop was an alien, neutral but still a foreigner, and therefore could not be trusted. This attitude of mind was engendered by widespread rumour of the existence of a clandestine Fifth Column, made up of Nazi agents secretly infiltrated into Britain. Fortunately, the British sense of humour saved us from complete panic. A drawing appeared in *Punch* of a heavily armed 'nun' asking another 'nun' for directions. The second Sister of Mercy replies, 'Sorry I can't help you. I'm a German parachutist, meinself.'

One result of the rumours of impending invasion was that all the signposts on Romney Marsh and other places were taken down. This only hindered the legitimate movements of British troops and civilians unfamiliar with the area. Long after the war I was surprised to see that there was still a dearth of signposts on the twisting roads across the Marsh. On asking a local inhabitant why this was so, he replied cryptically, 'Ah well! You never know . . . '

The Luftwaffe's attacks on the slow-moving British convoys began to increase. These raids were directed against shipping proceeding towards our east coast ports, including the Port of London. As soon as the German Army had secured the French coastal-defence guns in the Pas de Calais area, they started shelling these beleaguered convoys. Many British merchant seamen died in the attacks and their bodies started to be washed up along our shores. Moreover, our beaches were becoming a grim sight, with most of them closed to civilians, covered with barbed wire, and daily sown with mines.

In the midst of all this, I had to leave home to go to London to take my exams for entrance into London University. I had been preparing for the exams when I was not engaged in civil defence duties. I thought that, if I passed them, the RAF would surely want me.

The memory of that slow train journey to Charing Cross will remain with me always. The grubby green Southern Railway carriages were jammed with troops from Dunkirk, most of them asleep, while others sat, smoked and stared silently out of the windows. By the look on their faces, I could see that they were still in shock, hardly believing that they were back in Britain.

Some of the carriages smelt unmistakably of French cigarettes. These compartments were filled with troops in horizon-blue uniforms, for some 140,000 of the soldiers who were brought back from Dunkirk were the remnants of the huge French Army, which was mainly made up of reservists with a tough backbone of regular soldiers.

These were the troops whose generals had been unable to cope with the shock of the blitzkrieg, and whose chain of command had disintegrated under the shock of battle. They were from the seasoned rear-guard, who had fought beside British troops to bring the German advance to a halt, and they had held, between them, the shrinking battle perimeter of Dunkirk for nine long days. They deserved to be rescued. They lived to fight again, but the next time that they would set out from Britain would be to win back their honour at Bir Hacheim in North Africa, and to be among the first to land on the Normandy beaches on 6 June 1944.

All the way on that slow journey up to London, wherever back gardens lined the railway tracks, groups of women and children and elderly men wearing their 1914–1918 medals stood and waved little paper Union Jacks, shouting greetings to the battle-weary men inside the trains.

Most of the soldiers were too exhausted to wave back, and many of them slept on till we arrived at Charing Cross station, where large crowds were gathered to welcome them home. The feeling of relief that the British Expeditionary Force was safely back in Britain was so strong I could almost taste it.

Although I was not a serviceman, in some small way I felt as though I was a part of them, and I wept silently for their suffering and for the warmth of the welcome for this battered army.

As I got off the train, the air-raid sirens sounded but nobody took cover. They just waited, looking hopefully for their menfolk among the mass of returning soldiers. Whenever they found them, their joy was overwhelming.

As these couples hugged each other and wept, I felt like an eavesdropper, and I hurried out of the station.

In London, I stayed with my delightful new sister-in-law, Mona, near Notting Hill Gate and, to my surprise, I passed my examinations with credits in every subject. This made no difference to the next RAF recruiting officer. From his point of view, my father was a registered alien and that was that. I pointed out that my brother was in the Honourable Artillery Company, one of the oldest and most prestigious regiments in the British Army, but the recruiting officer remained firm.

Meanwhile, my parents had been summarily ordered to leave Folkestone, which of course was in the 'front line'. They sold up Wellfield, their comfortable home, at a ridiculously low price to a war-profiteer and distributed all the pets, including the alcoholic parrakeet, among a few sympathetic friends and neighbours.

Ma arranged for some of their fine furniture and the lovely porcelain and silver they had painstakingly collected over the years to be stored in London until they found suitable accommodation. They had to sell the rest of their possessions for a fraction of what they were worth. They were given no alternative.

My brother and I were furious. There was no redress from the local authorities and no compensation was ever paid. The sole explanation given to my parents was a sneering, 'Don't you know there's a war on?'

My father was not allowed to possess a wireless set or a bicycle, and his car had to be sold immediately or it would be confiscated. Not one of my parents' so-called friends stood up for them and protested against this cavalier treatment. My mother and father were railroaded out of Folkestone as though they had a contagious disease, and no apology was ever made.

Chapter Ten

Not All Right on the Night

The Battle of Britain had started on 15 August. Every morning the air-raid sirens howled their disheartening dirge and, moments later, the skies above Kent and the south-eastern approaches to London were filled with aircraft. It was hard to make out which ones were British and which were German, because most of the big air battles were fought at altitudes at which the planes were seen only dimly. Their position was marked by trailing streams of vapour, drawing complex patterns across the summer skies.

At times, individual aircraft from both sides of the battle would wing over and dive lower. They pursued each other relentlessly, with guns chattering and streams of fiery tracer-shells arcing towards the ground as the bullets and cannon shells lost velocity.

Everyone watched, whether these separate duels to the death took place high up against the blue background of the sky or in a deadly hedge-hopping game of tag across the ripening cornfields, the woods or the rooftops. Only when the British fighters found themselves approaching the great London barrage of silver kite-balloons would they break off combat, and let the anti-aircraft guns take up the fight.

Then the skies became filled with the dark puff-balls of exploding shells, raining steel fragments and shrapnel on to the streets below. If you were wise, you kept your head down and sought shelter below ground. But the spectacle of RAF fighter pilots engaging such incredible odds, sometimes as much as ten to one in favour of the Luftwaffe, was too stirring to miss. Insane though it may sound today, most of us felt that we were letting our side down if we did not watch our gallant defenders with heartfelt thanks for their sacrifice and with positive prayers for their safety.

They were unique days and nights, the latter made more frightening by the distinctive, desynchronized drone of the German bombers' engines as they circled high above London among the sweeping beams of the searchlights and the flashes of the exploding shells.

We were now living in London and I wanted to get a temporary job while I waited for the RAF to relent. But since Dunkirk and the collapse of France, the British government had become even more paranoid about foreigners. Moreover, the emergency measures of the Defence of the Realm Act now precluded me even from studying physics at London University, as this branch of science had become a prohibited area of employment or study for anyone except pure-bred Brits. The son of a Peruvian aeronautical engineer was highly suspect. That meant goodbye to a career in physics, aeronautics or ballistics.

I went to the Labour Exchange in the City and explained my position. I was immediately offered a job. It was as a mortuary attendant. I said I was allergic to formaldehyde, adding that I thought opportunities to talk to the customers were too limited and that as a result my stammer might return.

I was then offered a job in Fleet Street, as an apprentice at a photographic press agency. It would pay the successful applicant £4 a week. I went along for an interview with the boss, Mr Bert Garai. I found him an honest, kindly man. He liked what he saw, and hired me on the spot.

Mr Garai was a middle-aged middle-European, small and neatly dressed, with shrewd eyes and a Hungarian sense of survival. From small beginnings before the First

World War, he had built up a first-rate international photographic agency. This provided newspapers, magazines and the general public with pictures of accidents, disasters, civil riots, royal occasions, horse races, football matches, weddings, christenings, funerals, dog shows, and other newsworthy events. Keystone Press employed some of the best press photographers in the world. According to Mr Garai, I was going to be trained to become one of them.

Having just read *The Street of Adventure*, about newspaper work in Fleet Street, I shook hands on the deal after first explaining to Mr Garai that I only intended to work for him until the RAF finally accepted me. There was a wealth of wisdom in his answer. 'God willing,' he said.

I worked hard, travelling to Fleet Street every morning from our new flat at Castelnau Mansions on the Surrey side of Hammersmith Bridge, where my parents had made their London home. In the evenings I practised drumming, a hobby I had acquired, along with a basic drum kit.

This musical event took place in a small back room in the flat, with muffled drums and a portable, wind-up gramophone with a pillowcase stuffed into its speaker. It was a dedicated affair as I almost-silently pounded out an accompaniment to any jazz record I could buy second-hand. I had taken up drumming early in 1940. Jack Filmer, a talented young cockney musician who was working in Folkestone, had given me music lessons. His teaching skill had turned me into a good drummer and I soon found myself doing gigs with other young musicians waiting for their call-up.

Through these one-night stands I met Tony Sherwood, a jazz pianist of my own age, who played boogie better than anyone I have ever heard. He was an apprentice draughtsman at the Hawker Aircraft Company at Kingston by day and a jazz pianist by night. We became close friends.

I stayed with Keystone Press in a whirl of activity for about six months. When they tried me out as a camera operator, they found I was not much of a press photographer. This was because I became too excited by whatever event I was covering and sometimes forgot to take pictures. The other professional photographers, a tough bunch of cynics, sensed my total amateurism and dropped their used flash-bulbs behind me, just as I was about to press the shutter-release.

These glass bulbs were the same size as those used in a household lamp. When dropped, they went off with a loud bang. My resulting jiggle of the big Graphlex Press camera caused me to finish up with a fine collection of headless notables.

My boss wisely put me to work in the library and caption-writing department, where I did a reasonable job for the agency until the great fire-raid of 1941, when, like most of the offices in the area around St Paul's cathedral, our premises were gutted by incendiary bombs. Mr Garai wept at the sight of the work of a lifetime in smoking ruins. The fire had destroyed over a quarter of a million negatives of unique historical value in their coverage of the great events of the twentieth century.

Meanwhile, the Ministry of Information had researched my background, following my application for a press pass. In their opinion, as the son of a Peruvian, I was not to be trusted. An immediate prohibition order was placed on me, and I was refused the MOI security pass. Mr Garai told me, sadly, that my budding press career was over. He gave me £5 as a parting gift.

I next tried playing drums as a whole-time occupation with Tony Sherwood. We had some hilarious times, finishing up by working in a trio at the Rougemont Hotel in Exeter. I featured a solo act, drumming on a line of bottles filled with different levels of water to alter their tone, and hung on strings behind me. As often as not the bottles broke in the middle of a frenzied 'drum-break'. This resulted in thunderous applause and sopping wet trousers.

We got little money but lived for free in the attic of the hotel, and we did fire-watching three nights a week. That job finished when the Luftwaffe tried to destroy Exeter. Obviously Goering had it in for me.

On our arrival back in London, we found that Tony's call-up papers for his aircrew training with the RAF had arrived. It looked as though our partnership would have to end. We decided to play together for one last time. This gig took place in a small West End night-club near the Windmill Theatre. At ten o'clock an air-raid started and built up into a major attempt to set the centre of London on fire. At midnight, the club received a direct hit. We both would have been killed for sure, but a couple of minutes before the bomb smashed through the roof we had been ordered down into the cellar. As we reached the bottom of the cellar steps, the world seemed to cave in above us. We did not even hear the bomb explode.

Tony and I managed to break out of the wreckage unscathed apart from a few bruises and minor cuts but covered from head to foot in grey dust. Others were not so fortunate, nor were the people in the place next door, which was reduced to rubble. Fires burned everywhere round us.

When the firemen finished pulling the dead and dying from the piles of bricks and splintered wood, they found my drum kit still intact under a pile of plaster and dust. The friendly stage-door keeper at the Windmill temporarily stored it for me.

As there was no public transport running, I walked to Hammersmith from the West End, seven miles through streets littered with broken glass. When I reached Castelnau Mansions at dawn, there was no glass in the front windows. Inside was a sooty shambles. Ma and Pop were shaken but unhurt. They were drinking cups of tea when I arrived. We cuddled together, weeping silently. Then we set about clearing up the flat.

Ma told me, 'When we heard the bombs coming, we just stood in the hallway and held each other tight. We didn't hear the explosion. One landed on the bank of the reservoir opposite. The sitting-room windows blew in, and all the soot came down the chimney. What a mess!

'We both prayed that you and Tony Sherwood would come through it alive.'

Pop added, 'We could read a newspaper by the light of the fires in the West End. It must be the worst raid London has ever had.'

The next day Tony Sherwood went off to his RAF training camp and, a week later, I collected my drums and got a job playing with Prince Cox's Travelling Circus, touring the West Country. I also did some inept clowning and even got laughs from the unsophisticated audiences. The small circus was not exactly Barnum and Bailey's, and we were reduced to playing village halls because travelling around with the Big Top tent was far too complicated in the restrictive wartime conditions.

Eventually the show went broke. Presumably, most of the animals were sold off, put down by the vet or eaten. So ended my brief career in the circus. But I had learned a bit more about life, including making love for the first time to a darling girl contortionist. That amazing girl could twist her body into a knot. Making love to her was an extraordinary experience. I could not believe that anything could be so exciting, physically, without breaking something. However, I did sprain my back.

On my return to London, a friend told me about an actor-manager who was auditioning for a tour of *Sweet Lavender* by Sir Arthur Pinero. After the unbelievable interlude with the lovely contortionist, I was ready to try anything. I read the part of the juvenile lead, Clement Hale, and Frank Forbes Robertson, the producer, hired me on the spot.

Two weeks later, we opened on the Monday night in Cardiff at the Playhouse Theatre. On Saturday night we closed. Once again, the Luftwaffe had pursued me. Apparently, the raid that night flattened part of the city. That put paid to the play.

It was not all Goering's fault. *Sweet Lavender* was a light piece from another era. It was dated and hardly suitable for a nation aroused to war. Moreover, owing to the shortage of male artists because of conscription, Frank Forbes Robertson had been forced to make do with three amateurs. One was a failed medical student, the second was a young man recovering from a nervous breakdown, and the third was me, with a strained back.

The play was a disaster. On the first night, the nervous young actor playing Horace Bream, the part of a voluble American, made his entrance and stood centre-stage, *speechless*. His mouth opened and shut like an expiring cod. Poor man, it was the worst case of stage-fright I have ever seen.

Frank Forbes Robertson was magnificent. Playing the character part of Dick Fennell, the older, worldly-wise man in the play, he immediately took command. He not only provided the panic-stricken player with a chair, into which he slumped, but also somehow conveyed the sense of the missing lines to the bewildered audience. Both he and I filled in the embarrassing silence with a lot of frenzied stage business, spilling the tea, dropping a teacup, handing round cake and, together, folding the large tablecloth while, all the time, he kept up a running flow of impromptu lines, as though he was asking questions of the terrified actor. To these our speechless friend mutely nodded, or shook his head, as though suffering from terminal laryngitis.

After an incident-packed three minutes, which seemed to me more like three hours, Horace Bream stood up and, still mute, shakily left the stage. As this character's lines were vital to the plot of the play, the audience was left in a kind of vacuum, which we filled in as best we could as the opportunity presented itself. Sir Arthur Pinero would never have recognized his minor masterpiece.

To compound the confusion, I was late for my next entrance because I failed to make a quick change from a tight-trousered tweed suit into full evening dress with even narrower trousers. I had forgotten to bring the button-hook from my top-floor dressing-room and therefore, with my sprained back, I could not undo the Edwardian high-buttoned boots I was wearing.

The only way I could make the change in time was to rip up the narrow tweed trousers and peel them off, and then tear the tight evening dress pants up their seams, like peeling the skins on a banana, and slide them over those immovable brown boots. All the time, I could hear the cue for my entrance getting nearer and nearer. I heard the fateful words spoken as I was still desperately tucking the loose, flapping halves of my evening dress trousers into my thick grey woollen socks. I was embarrassingly late for my entrance.

At last, with as much nonchalance as I could muster, I opened the door and strode on to the stage. Fortunately the door, which opened down-stage, concealed the state of my trousers, and by nipping behind a large sofa I managed to hide my brown button-boots from the audience.

Unfortunately we had not rehearsed such a move, and it threw the rest of the already shaken cast into further confusion. I continued to deliver my lines from behind the sofa until I was physically forced out from behind it by Mrs Frank Forbes Robertson, a tall and powerfully built actress who was playing the heroine's aunt.

The audience gave a shriek of laughter as I stood revealed, with my tight evening dress trousers tucked into grey woollen socks above the brown button-boots. I must have looked like a Victorian man-about-town about to embark on a formal evening bicycle ride.

However, the look of taut despair on my face registered with the kindly Welsh audience who quickly smothered their giggles. As their laughter died down, I spoke my next lines in ringing tones. 'Come, Minnie,' I said, offering my arm to Mrs Forbes Robertson, 'allow me to escort you to the opera.' For me, it was a moment of theatrical triumph, as I regained the attention of the audience.

With my other hand, I flipped open my opera hat and placed it on my head. Or at least I thought I had flipped it open. Instead, the collapsible opera hat had opened on only one side. It must have looked like the one worn by Harpo Marx.

The final blow to my stage dignity came as we moved towards the door. At this point my evening trousers spontaneously released themselves from their retaining socks and flapped about on either side of my legs. A great roar of laughter rang out from the audience. So much for Act I!

Worse was to come. Even though Horace Bream, after two stiff whiskies, intermittently regained his voice, the front-of-house curtain refused to come down over the dramatic closing lines of Act II, when Clement Hale's father is supposed to collapse with a heart attack.

As I hurled myself across the stage to gather my stricken father into my arms, the curtain stuck half way, despite my despairing cries of, 'Father! ... Father! ... Father!' To which I added in despair, 'Speak to me, Father ... for Heaven's sake, speak to me ... For God's sake, somebody, do something!'

Still nothing happened. We could hear the stage crew in the flies above our heads swearing lustily as they struggled with the ropes. So could the audience. There seemed to be only one thing left to do. I would have to take my supposedly dying father off the stage.

The only way I knew of carrying an adult person was to use the method taught me by the St John Ambulance Brigade. To the delight of the audience, I picked up the limp, elderly actor in a fireman's lift and carried him off-stage draped over my shoulder.

It did not do my back much good, and much chastened, I returned home by train, with yet another air-raid thundering overhead. Understandably, I was in two minds about ever appearing on a stage again. One thing was clear to me: I had not stammered. This was probably due to all the adrenaline generated by the constant state of emergency in which that play had been performed.

Back in London I found that the RAF had called me up as a conscript, after refusing so often to accept me as a volunteer. On the date specified, I went to RAF HQ Uxbridge and passed the medical, only to be told yet again that because my father was a Peruvian I would have to wait for a final decision, which was to be made by a special board.

Not long after this I got married. This unexpected move by their nineteen-year-old son must have shaken my parents, but they both took it in good part. After all, as I explained to them, if I was old enough to fight and possibly get killed, I was also old enough to get married and have children.

My bride was a very attractive young French woman, Marie Barradell, who, together with her elderly English father and French mother, had escaped from France on the last ship to leave the small port near Biarritz, next to the Spanish border.

I had first met Marie when as a girl of seventeen she had stayed with friends of ours, the Scotts, who used to take in foreign students at their rambling Victorian house in Sandgate. My brother was a friend of the elder Scott boy, Laurie, and my chum was the younger one, Barney. The pretty French girl was very taken with Barney Scott, who was the same age as herself. Being only fourteen years old at the time, I had to be content with gazing longingly at her. I do not think she even noticed me. Anyway, at that time I had not learnt to speak properly, so I did not stand much of a chance with girls.

Marie Barradell was very talented, being a student at the Paris Conservatoire and a pupil of the famous French teacher of pianoforte, Marguerite Long. When I met Marie again, it was in 1941, in London, just after my return from Cardiff. She had blossomed into an extremely attractive and apparently very sophisticated young woman. The early promise of her musical talent was fulfilled by her winning the coveted Medaille d'Or, the highest award for pianoforte that could be given to an artiste of the Paris Conservatoire.

I was completely bowled over by her and, to my amazement, Marie took an interest in me. Now that I could speak, I amused and intrigued her with my extravagant descriptions of life in Fleet Street as a photographic journalist, as a drummer on tour, and as an actor in the disastrous play in Cardiff. Making her laugh was quite an achievement. Marie, who spoke excellent English, had so devoted her life to the practice of pianoforte that she had not been given much opportunity to see the funny side of life.

Marie was unofficially engaged to Barney Scott. I had no intention of cheating on my boyhood friend, but, before either of us knew what was happening, Marie and I found ourselves passionately in love, with no chance of pulling back from a complicated liaison.

When, in fairness, I told Barney, he beat me up. I tried to defend myself, but I did not hit back, as I happened to like the guy. Had he been a Frenchman, he probably would have shot me. The British tend to express their disapproval in these matters by thumping the offending party. It was undignified, unnecessary and painful.

Marie broke off her unofficial engagement and I got an emergency marriage licence from the bishop's office at Westminster Abbey, which was not hard to obtain in wartime. We got married in a small church in Barnes.

Both our families were shaken when we told them, but they recovered quickly and set about helping us to find a home. This was not too difficult as London had emptied rapidly during the air-raids, with many wealthy people running away to the country. We soon found a tiny flat in Kensington and set up our first home, and it was not long before Marie became pregnant.

I had managed to support us with small acting jobs, working as an extra in films and a few engagements as a drummer. Then I landed my first real acting job. This was with Robert Atkins, the Shakespearean actor-manager, who auditioned me for an extended season in Manchester and in Regent's Park Open Air Theatre. My pay was £8 a week. It looked as though my fate was sealed. The RAF evidently had finally refused me, as nothing further had been heard from them, so I gave up trying to enlist and became a fully fledged Shakespearean actor.

My new employer was quite different from my last producer. Whereas Frank Forbes Robertson was tall, gaunt, and immediately recognizable as a traditional 'actor-laddie', Robert Atkins was powerfully stocky in build, with a beaming, hook-nosed, shaggy-browed face and shining bald head. Far from looking like a distinguished actor, he gave the impression of being a bank manager or Mine Host of the Victorian pub he often frequented, or even a bishop in mufti. Until he spoke! Then his deep, rolling, unmistakable voice, which only those who worked for him and loved him could imitate, made the listener aware that here was a fine actor and a great personality as well.

Robert Atkins was unique. He was the only actor-manager who truly brought Shakespeare to the people, with his many open-air performances all over Britain. Furthermore, he was a fine director of Shakespearean plays at the Old Vic, Sadlers' Wells, and Stratford-upon-Avon.

Stories about Robert are legion. I was involved in some of them. When I played Lorenzo in *The Merchant of Venice* at the Westminster Theatre, we wore Elizabethan costumes. Helen Cherry was playing Jessica, Shylock's daughter, who elopes with Lorenzo.

'She's too tall for you, Michael, old son. You'll have to wear lifts,' said Robert. Then, seeing my puzzlement, he added, 'They're pieces of triangular cork that you shove in your boots. They'll make you a good two inches taller.'

I got them from Bermans, the costumiers, and put them into my thigh-boots. Sure enough, miraculously I became a good six feet tall. However, when I walked, they tended to thrust me forward at an angle, as though I was leaning into a strong wind.

As I made my first entrance at the dress rehearsal, there was a howl of laughter from the other players. Robert walked down to the footlights, chortling. 'You'll have to learn to master that leaning effect, Michael. Remember, old son, you're supposed to be in Venice, not bloody Pisa.'

I had worked up to playing Lorenzo from small walk-on parts, in some of which I stood silently in the background as 'stage-dressing'. Robert took me aside. 'Don't just stand there like a constipated Guardsman. You're supposed to be listening to the other players, so react, Michael, react.'

That night on stage, I reacted to everything that happened and to every word uttered. It was a mute bravura solo performance. The audience were quite taken aback by the reactions of this strange young man who seemed to feel so deeply every emotion expressed by the rest of the cast. In the end, their eyes were fixed solely on me, as though mesmerized by a basilisk. When I exited I even got scattered applause. Robert will be pleased, I thought.

He was not. 'Michael, you looked as though you had bloody St Vitus's dance. For God's sake give the other actors a chance. Just react gently, as though you are interested in what is happening. Don't look as though you are being tortured to death.'

I learnt more about acting from Robert Atkins in one season than I would have gained from four years at drama school.

We played at some extraordinary venues. At Manchester we performed in front of the Victorian bandstand in Platts Fields. On one memorable afternoon it rained so heavily that we had to move the cast and audience into the stately Elizabethan manor house which graces the park. It was quite enthralling to play *A Midsummer Night's Dream* in such an appropriate setting.

We then moved to Boggart Hole Clough and worked beside another iron-work bandstand. Our next venue was at Eltham Park in south London, and a third bandstand. Finally, as autumn approached, encouraged by the excellent notices we had attracted with our repertoire of *Twelfth Night*, *The Taming of the Shrew*, and *A Midsummer Night's Dream*, all of which the critics had enjoyed, we moved into a real theatre in the West End of London. After all, the Westminster Theatre, near Buckingham Palace, is *almost* in the West End!

Chapter Eleven

The Reluctant Deserter

At this point in my life a sense of humour was invaluable to me. First, there was plenty of tension in my new family. The Barradells, although highly intelligent, were almost without a sense of the ridiculous. I was so accustomed to humour being the leavening in my own family life that the almost non-existent sense of humour among my new family greatly disturbed me. Life with my in-laws usually seemed to be hovering on the brink of melodrama. The most excitable of my in-laws was Papa Barradell, which was strange because he was an Englishman and had spent his whole working life as an accountant, rising eventually to become chief accountant at the London Metropolitan Water Board, from which responsible position he had retired at an early age so that he could live in France.

Mama Barradell was delightful, a kindly intellectual who still showed, at the age of sixty, every sign of her startling youthful attractiveness, which early photographs confirmed. Marie was obviously her daughter, blessed with the same musical gifts and extreme feminine sex-appeal. The only quality these women lacked was the ability to see the funny side of their own lives.

Not that the Barradells had much to laugh about. Firstly, they had lost everything, or thought they had, when through no fault of their own they had been forced to leave their home, a beautiful apartment in Paris in the Rue des Martyres, to make their escape to Britain. Until then, their life had been a tranquil round of typically Parisian bourgeois elegance among their well-heeled peers and the warmth of their close relatives.

I liked, but was somewhat chary of, my English father-in-law who, though he was a kindly and courteous man, had little tolerance for anyone who did not share his own, very decided opinions. These included a distrust of coloured people, Freemasons and Jews and a dislike of all foreigners except his French in-laws.

I can hardly blame him for his wary attitude towards me, because Marie was his adored only child and I had, as he saw it, taken her from him. Furthermore, I was half-Peruvian and, once having seen me naked in the bathroom and noticing that I was circumcised, my father-in-law had the deepest suspicions that I was probably coloured and Jewish as well.

As I had been brought up without prejudice against race, colour, creed or religion, my family being well-balanced mongrels from way back, I found this hard to take or understand. The result was a lot of family tension although, outwardly at least, our contrasting parents got along together quite well.

This family stress was relieved by the arrival of our daughter, Elaine, a beautiful bundle of chortling babyhood who smiled almost as soon as she could breathe. Elaine was the most good-natured of babies, which was a miracle because both she and Marie nearly died of a fever which, at that time, in the overcrowded wartime hospitals, was assuming epidemic proportions among young nursing mothers and their babies.

Elaine, being the Barradells' only grandchild, was nearly suffocated by love and cooing affection, but our cheerful little daughter bore it all with great tolerance and a beaming smile.

With the air-raids, the rationing, which had become stricter than ever and now was at a survival level, and the depressing news from many outposts of the British Empire, beleaguered by the Italians and the Japanese, life in Britain was highly distressing. Daily I thanked the Almighty that my theatrical work, although a considerable strain on my nervous system, was full of opportunities for laughter.

Like *Sweet Lavender* in Cardiff, our long season of Shakespearean comedies was not without moments of crisis. On the opening night, Helen Cherry and I were faced with such a moment during the opening lines of the moonlight scene in *The Merchant*. When we made our entrance, hand in hand, the epitome of Shakespearean lovers, the audience honoured us with a round of applause. I must admit, in all modesty, that we did look good. We were young, vibrant with controlled first-night nerves and, under our make-up, we were glowing with health. Helen was radiantly beautiful and I looked tall, slim and ardent, having at last mastered the art of using lifts in my thigh-boots by walking forwards while leaning backwards, in itself no mean feat.

This welcome petered out when, for no apparent reason, the front curtains descended abruptly in front of us. The heavy velvet curtains not only came down to stage level but continued to descend, draping themselves into a thick crimson pile until the top retaining-bar complete with its long manila-rope lines, lay on top of it. Over the top of this mound of curtaining we both gazed fixedly at the audience, still hand in hand but struck dumb with shock. Memories of the traumatic Pinero play flashed through my mind.

The spell was broken by Robert Atkins, whose bald head shone in the spotlight as he leaned out from the wings. He looked up, purple with fury, and shook his fist at the fly-gallery above our heads, roaring out the threatening words, 'I'll tear your bloody cock off!'

The audience collapsed into yells of laughter. When they died down, Robert, completely unabashed, said in that melodious diapason of his, 'Sorry about that, ladies and gentlemen.' Then, turning to us, he said, 'Carry on, my dears,' and withdrew from sight.

Amazingly we did carry on, without a further hitch. When we came to the end of our part in the scene, with the words 'Mark the music', there was enthusiastic applause.

In spite of this mishap, it turned out to be a most successful first night. James Agate, the theatre critic known for his witty sarcasm and sometimes vitriolic reviews, loved the whole production, seemingly without reservation. He even singled out Helen and me for special attention, complimenting us jointly on the clarity, poetry and youthful ebullience of our performance.

I do not know which one of us Mr Agate fancied but he was very kind. Evidently, the great man had not noticed that I was wearing lifts, and that, having taken them out of my boots during the interval because they were so uncomfortable, I had forgotten to put them back for my final scenes. Consequently, in Act III, Lorenzo was two inches shorter. But perhaps Mr Agate had left before the end of the play to write his review.

We had almost completed our successful season of plays at the Westminster Theatre, and I was receiving offers to test for various film productions. Apart from the war, things began to look rosy.

We still had the odd trauma during our production of *The Merchant of Venice*, but already we were rehearsing *King Henry the Fourth*, *Part One*, in which I was cast as Poins, Prince Hal's friend, a plum role for a juvenile actor.

One night I was playing the abduction scene in *The Merchant* when a series of mishaps clouded my elopement with the beautiful Jessica. I was wearing a mask and domino and carrying a lantern. In addition I was armed with a sword and was lumbered with the lifts in my thigh-boots.

Jessica had just dropped the casket containing Shylock's wealth from the window into my waiting hands beneath. I had caught it neatly as, by some minor miracle, I had managed to do every performance, and she hastened down backstage to greet me at stage-level. As she appeared in the archway, looking adorable in her elopement disguise of boy's clothes, with a triumphant laugh I spoke my lines:

> What, art thou come? On, gentlemen; away!
> Our masquing mates by this time for us stay.

These words are typical of some of the weaker exit lines that the great playwright wrote to get his players off the stage. The only way you can make an effective retreat with lines like these is to give a merry whoop of joy and exit laughing, hopefully to applause.

To further the dramatic action as Helen stood so invitingly in the doorway, instead of hurrying across the stage to meet her as I usually did, I decided on the spur of the moment to cover the distance in one athletic leap, in the style of Errol Flynn. It was a mistake.

With those lifts in my boots my balance was not too good. Moreover, at that crucial moment my mask slipped and obscured my vision. When one thing goes wrong, others quickly follow. My sheathed sword, which I normally steadied with my left hand, for that moment was unfettered and swung between my leaping legs just as I took off for that spectacular jump.

Blinded by the slipped mask and neatly tripped by my own sword, I flew horizontally across the short distance separating Lorenzo from his love, and hit Jessica about mid-section in a spectacular rugby tackle.

Helen muttered, 'Christ!' and fell flat on her back, with me on top of her. It looked exactly as though I was committing instant rape. This also occurred to some wag in the upper gallery, who shouted out, 'Wait for it, mate!'

Somehow, we picked ourselves up and managed to exit in a dignified manner. It says a lot for Helen's tolerance that she did not hit me.

Another unrehearsed event involved a young Irish actor, Dominic Fitzpatrick. This pleasant, highly strung lad got £5 a week, because that was the minimum Equity rate for a walk-on actor at the time but, because he sent most of it home to his ailing mother, he never seemed to get enough to eat. He lived mainly on milk and the nourishing food provided by a kind young actress. Dominic also helped to stage-manage the plays and he was a general understudy to just about everyone in the cast, excluding the women.

One night Nigel Clarke, an experienced middle-aged actor who was playing Antonio, had a bad attack of laryngitis and Dominic had to go on for him. We shared the same dressing-room and liked each other, so I helped him make up for the part. This required the application of crêpe hair to his youthful face. Without a moustache and beard Dominic would look the teenager he was.

I had never used crêpe hair before, although I had seen it in Nigel Clarke's make-up box. It consisted of a tight plait of curly hair, interwoven with string. The approved method of preparing it for sticking on the face with spirit-gum was first to release the plaits from the retaining web of string and then to teazle the hair straight over a steaming kettle. It was then combed and finally stuck on to the actor's face.

Neither of us knew this. Furthermore, time was too short to buy a proper false beard. So I separated the tightly curled strings of hair, cut them into three-inch strips and stuck them close together on Dominic's face, using a lot of spirit-gum. In all, it took a surprising two feet of crêpe hair to make my friend's beard. By the time I had finished sticking on the hair, he looked more like an Assyrian wall-painting than a Venetian merchant. The beard obviously needed trimming.

Dominic's youthful features were now heavily disguised behind a swarthy make-up and that short, crisply curled, dense black beard, and, though I say it myself, by the time I had shaped that thick mass of crinkly black hair, he looked every bit the part of a merchant-adventurer: hairy but authentic.

Dominic thanked me warmly, and strode on to the stage, determined to make a hit with his first real part in a Shakespearean masterpiece. In fact, from the moment the curtain rose, he did a masterly job. His Antonio was dignified and well-controlled in performance, though somewhat different from Nigel Clarke's interpretation in the delivery and vocal emphasis of his lines.

Robert was delighted. 'That boy will go far,' he said in solemn and prophetic tones.

All would have gone swimmingly but for my failure to follow the standard procedure for dealing with crêpe hair. The heat of the stage lighting did what I had failed to do. It uncurled the tightly wrinkled mass of false hair. The clearly visible result was that Dominic's beard started to *grow*. There was a murmur of interest among the audience as they first noticed this. They quickly became riveted to what is, basically, a rather dull, plot-filled scene at the beginning of *The Merchant of Venice*.

Salarino and Salanio, Antonio's two friends who set up the plot of the play with him, were equally fascinated by Dominic's rapidly lengthening beard. Mesmerized by the growing hair, they continued to speak their lines almost automatically but could do nothing to help. They did not even dare warn the young actor of his plight in case he fluffed his lines.

Dominic himself was completely wrapped in his role and proudly attributed the audience's breathless attention to his excellent handling of the part. By the time he approached the end of the scene, his sweat-glistening beard was a full nine inches in length and still growing. When he finally made his exit his beard was a good foot long. He left the stage to a storm of delighted applause.

By now, Marie and Elaine had fully recovered from their fever and we were staying in the same house as my in-laws in St George's Square. We had a tiny flat above their larger apartment. Life seemed to be slowly settling down into a pattern.

Part of the day was spent searching for the few articles of unrationed food that could be found. None of us could afford to buy from the flourishing black market, from which so many war-profiteers made their fortunes. But thanks to my mother-in-law's shrewd housekeeping we managed somehow. Mama Barradell also added to the small knowledge of cooking that I already had gained from my mother. I am much indebted to her for that.

Marie was not a good cook, having devoted her life to the pianoforte. She continued to practise for six hours every day to prepare herself for the concerts she was giving on behalf of the Free French, while Grandmère Barradell looked after Elaine. I spent much of the day rehearsing the new play, and often, during the many air-raids, most of which seemed to occur after midnight, we would spend hours *en famille* huddled in the basement stair-well, which seemed to be the safest place.

Weekly basic rations were: one egg, 4 ounces of bacon, half a pound of meat, 4 ounces of margarine or butter, 4 ounces of sugar, and a quarter of a pound of tea or coffee. We were also allowed a half-pint of milk a day. Only children and nursing mothers got an extra ration of milk and some vitaminized orange juice. Fruit was sometimes available in season.

On a points system, the odd tin of salmon, baked beans, tinned peas, Spam, etc., could also be obtained, but only if they were in stock at your friendly grocer's. In addition, if you knew the butcher well, he occasionally would slip a half-pound packet of sausages into the shopping bag. Otherwise potatoes, carrots, swedes and greens helped to make up the bulk of the weekly shopping. Even bread was rationed, and soon potatoes were added to this strict system of distribution. Shoes and clothing were on ration cards and consequently there was a black market in these as well.

Petrol rationing did not affect us as none of us had a car. Bicycles were the best way to get about but there was difficulty with replacing tyres, owing to the rubber shortage. All this, of course, was because the ships of our Merchant Navy bringing vital supplies across the

Atlantic were being decimated by the German U-boats, with appalling losses among our gallant seamen.

Therefore most of us tolerated the strict rationing and did the best we could, except for the black marketeers, whom most people would have liked to see imprisoned. Only the wealthy and the families of some bureaucrats did not feel the pinch because there were a lot of forged coupons about, and even genuine ration-book pages could be bought by those who were unscrupulous enough to use them. There were quite a few rich people living high off the hog.

In June 1942 Tobruk in North Africa had fallen to Rommel, and the Afrika Korps was within striking distance of Cairo. The Germans had advanced over a thousand miles into Russia since their attack in 1941. In accordance with the procedures that Winston Churchill had laid down in 1940, a Day of National Prayer was declared directly after each major disaster. The Fall of France, the Japanese invasion of Singapore, the loss of Hong Kong, the sinking of the *Repulse* and *Prince of Wales* by the Japanese, and the mass retreat of British forces in North Africa had each triggered a fervent religious reaction. Spiritually, it was an amazing time, for this, like the Battle of Britain, was a people's war.

Meanwhile, my career as a Shakespearean actor was flourishing. Then, one night in October 1942, I was arrested *as a deserter*!

I had just walked off stage, after the elopement scene in *The Merchant*. Waiting for me in the wings was Robert. He was accompanied by two RAF service policemen – a corporal and an aircraftsman. My heart leaped with excitement. At last the RAF had accepted me. I thought how nice it was of them to send me word personally. Innocently I beamed at them.

Before Robert could speak, the corporal rudely pushed him aside. 'Michael Bentin, I arrest you as a deserter from His Majesty's Royal Air Force. You have been absent without leave for sixty-five days.' By the tone of his voice he obviously enjoyed his work.

I was speechless with shock, but anger soon took its place. After all my efforts to volunteer over a period of more than eighteen months, this was too much.

Robert interjected. He was almost as angry as me. 'Balls!' he said, addressing the corporal. 'Mr Bentin has been trying to enlist in the Royal Air Force. He has been refused too many times. How can he be a deserter? Michael is trying to get *into* the RAF, not trying to get *out*.'

The corporal was adamant. 'You'll have to come with us.' He turned to his assistant 'Take his sword, Fred. He might do himself a mischief.'

'I'll have to change,' I protested. 'And I must finish the play.'

'At least grant us that courtesy.' Robert's voice was loaded with suppressed fury.

Reluctantly, the corporal agreed, but warned his colleague, 'Watch him, Fred. The deserter might do a moonlight flit through the toilet window.'

We finished *The Merchant* with the RAF watching me intently from the wings. When the curtain came down, they were waiting to escort me. The cast gave me shocked encouragement.

Dominic shouted, 'The English are all the bloody same, Mike.' He was a true-green Irishman.

Helen kissed me. 'We all know it's a silly mistake, Michael. I'm sure they will sort it out.'

The policemen insisted that I accompanied them dressed as I was. I believe that if they could have found an excuse to handcuff me, they would have done so.

Robert and the entire cast saw me off, waving and shouting a warm *au revoir*.

With my battered trenchcoat over my doublet and hose, and still in my thigh-boots, complete with lifts, I was driven to the offices of the DAPM, the Deputy Assistant Provost Marshal. These were located in an elegant block of recently built apartments in Kensington. Once inside the building I was put directly into a cell. I was shaken and depressed. The whole affair was so shaming.

Oh God, I thought, why must the British always treat my family like shit?

Then a still small voice inside my head told me what to do. I started to laugh.

'What's so bloody funny?' snapped the corporal.

Summoning my small store of Castilian Spanish, I said, '*Yo no hablo Ingles. Yo soy Peruano.*'

'What did you say?' The corporal thought I was being insolent.

'I don't speak English,' I explained. 'I am a Peruvian subject.'

Thrusting his face as close to mine as the bars would permit, the bully growled, 'You're bluffin'!'

'*Yo deseo inmediatamente la presencia de nuestro Embajador en Londres, Su Excelencia Don Miguel Benavides. Pronto!*'

'What does that gibberish mean?' The corporal was getting rattled.

'I am asking for the presence of our Peruvian Ambassador in London, Señor Benavides.' I emphasized every syllable.

The corporal blinked at that. He summoned aid. 'Get me his papers, Fred. We'll soon see what's what.'

Fred obliged, and handed the corporal my documents. He quickly perused them and found the bit which stated that my father was Peruvian. At least he could read. He was shaken for, like all bullies, his confidence was only on the surface. He started sweating, then he muttered the immortal line, 'Jesus Christ, Fred. 'E really is a bloody wog.'

The DAPM, a stocky and self-important flight-lieutenant, was summoned and duly appeared, seething with anger that he had been disturbed in the middle of the night.

'What the hell is this all about?' he demanded. 'Can't this wait till the morning, on defaulters' parade?'

The alarmed corporal took him aside and explained the situation in a whisper. The DAPM looked decidedly uncomfortable. He came over and spoke to me through the bars of the cell.

'There seems to be some confusion, Mr, er, Benskin. You see, there's a war on.' As he offered me that hoary old excuse for stupidity and injustice his tone was conciliatory.

'You could say that,' I replied icily. 'Now, get me the Peruvian Ambassador!'

The DAPM telephoned the Peruvian Embassy and was given the number of the Residency, where he finally contacted the ambassador. Being a family friend, His Excellency was very angry.

I began to enjoy myself. After all, I could dine out on this episode for years. I was released from the cell and offered a chair. Fred even brought me a cup of tea. Twenty minutes later the ambassador arrived. He was wearing a mink-lined overcoat. He had dressed hurriedly, and I could see that he was seething with indignation.

Ignoring the fawning service policemen, he came straight to the point. '*Qué pasa, Miguelito?*'

I told him in English. He heard me out, muttering '*Claro*' under his breath at each stage of that night's insulting behaviour.

At last he turned to the anxious gaolers. His tone was unequivocal. 'Not one British ship into the port of Callao will go until the honour of this young man has been vindicated.' He spoke with great authority. I was proud of him, and proud that I was half-Peruvian.

The service policemen grovelled. It was very satisfying after all those years of rudeness and insults.

I was driven back to my anxious family in St George's Square in the DAPM's staff car. A thought struck me and I started laughing. I realized that, had things gone otherwise, I would have been the first person to appear on defaulters' parade wearing an Elizabethan doublet and hose for nearly four hundred years.

A week later I was telephoned by the personal assistant to Group-Captain Gilligan, the commanding officer of the RAF Aircrew Reception Centre. Would I be so kind as to come over to their headquarters in Regent's Park as soon as possible?

I asked one question, 'Is that A.H.H. Gilligan, the ex-captain of the English cricket team?'

I was told that it was.

'How about tomorrow?' I asked. I was excited. A.H.H. Gilligan was one of the famous cricketing twins and, as a keen player, I was delighted to have the opportunity to meet him. Perhaps he would understand how anxious I was to become a member of RAF aircrew.

The next morning I was driven in style in an RAF staff car to meet my fate.

The great man was charm and courtesy itself. 'Sit down, Mr Bentin.' He waved me to a chair opposite his desk. I sat down and waited expectantly. This man was everything I had ever imagined him to be: tall, distinguished and every inch an English gentleman.

He looked at me quizzically. 'First of all, I cannot say how sorry I am that this has happened.' He indicated a pile of files on his desk. 'Apparently you had volunteered, unsuccessfully, over a dozen times before your call-up.'

I nodded.

'You're an old Etonian, aren't you?'

'Yes, sir. Mr Hope-Jones was M'tutor. He is also my godfather. I know he will vouch for me.'

'No need, my boy. Your ambassador has already been most insistent about your bona fides.' He looked at me keenly; obviously his next question would decide my destiny.

'When you were at Eton, were you a dry bob or a wet bob?'

I was surprised that the Group-Captain was asking me whether I played cricket or rowed for the school.

'A dry bob, sir.'

A.H.H.G. positively beamed. 'Bowler or batsman?'

'Bowler, sir. I am a medium-paced spin bowler.'

The Group-Captain glowed with pleasure. 'Can you bowl the chinaman?'

For non-cricketers, that meant, could I bowl a difficult-to-play spinner, called either the googly or the chinaman.

'Five times out of six,' I replied truthfully.

'Splendid! Absolutely first class! We must have you in the RAF. You do still want to join the Royal Air Force, I hope?'

'Absolutely, sir,' I replied.

At that wonderful moment, I realized that I could have been Adolf Hitler's illegitimate son but, so long as I could bowl the chinaman five times out of six, I was apparently needed by the Royal Air Force. But then, of course, there was a war on.

Chapter Twelve

Close Encounter of the Fatal Kind

My first week in the Royal Air Force stands out in my memory like a solar prominence. We were an intake of some 1,800 aircrew cadets, most of us about the same age. Anyone older than thirty was referred to as 'Pop'.

We came from all parts of the British Isles and from the Empire. Australians, New Zealanders, Canadians, Rhodesians and South Africans quickly found their fellow countrymen among the milling mass of cadets. These young men came from the wide-open spaces of the earth and were accustomed to travelling many miles from home, often staying away for weeks at a time. The young British concept of home-life was far more restricted, and the majority of these cadets had previously travelled only as far as the seaside and back.

Most of our aircrew cadets had been educated at local schools in England, Scotland, Northern Ireland and Wales and, in the case of British grammar schools, this standard was very high. It often exceeded the academic level, especially in mathematics, achieved by pupils from expensive public schools.

A knowledge of spherical trigonometry was necessary for key aircrew, especially for navigators. Therefore, the educational standards required were reasonably high, except for those cadets who were to become air-gunners. This category of aircrew received only basic training in order to get them into the air and fighting as quickly as possible, to replenish the dwindling ranks of gallant air-gunners who suffered the highest casualty rate of the war in the air. They lost over 30,000 killed, as well as thousands who were badly wounded or became prisoners of war. The operational life of these brave men could be measured in *weeks*. Owing to the inadequacy and short range of their guns, they were cannon-fodder for the enemy fighters, who were armed with much more powerful weapons.

I was delighted to find that there was little or no snobbery among aircrew cadets, and little prejudice against foreigners. This was due to our common denominator: no matter what our social, economic, ethnic or religious background, we all wanted to fly. That driving force had brought us from all over the free world to form the nucleus of the RAF's striking force.

Of my intake alone, 80 per cent were destined to die in the air or on impact with the ground. That was how high the cost of regaining command of the air in the Second World War was to become.

My first hours in the RAF were occupied by kitting up with a scratchy blue uniform and heavy greatcoat and trying to become accustomed to wearing boots which, at first, felt as if my feet had been encased in hardened cement.

My hair was cut by a demon-barber who in civilian life must have been a sheep-shearer. Shorn and uniformly clothed, I marched out, with my near-naked head now covered jauntily by a blue side-cap. This headgear bore the aircrew cadets' white flash in front and, because of its shape, was known as the Cunt Hat.

We were marched in Flights of 300 cadets to the HQ at Abbey Lodge, and on arrival were instructed to fill in the first of a seemingly endless stream of forms. As I continued, throughout my service career, to deal with the abundant documentary side of warfare, I came to believe that whichever side first ran out of paper would surrender.

We were interviewed by accountant officers, a strange breed of RAF personnel, who did not know one end of an aeroplane from the other. Mine asked me whether I would make a voluntary contribution from my pay to add to the shamefully small family allowance that His Majesty's Treasury saw fit to dole out to the dependants of those who were fighting on its behalf.

Like most of the married airmen, or those with dependent parents, I agreed to do so, and another few shillings a week was grabbed back from the already miserly sum we received as aircrew cadets. After deducting the allowance that I made over to my wife and child, I had exactly ten shillings a week to pay for any extras not provided for by the RAF. Practically every other married cadet without independent means was in the same situation.

Servicemen in the Royal Navy, the Marines and the Army were treated in the same miserly fashion. The marvellous thing was that, in the spirit of comradeship, we all made the best of it. At least, we aircrew cadets had clean sheets in which to sleep. That, in wartime, was a great luxury.

At the interviews with the accountant officer one cadet, named Woolf, who was sitting at the desk next to me, flatly refused to respond to the officer's attempt to make him part with even a shilling of his pay to add to his family allowance. The flight-lieutenant was making such a persuasive effort to extract money from the young cadet that I felt he must be on a percentage of the take. His final plea was pitched in a 'hearts and flowers' tone: 'But don't you realize, Aircraftman Woolf, what those few extra shillings a week might mean to your wife? It could provide her with some small luxury to make her life a little easier.'

Aircraftman Second Class Woolf's eyes gleamed as he administered a satisfying *coup de grâce*: 'Sir, I'm already allowing my wife £10,000 a year and I consider that's quite enough.'

We aircrew cadets were billeted all round Regent's Park in blocks of empty luxury flats. These had been abandoned by their well-off residents, who had moved to the safer countryside the moment the first air-raids hit London. It may seem strange that such valuable recruits were thereby exposed to heavy German air-raids on the capital city, when so many country-based establishments could have accommodated them more easily and more securely.

In these luxury apartments, which had been stripped bare, we slept, six or ten in a room, on iron beds, our few possessions neatly stowed away in our lockers, and our ablutions performed in what had once been expensive bathrooms.

I noticed that after lights out, there sometimes was the sound of muffled weeping coming from other beds in the room. If it went on too long, as some unfortunate home-sick youngster gave vent to his feelings, I would slip quietly out of bed and try to comfort him. It seemed to help, and I usually managed to get over to the sufferer the fact that there was nothing shameful in feeling homesick, and that I had reacted in the same way at boarding school. I also pointed out that it was only a temporary form of misery.

Rumour had it that the valuable properties in which we were billeted were owned by a consortium of wealthy businessmen, some of whom were in uniform, and that a number of these tycoons were even part of the upper echelon of the establishment which ran the RAF Aircrew Reception Centre.

Certainly, the whole place was run on lines totally unlike any other RAF establishment that I came across during my years in the service. For example, ACRC Regent's Park ran large pig farms. These were supposed to provide extra bacon, ham and nutritious sausages for the aircrew cadets, none of which fare I ever saw being issued to, or consumed by, my comrades-in-arms. We all ate the standard ration of bacon, Spam, and tasteless 'soya links', as we called the service-issue sausages.

For servicemen, we ate reasonably well, probably in

excess of the civilian rations, and there was much waste, which went to feed the pigs. There was also talk of a small fishing industry on the east coast operated by the same businessmen in uniform hierarchy but, once again, I never saw any evidence of fresh fish in our airmen's mess.

Another scheme that did not measure up to close scrutiny was the employment of aircrew cadets to dig ditches and lay drainage at a building site near London. Could this have been yet another property development for the same consortium? Certainly, today, housing developments cover the site.

This gross misemployment of aircrew cadets, who should have been receiving extra instruction in wireless telegraphy and navigation to ease any bottlenecks in the flow of aircrew training, infuriated us eager young airmen.

The excuse given to us was that it was being done to keep us fit. Presumably the same excuse applied to us having to tend the pigs and clean out their pens. In the winter, many cadets working on the exposed building site went sick with influenza. Some even contracted pleurisy or pneumonia.

Apparently, towards the end of hostilities, there was a heavy crackdown on these rackets by the RAF service police, criminal investigation branch, and a distinguished air-commodore, who was closely involved with RAF Training Command, and who had been one of the originators of these schemes, resigned. He was only part of the clandestine profiteering that was going on throughout the war. However, I believe that Group-Captain A.H.H. Gilligan, among other senior officers, was not party to this type of fraud.

One problem that must have given the RAF a headache was how to keep thousands of fit and horny young men occupied without giving us leave to visit the flesh-pots of London. Our time, from early rising at 6.30 to lights out at ten, was jam-packed with activity, endless drills, physical training and tests, lectures and other basic training.

We were shown films about the dangers of venereal disease which were guaranteed to put innocents off sex for life. Another solution to the problem of youthful sexual desire was reputed to be the clandestine administration of a sedative in our tea. I was determined to find out if this was true and, as our mess was located in the restaurant at the London zoo, right next to the gibbons' cage, I fed those friendly apes with fruit cake soaked in our issue tea, which was rumoured to contain chloral hydrate.

If such a sedative had been administered, we could not taste it. This was because the tea was so strong it stained your teeth. The gibbons seemed to enjoy the tea-soaked cake, but I understand that they did not mate that season. Certainly, most of the cadets did not. But that could have been the sheer lack of opportunity.

Owing to the bottleneck in the flow of overseas air-crew cadet training caused by the shortage of troop-ships, which were being sunk in convoys at a fearful rate, the ITWs (Initial Training Wings) were full. I was one of the cadets who was kept at Regent's Park to continue with my basic training without moving on to an ITW. I was also one of those cadets who were to be sent *directly* for overseas training.

One day there were signs that we were to be issued with tropical kit. This meant that we would be trained in Canada. If the cadets were issued with Arctic kit, it meant they were going to be shipped to Rhodesia or South Africa. I suppose this puerile device was used to 'fool the Hun'. Much later, when I served with the Poles in Bomber Command, we used the same sort of ploy by calling our sea-mining operations against U-boat bases 'gardening', and we even referred to the parachute mines as 'vegetables'. What supreme folly war turned out to be.

Though I was a bare twenty-minute underground-train ride from my home in St George's Square, I was not allowed to see my family, nor were they allowed to come and see me. I could only telephone my wife or my parents, and even then I had to be very careful what I said. Posters threatening all sorts of dire penalties were displayed every-where at 'Arsy-Tarcy', as the ACRC was called. 'Careless Talk Costs Lives' the posters proclaimed, quite rightly when military secrets were involved, but they seemed to be superfluous as far as we ignorant cadets were concerned.

The seemingly endless bottleneck in my training nearly cost me my life but, on the other hand, it may well have been the reason I survived the war. It all started with an inoculation of ATT/TAB, the standard medical procedure administered to all aircrew cadets on their initiation into the service. Theoretically it protected us from typhus, tetanus, typhoid and paratyphoid. Understandably, in view of what happened, I am somewhat hazy about when I was inoculated, but I seem to remember that this was a *second* lot of injections, probably because we were to be sent directly overseas for flying training.

I was one of the last three cadets in the Flight passing through the hands of the medical orderlies who were giving us the jabs. I distinctly remember seeing the cor-poral who inoculated me change the bottle of serum, which was nearly empty, for a new one. The three of us on the end of the line then got jabbed, an unpleasant procedure administered without any finesse. We received just one wipe with an alcohol-soaked swab, and then it was straight in with the large hypodermic needle.

The drill instructor, a repellent little bully, ordered us to scrub out the billets to leave them clean for the next intake of cadets. 'It'll do your bloody arms good. They won't stiffen up. Come on, let's 'ave yer. At the double.'

In the middle of scrubbing the floor I passed out. When I recovered, I found myself sitting propped up against the wall. One of my mates was trying to get me to drink some water. My head was swimming and I could not focus my eyes properly. I was starting to hurt all over.

'You'd better report sick, mate,' my helper said. 'You look bloody awful.'

I remember that he helped me to gather my kit together. I felt so giddy and sick that I could hardly stand up, but

I was determined to make it alone to the medical officer. I was due for a weekend pass, and I did not want to miss the chance to see my family.

The distance to the nearest RAF sick quarters was a few hundred yards at most. It might just as well have been miles. Every few yards I had to stop and hang on to the wall to steady myself and eventually I accepted the offer of help from a passing cadet. I noticed that no civilians offered to help. Perhaps they thought I was drunk.

My memories of the next nightmare hours are too hazy to recall in detail, but I do remember being taken by ambulance to the central sick quarters at Abbey Lodge. From then on, it was like drowning in an ocean of seething pain.

I had in fact been given the *cultures* of typhus, tetanus, typhoid and paratyphoid at one and the same time. It is a miracle that I survived. Apparently the new bottle of 'serum' had not been properly heat-treated, which I believe was the method by which these serums were obtained from the live cultures.

The other two cadets who had received their inoculations from the same bottle were affected in the same way. I heard later that one of them died, and I know that the other, a nice lad from Weymouth, a cobbler by trade, was invalided out of the service.

In fairness to the RAF medical service, the doctors did everything they could to keep us alive. I was given a lumbar-puncture without any form of anaesthetic, either general or local, and screamed in agony. This drawing-off of spinal fluid was carried out to determine whether I was suffering from cerebro-spinal meningitis. It was only when I began to exhibit the symptoms of tetanus, i.e. lock-jaw, that it dawned on the doctors what was wrong.

My back arched with the strain until it was bent like a bow. Suddenly the agonizing pain stopped, as though cut off with a knife. I felt myself slipping backwards into a black void. I realized with complete clarity that I was dying. There was an instant of panic and a sense of blind fury that I had been killed so needlessly. I also felt a despairing sense of regret and, illogically, an acceptance of the fact of my death, bringing with it unconsciousness and a complete black-out.

I next became aware that I was suspended between light and darkness. Above and around me there seemed to be an infinite expanse of bright light, more intense than anything I had ever seen while, below me, I appeared to be hovering over a bottomless pit of velvet darkness. Strangely there was no sense of vertigo, a condition I often experience and dread. I sensed that I was floating between two extremes, suspended in space-time. I was waiting. I was past emotion, beyond fear.

There was no longer any sense of regret, only a sensation of overpowering *awe*. Infinite peace surrounded me. I believe that this was that stage of peace, which passeth all understanding. I felt that I was in the presence of God, not the conventional form of the Almighty, which religion had taught me, but rather a sense of being an infinitely small part of something infinitely vast. This was all space, all time, the totality of being.

I have no idea how long I remained there, but I do remember the sudden sensation of being drawn backwards, as though someone, or something, was pulling me. I seemed to be hurtling downwards through infinity. I slowly opened my eyes and tried to focus them. Everything was a blur. Into my hazy vision came a face. It was the beautiful face of a young woman. My God, I thought, it's an angel.

The lovely face had an equally lovely voice. 'Hello, dear,' she said with a wonderful smile. 'You *have* been a long way.'

Yes, I thought, you're right. I have been *all the way*.

Vaguely I could hear voices. These belonged to two RAF chaplains. They had been called in to the side of the three dying airmen, of whom I was one. One had already died, and the surviving two were in a critical condition. There was some confusion in my case because of my

Anglo-Peruvian dual nationality, which had been marked on my documents. Through a haze of semi-consciousness, I could hear the conversation. It fascinated me.

'His mother's English. He's Protestant, for sure.'

'His father's Peruvian. It says so on his documents.'

The discussion became quite heated as each chaplain argued for the custody of my soul.

I made a supreme effort to speak. The hoarse rattle that was my voice drew them to my bedside.

They both bent over me.

'How are you feeling, my son?' asked the padre who, I could see, wore the four rings of a group-captain on his sleeves.

'Feeling better, laddie?' enquired the Protestant chaplain, who was an air-commodore, with one broad ring.

Close proximity to death does tend to make you see things in their true proportion. To give different ranks to chaplains struck me as ludicrous. What position would God hold in the RAF hierarchy? I respected their religious beliefs but, in that context, I could not take them seriously.

I could not resist the impulse. I croaked, 'I'm alive. Piss off!'

My parents, Marie and my mother-in-law were now allowed in to see me. They had been summoned by the RAF matron when it looked as though I would not last the night. I was overjoyed to see them, but I was too weak to show it other than by a silent stream of tears.

The doctors were giving me analgesic drugs to lessen the trauma but my whole body felt as though it had been put on the rack. Every joint and muscle ached atrociously. The infinite peace I had felt all around me when I was torn from my body or, if you prefer it, when I was dying, was in stark contrast to the pain that now assailed me.

Pop gave me healing then and there which helped me considerably, and Ma, who somehow could always make the best of a bad bargain, actually got me giggling. On being told what had happened she asked the matron, 'Are you sure your RAF medical orderlies aren't members of the Luftwaffe?'

It was a long time before I was able to get off my back. Blessedly, the pain lessened until it was the sort of dull ache in my muscles and joints that one gets with a bad attack of influenza. My weight, which had been a steady 10 stone, had dropped to under 7 stone, a loss of 40 pounds. At my peak of physical fitness there had been no spare flesh on me, and every ounce had been concentrated in muscle and sinew. Now I was a physical wreck, barely able to walk.

It took months to get me back to my previous weight, and never again would my body achieve the excellent physical health that it once had enjoyed. My eyesight was badly affected. It had been slightly weakened by hours of study in poor lighting at Eton, but it was still passable when I was inducted into the RAF. Now it was 6/60 both eyes, which was far below the minimum requirements for aircrew.

It was goodbye to all those youthful dreams of flight. It was also nearly the end of my service career. The RAF, having done its worst, now wanted to give me the heave-ho. My physical state was their excuse, and I had to admit that they had a point. For one thing the poisonous toxins with which I had been inoculated now started to work their way out of my body. This manifested in a series of appalling abscesses bursting out of my groin, my neck, my face and one of my arms. I was told officially that I was to be invalided out of the service.

The official medical description given to my condition was 'myositis'. All that means is 'chronic inflammation of the musculature'. In other words the RAF were not going to admit to the real reason for our condition.

The Chief Medical Officer told me I would be invalided out of the service immediately on full pension.

'No, I bloody well won't,' I told him.

'That is a decision for your superior officers to make,' he replied angrily.

'I've spent the past two years getting *into* the RAF, and I am not going to be slung out on my ear in order to cover up your medical mistakes.'

'How dare you talk to me like that, Bentin,' he roared.

'I am a Peruvian subject and I demand to see the Peruvian Ambassador,' I said, using a ploy that was to save me from much grief throughout my service career.

Within hours I was granted an interview with the station commander who, thank God, was still Group-Captain A.H.H. Gilligan.

'I'm terribly sorry that things have turned out so badly for you, Bentin,' he said. 'How can the RAF make some amends for what has happened here through no fault of your own?'

Obviously he knew the score. It was almost as though he had rehearsed the lines.

'You can keep me in the RAF, sir,' I said simply. 'That is all I want. I know I won't measure up to the medical requirements for aircrew any more but, surely, with proper physical training, I can regain most of my health. I want to do some useful job directly connected with aircrew and flying. I understand the service needs flying control personnel, armourers, and air-sea rescue crews. I am qualified for that type of work. I've learnt a lot about aircraft and their operation, and I've been brought up with guns and small boats.'

The Group-Captain was not a fool. He knew that one keen serviceman, even if he was not completely fit, was worth many reluctant conscripts. But his next question startled me.

'What about RAF Intelligence?' he asked, consulting my documents. 'I see that you speak French and some Spanish. That would go a long way towards influencing the Intelligence section. Would you like me to start the ball rolling in that direction? It would mean that you would have to take a commission. That is the least the RAF can do.'

I started to laugh.

'What's so funny, Bentin?'

'I'm sorry, sir. Last year you were interviewing me as a supposed deserter. Now you are offering me a job in British Intelligence. This really is a mad war.'

He, too, started to laugh. 'I see your point. But first we'll have to get you fit. When you have reached a stage of physical fitness commensurate with the requirements of the service I will recommend you for a commission. Meantime, I'll set up an interview with RAF Intelligence. But, understand me well, Bentin, for you operational flying is out.'

I spent the spring and the early part of the summer of 1943 as a supernumerary airman attached to ACRC as part of the International Squadron, presumably in deference to my dual nationality. This attachment lasted over four months. It meant that, in all, I had spent over six months of my service career either sick or convalescent. But, slowly, my body got back to its normal weight.

Chapter Thirteen

Officers and Gentlemen

The interview with the Intelligence board was less formal than I had imagined. The panel consisted of two middle-aged RAF officers and an Army captain. Evidently they had gone deeply into my background. They knew a lot about my father and about my family in South America. Nevertheless they wanted these matters confirmed by me, presumably as a cross-checking procedure. They appeared to be relaxed, but they were evidently cautious men who knew the value of security. Anyone lying to them would have been given short shrift. There was no room for mistakes.

Everything that had held me back for so long from joining the RAF now seemed to count in my favour. The Peruvian connection was a big plus, and so was the fact that my family had contacts with Spain. Another apparent advantage was that I was married to a Frenchwoman who also had dual nationality, her father being British.

Even my experience as an actor seemed to be in my favour. Obviously a performer had at least one of the talents necessary to be an undercover agent. An experienced actor can quickly enter into another persona and pass himself, or herself, off as someone else. Furthermore, being accustomed to memorizing lines in plays, a performer can memorize the cover story which is a vital requirement if that new persona is to be credible under close interrogation.

At my interview the Army officer spoke to me in French. We had a lengthy conversation which must have disappointed him because I knew so little about France, having been there for a couple of trips only. Moreover, although my accent in both Spanish and French is impeccable, my colloquial vocabulary was insufficient to fool a Frenchman. I could pass for French to a German who was not a skilled linguist, but I could never have fooled the Milice, the Vichy-French police who caught many Allied agents. A local policeman makes an excellent counter-spy.

I told the interviewing board about my struggle to get into the RAF and why I wanted to continue in the service. I found myself at ease with these intelligent men. They were willing enough to use me, but my recent RAF history of poor health, coupled with my lack of knowledge of France and of the current French idiom, must have decided them to keep me, for the time being at least, home-based in Britain.

At the end of that long interview I was told to report back to ACRC and wait for further orders. These came within a month. They arrived in the middle of a game of table-tennis, in which I was fast becoming expert because it was about all there was to do in the International Squadron, which was an exotic name for a holding unit, where airmen waited for a decision about their future.

Group-Captain Gilligan had seen to it that I had a forty-eight-hour pass to say goodbye to my family, and, two days later, I was on my way to Cosford, an RAF station in the West Midlands, where aircraftmen, corporals, sergeants, flight-sergeants and warrant-officers were turned from 'the ranks' into 'officers and gentlemen'. It did not matter what their trade was or what skills they possessed; each and every one of us had to go through the same rigmarole before being commissioned. This intensive officer's training course took up a whole month and was almost entirely a waste of time, especially at that stage in the war when everyone who was qualified to do his or her job was badly needed.

Promotion to commissioned rank was not all rosy. For starters, the commissioned officer now had to pay for all his uniform other than the issue battle-dress which, eventually, we all wore. He also had to find money for his mess bills. In the sergeants' mess these were minimal and in the airmen's mess non-existent.

A new APO (Acting Pilot Officer) also got lumbered with a useless, obsolete camp kit, which he had to buy out of the small allowance granted for 'kitting out'. This impractical contraption consisted of a canvas and wood folding bed, a folding chair, a collapsible bath and wash-basin, and a canvas water-bucket. The whole outfit weighed some 60 pounds and must have been designed for the Crimean War, when officers had a number of servants to tend them.

Nevertheless, it was mandatory to purchase the whole kit and to lug the idiotic encumbrance around wherever you went overseas. I stored mine back home, went to the nearest American unit and begged for one of their neat, lightweight, roll-up safari beds. By that stage of the war, I had no pride left. Eventually it went everywhere with me overseas, where I washed myself and my clothes in empty petrol tins.

The latter invaluable tip was given to me by an old sweat attached to the International Squadron at ACRC. The marvellous old airman, who had dyed his hair from its actual whiteness to jet black and constantly lied about his age, had been in the RAF for so long that his uniform had faded to a bluish-grey. His buttons had been polished so often that the insignia of the RAF eagle on them was worn smooth, with tiny holes in the brass. He was a gold-mine of service information. During that wasted time at ACRC he had taught me a lot about the way the RAF really worked.

'Never volunteer. The bloody brass never tell you what you are volunteerin' for till after you've bloody volunteered.' Wise words from a wise man.

I came across quite a few of this splendid breed of old sweats over the next few years. They were all remarkably alike. Each one of them had lied about his age and dyed his hair to remain in, or to get back into, the RAF. Some of them had been in the previous service, the RFC (Royal Flying Corps), in the First World War. They wore their service ribbons to prove it. All of them also wore many long-service stripes.

These men usually worked in some obscure job such as being in charge of the large furnaces with which each pre-war RAF station was equipped. Here they reigned alone, without question or interference. Inside the buildings which housed the big boilers they made themselves comfortable. I do not think any of them was married, had a family of his own, or even living relatives. They struck me as being very lonely. I doubt if they ever took leave. Their whole life was the service, and they were more than content for it to remain that way. They were seldom 'posted', i.e. being sent from one unit to another, as they knew how to avoid it. I was posted so often during my wartime service that I felt like a wrongly addressed postcard.

Under the welcome guidance of a batman of this unique breed, I got the best out of those four weeks at Cosford. On his advice I managed to dodge most of the lectures and spent my time more rewardingly with the armourers, familiarizing myself with all the service weaponry. As I could shoot straight I got on well with them. I also went for long walks and did physical training in the gym whenever I could, for I was determined to get as fit as possible.

One simple device which the old sweat taught me for avoiding unnecessary bullshit was to stride purposefully about the place with a sheaf of papers in my hands, as though engaged on some important mission. No-one ever stopped or questioned me when I followed his excellent advice.

We were drilled endlessly, and were also required to take command in such drills, ordering our squads to perform all the evolutions in the drill manual. As an actor, I quite enjoyed doing this. Thanks to my experience with Robert Atkins in the open-air theatres, I now had a voice that carried further and was considerably easier to understand than those of the bellowing drill sergeants. Once I got the hang of it, I became so good at drilling the other cadets that some idiot suggested I should remain at Cosford as a sergeant drill instructor.

Fortunately, having been selected for Intelligence duties which, next to aircrew, had Number One priority, I managed to escape that dreary fate.

We also route-marched, sometimes as far as six miles out and back. To my amazement, I found myself enjoying the sensation of being part of a squadron of 500 cadets, marching along in battle-order, our rifles slung over our shoulders, belting out the old airmen's songs.

When we were not being drilled or drilling our own squads, we were lectured on such vital disciplinary measures as how to represent an airman at a court martial. This was something I did later on two occasions, and somehow managed to get both culprits, who were guilty as hell, off the hook. Otherwise they would have gone to gaol. As they were both aircrew, I thought this would be a stupid waste of valuable airmen at a time when we needed everyone who could fly.

We also received instruction in 'points of rank and uniform', such as the reason for and the exact width of the rings in each officer's badge of rank, though what this had to do with fighting a war I could not imagine. We also learnt how to site and dig an 'Otway pit', which was a service field latrine. At least I could see the point of that. One needed somewhere to put all the bullshit.

It soon became obvious to me that, in any wartime organization, there are two main categories of servicemen. There are those who actually do the fighting, including those who directly or indirectly assist them to carry out their hazardous missions, and there are those who hinder them from carrying out their tasks and make their lives unnecessarily miserable by bombarding them with bumph and bullshit.

It was only when we embarked on practical arms drill and the use of weapons, spending hours on the rifle-range, that the Cosford course for officer cadets began to make sense. Even then, the mandatory twelve rounds of Argentine ammunition which we were allowed to fire from our ludicrously underpowered .38-inch Smith & Wesson revolvers hardly qualified us as expert hand-gunners, a skill which we might well have to use overseas in the future invasion of Europe.

Luckily, during my convalescence at ACRC, I had made the acquaintance of the armourer sergeant, who used to take me down to the range under Baker Street station to shoot off as many rounds of hand-gun ammunition as he had available. With this experience of practical pistol shooting, and my father's previous tuition in the safe use of firearms, I now managed to outshoot every other cadet on the course with the exception of one Canadian, an Australian, and another Englishman, all of whom were as experienced as I was with firearms.

One thing is certain, we shot as well as, and some-times even better than, the instructors. During one of these shooting sessions, by sheer chance, I saved a cadet from being badly injured. This youngster was next to me and I heard his gun misfire.

Whether this was an unconscious reflex action or the result of those sessions of shooting with hand-guns at the Baker Street range, I do not know. It also could have been a psychic warning. I just *knew* that the bullet was stuck half way up the barrel of his revolver. If he fired the next shot, his hand would be blown off as the gun, with its barrel blocked, exploded like a hand-grenade. Before anyone, including the firearms instructor, could move, I had knocked the revolver out of the sur-prised cadet's hand. It all happened so fast I did not even have time to shout a warning.

The sergeant armourer was furious until I told him what had happened. 'It's that Argentine ammunition,' he said. 'It's either no bloody good or some bloody dago has sabotaged some of it.'

He picked up the gun and, sure enough, there was a .38 slug stuck half way up the barrel. 'You'd have lost your bloody hand, for sure,' he told the cadet.

He turned to me. 'Thanks, mate, I mean, sir. I'll get you some decent ammunition.'

'One other thing, sergeant,' I said. 'Don't forget, I'm a bloody dago, too.'

From then on, I was allowed to shoot as many rounds as I wanted to.

The permanent staff at Cosford had made themselves a nice, safe career in the service. Most of them had their wives, and even their families, living near the camp. Rations were both plentiful and the best obtainable, and the food was well cooked by the skilled catering corps, who had also found themselves a cushy billet.

What a contrast was the life of operational aircrew and their hard-working ground crews. Except when they were on permanent pre-war RAF stations, they had to endure the most primitive conditions, half-frozen in winter and usually bogged down in mud during the spring rains. And, unlike the staff at Cosford, they seldom saw their wives and families, except during short periods of leave.

I was not the only cadet to feel little patience or respect for the pompous teaching staff at this RAF station.

We were allowed to attend the officers' mess from time to time, so that we could be tutored in how to pass the port in the correct direction, to the left. There we learnt such useful fighting phrases as 'The port is with you.' We also were taught how to toast His Majesty the King, and which knife and fork to use for each course.

After four weeks of this nonsense I was commissioned and kitted out, including that compulsory camp furniture, and I was given seven days' leave in which to pick up my new uniform. Armed with a first-class rail-pass, for I was now a British officer, I went home. That, at least, was a joyous relief. Just to be with my family, and especially my wife and child, was quite sufficient for me. I loved them all very much.

I also made a point of visiting ACRC to thank the Matron and her nursing staff for everything they had done for me. While I was there, I telephoned Group-Captain Gilligan to pay my respects. But for him, I would have been a civilian again.

Ma and Pop were delighted to see me, but my father had grave news. My cousin John was missing, believed killed in action. That was a bitter blow for everyone who had known and loved him.

Both my father and my cousin Joan, John's sister, had had detailed clairvoyant visions of what had happened to him, which turned out later to be absolutely accurate. I consider those psychic experiences to be remarkable evidence of the survival of the human entity after death.

That was the thought that I took with me when I reported in August 1943 to The Towers, Highgate, in north London. It was a large Victorian mansion, set in extensive grounds, and surrounded by high, barbed-wire-topped walls, patrolled day and night by armed guards and RAF police dogs. This was where I was to be trained in the special techniques employed by RAF Intelligence and in other top-secret methods of waging clandestine war. I was twenty-one years old, one of the two youngest Intelligence officers in the Royal Air Force.

Chapter Fourteen

Cloaks and Daggers

The Intelligence school was quite unlike Cosford. Whereas the RAF commissioning course had been one long bore, bar the weapons training, The Towers was the venue for a whole collection of Allied officers who were there to learn, as quickly as possible, the important techniques for evasion and escape.

This was the top-secret course devised by MI9, the Military Intelligence inter-service organization which had originally been devised by two British Army officers, Captain Airey Neave and Captain Tom Jarrett, each of whom had broken out of a German top-security prison camp. They had both made a 'home run', i.e. an escape back to Britain, despite the fact that these POW camps, in Neave's case Colditz Castle, had been made especially secure in order to contain previous escapers like themselves.

These brave men were eventually responsible for the escape or evasion of well over two thousand Allied servicemen, mainly aircrew, who made their way home via 'underground' escape routes operated by our agents in Europe with the assistance of the gallant Resistance groups in the Netherlands, Belgium and France. Although I had not known it at the time, Captain Airey Neave had been one of the officers who had interviewed me for Intelligence work.

On my arrival at The Towers, my service identity card was cross-checked by an RAF service policeman. He was accompanied by a German shepherd dog of noble proportions. I have always loved dogs, especially Alsatians. We find great pleasure in each other's company. This fine animal was no exception. Before the RAF dog handler could stop me, I was stroking that handsome dog, who welcomed me by licking my hand. I probably ruined months of training by that instinctive gesture, but that is how I always greeted my canine friends.

From that moment on, I knew that this course would be a marvellous experience, as indeed it turned out to be. In those few weeks I met colleagues from all over the world and found a common bond. We all felt the same way about the war. We all realized that we were fighting evil in its most terrifying form: that of the archetypal demonic force within man. To me, there seemed to be no other way that the Germans, a rational, hard-working and religious people, could have been led down such a sadistically destructive path by a group of insane fanatics.

My comrades-in-arms came from the United Kingdom, France, Belgium, Norway, the Netherlands, Poland, Czechoslovakia and the United States. All the officers from the European countries had escaped from the Nazis, some during the invasion of the Netherlands and the collapse of France, while others had reached Britain by circuitous routes long after their countries had been taken over by the Wehrmacht.

Our American colleagues, two of whom were of senior rank and somewhat older than most of us, came from the OSS, the clandestine Office of Strategic Services which later became the CIA. As yet, our comrades from the United States had not met the Nazis face to face. They believed that Hitler and his whole hierarchy were misguided militarist geopoliticians, and that a viable peace treaty could be negotiated with them from strength. Like most Americans, they were convinced there was good in all men, even the Nazis.

One of the Americans, US Navy Commander Bill Casey, many years later became the Director of the CIA and, forty years after that MI9 course in London, sent me greetings while I was living in California. What an encyclopaedic memory he must have had.

We were given lectures by two veteran escapers from the First World War, Flight-Lieutenant Durnsford-Smith, author of the pre-war bestseller *The Tunnellers of Holzminden*, and Squadron-Leader Evan-Smith, author of another successful book, *The Road to Endor*. When we were asked if we had read either of these books I was the only member of the course who happened to have enjoyed both of them. When the authors asked me why I had read them, pre-war, I answered truthfully, 'My mother recommended them.'

After the shout of laughter that followed, I explained that my mother was a great reader of true-life adventure stories and a knowledgeable student of criminology.

'Into which category would you place these books, Bentin?' Flight-Lieutenant Durnsford-Smith enquired.

'Both categories, sir. What each of you did was highly adventurous and, as far as the enemy was concerned, you were both guilty of attempting to escape from what the Germans considered to be the legitimate confinement of prisoners of war under the terms of the Geneva Convention. Therefore they would have shot you, if they had had a chance, during your escape.'

It says a lot for the general atmosphere at The Towers that this was not frowned upon as an impertinence from a junior officer. Instead, my remark became a topic for discussion. That was what fascinated me about the whole Intelligence course. It was a deeply serious affair, dealing with matters of life and death.

At this point, let me clarify the difference between an 'evader' and an 'escaper'. The first category refers to someone who is *avoiding* capture, after having been shot down, or one who has been landed clandestinely behind the enemy lines. The second category refers to those who already have been captured, and who have subsequently escaped. In other words, an escaper is one who is trying to avoid recapture. The prime objective of both escapers and evaders is to get out of enemy-occupied territory as quickly as possible and to rejoin their units.

The only effective underground escape routes in operation in Europe at that time ran from the Netherlands, through Belgium and into France, where they continued through both the German-occupied north and the Vichy-governed middle and southern portions. Eventually, these long escape routes ended at the Spanish or Swiss frontiers.

The two main underground routes running through France were called Comet and O'Leary. These were operated by local Resistance movements and were organized, for liaison purposes, by British-trained personnel who were dropped by parachute or flown in by Lysander aircraft operating from Tempsford in Bedfordshire.

Comet was largely in the capable hands of an English-woman married to a French count. O'Leary was under the control of 'Lieutenant-Commander Patrick O'Leary' who was actually a Belgian Army surgeon, Major Albert Guerrisse. Both were captured by the Abwehr (counter-espionage), and the Belgian suffered brutal interrogation by the Gestapo. He survived the horrors of Dachau concentration camp and was able to give damning evidence against the Nazi war criminals at the Nuremberg trials.

There was considerable panic at HQ in Britain when the news broke that almost the entire escape operation in the Blois and Tours area had fallen into enemy hands. Everyone in that Resistance cell was suspected: the priest, the mayor, the doctor, the dentist, and many others. All of these were French. But, in the end, it turned out to be an Englishman who had betrayed them. He was a British serviceman, Sergeant Cole, who had gone to ground during the evacuation of Allied troops at Dunkirk. He had absconded with the mess funds, which were considerable, and set himself up by going undercover with a French girlfriend.

At that time news had reached Britain that two British officers who had evaded capture during the collapse of

France had been helped to cross from enemy-occupied territory into Vichy France by an Englishman claiming to be a British officer, 'Captain' Cole.

MI9 was interested in this information and one of their operatives in France managed to contact this man. In fact there *was* a Captain Cole in the Army list who, after Dunkirk, had been reported missing, believed killed in action.

Because of that coincidence, Sergeant Cole successfully passed muster. Even though neither 'Pat O'Leary' nor Airey Neave was fully convinced, they had so much on their hands while they were setting up the escape routes that a full investigation into Cole's background was never carried out. It was the only big mistake that MI9 made throughout the war in Europe, and was to cost the lives of some of our best operatives in France, and the capture of Albert Guerrisse as well.

The principles of evasion, i.e. avoiding capture, were basically simple. It was part of our job, as Intelligence officers, to pass these techniques on to Allied aircrew.

The most vulnerable moment is directly after the airman has landed by parachute or has made a successful emergency landing in enemy-held territory. At that point, understandably, he is in a state of shock. Therefore the first rule is to get out of sight and under cover as quickly as possible. Obviously, if the airman is severely wounded this course of action is impractical. In that case, the next move must be dictated by common sense. Better a live airman, fully recovered from his wounds and willing to attempt to escape from a German prison camp, than an evader who has bled to death in concealment. It is also vitally important to bury or hide the parachute. If a parachute is found too quickly, the person who used it cannot be far away. The longer it can remain undiscovered the better.

The next move is to lie low and, if the hiding-place is sufficiently secure, to try to get some sleep. This is why a dense wood is a favourite choice for concealment. Naturally, moving to a hiding place is much safer by night.

Most RAF bomber and intruder actions were nocturnal, whereas the American bomber assault was carried out in daylight. This made American attempts at evasion much harder.

After resting up and taking advantage of the opportunity to get over the worst of the shock, the evader should eat some of the emergency rations and use the water-purifying tablets in his escape-pack to treat any water he finds. Then he should use his silk map and small compass to orientate himself as accurately as possible.

If he has landed in enemy-occupied territory such as the Netherlands, Belgium or France, he must stay concealed until dawn, and then, from hiding, observe the movements of any local people in the area such as farm-labourers. This can apply only when he is concealed in the countryside. If he has come down in the vicinity of a town, he will either have been captured almost immediately or have been contacted, aided and concealed by a sympathetic member of a local Resistance group.

An all-important rule is: never approach anyone and ask for help unless he or she is alone. A person who would assist you when alone is often chary of doing so if he or she is accompanied by someone else. The evader, or escaper, should always remember that their helpers' lives would almost certainly be forfeit if they were caught.

Another basic rule is to rely on the survival instinct, but to filter such intuition through rational thinking. Above all, do not panic! Always behave as naturally as possible. Never run when you can walk. Lay up during the day, and only travel by night when it is safe to do so. Fear is the worse enemy. Be cautious, not fearful.

Lastly, the evader/escaper must remember that the chances of success are much increased after contact has been made with the Resistance. Trust them, but only answer such questions as are necessary to establish your bona fides as an Allied airman. The Abwehr had skilled operatives who trapped members of the Resistance by posing as shot-down Allied airmen. The cardinal rule is: at all times, listen to your instinct.

The most important point that each of these exceptional men made to us was that 'Escaping from, or evading, the enemy is primarily a state of mind. If you are determined to do so, your chances of success are very greatly increased.'

There were many ingenious escape-aids available. The imagination used in devising them was quite extraordinary. Most of the following were sent to prisoner-of-war camps hidden inside Red Cross parcels. Sizeable compasses were concealed in shaving brushes. Large silk maps were slipped inside gramophone record covers. Strong wire-cutters were also sent in these parcels, each separate limb of the cutter being hidden inside a hollowed-out cricket or baseball bat. The German guards never discovered this device but they sometimes confiscated the bats, with the excuse that they might be used as weapons. Even small radios were smuggled into prison camps. Their various components which, in those days, included valves and batteries, were contained in tins of jam, Spam, and other food packs.

Obviously, escaping was much harder than evading the enemy before capture, because all the security measures of the prisoner-of-war camp first had to be circumvented. Yet there were many attempts to escape. All of them were aided by the ingenuity of MI9. Some of these attempts were successful, and the stories of how these brave men got away to Sweden, Switzerland and Spain makes exciting reading.

Prisoner-made civilian clothing, or even military uniforms, were often used in these attempts, as had been the case with Colonel Airey Neave's famous escape from Colditz Castle, when he disguised himself as a German NCO and simply walked out.

Each prison camp held Allied prisoners who were skilled with needle and thread, and MI9 provided special grey woollen blankets for the prisoners. These were allowed under the terms of the Geneva Convention, but MI9 modified them by printing on the material, with invisible ink, the complete pattern of the clothing or uniform.

By dipping the blanket into a pail of warm water, to which had been added certain chemicals, which had been hidden inside jam pots or Klim dried-milk tins, not only did the pattern become permanently visible but the colour of the blanket changed to dark-blue, brown or field-grey, as the clothing or uniform required.

Other Red Cross parcels contained forged documents or, alternatively, the ink, pens and rubber-stamps required by prison-camp forgers to produce their own papers. These skilled forgeries were of *Ausweise* (identity cards), which were issued to the hundreds of thousands of skilled foreign artisans who were working in Europe on German war production.

In addition, false orders were produced, justifying the long journeys undertaken by some escapers, who often travelled right across Europe.

Even tiny cameras and miniature film, photographic printing-paper and all the necessary developing and fixing chemicals were smuggled into prison camps inside tins of food, tubes of toothpaste, and cakes of shaving soap.

Inside each POW camp there was a complete escape industry in progress under the command of the senior British and Allied officers, whose job was to organize an escape committee. These committees organized, co-ordinated and controlled all individual or team attempts to escape, so that one did not interfere with the other. All plans to escape had first to be approved by this group of experienced officers, and their decision was final. Hare-brained schemes were rejected outright. Only carefully planned escapes were allowed, sometimes taking months to accomplish.

When posted to our operational units, we were to pass on to aircrew only the information and equipment that concerned them, including their personal evasion kits, containing emergency rations, rubber water-bottle, purifying tablets, compass, maps, and local money, to be used should they have to evade capture. If they failed, were taken prisoner and, subsequently, tried to escape, the appropriate information and other escape-aids would be made available to them by the escape committees inside their prison camps.

Primarily, we had to get across to Allied aircrew the feasibility of evasion and of escape, if captured.

I was delighted when, years after the war, various Allied aircrew, whom I met at RAF functions and whom I had briefed and served alongside from 1943 onwards, told me that I had been of help to their personal survival during operations. That made it all seem worthwhile.

One factor emerged again and again during our conversations at The Towers. This was the number of times that some hitherto unsuspected sixth sense or, as I thought of it, psychic awareness, had saved the participants from capture and death during their escape from Europe.

Here is one example of the sort of thing I was told by men I could trust. A Belgian officer related: 'I was asleep in the back room of a friend's house. In the middle of the night, I woke up. I heard my mother's voice telling me to get out of the place as fast as I could. I put on my pants and shoes, grabbed the rest of my things and went out through the window, which overlooked a small garden.

'As I climbed over the fence into a back alley, I heard cars pulling up, followed by shouts and the front door being kicked open. It was the Gestapo. I heard later that they had never troubled the occupants of that house before. I also heard that my friend and his wife were taken away for questioning. I don't know what happened to them. Had I not been woken by my mother's voice, I would have been caught for sure. I am certain it was her voice, even though she had been dead for eight years.'

My final interview with the super-efficient staff at The Towers was friendly and they seemed to be pleased with me. They wished me luck, handed me a rail-warrant for my coming journey, and told me where I was to be posted. It was to RAF Hemswell, the Lincolnshire airfield which housed Numbers 300 and 305 Squadrons, whose aircrew flew Vickers Wellington bombers. Both these squadrons were Polish.

It was the start of a long and devoted friendship with some of the bravest men and women I have ever known.

Chapter Fifteen

My 'Bleddy' Marvellous Poles

I arrived at Lincoln railway station to be met by a chirpy cockney WAAF driver. On the way to Hemswell, she told me how much she liked the Poles. 'They've lost everything, sir. But they are ever so nice and cheerful. It makes us all want to mother them.'

At Hemswell I was told to familiarize myself with the air and ground crews, the airfield, its personnel and the operational procedures then in force. Shortly after I arrived, 305 Squadron was posted away, to convert their aircrews to fly B-25 Mitchell bombers for operations with the Second Tactical Air Force. At the same time, 300 Squadron moved from its station at Hemswell, with the large pre-war mess halls and comfortable billets, to a small satellite airfield which had just been completed. This was sited four miles further down the road towards Lincoln.

The satellite airfield was called Ingham, after the tiny village nearby. It was made up of a number of arable fields with their dividing drystone walls removed to form a large rectangular landing ground. This area was left covered with grass and, unlike RAF Hemswell, Ingham was not equipped with concrete runways.

The new airfield was surrounded by an asphalt taxi-track, dotted with numerous tarred hard-standings on which the sturdy Wellingtons were serviced. The hangars were temporary hemispherical structures, roofed with corrugated iron sheets which were laid over a curved network of latticed steel frames.

After heavy rain the whole area, including the primitive living quarters of small huts, became a sea of mud. The Wellingtons, carrying bombs, ammunition and full petrol-tanks, found it difficult to become airborne as they thundered along the sodden grass runways.

Everyone – officers, NCOs, Airmen and WAAFs – lived in Nissen huts, squat structures made of brick, wood and asbestos cladding, some of which were rectangular in shape while others were miniature versions of the low, domed hangars, roofed with either tarred felt or sheets of corrugated iron.

In winter they were bitterly cold, despite the red-hot glow from the pot-bellied iron stove which was placed on a brick pad in the centre of each hut. These stoves were kept going day and night, the tall, blacked-tin chimney-pipes which stuck out of the roofs discharging wisps of sooty smoke into the chilly Lincolnshire air.

My first operational briefing was for a night raid on Düsseldorf in the Ruhr, the 'Happy Valley' as it was called with typically cynical RAF understatement. According to the returning aircrews, the valley of the Ruhr was anything but happy for them because of its deadly barrage of heavy and light flak, the concentrated anti-aircraft fire of thousands of 88-mm guns and a huge number of lighter automatic cannon which protected the vital steel industries of the Ruhr.

The heavy flak guns were capable of reaching 35,000 feet, well over twice the altitude of 16,000 feet at which the Wellington twin-engined bombers carried out their attacks. The heavier four-engined Lancasters and Halifaxes bombed from around 20,000 feet. The other heavy bombers, the Stirlings, though powered by four engines, flew at the same operational altitude as the Wellingtons. Being much slower than the Lancs and Halis, and a bigger target than the Wellingtons, their losses during the winter of 1943–4 were appalling.

It was the Poles who first taught me how to fight a war. They waged it twenty-four hours a day, seven days a week, waking and sleeping, in daydreams or in nightmares. As one good friend, Flight-Lieutenant Roman Statmuller, explained, 'You must fight these bleddy Nazis all the time, every bleddy day, every bleddy night. Think about destroying them, Mike, when you eat, when you drink, even when you make love. Only when they are finished for ever can we afford to stop fighting the bleddy bastards.'

At Ingham I was thrown into the deep end of operations. A bright ex-advertising man who was my senior Intelligence Officer (IO) taught me how to present an operation pictorially, and my own drawing and acting experience helped me as well. I soon was able to give the aircrews of 300 Squadron a clear presentation of the purpose, character and hazards of each operation.

By the late autumn of 1943, the Bomber Command assault on Germany had made devastating raids as far as Berlin. Each night, operations by RAF bomber groups were being carried out all over the Third Reich. In the case of 300 Squadron, they reached as far eastwards as Posen in East Prussia, which lay beyond the old Polish corridor. For this special operation our Wellingtons had to be fitted with long-range tanks. These consisted of two long rubber cylinders like huge black sausages, each weighing over 1,800 pounds when filled with fuel. They were stowed on either side of the bomb-bay. If these tanks were hit, the Wellington would blow up like a huge firework.

One of our aircraft failed to return from this long-range raid, having been shot down over the target area. After that raid, Bomber Command decided to use the Polish squadron for dropping mines on the approaches to the German U-boat bases at Brest, Lorient, and St Nazaire. These well-defined targets were located on the Atlantic coastline of Brittany, in the Bay of Biscay.

By this time I knew most of the aircrews, and counted many of them as friends. On their part, they accepted me as someone who knew about their aircraft and what it was capable of doing. I had obtained this knowledge by the simple process of asking the ground crews to show me over every inch of the Mark X Wellingtons they were servicing.

I also spent what little spare time I had learning instrument flying in our Link trainer. The Lear/Link blind-flying trainer was a small facsimile of an aircraft, firmly attached to the ground and sited inside a specially built Nissen hut on each operational airfield. Unless pilots were experienced in instrument flying, they soon lost control in the zero-visibility conditions of flying in cloud. The Link was the progenitor of today's flight simulators but, of course, nowhere near as complex.

The aerial mine-laying operations I briefed were limited to not more than three aircraft per night so as to draw minimum attention to the mining. The whole operation required precision flying. When they had checked their exact position by taking a compass bearing on a lighthouse on an unmistakably shaped island off the south coast of Brittany the pilots set course almost due east to fly along the narrow swept channel, which the Germans kept free of mines so that their U-boats could pass safely in and out of port between their own mine-fields.

Because the mines carried by our Wellingtons were dropped by parachute, an exact altitude of 1,000 feet for their release had to be strictly maintained. If the mines were dropped too high, their parachutes could drift out of the swept Channel area and would only reinforce the German mine-fields. On the other hand, if the mines were dropped too low, their parachutes would not have sufficient time to open and the thin-skinned weapons would break up on impact with the water. Their metal casings had to be made as light as possible so that the maximum amount of explosive could be carried for a given airborne weight.

The whole operation was a tricky one, not only from the point of view of airmanship and pinpoint navigation, but also because of the vulnerability of the low-flying aircraft to anti-aircraft fire. This came from numerous heavily armed flak ships that patrolled the narrow sea-lane.

These difficult operations against the U-boat bases had to be carried out in conditions of clear visibility, usually just before, during, and directly after the full moon. The Wellingtons had to fly a straight and steady course at 1,000 feet altitude for well over a minute throughout the last part of the operation in order to drop their mines accurately. This made them easy targets for the ship-mounted flak guns. Therefore, the sooner the last part of the drop was accomplished the better chance the aircraft had of survival.

This also meant that from my point of view, as the briefing officer, the clearer, simpler and more accurate the information I gave these aircrews, the more chance they had of carrying out their mission and returning safely.

I volunteered to fly with them on each and every operation but was turned down. This was not the air-crews' fault. They were more than willing to take me along. However, during my first week at Hemswell, three non-flying officers from the group had been lost aboard bomber aircraft when the planes were shot down over the Ruhr. These had included a medical officer, a padre, and an Intelligence officer. It was decided at Command level that an embargo on all non-flying personnel taking part in operations over enemy territory should be enforced. This applied especially to Intelligence personnel; even an inexperienced IO like me already possessed secret information which Command did not wish to risk being extracted by the enemy.

The Germans specialized in obtaining information from newly shot down aircrew, and had established a special transit camp for captured Allied aircrew. Torture was not used, but trained English-speaking German Intelligence officers, posing as Allied POWs, were infiltrated among the new prisoners. Their aim was to gain their confidence and to gather information about their units and operational procedures. They were extremely effective and had become an acute problem.

At each briefing, I warned my aircrews about this procedure, which was effective only when the Allied aircrew were unprepared for this type of 'interrogation'. Under the Geneva Convention, the only information that a POW was required to give was his name, rank and service number. The rest was illegally extracted.

This new embargo from Command did not mean that I was not allowed to fly with my 'bleddy Poles', but it limited such flying to 'bull's eyes' – practice night 'bombing' flights in Britain – local cross-country familiarization-flights with new crews, and square searches, i.e. looking for dinghies containing aircrew shot down round our coasts.

I flew whenever I got the chance, and the Polish crews were confident that I knew what I was doing. Thanks to my unofficial time spent in the Link trainer, I was becoming a competent instrument pilot, and this went over well with the crews. To my delight the pilots, especially Roman Statmuller, would let me fly the Wellington for hours at a time.

One motive I had for this extra effort was the hope that I might still be accepted by the Air Transport Auxiliary (ATA), which ferried aircraft of every type from the factory airfields to the bases that required them. They used pilots declared unfit for operational flying, either because of severe wounds or because their eyesight was not up to standard. This type of flying allowed for corrected vision, i.e. prescription goggles or glasses could be worn if necessary.

My ambition to fly with the ATA was backed by our Commanding Officer, Wing-Commander Baron Kuharski, himself a keen flyer. Another surprisingly helpful supporter was our Number 1 Group Senior Air Staff Officer, Air-Commodore Cozens. Both these men, to whom flying meant so much, recognized a frustrated 'penguin' when they saw one and both of them encouraged me to apply for the job. I was even sent to London to pick up a pair of lensed goggles which the medical officer had ordered on my behalf. With them, I could enjoy the same acuity of vision I had with my ordinary spectacles.

Meanwhile, I continued to brief my Poles on their various operations, most of which were confined to mining the U-boat ports in Brittany and attacking the patrol-boat bases around the Texel on the northern Dutch coast. From all these operations every one of our aircraft returned safely.

By now I had acquired the habit of remaining behind in the Intelligence Operations hut after the briefing was over, ostensibly to wait for early returns, i.e. aircraft that, for one reason or another, had been forced to abort their mission. Actually I stayed alone, sitting silently in front of the large plastic-sheathed map of Europe, in order to follow the whole operation in my mind from start to finish.

I probably would have been certified insane by the medical officer, had he known the real reason for this lonely vigil. I believed that, by concentrating on the progress of the aircrews and their aircraft throughout the whole operation, I would, in a sense, be helping to protect them from harm. Being trained in navigation, and having flown with the crews, I could visualize the whole route in and out of the target area. I also had a fair idea of the hazards they would encounter. By positive thinking I hoped to aid my friends to the best of my ability. If I was not allowed to fly with them physically on operations, at least I would accompany them mentally.

After serving several months at Ingham, I was posted to nearby RAF Wickenby as operational Intelligence officer attached to Numbers 12 and 626 Squadrons, which flew Lancaster bombers, and with mutual regret my 'bleddy' Poles and I said goodbye.

Chapter Sixteen

The Slaughter of the Innocents

On the way to Wickenby I visited Lincoln cathedral. I needed to pray. I hated leaving my Poles. They had made me welcome and let me fly with them. I felt one with their cause. Now I was being pitchforked into a very different situation and I wanted to make sure that I started my new job on the right foot: hence my need for a word with the Almighty.

The grey bulk of the cathedral rose out of the early-morning mist like a stone battleship. The soaring pillars of the Gothic nave exuded power and tranquillity, a rare combination in wartime. As soon as I entered I could feel the sense of peace. To my surprise, the cathedral was almost deserted. I had expected it to be full of people seeking solace from the tensions of war.

By the winter of 1943, our bomber losses were mounting with the increasing savagery of the RAF's night offensive on Germany. Raids of more than five hundred aircraft at a time over each target area were a common occurrence. The first devastating thousand-bomber raid on Cologne in 1942 had signalled the start of Air Marshal Sir Arthur Harris's all-night offensive against the industrial heart of the Third Reich.

Not only the huge manufacturing complex of the Ruhr but all Germany's major cities were now considered to be legitimate targets. By day the US Eighth Air Force pounded the targets with hundreds of their heavily armed, high-altitude B-17 Flying Fortresses and B-24 Liberator bombers. By night the RAF took over the offensive. The sky on operational nights was filled with the thunder of our aircraft as the Halifaxes, Lancasters, Mosquitoes and Stirlings gathered over the east coast before setting course for Germany, led by twin-engined Mosquito pathfinders.

I came out of Lincoln cathedral filled with a new resolve. Thirty minutes later, I reported to the guard room at RAF Wickenby, and was directed to the Intelligence section. In the operations building I handed over my orders to the Senior Intelligence Officer, Squadron-Leader Williams, a gaunt, grey-haired First World War pilot. Among his medal ribbons I noted the Military Cross.

'Glad to have you with us, Bentin. We are at full stretch here. Your experience with the Poles will come in handy. Just sling your kit into your hut and then come straight back. We've got a long day ahead of us.'

An hour later I was helping to pin up the required briefing information for that night's maximum-effort operation deep into the heart of Germany.

What manner of men and women made up the air and ground crews of bomber stations such as RAF Wickenby? In essence, the aircrews were much the same as those I had met previously at the Aircrew Reception Centre in Regent's Park. However, there was now a discernible difference in their attitude. Having experienced the grim side of their job, they had changed from being enthusiastic young men who were mad about flying to something much harder. Many of them had seen their comrades killed in air accidents during training, while others had watched their mates die horribly in the nightly holocaust over Europe.

First and foremost, aircrew were intent on survival. Their faces showed the strain. The eagerness of youth and the excitement of flight had taken second place to a dogged determination to make it through their first tour of thirty operations. If they did so, their prospects of survival were healthier, for after completing that first tour they would be posted to a safer job as instructors until they were needed for their second tour some six months later. Leonard Cheshire went on to complete a third and even a fourth tour of operations, in his case winning the Victoria Cross for having completed over a hundred operational sorties over Europe.

When you consider that their chances of getting through that first thirty operations over enemy territory were frighteningly slim, and that the outcome was determined by aircrew giving 100 per cent concentrated effort throughout their whole tour, you realize just how much stress they were under. Lack of concentration on the part of any member of the crew could spell death for them all. Their survival rate was depressingly low.

There is no doubt in my mind that luck played a big part in these operations, but morale was another factor that determined the odds. Some aircrews were lost because one of them had received a 'Dear John' letter from his wife, fiancée or girlfriend telling him that she had been unfaithful. That would badly affect his concentration.

Sheer skill played the most important role in the whole business of survival. An experienced, gifted pilot, a first-class navigator, a well-trained flight-engineer, each with a cool head in an emergency, were all essential ingredients in surviving those thirty operations. Alert and straight-shooting gunners and a good wireless operator generated excellent morale, and an efficient bomb-aimer made each and every operation worthwhile. Such a crew usually made it back home. But not always. They still needed luck on their side.

With hundreds of our aircraft flying without navigation lights there was always the danger of mid-air collision. It is astonishing that more bombers did not suffer this sort of accident at night or in bad visibility. Over the target area there was also the danger of being hit by bombs and showers of incendiaries dropped by their own comrades above them. Many of our planes suffered from this target hazard.

Bad weather brought down many of our aircraft, especially on their return to Britain when the pilots were near exhaustion after over seven hours of operational flying. On the night of 16–17 December 1943, after a heavy raid on Berlin, in addition to many casualties over Germany, the RAF lost twenty-eight Lancasters, mainly owing to mid-air collisions while approaching their bases or by aircraft flying into high ground during unexpected fog and low cloud. There were pathetically few survivors. One of our 12 Squadron aircraft crashed within sight of Wickenby, with the loss of all seven of the crew.

Only the bomber crews themselves knew how lucky they were to return safely from those terrible winter operations over Europe. Bomber Command alone suffered over 55,000 killed during the six years of war, many of them in the middle of this long winter air battle.

Our aircraft were well serviced, and more and more of these dedicated ground crews were made up of WAAF personnel. Without their skills and the care they took in their expert trades in all weathers and in all conditions, which were often appalling, the whole RAF bomber offensive would have ground to a halt. It was an extraordinary example of group effort and application.

The team effort was nowhere more evident than in the parachute-packing sections of each RAF bomber station, where the lives of each member of the aircrew literally depended on the concentration of the expert packers, most of whom were WAAF. Part of their motto, which summed up their philosophy, was, 'My heart is with you at the jump.'

There were very few cases of parachutes failing to open properly, and these accidents were usually associated with battle damage to the canopy or shroud lines, or were caused by jumping from too low an altitude.

I have been asked, mainly by people who were not involved in the wartime services or who were not even born then, 'Didn't you have a fabulous time with all those WAAFs and other servicewomen? Wartime sex must have been so available, and on such a large scale. What a life you must have had! Go on, admit it.'

In my case, the idea of romantic love appealed much more than sex for its own sake. So, in the service, I put it out of my mind. Moreover, I was very much in love with my wife and therefore did not respond when I knew the opportunities for extra-marital sex were there. This was often the case among contemporaries who, like me, were newly married. In wartime, there were other priorities. Survival was the strongest instinct. We had to win the war or perish.

Owing to the rapport I had with aircrews, a new and grisly paranormal ability had manifested for me during this eventful period with Bomber Command. To put it simply, I could tell which members of the aircrews would die that night. I could not tell which ones would be wounded and survive or be shot down and taken prisoner. My foreknowledge applied solely to the ones who would die. As this fact became increasingly clear, I went to see the chaplain. I explained the problem and begged him to pray with me that the dreadful burden should be taken away.

The chaplain, a wise man who had been a subaltern in the Guards during the Battle of the Somme and who had taken Holy Orders some years after the Armistice, heard me out in silence. He was not in the least surprised by my petition. 'You wouldn't be the first person who has come to me with a similar request,' he said, and went on to explain why he thought this strange phenomenon occurred.

'It happens because you are so close to aircrew. Somehow, like others before you, you catch a terrifying glimpse of their future. How does it manifest for you, Michael?'

'Their faces have the look of death,' I said. 'I can't be more explicit than that. It is just that I *know*. I wish to God that I didn't.'

'Then we will pray together.'

Which is what we did and, blessedly, those appalling previsions ceased.

This grim time had its bizarre moments. Without my sense of the ridiculous I would have been lost, a basket-case of nervous depression. One terrible night everything went wrong. One of the first pilots to return was a squadron-leader whose Lanc had been shot up and he had two badly wounded aboard. He landed on three engines.

After debriefing, he stormed into the Intelligence hut. 'Christ, what a cock-up! The route markers were wrong. The flak was the worst I've ever seen, and the bloody target was obscured. The bloody weather forecast was miles out. Jesus, what a goddamn awful night. Get me Group HQ. I want to tear them off a monumental strip.'

I tried to get through to Bawtry, our Group HQ, but somehow I was connected to Bomber Command's operations room. Before I could tell the operator there had been a mistake, the seething squadron-leader had snatched the phone from me.

'What stupid bastard planned this bloody raid?' he yelled down the phone. 'Everything that could go wrong went bloody wrong. The stupid moron in charge of planning this sort of mass murder should be shot . . . etc.' He raved on in the same vein for another two minutes. Eventually he ran out of breath.

'Do you know who you are speaking to?' asked a cold voice at the other end of the line.

'No, I don't. And I don't bloody well care.'

'This is Air Chief Marshal Sir Arthur Harris, C-in-C Bomber Command.'

There was a short silence at our end of the line. Then the squadron-leader asked hoarsely, 'Do you know who *you* are talking to, sir?'

'No, I don't,' replied the Commander-in-Chief.

'Thank Christ for that,' the pilot muttered and put down the phone.

Bomber Command tried all day to trace the call, phoning all round Number 1 Group. When it came to my turn, as the Duty Intelligence Officer I told them I had no idea what they were talking about.

Another odd incident that stands out in my memory concerned the loss of eleven Elsan chemical toilets during one night's raid on Berlin. The Adjutant of 626 Squadron and the station equipment officer sought my help. The equipment officer asked, 'How the hell am I going to justify the inexplicable loss of *eleven* tin toilets out of sixteen of our aircraft over Berlin in one night?'

I thought for a moment. 'How about if the aircraft had to be lightened at all costs? There were heavy headwinds that night. The pilots were concerned that they might not have enough fuel left to make it back. So they chucked out the toilets. How does that sound?'

'They'll never believe it.' They almost spoke the words together.

'All right, gentlemen. What else can you give as an excuse? Your best bet is that the aircrews had to lighten their aircraft. A full Elsan would be their first choice.'

The equipment officer looked at me. 'How the hell do you know they were full?'

I looked him straight in the eyes. 'Take my word for it. If they were dropped over Berlin, they were full.'

We had a number of Australian aircrew on our strength, and I had heard about this incident from one of them. He had told me gleefully that it was an Aussie operation.

There was a sequel. About a month afterwards, we were visited by an official from the Swiss Red Cross. He was accompanied by an officer from the RAF's Special Investigation Branch. As the Duty Intelligence Officer on the night of the operation when the Elsans had gone missing, I was cross-examined minutely. I was told that one of the eleven offending chemical toilets, which had whistled down from 20,000 feet on to the burning German capital, had disintegrated on impact, covering an unfortunate German with its contents. Part of the flattened tin toilet had been recovered. It had official identification numerals stamped upon it, and the German government complained to the Swiss Red Cross. At Geneva's request, it was traced back by the RAF Special Investigation Branch to our Bomber Wing.

The German government officially accused the Royal Air Force of using 'bacteriological warfare', in direct contravention of the terms of the Geneva Convention and the Treaty of the Hague on the conduct of war. Coming from the Nazis, that took my breath away. What a bloody nerve!

Another occurrence was even more extraordinary. One night, I was being driven round the airfield by the orderly sergeant to check up on the beacons. This job was known as 'beacon bashing'. It was a necessary procedure to make sure that the big automatic generators were functioning properly, flashing out their appropriate Morse-code light-signal to help guide aircraft at night.

Half way round the perimeter track, in the gale-swept darkness, I made out a large billowing white shape. For a moment I thought it was a paranormal manifestation, then I realized it was an open parachute which had been trapped by the wire perimeter-fence.

We got out of the car and hurried over to it. Harnessed to the parachute was a semi-conscious airman. I sent the orderly sergeant back for the medical officer and the 'blood wagon', while I gave what comfort I could. To my astonishment, the delirious airman kept muttering, '*Kamerad!* . . . *Kamerad!*' This was odd, because he was wearing RAF flying kit.

The medical officer soon arrived with the ambulance and rushed the injured airman to station sick quarters. Later that day I found out what had happened. The battered parachutist was a sergeant rear-gunner from one of our own aircraft. He had been in his aircraft waiting for 'press tit time' and had dozed off in his rear-turret. This was unusual for an experienced air-gunner but after two consecutive nights on operations, he was exhausted. As he fell asleep he must have accidentally dislodged the jack-plug of the radio-telephone system. When his pilot had been told that the night's operation was scrubbed owing to the appalling weather conditions, he had checked out each of his crew on the closed-circuit R/T. They had all replied, except the rear-gunner.

The skipper assumed that the gunner had left his turret and got into the large truck which already contained aircrew from two other aircraft. It had never occurred to anyone to take a head count. The night was so dark and the weather so appalling that nobody had spotted the rear-gunner sleeping soundly in his darkened turret. They had driven off, leaving him alone in the Lanc.

Just after midnight, he had woken up. For a few moments in the pitch blackness, he was completely disorientated. The last thing the rear-gunner remembered, before dozing off, was that he was on an operation. Suddenly it dawned on him that the engines were silent. The howling gale outside must have sounded to him just like an aircraft in a dive. He tried to call up the skipper on the intercom and got no reply. He checked the equipment and, to his horror, saw that the R/T plug was disconnected.

Exhausted and confused, the panic-stricken gunner concluded that the aircraft had been abandoned by the rest of the crew. He believed he was crashing towards the ground. There was only one thing to do. As the silent engines were no longer providing power for the hydraulic system of the turret, the gunner manually cranked it round and bailed out backwards.

His helmeted head hit the asphalt hard-standing only three feet below the rear-turret. As he lost consciousness his reflex action was to pull the rip-cord to release the parachute. The drogue chute fell out of the pack. It was caught by the wind and, as it was intended to do, pulled out the rest of the parachute canopy. This immediately filled up with the full force of the gale, dragging the semi-conscious rear-gunner right across the airfield, badly bruising him in the process. The canopy eventually caught on the perimeter-fence, where we found him.

Even as I comforted him, the groggy young sergeant, who was convinced that he had bailed out over Europe, kept thanking me in schoolboy German, '*Danke schon, Kamerad! Danke schon!*'

I would have stayed on with this Bomber Wing indefinitely, but fate had decided otherwise.

Air-Commodore Cozens had been as good as his word when he had promised to help me get a job flying. He had approached the Air Transport Auxiliary on my behalf, recommending that they should test me for flight training. At his request, I was fitted with a pair of prescription-lensed goggles which enabled me to see quite well, and I felt confident that I would be able to pass the Air Transport Auxiliary flying test.

While I was in London being fitted for the goggles, I heard a magnificent story from the optometrist, which I believe to be true. One of our top night-fighting pilots had been plagued with eye trouble, and the RAF medical board wanted to experiment with the brand new moulded-glass contact-lenses. The pilot was duly fitted for one of the first pairs of these revolutionary optical aids.

They worked very well but, at first, were uncomfortable to wear. Nevertheless, the night-fighter ace persevered with them, wearing them even when he was not flying. His aircraft was a specially modified de Havilland Mosquito twin-engined night-fighter, and his navigator used to profit from unsuspecting fellow customers in saloon bars by telling them, 'My pilot has got a glass eye.'

Naturally, knowing nothing about the new glass contact-lenses, the incredulous customers would scoff at the idea. 'Don't be silly. Whoever heard of a pilot with a glass eye?'

Invariably they accepted a bet of double whiskies for the flyers if the pilot could prove this preposterous claim. The pilot would hold one of his eyelids wide open and, taking a coin from his pocket, would tap it against the glass surface of the contact-lens. The bet was won!

The amazed customers would pay up. After the whiskies had been rapidly disposed of, the same question would always be asked, 'But doesn't that glass eye make flying difficult?'

The pilot would take out the coin once again, hold the other eyelid wide open, and tap against the contact-lens fitted to his other eye, saying, 'Not half as much as this one does.'

Knowing that pilot, I am sure the tall tale is true.

To test my new Mark VIII prescription goggles, I was sent to a nearby training unit for assessment by the chief flying instructor. The test was scheduled for the next morning, and I was confident that I would make a good enough showing to proceed to the next step in becoming a transport pilot.

The morning was clear but misty, with thin cloud and an indefinite horizon. The instructor and I were strapped into the Miles Master training aircraft and carefully went through the cockpit drill together.

'Right,' said the instructor. 'Now let's see what you can do.'

We taxied out and took off, climbing to about 6,000 feet, where the instructor handed the aircraft over to me. He ordered me to perform a series of turns, followed by a practice stall and recovery. So far, all was well and good. However, with all the tension and excitement my goggles started to steam up. Instead of telling him, in my eagerness to prove that I could fly I started cheating.

Because the horizon was so unclear, and the goggles misty, I commenced flying on the instruments, which I could see clearly enough. I knew how to use the blind-flying panel because of those hours in the Link Trainer.

The instructor was no fool and must have twigged what I was doing. 'OK. Now, let's try a spin.'

I pulled the Master up into a savage stall and let her fall off on one wing. We immediately started to spin. I then realized why we were doing this manoeuvre. Some of my instruments went haywire. The Artificial Horizon, which I had relied upon for my stability in flight, toppled. It would be useless until I could straighten out the aircraft, and even then it would take some time to settle down. I recovered from the spin by reversing the controls as my previous instructors had taught me. We came out of it safely with plenty of height to spare.

The instructor still was not satisfied. 'Do a slow roll,' he ordered over the radio-telephone.

As soon as the Artificial Horizon had settled down, I obliged. Once again it toppled, leaving me trying to find a horizon in the duff visibility, and with my goggles misting up worse than ever. I had got away with my recovery from the vertical spin but this was quite different. Now I was rotating the aircraft round its horizontal axis in straight and level flight. To perform a proper slow roll I had to be able to see a clear horizon in order to orientate myself, and I could not distinguish one.

Suddenly I saw a straight line in front of me. Thankfully I lined up the nose of the aircraft with this horizon while I performed a neat roll. Or so I thought until I realized that the airspeed indicator was racing round the dial, and that the 'G' had started to build up rapidly. The 'horizon' I had picked out was a canal bank. We were rolling in a near vertical dive!

That instructor must have had nerves of steel, as we were losing height rapidly. He pulled us out and never said a word until we had landed.

'Lensed goggles or no lensed goggles, you can't see a fucking thing, Bentin. Stick with Intelligence. You know what you are doing there.'

Of course he was right to fail me, but I was still hopeful that I might be accepted as a navigator with ATA. When I was summoned to Number 9 Group HQ, I thought this was it: at last, I was going to be trained for aircrew.

My Senior Intelligence Officer at Wickenby, Willy Williams, was most reluctant to see me go and, as a parting gift, arranged for me to draw an 'Irvin' flight jacket and flying boots. The equipment officer gladly supplied them. He said that he 'owed me' for getting him out of trouble, along with the adjutant of 626 Squadron, over the problem of the missing Elsans. Apparently, my emergency lightening of the aircraft explanation had been accepted.

I went round to say goodbye to my aircrews, who wished me luck with ATA, and off I went to Number 9 Group HQ, Barton Hall, near Preston in Lancashire. There, a dismal shock awaited me. The long-awaited posting had nothing whatsoever to do with ATA training. Instead, I was to be trained as a fighter controller. In total bewilderment, I asked why I had been selected. I was told that I had passed the test with flying colours and had been rated the best on the course.

'What bloody test? What bloody course?'

Then I remembered. During a brief visit three months previously by a fighter affiliation team, which had gone round Bomber Command demonstrating German combat aircraft and their capabilities, I had been asked to test for fighter controlling. As this entailed a forty-eight-hour pass to London, I had volunteered, thinking that, with my standard of eyesight, I would not stand a chance of passing the test.

I duly reported to Adastra House in Kingsway, listened to a lecture which confirmed my doubts about my eyesight, and took the test. This was like pelmanism, an exercise in visualization and retention of memory patterns. It was precisely the sort of thing I had done so often, experimentally, with my father. It was all ridiculously easy.

When it was over, I told the examining board that, being subject to blinding migraine headaches, which were induced by flashing lights, I doubted whether I was a suitable subject for fighter controlling. I explained that having to watch a radar screen intently for any length of time was one certain way of bringing on a crippling attack. They duly noted this. I returned to Wickenby and thought no more about it. I had no idea that I had been chosen for the job.

When I reported my handicap to the Wing-Commander in charge, who was a textbook officer with little or no imagination, he was furious. He could not understand why I wanted to fly with the ATA or, alternatively, return to operational Intelligence when this new job offered me a safe attachment to a comfortable, nearly non-operational group. He was sure I was trying to pull a fast one. It never occurred to him that I was telling the truth.

'Why did you apply for the job in the first place?' he shouted. 'You must realize that your refusal to train as a fighter controller is rank insubordination.'

Faced with such bone-headed obstinacy, I lost my temper, which had been sharpened by the disappointment of not being accepted for ATA training. Furthermore, I decided to put my valid complaint in writing. When I handed it to him, it was received by the Wingco in icy silence.

I found out later that he was a regular and, like a number of other officers and airmen at Barton Hall, had wangled himself this cushy billet. By early 1944, bomber attacks on the Manchester and Liverpool areas had virtually ceased. Number 9 Group still held a few operational fighters on charge, just in case, but it was now more concerned with training than with defence.

I had not taken kindly to my treatment by the pompous Wingco, and I made the mistake of showing it. For some minor misdemeanour, I was made orderly officer for a fortnight. I took my orderly duties seriously, especially in view of the appalling lack of security that plagued this Group HQ. Every night the orderly sergeant and I would gather up the secret documents which we frequently found lying around the offices of the mighty, and return them to the Central Registry, carefully obtaining a receipt for each document, a copy of which I enclosed with my report. These reports were studiously ignored and the same lax attitude to basic security continued.

One night I found a thick file marked 'top secret' which, as usual, I returned to the Central Registry, keeping the receipt. The next morning I was rudely awakened by two service policemen. I was told that I was under close arrest, the charge being unspecified. I objected loudly. My new-found friend Ray Hodgkins came into my room to find out what the ruckus was about.

'Wait a bit,' he said firmly. 'An officer being placed under close arrest is entitled to an escort of his own rank. Secondly, the charge must be specified. Until that correct procedure is adopted with my brother officer, you two can piss off!'

They did so, muttering under their breath.

'All right, Mike,' sighed Ray. 'They'll be back, pronto, with the DAPM. What the hell is it all about?'

'Search me, mate,' I said miserably. 'I haven't a clue.'

Then the Guardian Angel got through. I turned out my uniform jacket pockets and found my receipt for the documents. 'I'm bloody sure this has got something to do with it. Ray, be a pal and hang on to it for me. Don't let anyone get it off you.'

Ray grinned. 'Over my dead body, Mike.' I knew he meant it.

Twenty minutes later, the service police escort returned with a pompous DAPM. By this time I was dressed and shaved.

'Flying Officer Bentin. I am placing you under close arrest. You are charged with dereliction of your duties as orderly officer, in that you failed to secure a top secret document and return it to the Central Registry.'

'What top secret document?' Ray was still there, determined to see that I got a fair shake. 'It is not specified.'

The DAPM was taken aback. 'It's *too* top secret for that.'

Ray gave a snort of disgust. He turned to me. 'Don't worry, Mike. I'll go bail for you.'

We shook hands and Ray winked. 'They can't touch you!' He patted his top pocket where he had put the receipt.

The next twenty-four hours were unpleasant to say the least. I was confined to my quarters, without any outside contact being allowed me. This was in contravention of normal service procedure, the excuse being given that this was a grave matter for Intelligence experts. It looked as if I was to be branded a traitor as well.

The next morning I was collected by a service police escort and marched into a court of inquiry. Evidently this was to be a 'kangaroo court', the preliminary to a full court martial.

I thought to myself, 'What a bloody weird way to run a war!'

The charge was read out and the Senior Air Staff Officer (SASO), as President of the Court, spoke in the voice of doom, 'If you have anything to say, Flying Officer, make your statement now!'

By the look on their faces, he and the rest of the court had already decided that I was guilty and, by the audible rumbling of someone's tummy, they were now ready to adjourn for a celebratory lunch. As far as they were concerned, I was a cooked goose.

'Is the name of this top secret document Operation Overlord?' I asked.

The SASO nearly had apoplexy. 'How do you know the title of this top secret document? You realize, of course, Flying Officer Bentley, that this is a very serious matter indeed.'

'Indeed I do, sir! That is why I obtained a receipt for it from the Central Registry. On several occasions. My reports are all on file.'

If I had exploded a grenade, I could not have had a more devastating effect. I certainly spoiled their lunch.

'Hand it over!' demanded the President, purple in the face. 'Now!'

'I haven't got it on me, sir. But, I assure you, it is in safe keeping.'

Again, I felt that still small voice at work within me. 'I will produce it at a subsequent court martial, which I now request by my right as a serving officer, under King's Regulations and Air Council Instructions.'

I was dismissed and taken back to my quarters. I was no longer under close, or even open arrest.

Ray met me. By his expression he had been worried. I gave him the OK sign. He looked relieved. 'I'm sorry you had to go through that bloody nonsense, Mike. How did it go?'

I told him. By the end of it Ray was grinning. 'I'm sure you've won. Let's see what happens next.'

We had not long to wait. Early next morning, a WAAF driver turned up and asked to see me. I was dressed and shaved, ready for anything.

'My orders are to drive you to Blackpool, sir.' I noticed that she was a perky little blonde. Ray came in to my room and eyed her approvingly. 'Things are looking up, Mike. You get all the luck.'

'Where in Blackpool are you taking me?' I asked.

'The hospital, sir!'

A medical board! So that was the way my opponents were going to play it.

We drove off in a smart staff car and chatted all the way to Blackpool about everything under the sun. When we got there, I was loath to say goodbye to such a pleasant companion. I told her so.

'My instructions are to wait for you, sir.'

'These medical boards take all day. You'd better find yourself a decent mess and have lunch. I won't be finished till late afternoon, that's for sure.'

'I was told you'd only be about an hour, sir.'

Her reply startled me. Thoughtfully, I walked into the hospital and reported to the desk. I was expected. I was taken up to the second floor by an orderly and ushered straight into an office. Behind an impressive desk sat a young medical officer. The flight-lieutenant wore horn-rimmed spectacles. His face was undistinguished, and he seemed ill at ease. I don't remember anything else about him, apart from what he said.

'Sit down, Bentin. Now let's get straight down to the matter in hand. I understand that you are finding your duties in the Royal Air Force too much for you to handle. Therefore, I am recommending you for an immediate discharge from the service on psychological grounds.'

Just like that! No preamble, no explanation. They were going to give me the heave-ho neatly and with no questions asked. I was being eliminated. For a moment I was stunned. Then that still small voice sounded loud and clear inside my head. 'Tell him to get stuffed!

'You are, I presume, a qualified medical practitioner?' I asked, seething with cold fury.

'Of course I am. I am also a practising psychiatrist.' He was all bristling indignation.

'Then tell me, doctor, precisely how you have arrived at your diagnosis without examining me physically, or even attempting to make a show of examining me psychologically?'

'How dare you imply that I am . . . ' He groped for the word.

'A phoney?' I suggested.

That shook him. Prompted by my guide, I followed up the advantage with the *coup de grâce*.

'I presume that you wish to continue your practice in civilian life, doctor?'

His head nodded, in automatic reaction.

'Good! Because this is what I am going to do. On my *first day* as a civilian, I intend to report you to the British Medical Association for malpractice.'

'You wouldn't dare!'

'Oh yes, I would. What is more, my family know a number of physicians on the board of the BMA. You've shown no mercy to me. In return, I'm not going to give you anything but grief. Say goodbye to your career, doctor!' I paused. 'Or tell me the truth. Someone at Group has been on the blower to you. Right?'

He was in trouble and he knew it. He was perspiring heavily. 'Something like that. I am only following orders.'

'That's what they always say.'

He was bereft of speech. I took mercy on the little sod. I spoke slowly, making every syllable count. 'Recommend me for a full medical board. Let the board make the decision, in London.' I leaned in close to his sweating face. His glasses were steaming up. On the advice of the still small voice, I played my trump card. 'Furthermore, I want to have an interview with the Peruvian Ambassador. If you care to examine my papers, you will find that I am also a Peruvian citizen. I will return to Barton Hall and wait for my posting to London for a full medical board. It's either that or the Peruvian Ambassador *and the BMA*. It's entirely up to you, doctor.'

When I got outside the hospital, I found that I too was soaked with perspiration, right through to my jacket. I could not believe that I had said those things. I knew that I had been 'guided' and was very grateful.

My driver was waiting for me. She smiled stunningly. I needed that. Thank you, darling, whoever you were, for giving me that gentle accolade. I felt like a returning knight who had caught a glimpse of the Holy Grail. Then the full ludicrousness of the whole business struck me, and I dissolved into helpless laughter.

All the way back to Barton Hall I sang every popular song I could remember. My driver joined in with me. We stopped warbling only when we drove in through the camp gates.

There is a strange epilogue to this story. Many years after the war, I was told that my service papers had been scrutinized by British Intelligence. Naturally, I was interested to know what had been made of the adverse report that must have been filed by the Group SASO or his subordinate regarding this whole episode. For the record, I would like to state that no such adverse report had ever been made. I think that proves my point.

Chapter Seventeen

Battle of the Robots

The Central Medical Board assessed me as A4B. This meant that I was fit for operational duties barring those which required good eyesight. That put paid to my dreams of flying with the ATA, but at last I was back in business as an Intelligence officer. I soon discovered that the Royal Air Force had strong inter-command rivalry. Bomber Command had resented my being posted to Fighter Command, who resolutely refused to allow me back. Instead, they now wished to retain my services as an Intelligence/Operations officer in the Second Tactical Air Force.

This meant that I had to be retrained for briefing tactical fighter operations. These used completely different techniques to those of long-range night bombers. My original MI9 training remained valid for the requirements of evasion and escape, so I did not have to relearn that facet of my job. Instead, I was sent to Kirton in Lindsey in Yorkshire for a month's experience with fighter tactics.

It was now May 1944. The invasion of Europe was imminent. Second Tactical Air Force decided that I needed battle training, my previous Cosford version of a battle course being considered hopelessly inadequate, which it was. I was posted to Grantham Battle Course, where I enjoyed getting fit and, having been issued with sufficient ammunition, I was able to reach proficiency with a wide variety of weapons, ranging from .303 rifles to sub-machine guns, semi-automatic pistols, and even hand-grenades. That assured me a fighting chance, should I ever have to use them in anger.

While I was on this excellent course, I met some hard men and learnt some tough lessons in the art of armed and unarmed combat. The murderous instructors who taught us the latter art all recommended we should 'kick 'im in the balls'.

My new orders posted me to Sussex, to 350 Squadron, L'Escadrille des Chasseurs, a crack Belgian unit commanded by Wing-Commander Michel Donnet, a stocky young count possessed of great courage, charm and good humour. Presumably, I had been selected for my ability to understand French. In fact 350 Squadron contained approximately equal proportions of French-speaking and Flemish-speaking Belgians. They all spoke English as well as their mother-tongues.

350 Squadron was equipped with Spitfire IXBs, a faster development of the original Spits which, together with the more numerous Hurricanes, had won the Battle of Britain. These aircraft could do up to 385 mph. They were excellent fighting machines.

Within days of my joining them the entire Squadron, together with all its ground staff and operational personnel, was ordered to move from Sussex to an airfield in Kent.

The D-Day landings – Operation Overlord – had by now taken place, but the Squadron's task was to intercept and destroy the increasing numbers of VI robot 'vengeance weapons' which were being launched against London and its suburbs from the Pas de Calais area. These flying bombs were killing hundreds of people in the opening phases of what came to be called 'the Second Battle of Britain'. I was astonished when I learnt that our new base was to be Hawkinge airfield, the setting for all my early dreams of flight.

Wingco Donnet was a man of immediate action. Twenty-four hours after the orders had been received I found myself, at dawn, seated in the front cockpit of our ageing communications flight Tiger Moth, taxiing out on to the grass runway. The pilot was F-O Van der Vecken, a tough Flemish airman who spoke French with a heavy *flammand* accent. We took off on a perfect day and headed east towards Folkestone. The little plane was not equipped with radio to communicate with the ground nor did it have an internal radio telephone. We communicated with each other by signals supported by loud shouts and banging on the fabric-covered, plywood top of the fuselage between our cockpits. What should have been a carefree trip across the rolling Sussex and Kentish downland rapidly turned into a nightmare, as the questing barrels of hundreds of hurriedly emplaced anti-aircraft guns tried to centre us in their sights.

How could those trigger-happy gunners mistake an antiquated little biplane clattering along at 85 mph for the sleek, squat V1 robot aerial-torpedoes, with that distinctively loud stutter of their impulse-jet motors, racketing overhead at approximately 400 mph? It still puzzles me.

Yelling, 'Hang on, Spy,' Van der Vecken dived our Tiger Moth down to the deck. We hedge-hopped hair-raisingly over the south Sussex Downs, missing trees, telegraph poles, church spires, power lines and the few scattered houses by only a few feet.

We bucketed across Romney Marsh while those restless gun barrels tried to follow our wildly weaving flight. We zoomed up and over the wooded escarpment at Lympne and buzzed across the old, familiar airfield, making for the North Downs. A steep climbing turn carried us over the crest of Tolworth Clump, the once beautiful copse of tall trees which had topped these rolling hills for centuries until they were levelled by order of some lunatic Army officer who apparently thought the Germans were using the clump as a sighting mark for their giant cross-Channel guns.

I banged on the plywood fairing and pointed out the most sheltered valleys. Van used them for cover and, by weaving and dodging along the rolling countryside of the Kentish Weald, we finally arrived at Hawkinge. Even then we were not home and dry. Van der Vecken came straight in just as a whole covey of V1s crackled loudly by, zooming close above us.

Van side-slipped the manoeuvrable little Tiger Moth into a perfect three-point landing. Before the propellor stopped turning we had leapt out and dived into the nearest air-raid trench, landing on top of a bevy of frightened WAAFs who were sheltering there. In my wildest dreams, I had never pictured my return to my favourite boyhood haunt like this!

It took 350 Squadron only forty-eight hours to convert from their Spitfire IXBs to flying the most powerful and considerably faster Spitfire XIVs. This heavier version of the Spit had a much longer nose, which made taxiing difficult, but its massive five-bladed propellor, backed by the huge Griffon 65 engine, gave the pilot a lot more power, and sped the new machine along at over 400 mph. With these Mark XIVs the Belgians could catch the elusive 'buzz bombs', as the V1s were now called.

All the time this conversion was in progress, the Squadron was powerless to stop the seemingly endless stream of 'vengeance' weapons, which, day and night, roared over our heads on their way inland. Only the huge deployment of anti-aircraft batteries between Deal and Lydd managed to stem part of that murderous flood.

On the third day of our move to Hawkinge, I briefed the first dawn patrol for a mid-Channel interception of the buzz bombs. Wingco Donnet led the attack, and promptly shot down two. Both crashed into the Channel, exploding violently on impact.

Each of these patrols lasted approximately one hour, but the patrols started at dawn and finished at sunset. The Squadron quickly racked up an impressive score, diving to pick up sufficient speed to catch the V1s and blowing them out of the sky. But a large proportion of these dreadful weapons still got through our defences.

In all, well over three thousand V1s reached the capital and its suburbs. God knows how many more of them the Germans actually launched from their 'ski-sites' as we referred to them. The race for the Pas de Calais, where the bulk of the V1 launching ramps were located, took precedence over the Allied advance on Paris. Heavy civilian casualties and massive damage in and around London necessitated the capture of the buzz-bomb launching sites as quickly as possible.

I was nearly killed by a buzz bomb which crashed close to our billet, a mile from the airfield. I was shaving in my bedroom when I heard the unmistakable sound of a V1 being pursued by one of our new Spitfires. The buzz bomb landed at the end of the back garden where, fortunately, a line of trees fringed the grounds. I do not remember hearing the explosion. My next conscious impression was of crawling out from below the iron bedstead where the blast had hurled me. Apart from small cuts and bruises, I was unharmed, although I was groggy with shock.

A few days later, a visiting fighter wing flew in to Hawkinge, using our airfield as an advanced base to join the Belgians in an extensive sweep across the Channel. As this would reach as far as Belgium, all the aircraft were fitted with extra long-range tanks. Some of the visiting Spitfires carried this extra fuel in a sledge-shaped tank, which fitted snugly underneath the belly of the aircraft.

When the fighter sweep was over, the Spitfires returned, some of them almost out of fuel. One aircraft had been badly shot up and had no hydraulic power. This meant that the aircraft had to land without the speed-retarding effect of its flaps. Nor could the pilot lower his undercarriage. He had been unable to jettison his extra belly-tank, owing to further damage and, because he was low on petrol, he had to come straight in for an emergency landing.

I was walking back to the mess along the northern perimeter of the airfield when he attempted his belly-landing. Coming in much faster than normal, the pilot pancaked near the middle of our grass airfield, careering towards me on his empty belly-tank, which acted as a toboggan. He must have been doing well over a hundred miles an hour on the slippery grass, rushing at me like an unstoppable juggernaut. I stood stock still, trying to gauge which side to jump as the damaged Spitfire screeched towards me. It suddenly shed both wings and lost its heavy engine and bent propellor-blades. These broke off to one side, missing the terrified pilot by inches.

The loss of weight cut down the hurtling speed of approach, but the remains of the fuselage were still approaching me at a fair lick. I could see the pilot's shocked expression. He was strapped into his armoured seat, with his legs up in the air, and nothing at all in front of him.

I found I could not move! I just stood there, rigid, with my legs paralysed, waiting for the impact that would cream the pilot and myself against the brick revetment behind me. Then, fifteen yards in front of me, the smoking Spitfire came to a halt.

My paralysis left and I staggered towards the pilot to try to release him from his seat in case the plane blew up. Two Belgian pilots, who had been watching the whole drama, raced up to assist. The pilot muttered, 'Jesus Christ!' and lapsed into shocked silence. Then he fainted. Amazingly, apart from a few bruises from his seat-straps, he was uninjured. An hour later, the four of us were enjoying a pint of bitter in the mess.

Another incident which nearly wiped me out happened when I was strolling round the southern perimeter of the airfield. It was a lovely day, just before noon, and I had stopped to admire the view. Below me was Caesar's Camp. The grass-covered mounds and deep ditches on its summit hide the remains of an old Norman bailey which once had crowned it. During a lull between flights of incoming buzz bombs, I stood there thinking how peaceful it looked. As I did so, I distinctly heard the sound of an approaching express train. For a moment I thought, 'That's bloody weird! The nearest railway line is down there, at least three miles away.'

Then it dawned on me that the sound was coming from an approaching large-calibre shell, fired from one of the giant German cross-Channel guns at Gris Nez. Before I could move, the huge missile exploded below me in a blinding flash of chrome-orange light.

Once again, I did not hear the sound; I just saw the huge flash. I felt myself lifted up by the blast and thrown backwards for several yards. When I recovered my senses, I was lying on my back in the soft grass. I was completely uninjured but stone deaf. It took about three days before I got back my hearing.

At the same time my brother was fighting the buzz bombs as a battery sergeant major in charge of an emplacement of 4.5-inch heavy anti-aircraft guns located on the Romney Marsh. He sent me a delightful drawing of my Guardian Angel with a bent halo and his eyes crossed, being taken away on a stretcher by two other angel-bearers. One of them is saying, 'Poor sod, he's had charge of young Bentin for six months.'

I was seriously worried about my tottering marriage. The stress of living under the constant rain of buzz bombs had put a great strain on us all. My wife did not know from day to day whether they would survive, or even if I was still alive. Luckily, Elaine was too young to feel the full horror of those continual raids. I missed my wife and my family terribly. I managed to phone her and my parents occasionally, and I wrote as often as I could. But I was dog-tired, and when I did get leave, we were too strung up to make it the carefree and joyous event that it should have been.

Meanwhile, the V1s roared across the Channel in great numbers. The worst time was when fog or low cloud muffled our airfield in a murky shroud. The buzz bombs still raced low overhead because they were pilotless and gyro-controlled. However, we were helpless, unable to get a fighter plane off the ground. Only the barrages of radar-controlled anti-aircraft fire occasionally scored a hit, in which case the crippled V1 crashed near us.

When the weather cleared, the whole Squadron would take off and try to down the invading robots, while spent shells and bullets fell like hail. Even our Air-Sea Rescue Flight took off to do battle with the robots. This outfit consisted of an old Spitfire Mark V, a Walrus biplane amphibian which could fly at 80 knots and was armed with one Vickers K .303 machine-gun, and an American Navy Grumman Avenger, which must have been stolen from the Yanks. This sort of frenzied mass interception often resulted in a dead cow or sheep. As soon as I heard about the casualty, with my CO's encouragement I dashed over and bought the remains with the mess funds. This ensured that our Belgian allies and the RAF ground crew had more than sufficient fresh meat. Our fine Belgian chef beamed at the sight of it, and excelled himself.

As with the first Battle of Britain, when the end came it was sudden. One day 350 and the other squadrons had been operating at maximum effort, and within forty-eight hours the battle of the buzz bombs was over. The Allies had captured the V1 launching sites.

Within a week I was posted away from the Belgians. Apparently they were getting ready for a triumphant return to Brussels and, understandably, they needed to have a Belgian 'Spy'. My replacement arrived, and I quickly briefed him on our operational techniques. Wingco Donnet gave me a warm send-off, and thanked me for my efforts.

With the cessation of the buzz-bomb raids on London, an intense reaction had set in throughout the capital. My French family, exhausted by the ordeal, were even more highly strung than normal. My short leave was an unhappy one but it was a constant joy to be with Elaine, who was now more than two years old. When I took her by bus to visit Ma and Pop in Barnes, we had a blissful reunion. My father told me a strange story:

'Your cousin Pedro wrote from Lima asking me to answer, psychometrically, some specific questions involving decisions and specific dates, all to do with the Bentin family business. I answered them as clearly as I had been impressed to do, and sent the letter off by return mail. Naturally, it was censored.

'The authorities held it up because, by some extraordinary chance, the dates I had written coincided with those of various important troop convoys sailing to the UK from the USA.

'A Special Branch Officer and a member of MI5 came to interrogate me. I explained the circumstances, but they were very reluctant to accept my claim that I was a psychic. Then I got a clear impression about the Special Branch Officer.

'I gave him the name of his mother, and told him at what age she had passed over with cancer. I also gave him some personal information which seemed to convince him that I was speaking the truth about being psychic and my reasons for writing those dates in my letter. He had a short, private conversation with his Intelligence colleague and they left us on the most friendly terms.

'The letter got through to Peru, and it proved to be accurate and helpful to the family.'

Within a week I was posted for a short attachment to North Weald, where a Czech fighter squadron was operating. I found them as friendly and dedicated as my 'bleddy' Poles. From there I was sent to Number 10 Group at Box, near Chippenham.

In the underground ops room I met the Wingco who had given me such a hard time at Number 9 Group, Barton Hall. To my surprise, he was courtesy itself. He beamed upon me as though I was a favourite nephew. He also avoided me whenever he could. I had no further trouble with him. Obviously he was playing it safe.

10 Group's ops room was concerned with operations over the Atlantic convoys in the Western Approaches. Nevertheless, information concerning the previous night's raids on London was passed to us every morning. A new terror weapon, the V2, a long-range rocket, precursor of all future intercontinental ballistic missiles, had started to

hurtle down on the Home Counties. There was no way of stopping them because they arrived without warning. The blast of their warheads, weighing one ton, was emphasized by the depth to which they penetrated on impact.

The sense of helplessness that I, like so many others, had felt with the progress of the V1s was as nothing to the frustration experienced with the unstoppable, strike-without-warning V2s. Each morning I would plot the co-ordinates of the positions where the rockets had exploded. Too often they were scattered around Westminster. Our flat in St George's Square was in that borough. I prayed a lot.

I spent a last short leave with my family prior to being posted to Helmond, near Eindhoven, in the Netherlands. This was as far as the Allied thrust had reached before it had petered out on the south bank of the Maas river.

I travelled aboard an old liner converted into a troop-transport in convoy to Zeebrugge. During the night there was a submarine alarm. I did not fancy the idea of being tucked away below if a torpedo should strike us, so I spent the rest of the voyage on deck. As we came in to Zeebrugge to anchor in the outer basin of the Belgian port, another troop-transport following close behind us struck a parachute mine. There was a huge explosion. A column of foaming grey water hurtled up higher than the masts. The sound of screaming carried across the water as the overladen ship went down with heavy loss of life. To make it even more dreadful, many of those aboard had been members of the women's services; their corpses floated on the surface of the outer harbour. It was bitterly ironic that it had happened within a few hundred yards of safety.

When I reported for duty at RAF Helmond, an advanced airfield within a few miles of the German front lines, 121 Wing of Typhoon ground-attack fighters was operating as anti-tank and anti-locomotive intruders on targets of opportunity in Western Germany.

I sensed a mounting tension around me. The Allies were poised to launch their giant offensive against the

Siegfried Line, the prime objective being the seizure of the all-important bridges across the Rhine.

After the disaster of the bridge at Arnhem, both Montgomery and his Commander-in-Chief, General Eisenhower, were determined that the Rhine bridges would be seized intact and held at all costs. Failure to achieve this objective would undoubtedly result in the loss of thousands of Allied soldiers and of huge quantities of armour and other vital war supplies.

The Hawker Typhoon was a fast gun platform, sturdy and able to absorb heavy punishment in the tradition of its predecessor, the Hawker Hurricane. After the Typhoons' massacre of German Panzers while they were retreating through the narrow Falaise Gap in Normandy, the Wehrmacht had developed an understandable terror of the rocket-firing Typhoons. They were able to prohibit practically all daylight transportation of war supplies to the Western Front.

I got on well with my Typhoon pilots and the ground crews. They knew I was a frustrated flyer, as interested in their aircraft as they were themselves. Like all youngsters with a common interest, we formed an instant bond.

The officers' mess at Helmond was located in part of a monastery. The other half was still used by the monks. One day the Father Abbot came to see us with a problem. The Squadron artist had decorated the front of our mess bar with copies of a luscious set of 'Varga girls', seductively clad centrefold paintings that had featured prominently in the American glossy magazine, *Esquire*. The Abbot, while appreciating the skill of the painter, asked us if we could be persuaded to cover the girls' prominent physical features with more clothes. He told us, 'They are upsetting the brethren.'

One night I climbed to the top of the monastery's bell-tower. From this vantage point I was able to see many miles behind the German front lines and follow the progress of a heavy raid on an industrial city. The raid must have been carried out by Lancasters and Halifaxes, as by this stage of the war the Stirlings had been relegated to airborne operations, towing gliders. I saw the red and green target indicators being dropped by Lancasters and Mosquitoes, the brightly sputtering flares cascading down from 6,000 feet above the blazing city. It was extraordinary to watch the receiving end of the sort of raid I had briefed during that appalling winter of 1943–4.

It was also a weird sensation when we crossed the Rhine, Germany's 'sacred' river, after all those long years of war. The whole operation had a strangely detached feeling of unreality. Almost as soon as we had crossed the river, orders came through that I was to be posted to another Typhoon Wing, which had lost an IO.

My new Typhoon Wing lived under canvas, and the weather was warm. I dumped my kit in the tent allocated to me, which I shared with another IO and, within a few hours, we were operating once more. I briefed the new crews on targets of opportunity. These targets were either enemy tanks, dug-in anti-tank guns or self-propelled guns, all of which were hidden on the edges of the numerous woods and were costing us a lot of our armour. Apart from locomotive-busting, this was the ideal use for the Typhoons.

Within a couple of days we were once more on our way, keeping up closely behind the armour. Our destination was Achmer-Hustedt airfield, which was located on the banks of the Dortmund–Ems canal. I did not have the slightest sense of being part of an Allied conquest. I only felt a numb relief that the whole bloody mess would shortly come to an end. The question was: how high a price would have to be paid before the final collapse of the Third Reich? At Achmer-Hustedt, I would begin to find out.

Almost as soon as we had arrived on this captured Luftwaffe airfield, our airmen began to fall as a result of sniper fire which must have been coming from the opposite bank of the canal which bordered the airfield.

What was odd was that we had heard no shots. Our MO's examination of one of the wounded men explained why. The injured airman had been hit by a small-calibre unjacketed lead bullet, similar to the .22 ammunition which, as a boy, I had used on small-bore rifle-ranges.

Someone had to go and look, acting as a decoy on the other side to draw fire and winkle them out. The Wingco delegated me for the job, because he could not spare any RAF Regiment officers, whom he needed in situ to command the battery of the 40-mm Bofors guns in case we were attacked by the Luftwaffe.

I was given a Ferret light armoured car, a driver, and an RAF Regiment sergeant, a tough, wiry Yorkshireman who had been a miner. Once we were on the other side of the canal bullets began to spatter against the armoured sides of the Ferret. Through the slit in the armoured windscreen, the driver saw movement in the upstairs window of a derelict farmhouse a few yards to the left of the narrow road in front of him.

He told the sergeant, who relayed the information to me. The resourceful NCO was well able to carry out the attack, but he let me make the decision.

'All right, Sergeant. Give that farmhouse a burst from the Besa. That should stir things up.'

The old campaigner let loose a long burst from our heavy-calibre Besa (BSA) machine-gun. The big bullets, some of them tracer, chopped into the flaking plaster of the old farmhouse, tearing out whole chunks of it along with a shower of splinters from the rotting beams. The enemy snipers threw their weapons out of the windows and surrendered.

'*Raus! Raus! Kommen sie hier, mit die Handen hoch!*' I shouted in my appalling German.

Out stumbled three small soldiers in outsize uniforms, weeping in terror. They could not have been more than twelve years old. Suddenly one of them tripped. He threw out his arms to stop himself falling. I automatically started to squeeze the trigger of my Schmeisser sub-machine-gun as I had been taught by our combat-instructors. Before I could fire, the sergeant knocked down the barrel. 'Nay, lad. They're nobbut bloody kids.'

I was shaken. My conditioned reflexes had betrayed me. I had nearly shot three children.

'What the hell can we do with them, Sergeant? They've just killed and wounded our men.'

The grizzled ex-miner gave a derisive snort. 'We'll start the little buggers off right.'

He took off his belt, grabbed each of the junior supermen in turn and belted him across the buttocks, six times each.

The boys howled. The ex-miner was a stern father, but afterwards, somehow, we all felt cleansed. The spanking changed the murderous brats into normal kids again. Two of them had pissed themselves in fright. The other was even worse off. The little sods stank. They had been certain we would kill them. Now they knew we would not. Killers do not spank kids' backsides.

We drove them back to the airfield. When it dawned on them that we were going to take them to the prisoner-of-war camp, they brightened up considerably. They were excited to see the much-dreaded Typhoons close to. It was eerie that, while their victims were barely stiff in death, these perverted children were excitedly pointing out and discussing the different features of their enemies' aircraft.

So illogical is war that had these youngsters been British, and our roles reversed, with the Nazis invading Britain as they so nearly did in 1940, their actions would have gone down in our history-books as heroic.

From Achmer-Hustedt we moved directly to Celle, a few miles to the north of Hanover. We had barely finished preparations for the Typhoons to fly in, when an MO from the 51st Highland Division drove into our new camp. I welcomed him as his car skidded to a halt. He looked grey with fatigue and wasted no time. 'Have you lot got any emergency rations, vitaminized chocolate,

Pop, c. 1915.

Ma, c. 1916.

Myself (*right*) with my mentor
brother Tony, c. 1926.
Hawkesworth Wheeler.

Myself aged ten, 1932.

Arrested as a 'deserter', 1942. The only British serviceman to be arrested in a doublet and hose for four hundred years. *Mik*.

F/O Bentin, 350 Squadron Intelligence Officer, painting the Red Indian motif on Mike Donnet's Spitfire XIV, Hawkinge, August 1944. A vital piece of the war effort. *Courtesy Roy Humphreys.*

In *Starlight Roof*, 1947, Hippodrome, Leicester Square, London. The exhausting chairback routine. *The Hulton Picture Company.*

Subtle underplaying by the original goons. *BBC Photograph Library*.

The original rubber casts of the Bumblies with their creator, 'Professor' Bentine, 1953. *Allen Newton*.

It's a Square World - the infamous sinking of the Houses of Parliament with a Chinese war junk and St Thomas's Hospital in the background. *BBC Photograph Library*.

(*Left to right*) Myself, Fusty, Suki, Richard, Gus and Clementina, 1964. *Jeffries Brothers Press Ltd*.

EXCLUSIVE BY HOVERCRAFT THROUGH THE AMAZON

THE Amazon, the last great unconquered region on earth, has been tamed — by a hovercraft. After travelling 1,300 miles on the first ever hover - journey through the immense rain forests I have to report that apart from the heat it's as easy as catching the bus to work — and no more dangerous.

It was easy as catching a bus to work, says the first man to do it MICHAEL BENTINE

mile journey in only five days.

Incredibly the hovercraft is the same one which formerly operated in the Solent between Southsea and the Isle of Wight.

How would our hovercraft

Amazon in a dug-out canoe and fall in you won't stand much chance with the flesh-stripping piranha fish.

But in a hovercraft you're safe from everything except bombs—and the Indians don't use them!

I first got the idea that such

By hovercraft through headwaters of the Amazon, 1968. It seemed like a good idea at the time. *News of the World.*

With some Potty fans

Conducting 'Thunder and Lightning Polka' with the Royal
Philharmonic, 1972 - a long way from drumming in 1940.
© *Thames Television.*

Potty 'Treasure Island' with Long John Potty Silver and Potty Jim
Hawkins. The first Potty programme. © *Thames Television.*

Bentines' autumn. Falling leaves and waistlines.
News of the World.

that sort of thing? We need it urgently. We've used up all ours.'

'Of course. But it'll take a bit of time to round up.'

I was curious. The middle-aged Scots doctor said, 'There's a concentration camp up the road. It's hell on earth. Get the stuff as quickly as possible. We need every ounce you can give us.'

He paused, coughing badly. I remember that he was chain-smoking. 'Jesus Christ, laddie, there are thousands of them, old men, women and children. It's ghastly.'

'What's this place called?'

'Belsen. Bergen-Belsen.'

We rushed the stuff together and I followed him with my Jeep and Geordie driver. The road wound its way through plantations of full-grown fir trees. They had been planted in long, straight rows. Exactly half way up many of the tree trunks were wooden nesting-boxes for the birds.

As we approached the gates to the concentration camp, there was an appalling feeling of evil. Nothing could prepare you for what was to come. Words alone cannot describe it. Many have tried to do so, and even inmates of that appalling place cannot succeed in conveying its full horror. I am not able to either. Only the photographs and the films of those scenes can convey a fraction of the spiritual nausea that gripped everyone who witnessed it.

A month afterwards, I flew to Denmark in our 'liberated' Messerschmitt 108. My pilot was a West Indian friend, Flight-Lieutenant Osmund 'Kelly' Kelsick, whose valued comradeship has endured through the years.

As we flew low over Belsen, flame-throwers, mounted on Bren-carriers, small tracked-vehicles, were being driven systematically through the big compound, burning everything to a cinder. They said it was to wipe out scrub-typhus. We knew it was to try to erase the memory of that unforgivable crime. It did not succeed.

Chapter Eighteen

The Guns Fall Silent

The cease-fire hit us head on. I was in the control caravan before dawn, watching the teleprinter clattering out 83 Group's instructions to advance the 'bomb line', (beyond which Allied aircraft were free to attack any observed activity), preparatory to defining the operational orders for that day. In mid-sentence it stopped. There was a short pause. Then the teleprinter tapped out, 'Stand by for a change of orders.'

Again the machine fell silent. Finally it printed:

> Cancel all previous instructions. The bomb line will not, repeat not be advanced. As from 01.00 hours today, a cease-fire is in operation. The following orders to be effective immediately. All 83 Group aircraft to be on stand-by, refuelled, and rearmed. 121 and 124 Wing aircraft to carry 4 x 60 lb rockets and extra fuel tanks. Targets: to be designated. Further details to follow.

'Jesus Christ,' muttered the teleprinter operator, 'it's over. The bloody war's over.'

The Flying Control officer added, 'When it happened I thought I'd say something historic. But I can't think of a bloody thing.'

There was no spontaneous demonstration of joy or, for that matter, any other emotion. There were no cries of 'Thank God!', 'The Lord be praised!' or even 'We've won!'

We were stunned. Subconsciously we had been expecting it, but when it finally happened, it was like running into a brick wall. I clearly remember we were chain-smoking.

'I'll tell the Wingco,' I volunteered, and hurried over to the CO's tent. It was empty. I made for my own bell tent, stumbled over an unseen guy-rope in the misty light and fell flat on my face. Even on that historic morning, bathos was not far away.

When I reached my tent, the pilot who shared it with me was still asleep. I pulled out my Schmeisser sub-machine-gun and stepped outside. I stood in silence for a moment and clicked back the firing-bolt. I pointed the gun up into the lightening sky, and squeezed the trigger hard. A loud burst rattled out, shattering the silence. I held down the trigger until I had fired the entire magazine of thirty-two rounds.

The whole Wing, in various states of dress, came tumbling out of their tents, swearing and cursing. Most of them were carrying weapons. 'Werewolves', fanatical SS hiding in the woods, had already killed a number of Allied servicemen while they were asleep. I knew that the distinctive 'cloth-ripping' sound of Schmeisser gun-fire would get things moving.

'It's over! *Fini! Terminado! Kaput!*' I yelled at the top of my voice. 'The fucking war is over!'

The babble of voices shut off like a tap.

'What the hell is going on, Spy?' Our East African Wingco, Jimmy Keep, rapped out behind me. The Commanding Officer had been for a pee in the woods. He was still doing up his flies. Over his shoulder was a hunting-rifle I had acquired for him.

I told him the gist of the teleprinter message. His lean, tanned face hardened. 'I don't trust those bastards as far as I can throw a Tiffie. All aircraft to be ready for immediate takeoff. Two aircraft to be on the end of the runway ready to press tit on my orders. Get me confirmation from Group, Spy. Immediately.'

The Wingco's mouth relaxed into a broad grin. 'War or no bloody war, this calls for a drink. When you've carried out my orders, Spy, come back for one. Don't just stand there, you mad Peruvian bastard. Get on with it!'

An hour later he handed me a steaming mug of rum-laced coffee. It tasted wonderful. 'What are you going to do after this lot?' he asked.

'I always wanted to be an aerodynamicist, like my father. The war stopped that.' I paused, uncertainly. 'I really don't know, sir. Maybe I'll carry on with my last job. I was an actor.'

'You certainly behaved like one, you stupid bastard, firing that Schmeisser. You could have restarted the whole bloody thing.'

'How about you, sir? What will you do, now it's over?' I liked this tough leader and respected his judgement.

'Go home to Africa and start a bloody airline or maybe go back to farming.' His eyes were focused far away. 'I've never allowed myself to think about it before.'

Atypically, he let his thoughts come tumbling out: 'Christ, man, Africa's a marvellous continent. A bloke's got room to breathe there. East Africa's a great place for a youngster like you to make a life for yourself and raise a family.'

'I've *got* a family, sir,' I said, the misery of my marriage flooding in. 'I have a small daughter. My wife is French. She's a concert pianist. I don't think she'd take kindly to Africa. Paris is more in her line.'

Despite anything I could do, my eyes filled with tears. I saluted and hurried out of the tent. Tears pouring down my face, I stumbled off into the woods. Out of sight of the airfield, I threw myself down on the dense under-growth and wept my heart out. I have no doubt that many others were doing the same.

Afterwards, I dozed off. Curled up among the thick ferns of the undergrowth, I slept for hours. It was not surprising. During those last, frenzied days of war I had averaged three hours' sleep a night. Like many of us, I had kept going on black coffee, alcohol, and benzedrine tablets given me by the MO. Eventually, nature demands full repayment for her loans.

That night we had a monumental piss-up. It was not a party in the ordinary sense of the word. I doubt whether many of us enjoyed it. It was simply a young person's way of releasing some of the unbearable tension. I do not remember anything about it, except that I did not seem to get drunk. I had too much adrenalin in me.

For the next few days nothing much happened. Our aircraft were kept in a state of readiness, with two Typhoons waiting for take-off at the appropriate end of the temporary runway. Celle airfield had been bombed and rocketed frequently, and our ground crews had laid a steel mesh runway while the networks of holes were being filled up.

A few 'werewolves' came out of the woods and surrendered. They were not much older than the boys I had nearly shot at Achmer-Hustedt. This time there was no grizzled RAF sergeant to spank some sense into them. We trucked the sullen little bastards to the nearest POW cage.

On the fifth day, without any prior notice, an American Air Force Dakota flew in. Out of it climbed a slim, attractive blonde woman, dressed in a fawn trouser suit. She wore a soft felt hat, with the broad brim pulled down. It was Marlene Dietrich, accompanied by some high brass and the inevitable gaggle of American press in battle dress. She wore no make-up. I sensed that she was under great stress.

She was driven away in a Jeep, with three other Jeeploads of armed escort and the rest of her entourage. The direction they took was towards Belsen. We heard that her sister had been reported as being one of the surviving inmates of that ghastly place.

When she returned there was no other woman in her party. White-faced and shaken, the famous actress politely refused our CO's offer of hospitality, reboarded the Dakota, and took off. I felt for her.

The Wingco sent for me and, to my surprise, ordered me to fly to our British base at Dunsfold, near Guildford, Surrey. He told me I had to deliver some top-secret documents to HQ Second Tactical Air Force. 'Take your time, Spy,' he said. 'I don't need you back right away.'

I flew back to England in a Dakota filled with ex-prisoners of war. They were thin and gaunt, still tense, only half-believing they were free. Most of the way they sat in silence and smoked, each of them deep in his own thoughts. This flight was part of a massive air-lift, ordered by Winston Churchill, to bring those poor devils back home as quickly as possible.

After we landed at Dunsfold I heard that the flight before us had crashed into high ground in thick cloud only a few miles from the airfield. There were no survivors. It seemed shockingly ironic to survive those long years of captivity only to die within sight of home.

When I opened the door of our flat in St George's Square my surprised reception confirmed my fears about our marriage. We made love, but I sensed it was over between us. I longed to be comforted in loving arms. Instead, it felt more like a wifely duty to bring me temporary relief from all that pent-up longing. But at least I held my adorable little daughter in my arms. I just hugged her and wept silently.

The short leave seemed unreal. The next day, 8 May, was VE Day (Victory in Europe Day). I excused myself, and went alone to Whitehall. The streets were so densely crowded I could hardly move. The noise was deafening. A surging mass of people, many of them in uniform, had flooded into the West End, headed for Buckingham Palace.

Almost breathless with the pressure, I found myself swept up in that spontaneous mass movement and involuntarily carried along towards the Palace. Somehow, the people around me sensed that I had just returned from the battle front. I realized why when later I looked into a mirror. A much older man, in a worn battle-dress, stared back at me, the features drawn, and the eyes still haunted by what they had seen.

My parents welcomed me with the warmth I longed for. After the tears, they told me my brother and his family were well. Our psychic friend, Eddie Partridge, had been right: we had *all* survived the war. Only later did we realize what those years had cost us.

With the help of both families, Marie and I were able to scrape together enough money to go down to Brighton for a couple of days. It was the last chance to rescue our marriage. Sadly, it failed. I do not blame anyone. It was the bloody war, no more, no less. We were not alone. Thousands of marriages failed, unable to bear the strain of long separation. Only the strongest ties of love survive that kind of stress; in our case it led to divorce.

Knowing that this probably would be the last time I would be with my wife and child, I left for Dunsfold and caught the next 83 Group courier-plane back to Germany. The temptation to desert was almost unbearable. I now knew why so many men took that path. To condemn those who did so is unrealistic. I believe I would have got away with desertion. After all, I was a volunteer of dual nationality, most reluctantly accepted by the RAF. I was deterred by the thought of my comrades. They would not have been able to argue *their* way out of such a charge.

So I returned to Germany, just as Jimmy Keep had guessed I would. I was told later by the chaplain that my CO had known for some time what was wrong. Apparently the chaplain had noticed that I received no mail from my wife. That was why I had been sent back with the despatches. They were of only minor importance. It just shows what a good CO Jimmy Keep was. Among all that battle stress, he found time to care about his men.

Within a few days of my return, we packed up and moved north. I remember the look on the faces of the surviving citizens of Hamburg when we trucked through that shattered city. As we lumbered through the maze of bomb craters that pock-marked the once stately avenues of Hamburg I realized that we were passing through a gigantic graveyard. The few survivors looked like zombies. They were past hate. They just stood in shocked silence. Only their unblinking eyes seemed to be half-alive. Their look of numb accusation was heart-rending as the RAF, which had destroyed their city, drove past them.

We were ordered to take over the German air base at Schleswig, a small picturesque town on the shores of the Baltic, not far from the Danish border. We were to be part of an occupying force to receive the surrender of the northern forces of the Luftwaffe returning from Norway and Denmark. This force was full of fanatical Nazis, and we had to disarm them. In the unlikely event that these well-armed and battle-hardened men should stage a coup, we would be outnumbered four to one. It was not a pleasant thought, so we put it out of our minds.

In the event, the Luftwaffe, and even their attendant SS forces, were as sick of war as we were ourselves. They were only too willing to co-operate but this was made harder by the decision of the Allied high brass to institute a 'non-fraternization' order which forbade all Allied personnel from establishing any sort of friendly relations with our erstwhile enemy.

I had a weird experience in connection with the 'non-frat' order when I was on my way to pick up a visiting military mission and escort them back to Schleswig. As my driver and I were passing through a small town we were flagged down by a young Guards officer. Despite his youth, he was a major.

'You are the first RAF personnel I've met in this area. I wonder if you could help me?'

'Certainly, sir. We're always willing to co-operate with the Army. How can I help you?'

The young major looked embarrassed. 'I've been put in charge of a Jerry baby-farm.'

'What the hell is that?'

'It's one of those places where Hitler was trying to realize his dream of an Aryan master-race. The whole camp is full of big, blonde, Boche girls who have been carrying out his crazy scheme by producing hundreds of so-called pure-Aryan babies.' The major was extremely uncomfortable. 'If I don't do something about the situation soon, all hell will break loose. That's where you come in. You can help me.'

I was intrigued. 'How?'

'Frankly, my chaps just can't cope. It's this bloody non-frat order. These Fräuleins are going stark raving mad. They've been used to regular, er . . . servicing by those bloody great SS bastards, and now their, er . . . supplies have been cut off so to speak.'

'How the hell do you expect me to help?'

'Well, er,' he paused. 'We all know that you RAF chaps are not as disciplined as my Guardsmen, and I thought that . . . perhaps?' He looked desperate, almost pleading.

I cut him off abruptly. 'Well, you bloody well thought wrong, sir.' I was willing to help inter-service relations, but not at the cost of a court martial. I took a deep breath.

'I agree with you, Major. The whole non-frat situation *is* getting out of hand. It's doomed to failure. Anyone can see that. But I'm sorry, sir, I can't help you out by trucking in a lot of randy airmen. We've got our own problems, believe me!'

Curiosity was getting the better of me and, by this time, my Geordie driver's eyes were bulging behind his thick steel-rimmed spectacles. 'It wouldn't do no harm to have a dekko, sir,' he said hoarsely.

'All right, I'll come along with you to . . . assess the situation, sir. But I can't promise to help.'

The major was only too delighted to let me see for myself.

As we drove into the large wooden-hutted camp I could see just how monumental his troubles were. Everywhere there were tall, blonde women in the uniform of the Third

Reich's Auxiliary Corps. The youngest among them were dressed as *Hitler jugend*. Most of them carried babies in their arms. Many were good looking. They all had the same hungry look and not because they were short of food. By their busty shapes you could see there was plenty of that.

The whole scene would have been funny if it had not been so obscenely pathetic. It was another example of the appalling outcome of Hitler's nightmare schemes.

'Jesus, look at all that crumpet,' muttered my Geordie corporal.

I saluted the beleaguered major. 'Good luck, sir. I can only suggest that you make a full report to your superiors . . . and pray.'

Visibly disappointed, the young camp commandant returned my salute and his teenage Guardsmen presented arms as we drove off.

I met the visiting commission as planned, and escorted them to Schleswig. Nothing seemed to matter any more. It was as though I was living in some sort of limbo. If it had not been for my West Indian friend, Kelly Kelsick, I would have had a nervous collapse.

'What you need, Mike, is a spot of leave. The Wingco has offered me a week in Brussels. Can you think of a good reason why you should go with me?'

My optimism returned. 'I'll say I need to see the Peruvian Consul to renew my passport. There *has* to be one in Brussels.'

The Wingco was no fool, but he went along with the idea. After all, my real job – teaching aircrew the vital MI9 evasion and escape techniques and briefing them for operations – was now over. About the only flying the Wing had to do was 'air testing', mainly to keep their hands in.

Now I was just a supernumerary Intelligence officer with little or nothing to do. The RAF Special Investigation Branch had taken over from where I had left off. Their job was to hunt down the Nazi war criminals among the surrendered Luftwaffe. For that you had to be fluent in German, a language I disliked and therefore was no good at. Moreover, my kindly CO had guessed how near I was to going over the edge.

'All right, Spy. Go and sow some wild oats in Brussels. Just don't come back with a dose of clap. Oh, and give my regards to your Peruvian Consul, if by some miracle there happens to be one there.' Jimmy Keep was one hell of a man.

Just before we left for Brussels, an incident occurred that completely changed my whole attitude to the war. Until then it had been a kind of personal crusade, which I had played by the rules.

I was duty officer, alone in the operations room at Schleswig airfield. A Fieseler Storch landed neatly outside the watch office. Out of the machine climbed a pilot, a tall flight-lieutenant who came into the office and brusquely asked, 'Are you the duty officer?'

'Yes. There's only me here at the moment. How can I help you?' He handed me some documents. At a glance I could see they were some sort of manifest.

'Sign these. I want to clear a Junkers 290 for immediate take-off. It's going to Farnborough. They want to examine and evaluate it.'

It all sounded official enough, but suddenly that still small voice sounded inside my head. By bitter experience I had learned not to ignore it. 'I presume this is the cargo manifest?'

'It is. Don't worry, it's been cleared. The papers are all in order. Go ahead and sign it.'

His tone was authoritative, yet he was not a senior officer. He also seemed over-eager to complete the chore.

'I'm afraid I can't do that. Not until I have read it and examined the cargo hold of that machine.'

The flight-lieutenant had a short fuse. 'Bloody hell, man! Just sign the thing. Here!' He indicated the space on the top copy of the triple document. He riled me. I was now certain there was something wrong.

'When I have examined the cargo.' I spoke very deliberately.

His face became red with anger. I think he had been drinking. 'You'll hear more about this.'

I had really upset his day. He stomped out of the watch office, started the Storch's engine and, without the customary safety checks, took off.

The still small voice continued to prompt me. I quickly cycled round the lengthy perimeter track to the opposite side of the airfield, where three of the big four-engined Junkers 290 transport planes were kept. A friendly sergeant-fitter was just putting the finishing touches to one of them. I knew him.

'Hello, sir. Want to have a look at a big bird? These bloody machines are a beautiful job. This one is due off to Farnborough this afternoon. We've been working on her all night.'

'Have you now? Yes, I'd like to look inside her.'

The sergeant looked flustered. 'What about one of the others, sir?'

I looked at the manifest. It was blank apart from the words 'Cargo: spare parts'.

'No, I'd like to look inside this one. In fact, Sergeant, that's an order.'

That was one of the few times I ever pulled rank in my service career. The sergeant, who was a regular, shrugged resignedly and ordered the rear-mounted loading ramp to be lowered. This was the first machine I had encountered with that device. It was impressive. So were the contents of the plane. I could see rolled-up carpets, packing-cases, ornately framed pictures, antique gilded furniture and, in the centre, the *pièce de résistance*, a small, beautifully built yacht, its masts and gear neatly stowed beside it.

'Thank you, Sergeant, I've seen enough. You can close her up now.'

'Nuffinck to do wiv me, sir. I'm just carrying out orders from high up.' The sergeant smiled nervously as he pointed in the direction of 83 Group HQ, a few miles down the road.

'That's all right, Sergeant. I quite understand. You're clear in my book.'

I quickly cycled back to the operations office and had barely settled down to my lone watch when the Storch returned. This time the engine was left ticking over, a risky business at best.

The pilot, a thick-set officer of surprisingly high rank, got out and strode into the office. There was no preamble. 'Are you the stupid bastard who won't sign the manifest?'

'That's me, sir. I can't sign it until I have checked the cargo.'

'It's already been checked. Just sign the bloody thing. That's an order!'

His face was even redder than that of my previous visitor. I think he too had been drinking.

'Very good, sir. But I am signing it under written protest.' The still small voice was most insistent. 'Shall I add the yacht and the other articles, sir?'

I thought the VIP was going to hit me. He certainly wanted to. After all, there were no visible witnesses. But he was not going to fall into that trap. Instead he snatched up the controversial manifest. He leant over the desk, his fuming face glaring into mine. 'Name? What's your bloody name, man?'

'Bentin, sir. It's a Peruvian name. I am a volunteer from South America, sir.'

'I don't give a shit what you are or where you come from, you little sod. I'm going to have your guts for garters.'

With that he slammed the door of the watch office, climbed into the Storch, revved up without even the most cursory of checks, and took off.

I breathed a long sigh and waited impatiently for my relief. I never heard another word about that morning's events. But then I did not expect to.

My sense of loyalty to my comrades-in-arms certainly did not include protecting high brass engaged in looting. Obtaining a weapon for one's commanding officer as I had done, came under the heading of 'legitimate spoils of war'. Yachts, carpets, antique furniture and fine art did not. If airmen were 'crimed' for nicking the odd crate of German wine or a German officer's watch, how come the high brass were immune? Looting is looting. Only the scale was different.

When Kelly and I went to Brussels, we took a case of Luftwaffe radio valves with us. I reckoned the Nazis owed us that much. With the money we got for them, we financed our short leave in Brussels, using most of the funds to treat as many Allied pilots as we could find to a decent meal and a bottle of wine. It was the nearest thing to a celebration we could dream up.

Those few days in the liberated Belgian capital were a revelation to me. Kelly was a cool, handsome man with great charm and presence. He had the sort of personality and looks that made the girls circle him like barracudas. I just went along for the ride. I had never met so many pretty girls.

In addition to the radio valves, we had 'liberated' a German Waffen SS combat-photographer's Imo movie-camera. The deceased owner had no further use for it. When we enquired where we could flog it, we found immediate interest.

'I know just the person who could use that,' Raymond, a Belgian night-club owner who had been admiring the Imo, told us. 'A friend of mine makes films. He could use this.'

Instantly I was interested. 'I was an actor, in Shake-spearean plays mainly. I'd like to see your friend's studio.'

'And so you shall,' said our helpful friend. The next day he collected us from the British officers' club and drove us to a big barn on the outskirts of Brussels.

'It's not exactly Hollywood,' remarked Kelly as we were ushered inside.

'I expect their film industry has just got going again,' I said. I explained that the Brussels-based film industry had been closed down for refusing to make propaganda films for the Nazis. Several well-known actors and directors had paid for their principles with their lives.

The studio interior of the capacious barn was conventional enough, as far as I could tell from my limited experience as a film extra. There was an overhead grid system holding the lighting equipment, and the centre of the studio was taken up by a couple of typical movie sets depicting a theatrical agent's office and a bedroom with a large brass bedstead.

The thing that struck me immediately was that there were no facilities for recording sound. Obviously the movie was low-budget, and was being shot mute, as in the silent era. Evidently the sound track would be recorded later.

Raymond introduced us to the producer-director, a harassed man who immediately examined the Imo camera. His cameraman did the same and, having pronounced himself satisfied, he quickly returned to the task of lighting the set, preparatory to a take.

Raymond completed the business side of the deal and was paid in cash. He deducted his substantial commission and handed us the rest. It was considerably more than we had expected.

At that moment, four actors and actresses, wearing robes over their costumes, returned from their dressing-rooms, which were temporary plywood enclosures at the side of the barn. Raymond was eager to get back to Brussels, but I insisted on remaining until the scene was shot.

The cameraman at last declared himself ready, and the director, who had been graphically instructing his cast out of earshot, gave his players the go-ahead.

Both the male and female actors immediately dropped their robes. They were stark naked. Physically, they were well equipped. They climbed on to the big brass bed. The director called out, 'Action!'

The small cast immediately obliged. Though this was a rehearsal, there was no lack of enthusiasm in their performances. They played their parts with professional zest. The only thing missing was dialogue. But then there did not seem to be much need for words. Somewhat shaken and unlike those dedicated performers, we quietly withdrew. Once outside, for the first time in many months we laughed till we cried. From then on a dark shadow seemed to be lifted from my mind.

Chapter Nineteen

My Best Friend, Sally

I had been married four years and was still in love. I had remained faithful to my wife, despite a collapsing marriage and a wealth of temptation. But that last leave in London had broken me. Then, unexpectedly, in Brussels I found a young woman who changed the direction of my life. She was a sergeant in the ATS, small and very pretty. We met on one of the overcrowded trams that used to run along the Avenue Louise. The severity of her smart uniform could not disguise her sex appeal. When our eyes met there was immediate rapport. Kelly thought her delightful. I was enchanted.

I had four days left before we had to get back to base. That lovely sergeant and I probably broke every rule in King's Regulations and Air Council Instructions, to the prejudice of good order and discipline. In the course of our brief, passionate affair, a powerful spell was broken. Suddenly I was free from that unhappy infatuation with my wife. Perhaps it was nature's way of clearing the slate. For months I had been drifting, careless of what happened to me. Like many others, the war had exhausted me, mentally and physically. Renewal of the experience of physical love reawakened my will to live.

Our part of Schleswig-Holstein was dotted with large plantations of half-grown fir trees. As a result of the wartime restrictions on hunting, the whole area had become overstocked with deer. The Wingco, brought up on an

East African farm, knew that overpopulated game needed culling. He shot a number but was too busy disarming the northern Luftwaffe to handle the whole herd.

Knowing I was experienced with guns and a good enough shot to ensure a quick kill, he delegated me to do the culling and, at the same time, to supply the mess with venison. On these daily stalks I took Sally, a beautiful German shepherd bitch. She proved to be a splendid hunting companion.

I had acquired her on the way through Germany. The Wing's official guard-dog handler, a corporal from our airfield security section, had given her to me. Sally had been renamed. Her former master had been an SS officer and she was still guarding his dead body when the corporal found her. She had been badly wounded by the mortar shell that had killed her German master. Our dog-handler had nursed her back to health and she repaid the corporal's care and kindness with total fidelity. I swear that Sally understood every word he said. When the corporal explained to her that I was to be her new master, she accepted me and gave me the same kind of devotion. From then on we were inseparable. Sally saved my life.

We were out hunting on a sultry day. I did not feel well. My limbs ached and I felt feverish. I was due to fly with Kelly later on that day and, rather than hang around waiting, I decided to go out shooting. Killing has never been a sport for me, but the culling needed doing and, like most young men, we were meat-hungry.

I did not realize that I was shivering until I missed an easy shot. Instead of a clean kill, I severely wounded the deer. The poor creature took off into the undergrowth. I had been taught by my father never to let a wounded animal suffer so I raced after it. It was a surprisingly long chase, and we were miles away from the airfield when I finally got the opportunity for a certain mercy shot. This time, I did not miss.

By then I was shivering badly with fever. I started back unsteadily, with Sally beside me. My eyesight was clouded and I felt giddy. I had no sense of dread or alarm, only a feeling of resignation. Everything was fuzzy and ill-defined. I vaguely remember that it was raining. Of one thing I was certain. I would never again hunt or kill another living creature. It was the first time I had inflicted needless suffering. I was disgusted with myself.

We were still a mile or so from the perimeter of the airfield, on the fringe of the half-grown forest, when I collapsed. Curled up in the wet ferns, I felt an over-whelming desire to sleep. Sally whined unhappily. Then I fainted. I do not know how long I was unconscious but my dog's insistent attentions woke me up. I vaguely realized what was happening. If I stayed there, I would die. I managed to stand up. Using my hunting rifle as a support, I hung on to Sally's collar, and she led me back. I was coughing, retching up blood. The last mile seemed like eternity. Within sight of the camp, I dropped. The last sound I heard was Sally barking.

The next thing I remember was being carried between two airmen. I heard one say, 'Don't worry, mate, you'll be all right now.' I do not remember anything else until I woke up in bed in my billet. Kelly and the MO were there. My splendid West Indian friend had been concerned when I had not returned from hunting.

He knew how much I enjoyed flying with him in the Messerschmitt 108. It was a treat I never missed. Eventually he telephoned the guardroom. They sent a service policeman to look for me. He set off in the direction of the woods and heard Sally barking. All our service police knew my dog. He called to her. She came directly and led him to where I was lying, hidden by the long grass. When my rescuer saw my condition, he ran back for help while Sally stood guard. Together with another airman, he got me back. They put me on my bed and called the MO.

I was too far gone to remember much. I recall the word 'pneumonia'. I remember being put in an ambulance. I was in a lot of pain, which made it punishing to breathe. Then, just as had happened to me before, in

1942, I abruptly left my body. The pain ceased. I was surrounded by intensely bright light. Had I been seeing through my physical eyes I would have been blinded instantly. Below me was an abyss of velvet darkness. It was as vivid as my memories of the first experience of dying. As before, I felt no fear. Most of all, there was the same overwhelming sense of awe.

After a while I felt myself being drawn back. There was the sensation of rapid acceleration, until I felt myself hurtling through space-time. Abruptly, I was back in my body. The pain was bearable and I could breathe more easily.

During the years of paranormal investigation I had become familiar with the fringe sensations of passing into a trance. Had I not experienced them, I would have been much more alarmed by what I believe to be the death experience. This does not mean that I had lost my natural fear of death, which is, after all, part of our survival instinct, and to this day I still retain it. But it is only a fear of the mechanism, the form of death, not a dread of death itself. From personal experience of that condition, I *know* there is nothing to fear.

I was down to a hundred pounds in weight. Once again I was a physical wreck. Kelly came to see me and was shaken by the change. Years later he told me that at the time he did not think I was going to make it. In fact I easily could have slipped away. Kelly sensed this and said, 'Come on, Mike. Don't let the bastards win. Get off that bloody bed. Show the buggers what you're made of!'

Good old Kelly! That deep, melodious voice of his had a unique, persuasive quality. It struck a chord in my failing will. I struggled out of bed and, helped by Kelly, I did a wobbly circuit of the room.

I was transferred to 8th Base General Hospital, near Minden in Westphalia, and put into a ward which I shared with five other young officers. I was the only one among us who was not aircrew. Each of us had finished up in this ward after reaching the limit of endurance. All of us had managed to keep going while the war was still being fought. Once hostilities were over, reaction had set in. The only difference was in the individual ways we had been affected by it.

Two occupants of the small ward were highly decorated. One wore a faded DFC, the other had been awarded the Conspicuous Gallantry Medal. The first patient had become hermetic, closed up inside a wall of silence. The other regularly 'bailed out' of his bed on to the floor when, in his nightmares, his aircraft burst into flames. They were tragic examples of the futility of war.

Another member of our select group had to be carefully watched. He had been a bomb-aimer on too many night operations over Europe. One of his spontaneous reactions was quite bizarre. Occasionally an inexperienced new nurse would accede to his shy request for a urine bottle. Once he had filled it, in his confused mind it became a bomb. When the unsuspecting nurse returned to remove the full bottle, she was lucky if she was not hit by flying glass when he deliberately slung itsat her. This only happened at night while the rest of us were asleep. By day we could keep a wary eye on him, and the staff nurses knew the score, too.

In comparison, my own troubles were minor. Apart from exhaustion and an emaciated body, which was being built up with diet and physiotherapy, I could not stop tears from flowing. I do not mean I wept. The constant flow that welled out of my tear-ducts had nothing to do with sorrow. Like the odd behaviour of the others in the ward, it was a result of having driven myself beyond the limits of endurance. With the constant loss of body fluids, I was often seized by violent cramp. Drugs and medications seemed to have no appreciable effect. I had to drink pints of water containing potassium and salt. Then, one morning, it simply cured itself, like a well running dry.

I received some mail from home and a morale-boosting visit from the lovely ATS sergeant, who had been posted to a nearby HQ. Two weeks later, I collected my kit from Schleswig before leaving for home. This gave me an opportunity to say goodbye to Sally, who joyously greeted me when I returned from 8th Base Hospital. I told her why I must go, and why she must stay. I am sure she understood me.

Sally had all northern Schleswig-Holstein for her domain. She was surrounded by affection and she had a strong sense of duty. Better that Sally should stay where she belonged than come with me to England to be greeted by six months in a cramped quarantine kennel, followed by the probability of living in a flat in London. Sally was a free-range dog not a spoilt pet. But it hurt both of us to say goodbye.

Years later, through an acquaintance, I was given news of her. Sally had lived out a full and rewarding life with the RAF at Schleswig, and she is buried on the airfield. No dog could have been a greater friend. I look forward to meeting her again. After Sally I never had another dog. Parting from her had been too painful.

Back in England, I telephoned my parents and asked them to pass the news of my return to the Barradells, whom I had not been able to contact. I also told them that I was being sent to Wroughton Hospital, which I believed was somewhere in Wiltshire. Twelve hours later, I was sitting in a small ward there, enjoying a welcoming cup of tea.

None of the staff seemed too sure what I was being treated for, but by the constant testing and re-testing of just about every function of my weary body, it seemed that they were trying to ascertain just how much damage had been done by my earlier brush with death.

As part of these tests I was sent to see a psychiatrist for evaluation. My only previous experience of a psychiatrist had been at Blackpool. It had not given me much confidence in that side of the medical profession. The psychiatrist at Wroughton Hospital did nothing to alter my opinion.

He was a small, intense man who made copious notes of my answers to a string of questions. These queries, as far as I could see, had little to do with evaluating my background as a human being but seemed to be solely intended to give a detailed profile of my sex-life. He then asked me to tell him what the shape of some ink blots meant to me. For the next half-hour I conjured up utterly ridiculous interpretations of those ink blots and gave them every weird and wonderful sexual connotation I was capable of deriving. The more outrageous my interpretations, the more excited my examiner became. Behind his thick glasses, I could see his myopic eyes shining with psychiatric fervour. When I left he thanked me profusely for my whole-hearted co-operation.

I requested an interview with the senior medical officer, a tough old physician with many years' experience of general practice before serving in the wartime RAF, and asked to see another psychiatrist.

A week later I went to see a psychiatrist who was quite different. He was a cheerful character and keen on flying. He gave me the confidence to tell him something of my story. He listened sympathetically and occasionally asked pertinent questions. He then gave me a clean bill of health. 'There's nothing wrong with you that a couple of years of peace and hard work won't sort out. My advice to you is to get fit as soon as you can. That bloody myositis, or whatever it was that nearly killed you in 1942, has done some damage. You must have the constitution of an ox to have survived it and the other misfortunes you've been through.

'But there's nothing wrong with your mind. You've got a lively imagination and an excellent sense of humour. They'll stand you in good stead. I'm recommending you for honourable discharge from the service on medical grounds, owing to the accumulated effects of the earlier myositis and the recent double-pneumonia. I am also recommending you for a disability pension.'

He smiled at my surprise. 'But somehow, Bentin, I don't think you'll need it.' His last remark made me feel much better.

My subsequent interview with the pensions assessor, a civil servant, confirmed my view of His Majesty's Treasury who, on a number of occasions, had been weeks late in paying my family allowance into my bank account.

'In view of your medical report, we are willing to grant you thirty shillings a week, subject to review every six months.' The weasel-faced assessor smiled complacently as though expecting applause for his munificent gesture.

'Thirty pieces of silver sounds about the going rate for what the service did to me with that bloody injection,' I said, carefully enunciating each word. 'Tell you what, mate . . . Why don't you stuff it!' I was in no mood for courtesy.

I wondered what sort of a pension they awarded to the dependants of servicemen who had died or to those who were disabled for life through such gross ineptitude. Evidently, as ex-servicemen, our usefulness was over. The only ones to benefit would be the regulars. They would be well looked after. Civilian volunteers, like myself, were to be discarded as rapidly and as cheaply as possible.

Therefore, my grateful thanks to that self-satisfied pensions assessor for shocking me into the firm resolve never again to rely on the authorities for any help whatsoever. It has stood me in good stead. From then on, I realized that I was on my own. I decided to do something worthwhile with my life, preferably without hurting fellow human beings. Then and there, with the invaluable aid of that still small voice, I decided I would capitalize on my odd ability to make my contemporaries laugh. The reluctant jester was about to turn professional.

Chapter Twenty

The Jester Turns Pro

Being a shy person, as an important part of my survival pattern I had developed the ability to see life through the eyes of a clown, but although I had been a professional actor I had never been a professional comedian. First, I had to find out how much I knew about comedy.

For a whole week I let my mind wander through the long corridors of memory. A detailed review of many pieces of silent film comedy passed in front of my inner vision. I had cherished memories of Buster Keaton, Charlie Chaplin, Laurel and Hardy, Harry Langdon and Harold Lloyd. From watching them, I had learnt what little I knew of the art of visual comedy and could perform recognizable impersonations of them all. This was my stock in trade as a stammering schoolboy clown, and my defence against the loneliness of being shy. I made up my mind that if I became a professional comedian I would create my *own* style of comedy, using the brilliance and originality of those great performers as a guide.

I went to live with my parents on extended sick-leave while I sorted myself out. I was delighted to be with them, and I knew I could call on my mother's astute common sense and my father's wisdom while trying to put my life back into some sort of shape. I was waiting to be demobilized and I must have been a burden to my long-suffering mother and father because my nerves were still in a pretty jumpy state and I found it hard to sleep.

This temporary insomnia was not helped by the presence of a cricket which had taken up residence somewhere inside the walls of my parents' flat. Night after night, that insect 'cricked' away until I nearly went berserk. After the third sleepless night, I told my parents, and Ma sent for the pest exterminator.

The extermination team brought with them a large truck and a whole mass of equipment. By the size of it all, anyone would have concluded that we were infested with a plague of rats. Seeing our surprise, the chief exterminator, a large overalled man wearing a bowler hat, solemnly proclaimed, 'There may be more than one. Crickets are *very* tricky. They take a lot of exterminating.'

He started off by using a stethoscope to pinpoint the general area where the cricket was active. The little sod would not oblige at first, presumably having exhausted itself by its nightly performance.

'We'll 'ave to wake 'im up.' The big man started banging the walls. Suddenly the cricket was back, clicking away like a taxi-meter.

'Ah!' muttered the exterminator. 'We'll soon 'ave the little bugger out of there.'

His two assistants unloaded still more equipment from their truck. Their leader carefully drilled a half-inch hole right through the wall, at the spot where he had last heard the cricket. The assistants brought a heavy machine like a small boiler fitted with a powerful hand-pump. The master-craftsman threaded its long, flexible hose-pipe into the hole he had made and started to pump. While he did so, we could still hear the cricket chirping merrily away.

' 'E's taking far more insect powder than I thought. 'E must be a big 'un.'

The exterminator went on pumping for another few minutes, without result. The cricket continued to 'crick'. Then we heard some muffled coughing and a strangled choking sound. It seemed to come from the flat below. It was followed by a thud.

'My God,' cried Ma. 'It must be the old lady in the flat below. She's an asthmatic!'

We all dashed downstairs and frantically rang her door bell. There was no answer. While Ma rushed back upstairs to ring for the ambulance and inform the police, we put our shoulders to the front door and forced our way inside. No door could have withstood that big exterminator for long.

We found the old lady unconscious amid a cloud of fine insect powder which must have seeped into her flat through a hole in the cavity wall. She was pretty far gone but, by the time the ambulance men had arrived, we had succeeded in pulling her round. She was pathetically grateful, even when we explained the cause of her seizure. The police, who arrived later, asked for a full report from the exterminator. As he did not seem too put out by the whole incident, I can only surmise this sort of thing often happened.

When we had seen our stricken neighbour safely off to the hospital, we all returned upstairs. The cricket was still at it. My mother would not hear of the exterminator and his team trying any more of the deadly equipment. Instead, she gave them a cup of tea.

'Perhaps we should try prayer,' Ma said, half-joking, when they had gone.

'Good idea,' agreed Pop. We sat down and prayed for the cricket to leave.

Whether it was the lingering effect of the insect powder or the effectiveness of our prayers, I will never know, but the cricket left that night. Its 'cricks' gradually faded out until, around midnight, they stopped altogether. For which peace I was duly grateful to the Almighty.

At this point in my life, I was delighted to meet again my ex-partner, Tony Sherwood. We had a hilarious reunion and decided to team up as a double act.

My brother had written a very funny monologue which he used to perform as a party-piece in his sergeants' mess. It was a burlesque of those blood-curdling mid-European fairy stories which must have scared the hell out of generations of children. When Tony and I saw him perform it at a family party, we asked him if we could use his 'Russian Fairy Story' as the basis for our intended act.

Being generous to a fault, Bro was delighted to let us have it, especially when I suggested that Tony Sherwood and I should recite the piece in unison, with synchronized movements that exactly matched the action. Then and there, we tried it out and, though it was only a rough rehearsal, we all could see that it worked equally well for a double act. For which kindness, as for many others, I am deeply grateful to my brother.

In all, it took several weeks of rehearsal to get this short comedy piece running smoothly and to integrate it with our piano-and-drums jazz arrangement of the Russian song 'Black Eyes', with which we intended to finish the act. We called ourselves 'Sherwood and Forrest'. It was the only time, in all my years in show business, that I ever changed my name, although I did add an 'e' to Bentin.

The next problem was what to wear? We had already swapped our uniforms for civilian demob outfits. Both officers and other ranks were issued with a limited choice of a suit in blue, brown, or grey pinstripe, a tweed sports coat and a pair of trousers, three shirts, two pairs of shoes, black and brown, underwear, socks, a tie, and a choice of a raincoat or overcoat. For me, it was an embarrassment of riches for, apart from my threadbare uniform and much-worn battle-dress, RAF-issue shirts and underwear, worn shoes and darned socks, like many others I would have been naked. What few civilian clothes I had possessed were lost long ago in the bombing of London.

As a basic wardrobe for civilian life, this outfit could not be faulted. But, because of the limited choice of suits and jackets, ex-servicemen were instantly recognizable. There was no mistaking the material and the cut of a demob suit.

Somehow, we had to find costumes for our act. Our budget was strictly limited. Neither Tony nor I had drawn much in the way of our demobilization grant. This had been based on seniority, not on the hazards of wartime service under battle conditions. Both of us got about £55, which was pretty cheap for four years of our young lives. Nevertheless it was very welcome.

I designed several costumes and we finally decided on being dressed as Victorian undertakers, complete with very tall top hats wrapped in black crêpe. I cannot think why we settled on those outfits, but they looked very funny. We also used pale greasepaint make-up, so that we looked suitably ghoulish.

The trouble with funny costumes is that, although you can get a hilarious reception when you first appear, their exaggerated grotesqueness tends to pall. We had to work doubly hard to overcome this unforeseen handicap.

After weeks of rehearsal we managed to get an audition at Collins Music-Hall, a vaudeville theatre in Islington. When the fire-curtain was laboriously raised, we could dimly make out three people sitting in the cavernous darkness of the stalls. They were the manager, the licensee of the theatre and a theatrical agent.

It is never easy to be funny at ten o'clock in the morning, but we did our best. The audience heard us out in mute shock, and at the frenetic end of our act the silence was deafening. Down came the curtain, and that was that. As we packed up and left, the hatchet-faced agent told us, 'You're too fucking sophisticated.'

Undaunted, we tried other auditions without getting a single booking. We got plenty of laughs and encouragement from the hardened old pros among the stage staff, but it seemed that our act was too 'different' for safe inclusion in the surprisingly conservative programmes of the post-war music-hall.

Our final audition was at the Windmill, the small theatre in the West End which had become famous as the only nude show in town. Its proud boast, 'We never closed', referred to its unbroken record of performances throughout the London blitz and the rest of the war, including the dreadful V1 buzz bombs and the V2 rocket attacks.

In late 1946, when Sherwood and Forrest did their audition for Vivian Van Damm, the owner, he was about the only West End theatre licensee who gave unknown performers, especially young comedians, the chance to perform in his theatre. To our amazement, among a surprising number of failures at that audition, only two acts got booked. Sherwood and Forrest was one of them. The other was a stocky, ebullient young Welshman with a mop of unruly hair. His name was Harry Secombe.

The first thing Van Damm asked us was, 'Has your act been licensed by the Lord Chamberlain?'

We told him we had no idea this was necessary. We learnt it was a strict legal requirement that any theatrical performance, musical or otherwise, must first be licensed by the Lord Chamberlain. In those days this austere, almost God-like hangover from Victorian morality was the ultimate arbiter of 'public good taste'. His decisions were enforced by the antiquated and confused rules and regulations for censorship, which had encased the theatre and all other forms of public entertainment in a moral straitjacket.

The multiple prohibitions, restrictions and penalizations, including heavy fines and even imprisonment, were intended to suppress or eliminate blasphemy, obscenity (both in language and actions), lewdness, unlicensed performances under the influence of alcohol, exploitation of child performers, cruelty to performing animals, immorality (both on and off the stage, but within the confines of the theatre), and any other 'criminal' acts, both real or imaginary, which were deemed to come within the scope of the seemingly unlimited powers of the Lord Chamberlain's office.

The only area in which this organization was doing useful work was in its prevention of child exploitation and cruelty to animals. Everything else was an imposition on the public.

In addition to these stringent regulations, there was the added burden of fire regulations. These were reasonable and sensible precautions against the horrors of fire in a crowded public place. They also applied to the conditions under which each individual performance was given. The performers, or the theatre management, had to ensure that all costumes were fire-resistant and that nothing of an inflammable nature was used on stage.

Every word and gesture of our act had to be examined, clucked over for 'indecent double-meanings' and was finally passed by the Lord Chamberlain's office as suitable for public exhibition.

The Windmill's licensed nudes were allowed to appear in 'subdued light', provided that they did not move. The small, packed audience were mostly regular and dedicated voyeurs. Many of them had noticeable erections, which they handled during the nude tableaux. They were usually spotted by the nudes. As soon as the girls were offstage, they would inform the stage manager, 'Row three, seat six, elderly grey-haired gent. He's at it. Dirty old man.' If members of the audience were caught masturbating or exposing themselves, they were promptly ejected by a muscular commissionaire.

There was also a notice, prominently displayed in the foyer, which prohibited the use of binoculars, monoculars, opera-glasses, telescopes, and other artificial aids to vision. To circumvent this, one inventive member of the audience had a pair of ultra-short focal-length binoculars specially made to look like a pair of very thick glasses. This gave him close-up vision.

Wearing them, he managed to get past the vigilant commissionaire at the door but, unluckily, while wearing them his normal vision was impaired. Consequently he missed his footing and fell down the stairs, breaking a leg on the way. He was sternly reprimanded and his special glasses were confiscated until the ambulance arrived.

Directly after our successful audition, Tony Sherwood, who was late for a music lesson, left – most reluctantly as we both wanted to celebrate. I sensed an immediate rapport with Harry Secombe. We quickly sized each other up, and liked what we saw.

'What service were you in?' I asked him.

In those first years after the war, it was a question young men asked each other. Most ex-servicemen felt the bond of shared experience and, in addition, they might have had mutual friends in the forces. In that way I often found out what had happened to friends with whom I had lost contact. Sadly, many of them had been killed or were still missing.

'Army,' the curly-haired comedian replied. 'I was a bombardier in the Royal Artillery. I finished up in Italy and did a bit with CSE (the Army's entertainment unit). That's where I dreamt up my act. How about you, mate?'

'I was RAF. So was my partner. Both of us were aircrew volunteers. I failed my eyesight test, half way through training, and finished up in Intelligence.'

Harry laughed. It was the first time I was to hear his high-pitched giggle. 'Judging by your act, mate, *no-one* is going to believe that. By the way, which side were you on?'

I liked this funny, outgoing Welshman with the ready laugh. Here was someone who had been through the mill and come out the other side still chuckling. Harry Secombe was my kind of bloke. Our long-standing friendship has confirmed that first impression.

Harry was booked into the Windmill a few weeks before Tony and I were due to perform. I went to see his act, which seemed funnier every time I saw it. Performing at the 'Mill' could be quite an ordeal, because often you were faced with the same audience for most, if not all, of the six daily shows. Some stalwarts stayed on from ten o'clock in the morning until the last show, which finished at ten p.m., moving to seats nearer the stage as others left. They were not there to see the comedians. They had paid their money to goggle at the nudes. Why not? They were beautiful girls.

Tony and I played six shows a day, six days a week, for six weeks, a total of 216 shows during that short season. We had learned to perform the 'Russian Fairy Story' sometimes with very few laughs. This was because, although the act went well for the first couple of performances, by the end of the day many members of the audience had seen it six times.

We had another handicap. Because of the strict rules of the Lord Chamberlain's licence, once an act, play, or script had been passed, not one word of it could be changed. This regulation was particularly strictly enforced with anyone, especially a comedian, who was appearing at the Windmill because the nude show was already on the fringe of 'respectability'. Dirty-minded little men from the Lord Chamberlain's office periodically sat in the audience to make sure nothing was changed. They checked every word and gesture from copies of the detailed script that we had submitted to the Lord Chamberlain.

Many people have wondered whether there were opportunities for sex with all those nudes.

The answer is, 'No!' To the public, the Windmill might seem a sexual paradise. For the girls, it was more like a nunnery. They worked very long hours and were under constant surveillance.

We were not the only comedians on the bill at the 'Mill'. While we were there, Alfred Marks was a resident performer whose contract, unlike ours, was for more than one season. He worked as a versatile character-comedian and a singer. The possessor of a fine bass-baritone voice, and with a great gift for dialect comedy, this warm and friendly man had been demobbed from the RAF at about the same time as ourselves. He was, and still is, one of the best raconteurs in the business. His timing is impeccable.

For six weeks, during those long pauses between appearances at the 'Mill', Alfred, Tony and I often played chess in the roof-top canteen. Our enjoyment was somewhat curtailed by the intrusions of a 'kibbitzer', someone who watches your game and gives you unwanted advice on how to play it. Keith Lester was the 'Mill's' choreographer and, apart from the annoying habit of butting in on our games of chess, he was a friend.

One Friday, after he had screwed up an otherwise enjoyable game with his advice – 'Watch his bishop, dear boy, or it's mate in three' – I decided that the time had come to do something about it. I told Tony and Alfred about my plan to 'de-kibbitzize' Keith. They both thoroughly approved. Early on Saturday I bought two cheap chess sets, and spent all Sunday with Tony making my own version of chess. This consisted of sticking one of the chess boards on to a large plywood base, then cutting the second chess board into strips and adding these other black and white squares to the first board, thereby producing an impressive-looking, much larger board, two squares bigger all round.

Tony was a dab hand at carpentry, so the result looked authentic. We then set about modifying the pieces, so that there were four extra pawns on each side, plus four other new pieces as well. These consisted of two 'archbishops' and two 'grand knights' per side.

We made the 'archbishops' by attaching the four extra bishops' mitres to the tops of four castles and the 'grand knights' by doing the same thing with the four other knights' horse-heads. The result looked puzzling but professional.

On the Monday, there was no time to teach Alfred much more than the rudiments of the new game so we ad-libbed it.

Both of us, watched by an equally solemn Tony, played this new game with great concentration. No-one had the slightest idea what we were doing. For that matter, neither did we, but we played the game, which we called 'Pshessh', with evident confidence and great enjoyment.

During the game we would remark on each other's moves with cryptic comments such as, 'I see you prefer Plottnik's defence to the more conventional Kubalik gambit. That's an interesting ploy, Alfred.'

My solemn-faced opponent, with whom I would never play poker, replied, 'I learnt it from watching Skobolev. He mated Lubichev in six moves by the brilliant use of his crossed archbishops. I've used it ever since.'

About half way through the game, Keith swept gracefully into the canteen. Having been an excellent dancer in his prime, Keith Lester never merely walked into a room. He always 'entered'. Immediately, his eyes wandered towards the game in progress, and he was just about to make one of his 'kibbitzing' remarks when it dawned on him that this was not a conventional chess match. Unwilling to appear ignorant, he took his cup of lemon tea, sat down quietly and watched us.

When it was our turn to go on stage, we reluctantly left the board as it was. 'Please see nobody touches it, Keith, there's a good chap,' said Alfred as he left.

According to one of our friends, whom we had let in on the secret, Keith stared in fascination at the overcrowded chess board until we returned. Incredible though it may seem, Alfred, Tony and I kept up that game for a whole week.

By Friday, Keith thought he had grasped the essentials of the new game. He moved closer, ready to put in his 'kibbitz', and remarked languidly, 'Watch his archbishop, you headstrong boy. It could be mate in three!'

Tony, who had nonchalantly dropped explanatory hints about the intricacies of Pshessh to Keith during the week, exploded. When he laughed, he always closed his eyes and banged the nearest object. This happened to be the Pshessh board. The pieces flew everywhere. Alfred and I collapsed in hysterics. We laughed so much we nearly missed our cue.

To give Keith his due, he took it all in good part. Apparently he dined out on that story for years, but he never again 'kibbitzed'.

The other person in on the Pshessh secret was Gus Chevalier, who gave me an excellent piece of advice which I have followed religiously ever since. One day he saw me take a drink before going on to do the act. 'You are just starting in this business, Mike,' he said. 'I think you're going a long way in it. Maybe right to the top. Don't fuck it all up with booze.'

That was the best advice I ever had in show business. Since then, I have never touched a drop of liquor *before* a performance. I enjoy a glass of good wine with a meal, but I do not drink to excess, and never before a show. In show business you need your wits about you.

Gus Chevalier's warning makes good sense. I recommend his advice to anyone in or out of show business. Alcohol, in its way, is just as deadly as drugs.

When we finished our six-week stint at the 'Mill', Tony and I felt as though we had been through a baptism of fire. Through an audition we got a radio performance with one of the BBC's top shows, *Variety Bandbox*. It worked well. Then we realized that we had only one act. We were going to need a lot more material besides the 'Russian Fairy Story' if we were to go into radio, which was then the big medium and a sure formula for success if you broadcast well. Meanwhile, we got bookings for different gigs, playing Billy Butlin's holiday camps. These were only one-night stands, and we were not getting sufficient work to make a living at it.

What was more serious, our pitiful 'war service gratuities' had long since run out, and we were broke. I went to Snow Hill Labour Exchange in the City to see what the prospects of work as a journalist were. If they were good, I could continue with the act in the evenings. All I got was the same job offer I had turned down in 1940, as a mortuary attendant. I gave them the same answer, 'Sorry! There's no opportunity for conversation with the customers.'

Tony and I finally got a break on television, on Christmas Day 1946. We did two performances, without an audience, in the cramped BBC studio at Alexandra Palace. It was an interesting experience, because the director was 'half-cut' most of the time, having celebrated Christmas over-lavishly.

Sherwood and Forrest appeared in people's homes on the tiny 10-inch black and white screens of that era. I doubt whether more than 10,000 dedicated viewers saw us, and they were confined mainly to the London area. Nevertheless, it proved to be a milestone in what is laughingly referred to as my 'career' ('career' is also defined as 'A headlong rush, often downhill').

Shortly afterwards, Tony and I agreed to split up the act. He had been offered an excellent scholarship for two years at the Guildhall School of Music. He deserved it, and it would have been churlish of me to stand in his way. So I went solo.

I now had to find a new act, and that takes time.

I decided to stay with the general pantomime style of the silent comedians but to use my voice as well. I rehearsed an entirely non-existent language, a mixture of mock-Polish, pseudo-Russian and any other foreign-sounding tongues that appealed to my ear. The result was a fluent and incomprehensible flow of seemingly authentic gibberish, which I combined with graphic miming to point up what I was describing.

To try it out I went to Soho, where just about every language in the world is spoken, and I used it to do my shopping. Although the shopkeepers were unable to pinpoint where this voluble young man came from, they all understood what I was trying to describe. I had a wonderful time doing it and called my new language 'Slobodian'.

For a long time Alfred Marks was convinced I was speaking Russian. Slobodian became one of the most effective weapons in my comedy armoury. I suppose I was really looking for a way round my stammer which, since my wartime experiences, had returned in force. This post-war handicap was the main reason I had not returned to my original career as a Shakespearean actor with Robert Atkins.

The Nuffield Centre, a forces entertainment centre, served as the ideal try-out venue for new acts. Tony

Sherwood and I had tried out our 'Russian Fairy Story' at the Nuffield with great success, so I used the centre as a sounding-board for all the comedy ideas I was developing. The young servicemen and -women were a marvellous audience. They did not want to hear the tired jokes and comedy routines which they knew by heart from touring ENSA companies during the war. These youngsters loved original comedy, and they did not mind if you were not perfectly rehearsed, just so long as you were different.

I was not alone in my choice of the Nuffield. Many other young comedians and singers used it for the same reason. Mary Cook, a talented professional pianist who ran the entertainment side of the centre, was very astute, and kind-hearted too. She knew that things were tight for all of us young hopefuls so, although we were not paid for our efforts, she saw to it that there was always a large supply of sandwiches, coffee and tea to sustain us. For many of us, this was the best meal of the day. For some, it was the only one.

Many unknown performers, who later became world-famous, started in this way. My friends Peter Sellers, Benny Hill, Harry Secombe, Tommy Cooper and Tony Hancock were just a few of them. The full list read like a *Who's Who in Show Business*.

My new acts ranged from 'The District Attorney Sums Up', a wild burlesque of those American movie courtroom dramas where the brilliant young DA successfully proves his case, to a mad lecture in fluent Slobodian on the anatomy of the human body. I illustrated this latter bit of nonsense with large, graphic diagrams.

My version of the typical courtroom scene was a wild piece of comedy interspersed with ridiculous props as the criminal exhibits. These consisted of a rubber chicken, a bow and arrow fitted with a silencer, a six-fingered rubber glove which got milked, a trick glass into which the DA pours water that turns into wine, and various other visual insanities. This act was immensely successful. So was the 'Mad Slobodian Professor's Anatomy Lecture'.

Like all the other acts at the Nuffield, it had to be clean, but my Slobodian lecture was a bit cheeky. In those immediate post-war years, with the Lord Chamberlain at the peak of his powers, this was something of a breakthrough. It scraped in under the wire mainly because the dirty-minded officials could not understand what I was saying.

I believe they thought I actually was speaking some unfamiliar mid-European dialect. Nowadays, that illustrated lecture probably would be considered suitable for children above the age of twelve. In those days it was risqué. The Nuffield audience loved it.

Another favourite with them was my 'Imaginative Young Man with a Walking Stick'. This was a piece of very energetic pantomime, which I introduced by saying, 'Imagine a nervous and over-imaginative young man waiting for his girlfriend outside the stage door of the theatre where she works. He is carrying a walking stick and, as he impatiently passes the time till she appears, he imagines himself in all sorts of dramatic situations.'

The Nuffield pianist then ad-libbed some appropriate background music while I became a big-game fisherman trying to land a giant fish, a swashbuckling fencer in the Errol Flynn tradition, a hysterical Japanese soldier at bayonet practice, and various other equally energetic routines, during which I threw myself round the small stage like a rubber ball, using the walking stick as the motivating prop.

This act was rapturously received, and an agent gave me a couple of weeks in provincial variety to try it out for the first time professionally. These dates were not exactly an unqualified success. The older members of the audience at both Peterborough and Weston-super-Mare lapsed into bewildered silence, but the young people loudly enjoyed the novelty of my act.

The greatest encouragement came from the amused stagehands, who had never seen anything quite like it. The veteran performers on the bill also appreciated what

I was trying to do. They told me to keep at it, and they gave me a lot of sound advice. But I still had not found the magical formula that would launch my career as a solo comedian. I stumbled across that treasure trove by accident, or was it? Somehow, I do not think so.

My brother and sister-in-law and their baby son, John, were living in Barnes above a converted shop where an enterprising rubber company manufactured condoms. Like me, they were nearly broke, but these two very talented artists were managing to survive. They were both determined not to give up their art. Together, we were having a wonderful evening of laughter reviewing our various misfortunes, which is the best use for a sense of humour. I was melodramatically describing an incident that had occurred during the war, and was standing on an old wooden chair to illustrate the action. In doing so, I broke the back right off the elderly Victorian piece of furniture.

It fell to the floor and my brother, who was still laughing, bent down to pick it up. As it was one of only three chairs he should have been annoyed, but he was not.

'I should shoot you for doing that, Bro,' he said as he straightened up, holding the broken back of the dining-chair. Quite by chance, in the way that he had picked it up, the damaged chairback looked like a sub-machine-gun. My brother shook it as though he was recoiling from a burst of fire. We all laughed.

The three of us were in the sort of creative mood that children enjoy. Then and there, in turn, we grabbed the chairback from each other and held it in different ways to see if we could turn it into other objects. Amazingly, the simple shape left by the breakage could be used to illustrate all sorts of things, with only a word or two needed to emphasize the transformation.

During those few minutes, with the three of us trying to outdo each other, we must have devised a hundred different uses for that chairback. It became a comb, a plough, a pair of handcuffs, a guillotine, a flag, an axe, a saddle, a ship's rudder, prison bars, a road drill, and many other graphic shapes.

Suddenly it dawned on me what I had got in my hands. This chairback was an exponential development of my 'Imaginative Young Man with a Walking Stick'. Moreover, it did not need any lengthy explanation to set it up, and it instantly changed as you presented its different profiles to the audience. This was the act I had been looking for.

It took me two weeks to settle on the sequence of shapes that the chairback would represent. It may seem excessive, but the final editing of the material was a very important part. I had to make the shapes and forms into a flowing series of actions that would hold the attention of the audience without overtaxing their imagination or losing their interest. Once the choice had been made I rehearsed and rehearsed until the shapes, forms and movements merged into an easy-flowing montage.

Having got the sequence right, the illustrative words which accompanied it virtually wrote themselves. In its final form, the chairback became the subject of a melodramatic speech given by a hysterically nervous young man who is trying to sell the antique on behalf of a worthy charity.

In so doing, the young man gets carried away by the dramatic import of his own words. The chairback becomes whatever he is referring to, with a demonic life of its own, hurling him around the stage as he desperately tries to restrain it from taking him over.

Many years later, my friend Peter Sellers told me that my chairback had inspired him to perform his own memorable uncontrollable prosthetic arm routine as the mad Dr Strangelove in Stanley Kubrick's movie of that name.

In 1947, when I tried out 'The Chairback' for the first time at the Nuffield Centre, I had not the slightest idea how successful it would be. My four-minute action-packed performance literally had the audience on its feet cheering for an encore. It was also the most exhausting act I have ever done. In all, I performed 'The Chairback' some six thousand times over a period of eleven years, touring it right round the world. I could not perform it today to save my life.

While the Nuffield audience was still applauding, two men came back-stage to see me. One was in RAF uniform. I remember that they were still laughing. They introduced themselves as Monty Lyon and Dennis Selinger. They were theatrical agents. I sensed an immediate rapport with both of them.

Monty Lyon gave me his card. 'In all my years in show business, Mr Bentine, that is the most original comedy act I have seen. My partner and I would like you to have lunch with us. We have a proposition for you.'

'How about tomorrow?' I asked. Monty consulted his pocket diary. 'That would be difficult. How would Monday suit you?'

I nodded eagerly.

I went home in a happy haze. In the morning I told my parents what had happened. They were delighted. 'This is where it all starts, Michael. These men are going to help you. You can trust them.' Pop spoke in that tone of complete assurance which he used only when he had picked up the information psychically. I had never known him to be wrong in such cases.

My mother was more cautious. 'Be sure you get it in writing, darling.' Ma need not have worried. I enjoyed a gentlemen's agreement with both agents for many years without the three of us ever bothering about a written agency contract. We remained friends long after Monty Lyon retired.

On the Monday morning, I turned up at their office wearing my grey pinstripe demob suit.

It was a relaxed and cheerful meeting. They had both been in the RAF and we found that we had many mutual friends, including Alfred Marks, Jimmy Edwards and the writing teams of Dennis Norden and Frank Muir. Monty Lyon and Dennis Selinger had worked with them at RAF Henlow, where they had all been involved in camp concerts.

When we were fully relaxed and on first-name terms, Monty asked me whether I would audition for a new West End show produced by Val Parnell.

'But I've only got a four-minute act,' I protested weakly. 'I understand that most revue acts run three times that length.'

They both laughed. 'That's the first time we've ever had a prospective client raise an objection to the prospect of a West End show.'

Monty lit his pipe. 'Dennis and I both think that your chairback act is so completely different it will stand on its own.'

I remembered what Pop had said and stuck out my hand. 'If you think so, I'm willing to have a go.'

When the fire-curtain of the Prince of Wales Theatre rose for my audition and the stage lights came on, I found myself standing centre-stage peering out into the darkened auditorium.

'Whenever you are ready, Mr Bentine,' a powerful voice rumbled out from the stalls. It was Val Parnell. 'Take your time, lad!'

I took a deep breath, muttered a short prayer and went straight into my routine:

'Ladies and gentlemen, I am here tonight, in the cause of charity, in order to sell you this fine antique chair on behalf of those gallant men and women who, in our country's hour of darkest need, threw down their pens. Took up their guns . . . and . . . ' At this point, the chairback became the sub-machine-gun that had started the whole process.

I put my whole soul into my performance, the ever-changing shapes of the chairback hurling me from one situation to another like a demented puppet.

At the same time, to my surprise and delight, I heard loud laughter coming from behind the ultra-bright lights. It encouraged me to maximum effort. Yet I felt strangely detached, almost as though I was standing beside myself, watching someone else going through that frenzied routine.

I finished on the words, 'Was that your final bid, sir? Five pounds? Thank you very much indeed.'

'Well done, my boy,' said another voice which I later discovered belonged to Robert Nesbitt, the director. Down came the fire-curtain and the stage lights dimmed. I stood on the stage in the semi-darkness, my shirt sopping wet with perspiration already soaking through to my one and only suit.

Monty and Dennis, both grinning happily, soon reappeared. 'Well, Mike,' said Monty. 'You wowed them! You're to be in the new Vic Oliver show, *Starlight Roof*. You open in September at the Hippodrome, Leicester Square. That's three weeks from now. Come in tomorrow to sign the contract.'

I did not even think of asking how much I was to get for this undreamt-of break into the West End of London. When I got home Ma and Pop took it all far more calmly than I had done.

'I told you, you can trust your new agents,' said Pop.

'But get it in writing,' said Ma, and kissed me.

Chapter Twenty-one

A Gaggle of Goons

When I turned up for my first rehearsal with *Starlight Roof*, the cast of the show had already been hard at work for ten days. Inside the theatre there was a whirlpool of activity. During intervals in the rehearsals, I was introduced to the principal members of the large cast. According to the billing, *Starlight Roof* had 'A Host of Stars'. These were led by Vic Oliver, Pat Kirkwood and Fred Emney representing British show business, with American stars Marilyn Hightower, Jere McMahon, Wally Boag and Barbara Perry and, right at the bottom of the bill, two new names, Julie Andrews and Michael Bentine.

Vic Oliver was an Austrian who had been very successful on Broadway. This mid-European charmer was well-educated, a stylish comedian and an accomplished musician. After success on Broadway he had left America, had risen to fame in Britain during the mid-thirties and became a household name on radio during the war. He finished his comedy act by playing the violin, in his own words, 'Better than Jack Benny, but not quite as good as Jascha Heifetz'.

Pat Kirkwood was a young northerner with a broad smile and an effervescent personality. She could put over a song in the strident style of Ethel Merman but, as she said, 'I'm no bloody ballerina.'

Vic Oliver's co-star was Fred Emney, a moon-faced genial mountain of a man. His stage character of a jumbo-sized man about town was matched by his rumbling bellow of a voice, which emphasized his Rabelaisian, monocled image.

Among the American stars of the show, Marilyn High-tower was a small, exciting dancer. For one number, she wore a special pair of point-shoes, which seemed to have ball-bearings in their blocked toes, and she pirouetted on them as though she were an ice-skater.

Jere McMahon was an exponent of the Jerome Robbins school of modern American dance. Tall and elegant, the multi-talented Bostonian had been brought over to part-ner Pat Kirkwood. Bitingly witty, he seemed to have been born out of his time. With his Boston drawl, Jere McMahon could well have been the reincarnation of a Regency buck. Women adored him.

Wally Boag, who was described to me as 'the balloon man', arrived two days before the dress rehearsal. Wally was an eccentric dancer with rubber legs, which he could swing up higher than his ears. He was also an excellent comedian, and the first performer to present 'balloon-ology', the art of making model animals out of long sausage balloons.

Barbara Perry was a machine-gun-fast tap-dancer, using her feet as an instrument.

When I met the youngest member of the cast, Julie Andrews, a foal-like, eleven-year-old child with an extra-ordinary, soaring operatic voice, I was instantly drawn towards her. We got on well, Julie always addressing me as 'Mr Bentine', and with equal formality I called her 'Miss Andrews'. I came to love her very much, and still do. She is someone very special for all my family.

As a bonus, there was also a bevy of very pretty girl dancers, who formed the *corps de ballet*. I was twenty-five years old, and I felt as though I had stepped straight out of the nightmare of war into an exotic dream. I half-expected to wake up at any moment.

On the opening night my act worked very well. I hurled myself around the stage, totally concentrating on getting the routine right. Why I did not break something, I will never know. All the time I was aware of continuous laughter, which got louder and louder, spreading rapidly to most of that receptive first-night audience.

At the end of my act, I was wringing wet and hyper-adrenalated. With the laughter, the act seemed to take me over, and at the end of those few minutes I nearly fell off the stage with nervous exhaustion. Still dripping with perspiration, I phoned my parents and told them the good news. Ma was delighted, and Pop was relieved. I did not stay for the celebrations or any of the parties to which I had been invited, because I wanted to be alone with my thoughts. The first of these, on my way home by underground, was a heartfelt prayer of thanks to whoever was guiding me.

It took me over four hours to unwind. When I finally fell asleep at four o'clock in the morning, I slept for twelve hours, waking up just in time for a bath, 'breakfast' and the underground back to Leicester Square.

While I was dressing, Ma brought me the papers. The notices were excellent for the show. Moreover, 'Miss Andrews' and I both got honourable mentions. Several papers even spelt my name right. Julie had stopped the show with her rendering of 'Je suis Titania', an operatic coloratura piece that had the audience on their feet, cheering.

I got more than enough publicity to ensure that I was booked for the run of the show (I had had a two-week contract, with an option clause on the management's side). I received £30 a week, less 10 per cent for my agents. To me this was a fortune.

My parents wisely decided the time had come for me to move out and find a flat for myself nearer the theatre. They had put up with my fluctuating moods of elation and despair for long enough. They had also financed me, which had not been easy for them on their restricted income. Quite frankly, they now wanted some peace and quiet.

By the time I had found a roomy bed-sit and settled in, the show had been running for three months. I had got to know the whole of the cast, and had taken one or two of those pretty girls to dinner in Soho. My post-war depression had evaporated like morning mist. I felt that life was good, particularly as one of the girl dancers, a cool, slim blonde of outstanding prettiness, had become a close friend.

I had first noticed her looking sadly at a pair of new ballet shoes which she was 'breaking in'. I offered my services to ease the offending shoes, and she trustingly handed them over, believing me to be knowledgeable about such things. I softened them up so thoroughly that I ruined them for ever. Realizing that my intentions had been honest, she thanked me and started to giggle. She became helpless with laughter every time she looked at her brand-new 'ballet-boots', as she called them. 'They're not supposed to be soft all over. The toes are blocked, so that dancers can stand on point. Never mind, they'll do for rehearsal.'

I apologized and offered to pay for a new pair. The lovely girl would not hear of it. So I took her out to dinner instead. As she was very slim, I thought she would not eat much. I learnt that dancers, however thin, eat like horses. My charming dinner companion started at the top of the menu and worked her way right through to the coffee and Turkish Delight. I would have got off lighter by paying for new 'ballet boots'.

Clementina Stuart, whose full name was Clementina Theresa Gadesden Stuart-McCall, and I became good friends without the slightest inkling, on either side, that we would ever be more than that. For six months we thoroughly enjoyed each other's company and laughed a lot, neither of us realizing that we were falling in love.

Then, one day, I took Clementina to meet my parents. They were enchanted with her.

That evening, while we sat laughing together in my room, for the first time I kissed her. To my surprise, Clementina kissed me back. At that moment, I realized that I was in love with her. I proposed to her while we were watching the film *Mrs Miniver* at the Empire, Leicester Square. Before she could answer, I took it back. My Scottish love was not standing for that. Clementina made me propose to her every day for months before she finally said, 'Yes.' Life seemed perfect.

Then, one night at the Hippodrome, I got a phone call from the matron of the West London Hospital. My mother had been admitted for observation, and the surgeon had decided to perform an immediate operation. This had happened without my knowledge, because Pop did not want me to worry unnecessarily. Matron finished by saying, 'Can you come and see her as soon as possible? Your mother is very seriously ill.'

When I got to the hospital the next day, Matron took me aside and told me that Ma was dying. At the most, she might live another six months. She had inoperable stomach cancer. The tumours had spread throughout her body and there was nothing the surgeon or anyone else could do. Only then, with blinding clarity, did I realize what my mother meant to me.

When I went into the room where Ma was recovering from the exploratory operation, I put on as cheerful an act as I could muster, but I do not suppose it fooled her for a moment. Although she was exhausted, Ma, as always, gave me her best. She even managed to see a funny side to her situation.

I asked her if she needed anything. Ma told me she fancied an orange. She was reluctant to ask for one because, thanks to the needless extension of wartime rationing, even by Christmas 1947, citrus fruit was like gold dust. The only hope I had of finding oranges would be on the black market. I promised Ma I would bring her some fruit the next day.

I automatically gave two energetic performances, but my heart was not in them. During that dreadful evening, one of the stagehands, a tough cockney who was even more perceptive than the rest of that remarkable breed, remarked, 'You're not your usual cheery self, Mike. Anyfink I can do?'

I told him that my mother was dying, and asked him, 'Could you help me find some oranges? A couple of them would do.' I knew that many of the West End stagehands worked after the shows as porters in Covent Garden's all-night market.

'Don't worry about that, Mike. Me and me bruvvers will find you some Jaffas.'

My cockney friend was part of a family of 'garden' porters who worked the Hippodrome. His short, massively built father, the 'Old 'Un' as he was known, ruled his four witty sons 'wiv a rod of iron'. They loved him for it. These were the 'bruvvers' who would find me the oranges.

After the show I went straight to the all-night pub in the Garden, as arranged. It was a bitterly cold night and raining heavily. I was wearing my old trenchcoat. I sat in the pub until my chum arrived. At about two a.m., we set off on a tour of the fruit stores. Each brother slipped me a few oranges, which I stuffed into my trenchcoat. All of them refused payment or even the offer of a drink. Then it dawned on me that they were 'nicking' the fruit. 'What the hell!' I thought. 'It's for Ma.'

By three o'clock, my trenchcoat was bulging with juicy Jaffa navels, enough to keep Ma in oranges for a month. I tried to thank them, but my cockney friends would not hear of it. Just as I got to the end of the market my belt came adrift. A shower of oranges fell on the cobblestones and rolled embarrassingly around me. A young copper approached me. To my astonishment, he helped me pick up the fruit. He never spoke a word till I was once more trussed up like an overstuffed turkey. Then he said, 'Give your mum our love, mate!'

I left the Garden with tears running down my cheeks. I learnt later that the 'bruvvers' had spread the word around Covent Garden that help was needed. The oranges had not been nicked. They were donated by the market porters. So as not to embarrass me they had let me think they were stolen. Covent Garden was quite a place.

My mother was deeply touched by that generous gesture. Typically, she asked the nurses to distribute most of the fruit around the children's ward, but they saw to it that Ma got her share.

For me it proved again that the greatest kindness comes from those who work the hardest and can afford the least.

The show had now settled into its long run, a total of thirteen months. Most of the performances were full, with highly appreciative audiences. Acting on Ma's advice, I managed to make the most of life in spite of her illness, and Clementina was a great help to me, giving me loving support when I needed it so badly. When my mother was back in Barnes, I would go over as often as possible to give her all the news I could think of. Ma enjoyed every minute of that, especially when I told her that Clementina and I were going to get married.

'She's the one for you, Michael. Clementina is a lovely girl in every way.'

Amazingly, my mother still retained her invaluable sense of humour. Her greatest pleasure was sitting up in bed, watching people go by. As my parents' flat was on the first floor, almost next to Hammersmith Bridge, there was a constant flow of vehicles and people passing below her. Ma used to make up stories about them as they went by.

She had excellent eyesight and a splendid imagination. Several times a week, a funeral procession would cross Hammersmith Bridge on the way to Putney or Mortlake cemetery. Once, when I was there with her, a funeral went past, going back towards Hammersmith. It had passed the window about an hour earlier, proceeding slowly in the usual direction. Now it was returning, with the flower-decked coffin still aboard. Intrigued, Ma remarked, 'Either they got the day wrong or they went to the wrong cemetery or else the drive must have done someone the world of good.'

Ma hung on to life much longer than the doctors' prognosis had indicated. It was as though she was waiting for something to happen before she let go. Although she was in considerable discomfort, thankfully she was free of agonizing pain. Our splendid Indian physician saw to that.

Apart from my bouts of total effort in the show every night, I was writing material for Harry Secombe, who broadcast several times on *Variety Bandbox*, and who was performing in cabaret at various small night-clubs. Together, we dreamed up some original comedy, based on our mutual enjoyment of the movies. In one of the broadcasts our joint effort had clashed with the material the star of the show, Derek Roy, was using. Harry and I got a polite note from Derek's scriptwriter, Jimmy Grafton, pointing this out. He suggested we should discuss the matter in a friendly way over a drink at the Grafton Arms, a pub owned by his family.

In those days, the Grafton Arms was the epitome of public-house Victoriana. It only needed sawdust on the floor to make the illusion complete. The landlord, whom I had met once before through a mutual friend, lived over the pub and was anything but a traditional 'Mine Host'. An ex-major of airborne forces, this urbane, clever man was only a few years older than we were. The well-dressed City gent who came downstairs in response to the barman's loud shout of 'Jimmy, two blokes to see yer!' looked more like a Harley Street specialist or a successful banker than a third-generation publican.

He smiled and held out his hand, greeting us with the words, 'You blokes are being too bloody funny. You're upsetting the star of the show. I presume you two gentlemen drink?'

We nodded in unison.

'What will it be? Scotch, brandy, gin, or beer?'

'A pint of bitter, please,' we chorused.

Jimmy Grafton's smile broadened. 'A wise choice. At Grafton's we pride ourselves on our ales.'

'Cheers, mate.' Once again we spoke in unison, and downed the fine ale.

Jimmy laughed. It had an honest, fulsome ring to it. 'You two sound like twins. I'm an identical twin myself, so I should know.'

From that evening on, the Grafton Arms in Strutton Ground, Victoria, became our mecca.

Through Harry I met Spike Milligan. Spike was sitting on the edge of his bed wearing his army-issue woollen long-johns and army boots. This seemed to be totally in keeping with his persona. None of us thought it odd, especially as it was a cold day. But then all three of us had been through a long, bloody war and had experienced many strange sights, sounds and situations. War had not brutalized us, but it had made us expect the unexpected. Most people would have considered Spike unexpected.

Harry told me he had met Spike in Italy, before the Battle of Monte Cassino. Spike's battery had been over-zealous in hauling their Howitzer into a new emplacement on top of a cliff. The heavy weapon had run away from its gun-crew, trundled over the edge, and thundered down to land at the base of the cliff, close to another artillery unit, where Bombardier Secombe had dug in. Sergeant Milligan had been sent to retrieve the weapon. His first words to Harry were, 'Please may we have our gun back?'

Interviewers on radio and television often ask me to tell them about the early days of the Goons, expecting a flood of hilarious stories. Oddly enough, the specifics of being a Goon are hard to pin down. The enjoyment, and most of the shared laughter, came from being tuned in to each other rather than from outstandingly funny situations.

The Goon Show came about as the direct result of the evening Harry and I spent with Jimmy Grafton at the Grafton Arms. We took Spike to the pub to meet Jimmy, and later introduced Mine Host to the youthful Peter Sellers.

As fate would have it, I was the first of the Goons to make a hit in London's West End. I have a two-page centre-spread from *Picture Post* dated 5 November 1948, illustrated with pictures of myself and my chairback in action and headed 'What is a Goon?' In fact, I used a lot of my personal publicity to help my friends Harry Secombe, Peter Sellers and Spike Milligan to share the limelight as 'Goons', which was how we now thought of ourselves. Without our close friendship over those preparatory years there would have been no *Goon Show*. Yet the show itself did not emerge on BBC Radio until 1951. I would not have missed being with my good friends and *The Goon Show* for a fortune. So long live the Goons and all that we stood for, especially our dedicated attempts to show that 'sacred cows' *all* have hooves of clay.

Chapter Twenty-two

Palladium Nights

While I was courting Clementina, she took me to meet her ballet teacher, Mme Nadine Legat. This exceptional woman was the widow of Nicholas Legat, the most famous Imperial ballet master of the immediate pre-revolutionary era.

Nicholas and Nadine Legat had settled in England, where they set up an excellent ballet school. Unfortunately, the school's economic position was always precarious, especially after Nicholas Legat's death, because Nadine Legat was not a good businesswoman, and had surrounded herself with her large family, most of whom were living off the school fees. Even these were paid intermittently, because Mme Legat often handed out scholarships to promising pupils from impoverished families.

One of her few paying pupils had been Clementina. She had been born in East Africa and had been stranded in Britain with her grandmother when war broke out. Her grandmother, who adored her, owned a beautiful old manor house in Dorset, where they both lived in style.

By the time Clementina introduced me to her teacher, the Legat school had moved several times in the course of its checkered career and was then situated at Tunbridge Wells. Madame was a small, hyper-energetic woman with piercing eyes, her very presence demanding attention. Her powerful personality inspired the absolute devotion of her pupils, all of whom were in awe of her, and those of her students who had displeased her in some way were terrified of her.

Clementina's family had been badly shaken by our decision to marry, but my still small voice told me that in Madame I would find an ally. After an hour's conversation with her, which closely resembled a wartime Intelligence interrogation, she seemed convinced that I was neither a fortune hunter nor a sex-mad satyr. We also discussed my father's researches into the paranormal and the active part that I had played in them. Madame suddenly went over to the wall, turned upside down, and stood on her head. She remained in that position for about fifteen minutes without a break in our conversation.

At the end of the interview I knew that Nadine Legat and I would become friends. We remained so, with great affection on both sides, until her death some twenty years later.

Nadine Legat was one of the very few people, apart from my parents, who approved of our marriage, and Clementina had to fly out to Kenya to settle her family's doubts. Her father, Colonel Fred McCall, had forcefully voiced his objection to our marriage, 'I'll not have my daughter marrying a Peruvian clown.'

Faced with the *fait accompli*, my father-in-law, whom I later came to admire, respect and love, told his eldest daughter to make the best of a bad job. Fortunately, when we finally met, and he saw how much in love we were, he became my staunchest ally.

While Clementina was away in East Africa sorting out our marriage with her parents, I was working hard to turn my chairback routine into a commercial twelve-minute variety act, acceptable on the music-hall circuits around Britain. Monty Lyon got me work in night-clubs and several out-of-town dates but, by the time Clementina returned and we had set up our first home in Richmond, Surrey, we were £75 in the red. From then on it was quite a struggle to survive.

When we realized that Clementina was pregnant I was overjoyed that I would, once more, have a child of my own, but my practical Scottish wife was concerned that we were bringing our baby into a difficult world at a time when we were flat broke. However, the still small voice whispered to me to have faith, and that soon all would be well.

One weekend our finances had got into such a bad state that we were faced with the choice of huddling round the gas fire and living off two jacket potatoes and toast or spending the gas-meter money going down by train to see Mme Legat and enjoy her generous hospitality. We flipped a coin and Madame won.

The whole atmosphere cheered us up and, replete with over-generous helpings of Russian food and encouraged by everyone's good wishes, laughter and warmth, we nearly missed the last train back to London.

Saying a hurried goodbye to a Russian family is not easy. Russians always bid you farewell as though they are never going to see you again. Madame thoughtfully had provided us with packed leftovers, extra food, and a bottle of wine, all jammed into a capacious carrier-bag, along with a whole load of magazines to read in bed, where we spent a lot of our time keeping warm during that very cold winter.

As we pulled out of the station, and fell back against the hard third-class seats, to Clementina's horror we realized that this was a non-corridor train with no toilets, and it was a non-stop journey to Charing Cross. It would take nearly an hour to get there. My wife has never had 'long-range tanks', and very soon it became obvious that she would soon have to relieve herself.

One factor on our side was that we were the only occupants of the compartment. By now, Clementina was near to tears. I thought quickly, prayed, and inspiration came. I shouted, 'Old Mrs Henderson!'

My lovely pregnant wife looked at me as though I had gone raving mad but I was already rooting around inside the carrier-bag. As I pulled out the pile of magazines, I explained my plan. 'Mrs Henderson kept our local sweet shop in Folkestone. When I was a boy, I used to buy toffees there. The old lady always put them in paper-funnels, which she made out of old magazines. Your problem is solved, darling!' As I was speaking, I had torn out some sheets from *Life* magazine and was already fashioning a number of funnels out of its high-quality photogravure paper.

Clementina now got the giggles, which made things worse for her, but she realized that she had no alternative to my scheme. As fast as I made the paper funnels, my laughing wife filled them. Luckily, I was three funnels ahead of the game. As each one became full, I quickly substituted an empty one, neatly flipping the used funnel through the half-open window into the rain-swept darkness, as we sped through the Kentish countryside.

By now, we both were hysterical with laughter. Nevertheless, I am proud to say that neither of us spilt a drop. This unusual disposal-method was quite acceptable because even if we had been in a railway carriage fitted with a proper toilet, on British trains these opened directly on to the railway lines when they were flushed. Hence the notice: 'Please refrain from using the toilet when the train is standing in the station.'

We finished up, weak with laughter, and with only one spare funnel. God bless you, Mrs Henderson, wherever you are!

We were giggling all the way back by bus to our flat, and we fell asleep in each other's arms, still chuckling. One thing I learned that night: If you ever happen to find yourself in a similar dilemma, and there are magazines to hand, do not use anything but photogravure paper. Ordinary newsprint is, literally, a washout.

The next morning, I sailed through an audition and got the job. I cannot remember what it was, but it earned me enough to get us out of our temporary financial fix.

While I was out of work or, as we say in the theatre,

'resting', I decided to grow a beard. This made me look more mature and therefore I reasoned that it would give me more weight with the middle-aged people who made up the bulk of the music-hall audiences, and who seemed to resent younger comics. Whether I was right or wrong, the moustache and beard certainly seemed to give me more confidence on stage.

During this 'resting period', in June 1949, my mother had been suffering badly in the final stages of cancer. My mother loved Clementina dearly, and she was holding back from 'passing over' until she had seen our child.

Andrew Briger, Mme Legat's nephew, who was staying with us for the weekend, and I had rushed Clementina to the nursing home where she was booked as soon as her labour pains started. However, her labour continued for so long that she was hurriedly transferred to Kingston Hospital. As I was an over-anxious father, the matron advised me to leave, although I dearly wanted to see our child born. Reluctantly, I went home until the matron rang up to say that we now had a lovely little girl.

Andrew and I hurried over to Kingston and, within an hour, I was holding my new baby daughter in my arms. She was beautiful. Andrew had her in his arms as the godfather and, being Russian, wept happily. Marylla had given Clementina a hard time coming into the world but my exhausted wife agreed that it had all been worth it.

A week later, I took them both home by taxi, and as soon as possible we went over to see my parents. Ma was able to enjoy holding her new granddaughter. 'She's so beautiful,' she said, tears streaming from her eyes. 'You must both go down to the country and show off your lovely baby to some of Clementina's family.'

I did not like leaving my mother when she was so ill, but Ma insisted. So, with Clementina and Marylla in the sidecar of the motorcycle I now owned, we set off for Frome in Somerset to see Clementina's great-aunt, 'Granty Bertha'. This dear little old lady had been a splendid ally during our unpopular courting.

I telephoned to say that we had arrived safely, and was relieved to hear that Ma was comfortable. As she was asleep, I did not speak to her. While we were at Granty Bertha's, my brother telephoned me to say that Ma had died. 'Thank God, Bro, she just seemed to slip away. Pop needs us right now.'

Naturally we turned round and hurried home. All the way, I was cursing myself that I had not been there to help Ma over to the other side. Tony and Pop had been there at the end. My brother told me that our mother's last words were, 'I do so wish that you were both small babies again.'

This had puzzled him until I told Tony how much Ma had loved cuddling Marylla. Then, with Pop, we all went into the sitting-room and cried our eyes out. We all felt very close.

My mother's last months had been eased considerably with the help of a cheerful nurse. This down-to-earth northerner, Wynne, had been introduced to our family by an old friend of mine from wartime Bomber Command. My mother was very fond of her, and appreciated everything that Wynne did for her.

Being extremely practical, Ma had told my brother and me that when the time came for her to pass over, it would be a good idea for Wynne to stay on as housekeeper for Pop. We both respected her wishes, and there is no doubt that Wynne, who was a widow, helped my father adjust to his new life. A year later, they were married. From everyone's point of view this seemed a good thing. My mother was one of those rare people who saw clearly what had to be done and then did her best to see that it was done. It was typical of her to have been more worried about my father than about herself.

Strangely enough, from the moment my mother left her physical body, my working life took a sudden turn for the better. It was almost as though Ma was now pulling the strings.

Unexpectedly, a six-week season in West End cabaret

materialized, at the Embassy night-club in Mayfair. This was the result of a one-night appearance at the same venue. It ensured that the rent and grocery bills were paid. As my method of transportation was by motor-cycle and sidecar, the fuel bills for the nightly run to the West End and back were not too onerous, even though I was reduced to using black-market Methanol because the petrol ration was so paltry. Although the war had been over for four years, there was still no sign of any part of rationing being phased out.

While I was at the Embassy, that great clown Danny Kaye, who had been a smash-hit at the Palladium, often came into the club after his show. He always invited me to his table and we became friends, discussing comedy and its future role in the new craft of television, a subject on which we held exactly similar views. Danny loved Buster Keaton's work, and valued originality as his number one priority. He told me, 'Mike, I am fascinated by your act. You have developed a whole new style, based on the zany approach. But why not be more yourself? You are a good-looking guy, so why hide behind a beard and moustache?'

I explained my theory about needing to look older. Danny was unconvinced. 'One more thing, Michael, I notice that you are beginning to slip in some blue material to please the club audience. Take my advice, by all means be cheeky, but don't cater to the lowest element in your audience. Keep it clean!'

I liked Danny Kaye. I also admired him for his many professional qualities. He was an excellent actor and mimic and had taken London by storm at the Palladium. His parting remark to me before he returned to America was, 'You could play the London Palladium, Mike. The audience is a pushover compared to this lot, and you are doing pretty damn good here.'

Two months later, Danny's prediction was fulfilled. After my Embassy stint I was given a week's try-out at the Kingston Empire on a bill headed by Billy Cotton and his Band. The variety show was called *Wakey! Wakey!* which was Bill's opening catchphrase. I was so excited by this break, I forgot to eat properly and hurled myself into a whirlwind of rehearsal until I had altered my act from its cabaret form into a broader music-hall approach.

I 'knocked my brains out' on stage twice nightly. The audience loved it and Bill Cotton immediately offered me regular work on a long tour around Britain. I would gladly have accepted but, on Friday night, Val Parnell turned up at Kingston Empire with Monty Lyon. The act went particularly well that night, and a delighted Monty came back-stage to tell me that I was to open in two weeks' time at the London Palladium for a four-week season with the Ink Spots, the American singing act, who were topping the bill.

I was so excited and exhausted by trying to keep a bad bout of influenza at bay that I fainted. Monty drove me home and Clementina put me to bed, so I missed the Saturday show at Kingston. Nevertheless, Bill Cotton, who was a very nice man, paid me in full which he did not have to, 'No play, no pay' being the rule at that time. We certainly needed the money.

I always feel tense before a show, especially when it is a first night. On my first night at the Palladium I was close to running out of the theatre. Suddenly I felt my mother close to me. It was a very clear impression. The still small voice told me, 'This is for Clementina and Marylla. Everything's going to be all right. Just do your best.' Those words could have been Ma's.

At last, I found myself standing at the 'prompt' side of the stage. Harry Brack, the large stage-manager, a veteran of so many first nights at the Palladium, sensed my terror. He grinned at me and, in his deep, gravel voice, growled, 'Go on, Mike. They're a lovely lot out there tonight. Kick the shit out of 'em, mate.'

That did the trick. The reluctant jester was ready to do or die.

Harry Brack flashed the green light cue through to the

conductor and the orchestra went straight into 'Happy Days'. Four bars into the music I was on. I cannot remember a thing until I came off-stage, wringing wet, with thunderous applause and cheers ringing in my unbelieving ears. By the time I finished, walking off-stage with a sink-plunger on my head, impersonating a trolley-bus, the whole orchestra were laughing so much that the brass and woodwind sections could hardly play 'Happy Days'.

I was still trembling like a winning race-horse and rubbing myself down with a towel when a knock came at the dressing-room door. It was David Lewin, one of the top critics in the London press. He had a photographer with him. His beaming, spectacled face told me all I needed to know.

The next day, all the morning and evening papers gave me exciting write-ups. David Lewin devoted his whole column to me. A day later Monty rang me. 'I hope you are sitting down, Mike. Val Parnell has just told me. You are to open, five weeks from now, in *Folies-Bergère*. You are back at the London Hippodrome!'

Chapter Twenty-three

Four Musketeers

Folies-Bergère was like an up-market Windmill nude show, but it had cost a helluva lot more money to stage. The ingredients, a mixture of sex and show business, were the same. The scale was different. The ingenious scenic effects, giving the illusion of animated paintings, were reproduced straight from the Folies-Bergère in Paris by the French director.

It was the first time that this type of French nude show had been allowed in London by the Lord Chamberlain, and it caused a sensation. Only the speciality acts, which were slotted into the show between the spectacular scenes, could have been transported from any British music-hall without alteration. I was an example. Other than appearing in the 'walk-down' at the finale, I gave the same performance as at the Palladium the month before.

I was concerned that, as at the Windmill, the audience would include a high percentage of voyeurs. But, apart from the odd weirdo, the *Folies* audience turned out to be much the same representative mixture of the great British public that we had enjoyed in *Starlight Roof*. Moreover the *Folies-Bergère* was twice nightly, and the tickets were good only for a single performance. That made a tremendous difference.

Like Vivian Van Damm at the Windmill, Val Parnell was betting heavily on sex to put bums on seats, yet the show itself was not in the least bit bawdy in the way that comedians in the *Folies* could be in France, which was much more liberal about such matters, and in no way did it resemble the smutty, old-fashioned American burlesque shows. *Folies-Bergère* was colourful, spectacularly ingenious, and tastefully presented.

My act was successful for precisely the same reason that my Palladium debut had been a hit. The gallery first nighters were the 'secret ingredient', the uninhibited young audience, perched high up in the cheap seats, which were unreserved and for which they had to queue for hours on the opening night. Many of them were ex-servicemen and -women who apparently saw in me a kind of comedy in keeping with the fast tempo of their lives, which had been moulded by war. *They* made me a success, and for that I shall always be grateful to them. *Folies-Bergère* gave me the cachet and the professional reputation I needed to launch myself into a full-time show business career as an individual comedian with a completely different act.

Without that cachet in those days when young comedians were up against experienced old music-hall performers, each with his own distinctive style of comedy tuned by years of work in variety, a newcomer like myself had precious little chance of *quickly* building a professional reputation. I had been demobilized in March 1946, an out-of-work Shakespearean actor with a bad stammer. Yet, by a series of minor miracles, here I was co-starring at the *Folies-Bergère* with the princely salary of £75 a week.

Not counting my appearances at the Windmill, I performed my act in the West End of London for over thirty-two months, from 1947 to 1950, a total of over eight hundred performances. How's that for an example of 'guidance'? Which is what I shall always believe it to have been. Despite all my hard work, dedication and nail-biting anxiety, only the helping hand of my blessed Guardian Angel could have made it all happen.

One direct result of this good fortune was that we were going to be able to move from Richmond into a flat nearer the West End, but before we could do so Clementina was stricken with suspected appendicitis. She had been energetically spring-cleaning our Richmond flat prior to leaving it, when she was doubled over with excruciating stomach pains. The doctor was called. He examined her and immediately had her rushed by ambulance to Putney hospital where she was put under observation, pending an emergency operation.

Unfortunately, Clementina, during her spring-cleaning spree, had washed everything in sight, including her nighties, and the only dry garment she could find to wear was her brother George's old flannel pyjamas which, being a canny Scot, she was keeping for household cleaning.

When I dashed over to the hospital to see if there was anything I could do, Clementina asked me to get her some new nightwear. As we had to wait some time for the result of the tests they were giving her, I drove up to London in the old Wolseley car which we now used for transport, and bought my wife a nightie and a new dressing-gown from Jaeger. I then drove back to the hospital and gave these to Clementina, who put her brother's old pyjamas in the Jaeger box and gave it back to me, with instructions to keep the contents for cleaning-rags.

I was late, so instead of going home, I drove straight to the Hippodrome and, as usual, parked near the stage-door in Lisle Street, leaving the Jaeger box on the back seat of the car.

Halfway through the show, the stage-door keeper called me and asked me to come downstairs as there was a detective-sergeant to see me. I thought it was probably a request to do a free show for the police, which most artists did in exchange for being able to park, within reason, near their theatres.

Extending the Jaeger box, the detective, who was in plain clothes, said, 'Mr Bentine, the stage-doorman says that it is your car which has been broken into. I have just apprehended the suspect and charged him with breaking and entering your vehicle, a blue-grey Wolseley saloon, which is parked directly outside this theatre. Can you identify the contents of this box, which was in the possession of the suspect at the time I arrested him, and can you give me some idea of the value of the contents?'

'Certainly, officer. The Wolseley *is* my car, which with the permission of the theatre management I leave parked here during the shows, and the Jaeger box is mine. But there's only my brother-in-law's old flannel pyjamas in it which are virtually worthless.'

This last piece of information seemed to surprise the detective-sergeant.

'Nevertheless, sir, no matter what the contents of the box, Chummy is a third-time loser and I nabbed him red-handed. I must ask you to assist the police by giving a formal identification of your property in a court of law. You'll be hearing from the police in due course. Now, sir, if you will give me your full name and address . . . '

The next morning I went straight to the hospital to find Clementina talking to a smiling doctor. He greeted me with the words, 'You will be very relieved to hear that your wife is quite well. Mrs Bentine has not got appendicitis. We have discovered from our tests that your wife is pregnant. Congratulations!'

Our baby Marylla was now some six months old, and during this emergency was being cared for by our kind-hearted landlady, the mother of a close friend of Clementina. By this time I was quite capable of feeding, bathing and changing my baby daughter, having had plenty of experience with Elaine, who by now was growing up in France where her mother happily had remarried. From time to time I received news of her from my father, with whom Marie still kept in touch.

Several weeks later, I was summoned to appear as a material witness at Lambeth Assizes. The prosecuting counsel was a tall, gaunt man, not unlike my frightening prep-school headmaster. He wore half-moon glasses perched low on his hawk-like nose. His tone was brusque and emphatic: 'Mr Bentine, this box with the name Jaeger on it – does it seem familiar?'

'It looks like the box I had in my car.'

'Precisely! In fact, it *is* the box that was stolen from your car, and it was found in the possession of the defendant by the detective-sergeant. This is exhibit A.' The barrister looked around the court as though he had just made clear some obscure point of law.

'The contents of this box . . . Can you identify them?' He plunged his hand inside the cardboard box and swept up George's old pyjamas, exhibiting them to the court with the air of a magician producing a rabbit out of a top-hat.

The court sat in silence, trying to identify the shapeless mess of faded striped flannel.

'Mr Bentine, can you identify the contents of your box?'

I suddenly felt embarrassed. 'Yes, I can.'

'Ah! Then you do recognize them?'

'Yes, I do.'

The hawk-like counsel hovered over the incriminating evidence, savouring the moment before pouncing. 'Will you please describe them to the court?'

I gulped, my stammer rising in my throat. 'They are a pair of pyjamas.'

'Precisely. This pair of flannel pyjamas is exhibit B.' Once again, the prosecuting counsel showed the pathetic-looking garments to the court. 'Are they *your* pyjamas, Mr Bentine?'

'No, they are my wife's.'

'Your wife's pyjamas?'

'Well, when I say my wife's pyjamas . . . I mean that my wife had been wearing them. They are not my wife's actual pyjamas. They belong to my brother-in-law. They are his old ones.'

I now was floundering. There was silence in the court. Sensing that this was too good an opportunity to miss, the sarcastic old judge intervened. 'Mr Bentine, is your wife in the *habit* of wearing her brother's old flannel pyjamas?'

'No, sir. Not *usually*. My wife had got only this old pair of pyjamas to wear when she was rushed off to hospital.'

I stuttered as I explained the circumstances which had ended with Clementina being carted off to hospital. I had the distinct impression that all the women present thought that it was me who should have been in the dock and that I was probably a wife-beater as well.

I hurriedly continued, 'I bought her a nightie and a dressing-gown from Jaeger and took them to the hospital. That is why my brother-in-law's old flannel pyjamas were in the box. My wife was going to use them for cleaning-rags.'

The cynical old judge and the other members of the court were enjoying every minute of this case, but the shocked expression on the defendant's face when he realized that he was going to 'go down' for a two-year stretch for stealing such slim pickings graphically bore out the truth of that hoary old maxim 'Crime does not pay'! I felt very sorry for him.

By this time we had moved into our new home, a two-bedroom flat in Petty France, not far from the Grafton Arms. This made it much easier for me to get to the theatre, and I often crossed Victoria Street to meet Harry Secombe, Spike Milligan and Peter Sellers at Jimmy's family pub.

As a result of the publicity I had received and the piece in *Picture Post* about me, the term 'Goon' was catching on. Jimmy Grafton was a shrewd businessman and was not slow to use this publicity to act as leverage in his approaches to the BBC on our behalf.

Pat Dixon, who proved to be a splendid ally, was the most interested of all the BBC light entertainment producers, many of whom turned Jimmy down, without a hearing. Pat Dixon was well aware of the fact that, with the exception of Peter Sellers, who worked regularly on the *Ted Ray Show* as an impressionist, none of us had, so far, made any impact on radio, though Harry had appeared a few times on *Variety Bandbox*. Furthermore, Pat knew that while I had appeared many times in the West End neither Harry nor Spike had worked in West End shows, other than Harry's season at the Windmill in 1946 and Spike's appearance there with the Bill Hall Trio.

Nevertheless, Pat Dixon was an open-minded man and he agreed to meet Jimmy, to get to know us all and to see for himself what could be made out of our potential as a radio comedy team. Pat's vision and commitment were essential to the eventual broadcasting of *The Goon Show*.

In July 1950, when Marylla was thirteen months old, our son Stuart was born in Dorset. Clementina was staying with her family in the old manor house at Holwell, a few miles outside Sherborne.

Our new baby was definitely unwell, and the local doctors and consultants could not decide what was wrong. Little Stuart had great difficulty retaining his milk and was losing weight rapidly. He cried continually and was obviously in pain, so we decided to bring him up to London to see the paediatric specialists at Great Ormond Street Children's Hospital. However, they too were unable to prescribe a remedy.

Meanwhile, with the help of the McCall family, which still did not include my father-in-law, who was detained for some weeks in Africa, we set up a new home in Chelsea. This was rented accommodation in Cheyne Walk, which my new mother-in-law, Mary McCall, had found for us. It was part of a terrace directly facing the embankment.

The spacious accommodation of this tall house was arranged on five floors. The high-ceilinged, well-proportioned rooms were built round an imposing central staircase that wound its majestic way right up to the top bedrooms. The lovely house was airy, elegant, and full of light though in need of redecoration. Willing hands and a lick of paint soon rectified that.

The house also contained a British Restaurant on the ground floor. This was a hangover from wartime rationing which had continued throughout the stringent post-war socialist regime. The restaurant, which provided inexpensive bland food of the institutional school of British cooking, was an advantage to us as a family, because we had grown considerably in numbers. My in-laws included Clementina's mother and her two very pretty younger sisters, Rosamund and Theresa. That meant a lot of cooking so, institutionalized or not, the British Restaurant helped considerably.

We had to make our way in and out of the house past the crowded restaurant, and, at night, we had to keep an eye on a large boiler situated in the dank and gloomy bowels of a deep cellar. This was an essential operation because the furnace provided us with heating for the many old-fashioned radiators scattered about the five floors and also supplied all our hot water.

The house had a disturbingly eerie feeling in that dark, basement area, and I found that I had to steel myself to go down there to perform the necessary task. As the type of fuel we used was strictly rationed, we had to eke out our limited supplies of coal and coke, especially during the winter, by carefully regulating the operation of the basement boiler, so there was no escaping that depressing chore.

Stuart was still very sick and not expected to survive. My new mother-in-law consulted Mrs Boucher's Domestic Agency, which was famous for having the best nannies in Britain on its exclusive books and, as a result of this wise decision, Nurse Frances Barbara Forbes came into our lives. This proved to be one of the greatest strokes of good fortune that ever befell us.

Our small, super-efficient professional nurse, with her calm, gentle face and a will of iron, had been trained at Luton Children's Hospital where she had acquired her wide experience of seriously ill infants. After leaving the hospital, Nurse Forbes had become a children's nanny, but she hated that term. Frances Forbes was Mrs Boucher's Domestic Agency's star turn. In view of the fact that all her previous professional engagements had involved looking after the troubled and ailing children of the British aristocracy or the disturbed and often spoilt progeny of wealthy families, all of whom lived in large homes run by many domestic servants, we were told by Mrs Boucher that our theatrical family was very fortunate indeed to have obtained her services, which she emphasized would only be temporary.

Nurse Forbes came to stay with us for the very few weeks that the specialists had told us were left for our baby son's life. 'Nursie' remained with us as an integral, very much loved part of our family for nearly forty years.

Her first meeting with her small patient was momentous. She took his wasted little body into her arms and smiled lovingly at his pinched, tear-stained face. At the time, my small son had been crying for hours, yet from the moment Nursie held him, he stopped crying. She then said, 'There is nothing radically wrong with this dear little boy.'

Her words had a magical effect on Clementina, whose heart understandably was leaden with grief. My poor wife, who was nearly at the end of her endurance, cried, 'But, Nurse, the specialists have all said there is no hope for him.'

'Rubbish!'

Clementina told me later that Nursie then reached into her capacious hold-all, extracted several labelled medicine bottles and proceeded to mix up some mysterious concoction. She gently coaxed the exhausted baby, who had snuggled tightly against her, into swallowing a spoonful of her 'magic potion'. Shortly afterwards, our baby son settled into a deep sleep, blessedly freed at last from pain. Clementina told me it was the nearest thing to a miracle she had ever seen.

I must explain why I had not yet met our new nurse. My home-grown stage make-up, which I firmly believed I needed for my 'mad professor' act, was arresting. Heavily bearded and long-haired weirdos have now become a common sight, and nobody gives them a second glance. But in 1950 it was a very different matter. Most people were disturbed by the appearance of such *outré* individuals. Both Clementina and her mother were afraid that I might prove to be a deterrent to Nurse Forbes's desperately needed presence.

Consequently I was kept under wraps and discouraged from making an appearance until our new children's nurse had committed herself to a longer stay.

The circumstances in which I finally met her were unplanned. I had been performing in late-night cabaret and had slept till noon. I then had a leisurely bath, wrapped myself in a towel and stepped out on to the landing. In doing so, I nearly ran into Nurse Forbes.

For a moment I stood there indecisively, my mass of hair standing up round my head like a young Albert Einstein and my beard dripping with water. In the shock of this unexpected meeting, I had involuntarily released my grip on the bath-towel. It fell to the floor, revealing all.

Nurse Forbes did not even blink. With a warm smile, she said, 'You must be the father. Your son is doing splendidly. He is such a dear little boy.'

I hurriedly restored the towel round my waist, mumbled something appropriate to express my gratitude, joy and relief, and fled into our bedroom.

Clementina was there, unpacking some clothes. She looked worried. '*Please* don't let Nurse see you like that, darling.'

'Don't worry, love. I've just met her outside the bathroom.'

'Like that? You met her like that? But you're practically naked.'

'I *was* naked. The towel fell off.'

Hand to mouth, Clementina gasped. I reassured her, 'Nurse didn't turn a hair. I'm sure she'll stay.'

From the moment Nursie took charge of our two babies, they were in safe hands. After our son took his first, successfully retained, bottle of Ostermilk, in

Clementina's words, he 'swelled like a prune', reaching the proper body-weight for his age within a few weeks. A more contented baby would have been hard to find.

Her second achievement was when she discovered that Marylla was not progressing as well as she should. Marylla was another very contented baby, but evidently she was behind the normal childhood schedule for walking. By the time this became apparent, Marylla was nearly eighteen months old.

'I think you should get a specialist's opinion right away,' Nursie said.

Clementina went with her to Great Ormond Street, where our daughter was examined by an orthopaedic specialist who confirmed Nursie's diagnosis that Marylla was below normalcy in her muscular development, at least as far as her legs were concerned.

An excellent physiotherapist, Miss Mitchell, successfully treated our daughter's legs with electro-stimulation. Poor Marylla liked her therapist very much, but hated this treatment, which Miss Mitchell told her was 'Fairies running up and down your legs', but which felt to our child more like the stings of a horde of insects. She used to cry piteously when she had to go for these treatments. That was heart-rending, but the programme of physiotherapy worked extremely well, and soon Marylla was beginning to walk unaided. Nevertheless, our daughter never forgot the discomfort of those sessions.

By now, we all referred to the two babies, who looked like twins, as 'Fusty' and 'Gussy'. Pop had nicknamed Marylla *Fastidio*, which is Spanish for 'nuisance', before she was born, because Clementina had suffered from constant nausea.

When Marylla arrived, she was anything but a nuisance, being one of the sweetest of babies. Her nickname became shortened to 'Fasty', pronounced 'Fusty', and this stayed with her.

As soon as it became obvious that Stuart had got a healthy appetite and was lustily thriving under Nursie's care, we nicknamed him 'Gus', after the jolly, fat mouse in Walt Disney's *Cinderella*.

By this time, the *Folies* had come to an end, and I went on an extensive tour of the Moss Empire circuit, right round Britain. For some inexplicable reason, I always seemed to be booked in sequences such as Glasgow followed by Portsmouth, then north to Edinburgh with Bristol to follow, and so on, necessitating long journeys by car from one end of the country to the other. Oddly enough, I have found this to have been the identical experience of practically every other variety artist of that era.

This extensive driving meant that all these long road journeys had to be made on Sundays, in between engagements. If the artist went by train, he was faced with restricted Sunday rail services, often having to change at Crewe Junction, and wait for hours there, on the way up north or down south.

The motorways had not yet been built and the A roads were barely adequate for the post-war traffic. They were three-lane roads at best, with the central lane used as the passing-lane. In restricted visibility drivers took their lives in their hands if they chanced passing a slow-moving vehicle, of which there were many. Quite a number of my friends in show business were killed in this way.

Touring Britain was neither easy nor pleasant. Artists just had to make the best of it. As I was getting paid comparatively well for these variety appearances, I was able to afford small hotels, but most variety artists stayed in digs, i.e. private lodgings. These ranged from friendly and comfortable to miserably inhospitable, and the food they provided in the all-in weekly rate ranged from good home-cooking to inedible left-overs. The 'rule' seemed to be: the plainer the landladies' daughters, the better the digs, and the prettier the girls, the worse the lodgings.

During the 'hungry thirties', it was common practice for landladies to send their prettiest daughters to meet the Sunday trains in order to lure variety artists to their lodgings and sometimes their doom. Many landladies' daughters slapped paternity orders on visiting professionals. In these conditions it is hardly surprising that a list of good digs was a treasured possession. When I toured with Peter Sellers, who came from a family of old pros, we would stay at the best of these places.

Most of this touring took place in winter, when it always seemed to be raining. Grateful though I was for the work, which gave me the money to support my family, I missed them all very much. I tried to make up for my absence by returning home whenever possible loaded with presents, but it was a poor substitute for the joys of family life. I met many commercial travellers who had to pursue the same sort of life without the monetary rewards I was getting, so I counted my blessings.

Moreover, there were significant benefits connected with this phase of my life. First, there were the friendly and enthusiastic audiences. Second, there were the pros themselves. With a few notable exceptions, they were the nicest bunch of people I have ever met. Most of them were eccentrics like 'Monsieur' Eddie Gray, a wizard of a juggler. This 'red-nosed' comedian had been a long-time member of the Crazy Gang, the precursers of the Goons. Monsieur Eddie Gray was the only member of the Crazy Gang with whom I appeared on music-hall bills, and my friend, Dickie Henderson Junior, had already warned me about the sort of practical jokes he used to pull on unsuspecting victims.

We met at the Manchester Hippodrome where we were on the same bill. Off-stage, lacking a red-nose and obviously false moustache, Eddie Gray looked like any middle-aged businessman. As soon as I had sat down in the stalls, with my wild mop of dark hair and beard singling me out as a performer, a man wearing steel-rimmed spectacles with thick lenses approached me diffidently, his spiral-backed notebook and poised pen identifying him as a local journalist. He politely introduced himself. 'Mr Michael Bentine, isn't it? My name is Carstairs. I'm from the *Manchester Evening News*. Is it true that you have been taking drugs?'

The shock of that unexpected opening line threw me for a moment. Then I remembered Dickie Henderson's warning: 'To meet him, Mike, you would never suspect that Eddie Gray was not whatever he claims to be. He may represent himself as an undertaker looking for business, in which case he will measure you from head to toe, a policeman in plain clothes making inquiries into a case of rape, or the town medical officer who has to examine every artist on the bill, naked, due to a sudden outbreak of cholera. You never know what Eddie will be up to next.'

I took a deep breath. 'Monsieur Eddie Gray, I presume?'

He chuckled, his poker-faced expression relaxing into a warm smile. 'Someone has been talking about me, son. Pleased to meet you. I enjoyed your act at the Palladium. They tell me you are as barmy as I am.'

From that moment on we were good friends. I always enjoyed working on the same bills as Eddie Gray, and whenever I played Brighton, where he lived, he would pop in to see me. Practical jokers are not my favourite people because often there is a vicious streak in them, but with Eddie it was different. He had been through the worst of the First World War and had developed his odd sense of humour as a means of preserving his sanity.

I do not think he, or the rest of the Crazy Gang, had a vicious bone in their bodies. They just had the same sense of the ridiculous as we Goons had. We, too, could not resist taking the Mickey out of the pompous.

Eddie Gray was not the only eccentric I worked with in variety. Among many others, there was Vogelbein, a Danish animal-trainer, and his bears. At one time, Vogie, his wife and the bears all lived together in a converted bus, with the grizzlies kept in a cage at the back. My friend was fond of a drink and sometimes got carried away. He once pushed Joly, his fiercest bear, through the curtains behind me while I was in the middle of my act. With my over-sized, old-fashioned black dress-suit and my wild hair and beard, Joly probably mistook me for another bear, and she tried to nuzzle me. Even though she was chained, a 500-pound bear is an alarming sight, especially when she is standing at full stretch on her back legs, growling and pawing the air. The audience loved it, but then they did not know, as I did, that she had torn the head off a previous keeper!

Henry Vadden was another eccentric. He started his act by picking up in his teeth a metal table on which two pretty girl assistants were seated. His next stunt consisted of balancing a heavy cavalry sabre point-down on his forehead, which was heavily pock-marked from many similar performances, and then proving that the sword was sharp by letting it drop to the stage, where it remained quivering in the floorboards.

The finale of his act involved him spinning a full-size wooden cartwheel on the tip of a twelve-foot pole. He then knocked the pole aside and caught the heavy revolving wheel on a spike sticking out of the top of a crash-helmet on his head.

He surprised me one night by saying, 'Michael, you have had a scientific background. Can you tell me why I am having headaches?'

I told him that I thought his finishing trick with the cartwheel might have something to do with it. I had often watched this astonishing feat and wondered why it did not injure his neck.

Henry laughed, 'I didn't think that trick would fool you too, Michael. It's not a real cartwheel. An actual working cartwheel would weigh around one hundred and twenty pounds, maybe more. My wheel was specially made for me, without the steel rim. It's a fake.'

'How much does it weigh, Henry?'

'About ninety pounds.'

There were two daring trapeze artists who worked on stage without a net over a drop to the floorboards of at least fifteen feet. These two East Europeans spent the time between their evening shows sitting in their dressing-room working as cobblers, making fine boots and shoes.

There were pigeon acts, such as Edna Squire-Brown's. She worked nude on stage, with the intimate parts of her body covered by live pigeons. Rumour had it that one night some wag in the audience threw corn on the stage, causing the pigeons to leave their perches and ruining the act.

I met ventriloquists who, sitting alone in their dressing-rooms, often held long conversations with their dummies. Terry Hall, whose delightful dummy, Lenny the Lion, became famous on TV, told me a story which I am sure is true.

Another famous ventriloquist, Dennis Spicer, had been killed while driving at night on tour. His car had been in a head-on smash with another motorist, when one of the drivers had fallen asleep at the wheel. His dummy, 'Jimmy Green', was found in the wreck undamaged. About a year later, my friend Terry was having a drink in the bar of the theatre where he was working. He noticed that a couple sitting in the corner were pointing at him and evidently having a heated discussion. Terry overheard them.

'I tell you he *is*.'

'I'm sure you're wrong. He isn't.'

'Then I'm bloody well going to ask him.'

The man came over to the bar and stood next to Terry. 'Excuse me, mate. I wonder if you could settle an argument I'm having with the wife?'

'I'll try. What is it?'

'You *are* that ventriloquist who was killed in that car crash, aren't you?'

In Terry's words to me, 'It takes all sorts.'

During these long bouts of touring in variety I had to dash back to London to appear each Sunday in *The Goon Show*, which had now started its long run. At first these radio shows were called *Crazy People* and subtitled 'The Junior Crazy Gang'. We all violently opposed this title and subtitle, which had been dreamed up jointly by the BBC's publicity department and the *Radio Times*.

Not the least of these strong protests came from our producer and enthusiastic mentor, Pat Dixon, who had a stand-up row with the senior management over the billing. It was only with extreme reluctance that the BBC changed the title to *The Goon Show*.

These Sunday shows were enjoyable but they were hard work, especially on top of twelve shows a week in variety. I would start out from, say, Manchester, after the last show, and drive for six or seven hours on those old narrow A roads, arriving home at around six in the morning, and then have to be ready at the Aeolian Hall or the Playhouse Theatre to rehearse the show by ten o'clock.

Peter Sellers nearly killed himself when on a long journey south he fell asleep, ran off the road through a thick hedge and finished up in a ploughed field. Although his Triumph Gloria car was badly damaged, Peter fortunately got away with a few bruises but it shook him up badly. Nevertheless, he still played his part in the Sunday *Goon Show*. That is how much we all believed in what we were doing. The Goons really were like the Four Musketeers, and it is hard to feel closer to each other than that.

Chapter Twenty-four

An American Witch-hunt

The experience I had acquired by touring, and from working in the two long-running Hippodrome shows, helped in my second Palladium season. The bill was topped by Nat King Cole, one of the most enduring artists ever in show business, and his warm off-stage personality was exactly the same as his public image.

Once again I was surprised by the enthusiastic response from the Palladium audience. Danny Kaye, who was back in Britain on tour, told me that the Palladium was his favourite venue.

When I confessed how apprehensive I always felt before going on stage, Danny said, 'If you don't have that godawful hollowness in the pit of your stomach, Mike, and the feeling that you'd rather be anywhere else at that moment, including sitting in the electric chair waiting for someone to pull the switch, there's no boost to your adrenalin. Without that extra pzazz, there is no projection. With no projection, you give no performance. No matter how laid-back you appear to be, you have to project your personality in order to get across to the audience. That is part of the price you pay for being an artist. You have to accept that or get out of the business.'

Danny Kaye was a perfectionist who rehearsed till he dropped. His next words summed up his philosophy as an artist. 'It's always the same. You'll never escape from that tension, Mike, and it gets worse as you get older. The guy who says he never feels nervous before going on stage is either a liar or an asshole. He sure as hell isn't a performer.'

How right he was. Once I am on stage I feel fine but just before I go on I have to summon up every drop of spare adrenalin I have got. I am literally in a blue funk until I get out front. Practically every artist I know, of either sex, is the same.

Twin bookings for the United States, by Ed Sullivan for TV and by Jenny Grossinger, who was the owner of the Grossinger's holiday resort in the Catskill Mountains, were as unexpected as they were welcome. I would be the first Goon to play America. I also learnt from Monty Lyon that Lou Walters, a Broadway night-club owner, wanted me to play his new club, the Gilded Cage, which was opening shortly.

As Nursie was now in charge and seemed happy to stay on with us, it was practical, if heart-wrenching, for Clementina to leave the children and accompany me on this new adventure. Our large maisonette in Cheyne Walk was warm and secure, and fortunately various members of our family were staying there, so Nursie would not be alone.

Today when young British artists go to America they are preceded by a barrage of television, films and/or records. Prior to their appearances, the Beatles, the Rolling Stones, the Who, Elton John, Dudley Moore, Marty Feldman, John Cleese and the Monty Python team, Benny Hill and Patrick Macnee were all preceded by a massive exposure on the media *before* their arrival in America. Consequently, they were welcomed in the United States with open arms.

By contrast, Terry-Thomas, Tommy Cooper, Max Bygraves and I, being completely unknown to American audiences, were all greeted with a deafening silence. We had to prove ourselves. It was not easy.

Back in the early 1950s the average American believed

that all British people spoke a strangulated form of 'upper crust' English, interjecting every few words with 'Jolly old' and 'Don't yer know!', addressing everyone as 'Old chap', 'My good man' or 'My dear fellar'. Most Americans, especially New Yorkers, did not understand a word we spoke. The reason was simple. In Britain we had been bombarded by a continuous flood of American movies and records. In comparison, the reciprocal English media traffic across the Atlantic had been minimal.

The Americans had not acquired the same familiarity with our language as we had with theirs. It took me three appearances on the Ed Sullivan show before I started to make an impression. Except with the pros, such as Ray Block and his Orchestra, who provided the musical backing for the show and who fell about laughing at what I did, I had to fight every inch of the way. I was not alone in this. Norman Wisdom, Terry-Thomas, Jimmy Jewel and Ben Warriss, three top British acts at that time, all had the same tough experience. Only Tommy Cooper, who was universal in his unique visual comedy appeal, made an immediate hit on US television.

We flew to America in September 1951 in one of the BOAC's Boeing Stratocruisers, a four-engined, propeller-driven civil airliner conversion of a Boeing B-29 bomber, similar to the one that had dropped the atomic bombs on Hiroshima and Nagasaki. The airliner boasted two decks, with a downstairs bar, and was equipped with sleeper-couchettes like large luggage-lockers, set overhead in first class. We flew tourist class, which in those days was far less cramped than economy class is today. The trip to New York took sixteen hours, with two refuelling stops en route, the first at Shannon in the south of Ireland and the second in Nova Scotia.

The BOAC pilot told me, 'We only made it in such good time because we had a sixty-knot tail-wind.'

Our arrival in America had a considerable impact on the immigration authorities. My long curly hair, beard and moustache, plus my dark leather trenchcoat only needed a 'prop bomb' to convey the unmistakable impression of instant anarchist. To aggravate matters we arrived in the middle of the McCarthy witch-hunts for covert Communists and fellow travellers.

The fair-haired squeaky-clean US immigration officer fixed me with his piercing blue eyes and asked me bluntly, 'What are your political opinions, Mr Bentine?'

I was surprised by this question and stammered, 'I haven't really got any.'

His mouth tightened. 'You mean you're an anarchist?'

'Good lord no! If I have any political opinions, I suppose they are a kind of liberal conservatism.'

The immigration officer looked at me in stunned disbelief. He passed his hand through the stubble of his cropped hair. He was obviously trying hard to reconcile my wild appearance with my stated political persuasion. He probed deeper. 'What are you doing over here, Mr Bentine? You have a temporary, restricted working visa.'

'I've come to America to do some television appearances. I'm a comic.'

The officer's eyes bulged. For a moment he was speechless. Then he turned to his colleague in the next booth. 'Christ Almighty, George, this one actually admits he's a Commie.'

I hastened to say, 'I am not a communist. I meant to say that I am a comedian. I'm working in television for Ed Sullivan.'

Instantly the atmosphere changed. With a welcoming smile we were whisked through Immigration and waved past Customs. The magic words 'Ed Sullivan' unrolled an invisible red carpet.

Outside the airport arrival building there was a final irony. We had arrived in the middle of a barbers' strike. The parading pickets were carrying placards with the words 'Barbers demand a fair wage' and 'Hair cutting is an art'. They looked at me in undisguised horror. One of them grinned and shouted, 'Hey fellah, you want I should give you an estimate?'

I knew then that I would enjoy New York.

The tall, impressive hotel commissionaire warmly welcomed us with obvious appreciation of the cool loveliness of my English Rose wife, and the efficient bell-captain saw to it that our copious luggage was handled with consummate ease. The open sesame of the name Ed Sullivan apparently had preceded us.

The reason for this became obvious when I saw my good friend Hans Holzer, grinning happily behind the welcoming hotel staff. I had first met him in London in 1949. Being Austrian by birth and upbringing, he embraced us both with European ardour. 'Welcome to New York, my dears! I've already told the hotel director that you are really the Peruvian Ambassador to Britain incognito. I also told him that you were appearing on the Sullivan show. He instantly offered to give you a doubly reduced rate.'

As we had a few days free before the first Ed Sullivan show, Hans rushed us around New York on a whirlwind familiarization tour. Being a journalist with his own news service, our friend seemed to have access to almost every segment of New York's seething life. He had provided us both with press cards which enabled us to sail through police cordons, security guards, and any other official deterrent or hindrance as, wide-eyed with wonder, we followed our unstoppable friend in his progress around all the places in New York 'where the action was'.

Hans suavely introduced Clementina as 'Lady Bentine of the London *Times*'. This earned my wife immediate respect. I even heard one security guard mutter to another, 'Now there's a real lady, and a great piece of ass, too.' I have seldom heard a more sincere compliment.

Hans always says he loathes Manhattan, which he finds claustrophobic after London, Paris and Vienna, but he freely admits that it is profoundly stimulating, especially Broadway. Judging by the numbers of great American plays and musicals that have been generated there, I wholeheartedly agree with him. This certainly applied to New York in 1951.

Nevertheless, Manhattan is also deeply disturbing, and although I find much friendliness among New Yorkers, at first strangers, especially foreigners, tend to find themselves cloaked in a shroud of suspicion which they have to pierce before the average citizen's warmth becomes apparent.

One morning, when I was still asleep after a late-night rehearsal for my appearance at Lou Walters's new night club, Clementina set out for a brisk walk in Central Park. As she strolled through the lonelier parts of this oasis in the middle of teeming concrete canyons, a mounted policeman galloped up to her. As he reined in beside her he growled, 'What the hell do you think you are doing, young lady?' Obviously my conservatively dressed wife was not a hooker. Clementina was surprised at being summarily accosted by a cop. 'I am just enjoying a walk in your lovely park.' Her accent was unmistakable, her smile innocence itself.

'Not here you ain't, lady,' replied the policeman and, chatting in the friendliest fashion, he accompanied her out of Central Park into the safety of Park Avenue. His parting advice was worth recording, 'We are proud of our Central Park, mam. But, for nice people like you, lady, it just ain't healthy. De park is strictly for de boids.'

Clementina also distinguished herself when she was looking for a hairdressing salon on Fifth Avenue. She had previously singled out an establishment with an imposing façade of shining black marble framing its front window, in which there were several wigs on stands and a small selection of make-up, tastefully displayed. Having arranged to meet me there later, Clementina entered the salon.

She was greeted by a suave, immaculate gentleman dressed in a well-cut tailcoat. Accompanied by soothing background music, he addressed her, 'Good morning, madam. And how may I be of service to you?'

'I'd like a shampoo and set, please.'

The atmosphere curdled. 'This, madam, is a funeral parlour.'

Seeing her blushing confusion and recognizing her English accent, the manager realized that his visitor had made a genuine mistake. He immediately softened.

Clementina told me later, 'When I explained that I had arranged for my husband to come and pick me up there, the manager was most understanding. To pass the time he showed me around the place. After all, one day I could become a valued customer. It was most interesting. They have different grades of funerals at all prices. He showed me the large variety of caskets, ranging from plain pine to ornate, carved mahogany, with handles from brass to gold-plate. They have marvellous names for them such as the Princess, the Duchess and the Empress, which the manager said was the top of the line. Apparently you can be buried in a full suit of clothes or, more economically, in just a half-suit. They cater to all budgets. The wigs and make-up in the window are just a tasteful way of showing that the staff are highly skilled in restoring badly damaged faces. I had no idea what a complicated business it all was.'

From the hotel we moved to a small apartment which Hans had found for us on East 54th Street, overlooking the new United Nations building. It was called the Beaux Arts Apartments and was a 'good address', which Hans told us was important to have in New York. It was also reasonably priced and well run.

One morning I was woken by the door-bell. As it was not yet seven o'clock, I cursed and trundled sleepily across the living-room. At the door were two tall, powerfully built men wearing identical dark suits and hats who flashed some sort of identification at me and forced me back into the room.

I did not catch what one of them said. For a shocked moment, I thought they were gangsters intent on robbery, especially as one of them had frisked me to see if I was armed. This was quickly done as I do not like sleeping in a full suit of pyjamas and usually wear only a long pyjama-top or a short night-shirt.

I spoke as calmly as possible, 'Look, fellahs, my wife and I are British. We're not worth robbing.'

This nonplussed the original spokesman. 'Mr Bentine, we have no intention of harming you. We are FBI agents and we only wish to ask you a few questions.' Both the big men looked askance at me, weighing me up. I did my best to keep my temper, deliberately taking a deep, steadying breath. 'In that case, gentlemen, fire ahead.'

While one of them watched me warily, the other continued, 'Mr Bentine, did you send a letter to Professor Albert Einstein, addressed to the Institute of Advanced Study at Princeton?'

'Yes, I did. It was written by my father who is a scientist. I believe it contained some notes on his personal attitude to the Professor's new theory of the unified field, which is still in its formative state.'

The duo looked at me unblinking, evidently still assessing my potential as a threat to state security. The spokesman then asked me the 64,000-dollar question. 'Mr Bentine, specifically what are you doing in the United States?'

At this juncture, we were joined by Clementina who, hearing the sound of voices, had slipped a dressing-gown over her nightie and had stepped out of the bedroom to find out what was going on. Even first thing in the morning, my young wife looked delightful. Her air of puzzled innocence immediately defused the air of tension. I hurriedly explained the presence of the two FBI agents, and they formally introduced themselves. Clementina was intrigued to meet two members of the legendary FBI face to face.

Turning back to me, the spokesman asked again, 'What precisely are you doing in New York, Mr Bentine?'

'I am working for Ed Sullivan.'

Once again the magic words 'Ed Sullivan' caused a transformation in official attitudes.

'You mean *the* Ed Sullivan?'

'*The* Ed Sullivan.'

'Can you prove that, Mr Bentine?'

'I can show you my contract.'

'I mean, could you speak with Mr Sullivan by phone?'

'Right now?'

'Right now, Mr Bentine.'

I shrugged resignedly and rang the number Ed Sullivan had given me in case of any problems. I felt this could be classified as a problem.

Ed Sullivan answered the phone and immediately recognized my voice. I told him why I was calling. I give him full marks for his calm reaction. After all, it was only 7.15 a.m.

'The FBI? There must be some mistake, Mike. Put them on to me.'

I handed over the phone. The following one-sided conversation took place. I had to imagine the Sullivan end of the dialogue. During it, the FBI agent almost stood to attention. 'Yes, Mr Sullivan. No, Mr Sullivan. Yes, sir, we are quite happy that you vouch for Mr Bentine. Certainly, Mr Sullivan. Yes, sir, I certainly will give your regards to Mr Hoover. Goodbye, Mr Sullivan.'

The agent replaced the receiver and nodded to his colleague. 'I'm sorry that you've been troubled, Mr Bentine.'

'Oh, that's all right, gentlemen. I'm glad you got things straightened out. How about some coffee?'

Both agents were relieved that I had taken the matter in this way. As far as Clementina and I were concerned it had been a surprising rather than a disturbing experience, and we both could see the funny side of it. The agents joined us for a cup of coffee while I regaled them with some stories about British show business. On leaving, the original spokesman of the FBI duo asked me one last question, 'Could you get us tickets for the Sullivan show?'

Ed Sullivan chuckled when I told him the details of our

inadvertent brush with Federal law. 'Next time, Mike, try to call me a little later in the day.' He was a nice man and treated me well even though I did not turn out to be the smash hit he had expected. 'I guess it will take some time for the American public to catch up with you.' He was right.

This was at the end of 1951, and it was not until 1969 that my style of humour became acceptable in the United States. Nevertheless, many professional comedians and comedy writers saw and liked what I did, and I was invited to remain in America.

Having seen a write-up in Britain stating that I was 'in the dollars' in New York, Peter and Spike phoned me to ask whether I was returning to *The Goon Show*, which was soon due to start its next season. They both urged me to return as soon as I could because, in their words, 'You are so much a part of the Goons and your ideas and voices are so important to the show.'

I felt an intense loyalty to my friends, and told Spike and Peter that I would be back. I telephoned Dennis Selinger to confirm the new contract for *The Goon Show*.

Meanwhile, Clementina and I had grown to accept New York for what it was. As in every other great city, the material contrasts between the rich, the average hard-working citizen and the poor were clear for all to see. We were shocked to see how many tragic alcoholics haunted Third Avenue.

But here is an example of how New Yorkers, beneath their thin shell of streetwise toughness, can be warm and generous. I was buying some supplies from a delicatessen which was run by a tough Irishman whom Hans had recommended. A tramp – or, as the Americans would say, a 'hobo' – lurched through the door and stood swaying against the counter, half-drunk. It was a bitterly cold winter's day, and he was wearing an ancient overcoat, an old khaki scarf and frayed mittens. He obviously had not bathed for some time. His eyes were watery and unfocused, and his unshaven face was gaunt with hunger. My heart went out to him, but before I could do something practical for him, the Irishman addressed him as though he was a valued customer. 'Good morning, sir. What can I do for you today?'

The pathetic alcoholic croaked out, 'Could you make me a sandwich?'

When the substantial sandwich was ready, the Irishman carefully wrapped it in greaseproof paper and handed it over.

The tramp grunted his thanks and lurched out of the door.

The burly Irish manager grinned at me. 'You was about to make a big mistake and give him money. Sure, it would have only gone on more booze. Dat poor devil needed to *eat* sometin'. If not, dey don't last long around here, specially in de winter! It's as cold as a witch's tit. Now, Mr B, what was it you was wantin'?'

I liked that Irishman. He told me he could not understand why better provision for the destitute was not undertaken by such an advanced, wealthy society as the USA.

In 1951, we were fortunate in having friends among most of the ethnic groups in New York. All these friendships had flowered through my contacts in show business, which on the whole seems to be almost free of the racial prejudices that trouble the rest of the world. I am certain this is because of the many shared experiences in the stressful conditions that our profession often generates. Mutual difficulties and hardships quickly overcome the idiocy of xenophobia, which is largely generated by ignorance and indoctrination.

One close friend, Johnny Puleo, from the Borrah Minevitch Harmonica Gang with whom I had twice worked the Palladium, was a very small and marvellously funny Italian comedian. His warm personality and lightning wit drew me to him like a magnet. In this I was by no means alone. When you mention his name to anyone who knew him they seem to glow with pleasure.

Johnny took us to dinner in Little Italy and introduced us to some of his wide circle of friends. We ate magnificently in a typical Italian restaurant, deafeningly cheerful and warmly welcoming, which looked and felt as if it had been taken straight out of an American movie. Our host was an elderly, white-haired Sicilian of great charm. He was particularly taken with Clementina's English Rose qualities, and openly expressed his homage and appreciation. We all got along famously and the dinner was a hilarious success. I was particularly moved by the way each of his guests, young and old, expressed their affection and respect for him by kissing his hand and prefixing his name with the word 'Don'.

It was only when we were being driven back in our host's luxurious limousine that Johnny told us we had been privileged to meet the 'Capo di Capos' of the Sicilian Mafia families. We had accepted our host as a kindly, aristocratic philanthropist of the old school. The truth shook us considerably.

One magical moment for me was when we went to lunch at Lindy's restaurant for the first time. Like Sardy's, Lindy's was a rendezvous point for many show folk. There was a friendly rivalry between these two establishments over which of them made the best cheesecake and strudel. As far as I was concerned, they both won.

I tried to catch the eye of the head-waiter to get a table in the packed restaurant. Suddenly I heard a yell of 'Mike Bentine' coming from one of the booths. All eyes turned towards Judy Garland who had jumped up and rushed across to greet me. I had played a two-week season at the Liverpool Empire with this multi-talented artist only a few months before. Warm and wonderful Judy clasped me to her diminutive body and gave me a smacking kiss.

At the same time, I felt myself being banged on the back by Max Bygraves, with whom I had shared variety bills. I could hear the buzz of conjecture rising from the luncheon crowd as they tried to figure out who the mysterious bearded weirdo might be.

Our wide range of experiences confirmed my belief that the reinforced-concrete maze of this great city is best explored in the company of a friend who is a streetwise navigator and can provide the thread of local knowledge that ensures your safe passage in and out of the labyrinth.

The same thing applied to New York show business. By this time my original agent, Monty Lyon, had sold his agency to Lou and Leslie Grade. Dennis Selinger had stayed on, and handled me and Peter Sellers, among others. The Grade Agency itself was just starting up in New York, but as yet did not possess the know-how for placing British artists in the best possible setting for their acts. In America, and especially in New York, it was a case of horses for courses. A comedian could do very well in one club and only get by or 'bomb' in another just across the street. It depended on the clientele who frequented that particular club or who liked the ambience of a certain theatre.

When Hans and I saw the Gilded Cage, which was brand-new, without any acquired atmosphere and decorated in the kitsch style of the Gay Nineties, complete with a life-size doll of a girl on a swing, we both sensed that it would be wrong for me. The ideal spot for me would have been the Blue Angel, a much smaller and more intimate club in the same Broadway area, which catered for a much younger clientele.

However, Lou Walters, who had booked me after seeing my act at the Palladium, was so certain that I was right for his night-club that he would not release me from my contract. At the dress rehearsal, my act went over very well with the small band and the show-wise waiters, and it was a big hit with Ben Blue, a veteran comedian in the same show, whose speciality was a very funny 'mind-reading' act dressed as a Swami.

But as Ben Blue summed it up, 'American audiences generally are not as quick on the uptake as the ones in your British music-halls. Remember, Mike, a lot of them don't speak English as their first language. Their ears are not tuned in to what you are saying. So, you'll have to explain what you are going to do, and then do it. That's what I do in my Swami act. Stay with it, Mike! It's only a question of a slightly different presentation. Your Terry-Thomas had the same problem at first, until he exaggerated his whole personality into a caricature of what we Americans believe is a typical English gentleman.'

Witty and shrewd, Ben Blue proved to be a good friend, and his excellent advice was right. Lou Walters did not hold it against me that I had not fulfilled his expectations and we parted on very amicable terms.

By my third shot on the Ed Sullivan show I had changed my whole approach to the studio audience and had slowed down considerably. The result was that it went exceedingly well. Ed asked me if I had any more material ready to present, but I explained that I would not be happy to use untried ideas and would rather return to England and work up new material for presentation later on American TV. He understood my reluctance to go ahead without due presentation, and we, too, parted on the best possible terms.

The next morning I received a cable from my brother which said that Wynne, Pop's second wife, had died suddenly of a heart attack. I immediately telephoned Tony, who told me that our father was desolate, crushed by this second stroke of misfortune so soon after Ma's death. Tony thought the best thing for Pop to do was to fly out to us as a stopping place *en route* for Peru, where we both knew that the loving arms of our South American family would help him get over this latest blow.

We had moved into a larger apartment on the East Side only a few days before, so we were able to offer Pop comfortable accommodation for his stay in New York. I met Pop at the airport. He looked pale and exhausted. A bitterly cold spell had wrapped Manhattan in a freezing fog, and it was not doing my father's sensitive chest much good. We put him to bed and he slept the clock round.

I was very worried by his psychological condition. He

was letting himself drift down into a deep depression and unless we did something quickly, he would soon lose what remained of his will to live. After bringing in a doctor, who was a friend of the ever-helpful Hans, he agreed with Clementina and me that the best course of action was to bundle my father on to the next plane to Peru.

Pop became very emotional and pleaded with us to let him stay, but Clementina and I knew damned well that if we weakened he would die in New York within a few days. The next day, we bundled him up as warmly as possible and drove him to the airport. Suddenly he brightened up. He was thin and shaky but his spirits were rapidly rising. Once again, his old fascination with flight and aeroplanes was stirring. A kindly air hostess took charge of him and, after an emotional farewell, he was taken out to the plane in a wheelchair.

As we watched the large Boeing airliner start up its engines and taxi out into the darkness, I turned to Clementina. 'I hope to God we are doing the right thing.'

'So do I,' said my wife.

Twenty-four hours of worry and anxiety followed until at last we got a phone call from Lima. We were told that Pop was fine and was very excited to be back with his Peruvian family. Apparently twelve of them had gone to meet him at Jorge Chavez Airport at 2.40 in the morning. A week later, a letter arrived from my father thanking us for doing the right thing. Pop was to enjoy a full year of his family's love and devotion before he felt 'homesick' enough to return to Britain.

One experience that underlines the contrast between London and New York occurred when I was driving down Broadway in the company of Chaz Chase, one of my friends from *Folies-Bergère*. Unknowingly, I had exceeded the speed limit, which was then lower than it was in London.

A wailing siren announced our pursuit by a police car. I pulled over to the side of the road and waited for the cops to arrive. They were two very large policemen, armed with holstered revolvers and night-sticks. As one walked round the car, inspecting the tyres for excessive wear and noting down the number, the other stood on my side of the vehicle. When he finally spoke it was with a heavy Irish-American accent, 'All right, lead-foot, where's de fire?'

'I'm sorry, officer. I'm a stranger in town and I had no idea I was exceeding the speed limit.'

'Let me see yer droiver's loicence, sorr!'

I handed my international driving licence over. It seemed to be in order, but he still fined me then and there. It was something like $25, and I had the feeling that this was not strictly legal.

I was about to protest when Chaz muttered, 'Pay it, and don't ask for a receipt, Mike!'

The whole incident had an unpleasant feeling about it. I felt a lingering resentment at the policeman's bullying air.

A month later, unbearably homesick for the children, we were back in Britain, and the sharp contrast between the behaviour of the police on each side of the Atlantic was clearly demonstrated to me.

In my old Wolseley 14 saloon, I was driving down the Mall towards Buckingham Palace, admiring the approaching troop of Horse Guards who were trotting along on the other side of the road. In their shining helmets and long riding cloaks, with their swords sheathed beside their saddles, they made a splendid Ruritanian picture in the winter sunshine.

As I came abreast of them I slowed down so as not to alarm the horses with my noisy engine, which was rapidly coming to the end of its life. Suddenly, the whole exhaust assembly, which was red-hot, broke away from the engine manifold, crashed to the ground, rolling across the road right under the forelegs of the leading black stallion.

The startled horse reared up, throwing off its unsuspecting rider, who was the troop sergeant. He clattered on to the tarmac, his plumed helmet flying off into the path of a motorcyclist. The rider swerved and came off, tumbling towards the kerb as his bike skidded horizontally into a tree. Another troop-horse reared up, and a second Guardsman crashed to the ground, causing a car on the other side of the road to skid and clip the kerb, spinning the vehicle right round. To cap all this mayhem, an elderly lady who was waiting to cross the Mall screamed and fainted. I had pulled into the kerb and was staring goggle-eyed at the mischief my glowing exhaust-pipe had wrought.

As I started to get out to assist the fallen, a large British bobby held up his hand to halt the flow of traffic, and proceeded purposefully across the Mall towards me. He stopped beside my car and surveyed it. He fixed his eyes on my sweating face. Then he spoke, with all the majesty of the law in his words, 'We're not being very clever this morning, are we?'

I had come home to rejoin the Goons in the new series but was shocked to discover that another actor, whom I had never heard of, had been brought into the show without anyone telling me about it.

The BBC Light Entertainment Department treated me as a bloody-minded heretic when I objected to our close-knit team being enlarged without any prior consultation with me.

I decided to pull out of *The Goon Show* now that it had changed from our original conception of it. However, despite my desire to withdraw from the show as amicably as possible, someone in BBC Light Entertainment made a major issue of my leaving. Influenced by the Corporation's press release about the circumstances of my leaving *The Goon Show*, the national newspapers made quite a meal of it. The whole thing was blown up out of all proportion to the simple truth of the matter, and I soon found myself being cast as the villain of the piece. The whole business became most unpleasant and upset us all.

Luckily, I had plenty of work to occupy my mind and, apart from many music-hall appearances, I was able to go ahead with a project that was very dear to me. This was a remote-controlled children's puppet show about friendly extra-terrestrials.

I had noticed that every film about outer space or extra-terrestrial life invariably depicted all alien intelligences as being intensely hostile to us Earthlings and intent on taking over our world. These sensationalized movies seemed to me to cater to the hatred and mistrust of other races that had been the cornerstone of the Nazis' poisonous doctrine.

To combat the possible effect on young minds of this sort of pernicious racist propaganda, I devised, designed, and wrote a thirteen-part children's series about three friendly little aliens from outer space, cheerful ambassadors from the planet Bumble, who landed in their flying-saucer in the garden of an absent-minded professor of astronomy, with the express purpose of getting to know the children of the Earth, and learning how to play their games. *The Bumblies* had been born. They were the forerunners of *ET*, that enchanting extra-terrestrial puppet character whom Steven Spielberg made world-famous, some thirty years later.

Even now my short series of eleven-minute black and white puppet films are still fondly remembered by millions of adults who were children at the time. That is another example of the extraordinary power of television to impress images, concepts, and ideas on the minds of viewers, especially the young ones.

Despite their success, *The Bumblies* were never repeated, probably because I owned the films, not the BBC. In fact, I nearly went bankrupt making them, and I never recovered their cost. The BBC paid me £40 for each of the thirteen programmes, a total payment of £520 for the use of the whole series, which is approximately what *each* programme actually cost me. Fortunately, I was able to make up the deficit by working doubly hard on the music-hall circuit.

Even with this financial drawback, the Bumblies were well worth the great effort required to put them on film.

Angelo de Calferta, a very talented Spanish sculptor, modelled the attractive puppets from my original three-view designs. Richard Dendy, a well-known special effects expert, moulded them in Latex rubber, and his resident engineer fitted them out with special internal remote-control mechanisms which I had suggested for their animation. These original mechanisms gave the three contrasting Bumblies a peculiar life of their own.

The Bumblies had numbers instead of names. Bumbly One was their leader and the most intelligent one. Bumbly Two was the fattest and most jovial of the trio, and Bumbly Three was the dim one, who always got things wrong.

In the course of the series, I played Pirates with them, with a large pirate ship, which they conjured out of thin air by a thought process using their invention, the Bumblescope. We also played Cowboys and Indians, with costumes and props conjured up by the same method; and we followed this by playing King Arthur and the Knights of the Round Table, with jousting Bumblies riding on caparisoned roller-skates.

We made most of these films in the bitter cold of Richard Dendy's attic, and the last few episodes were filmed in my garage in Richmond. The final film was about motor-racing and featured Bumbly Three driving a racing-car round a table fitted out with a race-track, pit-stops, and a spectators' stand where Bumbly Two gave a sports commentary on the event.

One particular feature of the Bumblies that everyone remembers was that they all slept on the ceiling.

We finished filming the last episode just in time to complete the packing for our coming voyage to Australia where I had a year-long contract to appear on the Tivoli Circuit of music-halls. By then, there was no doubt about the success of *The Bumblies*. They had won their place in British television history.

A couple of days before we left the front door-bell rang and I opened the door to find a dapper, bowler-hatted

City gent, complete with pinstriped suit and tightly rolled umbrella.

He immediately handed me his card. 'Good morning, Mr Bentine. I am from the Ministry. May I come in? I won't take up much of your time.'

I explained that we were very busy but invited him in.

He came straight to the point. 'Mr Bentine, we at the Ministry are very intrigued by your Bumblies.'

I said that I was delighted to hear it, and waited politely for him to continue, expecting a request for a signed photograph of the Bumblies. I also noticed that the man from the Ministry seemed to be nervous as he glanced at our extensive packing-up operation. He continued, 'We would like to know how these puppets are being manipulated.'

I was completely taken aback. 'I'm sorry, that is a trade secret. The mechanisms have been made to my specifications and I don't see what business they are of your Ministry.'

'But it *is*! You see, Mr Bentine, we are certain that you are utilizing some sort of shielded remote-control device that we at the Ministry haven't used ourselves. How do you shield your remote-controlled puppets from the intense electromagnetic interference that must be generated inside a television studio?'

I could not believe what I was hearing. 'What Ministry do you work for?'

'The Ministry of Defence. It's on my card.'

I burst out laughing. I had a marvellous mental picture of Bumbly Three sitting in the nose-cone of an intercontinental ballistic missile with that idiotic smile on his genial face, saying, 'OK, fellars, here we go!'

I also realized why the confused man from the Ministry had looked so apprehensive. Seeing all the packing cases, trunks, and bulging suitcases lined up ready to go overseas, he must have thought that I was about to defect to Soviet Russia, taking the secret of my discoveries in shielded remote-control with me.

Chapter Twenty-five

A Sunburnt Country

The steam siren of P&O's newest liner, SS *Oronsay*, blew deafeningly. Four-year-old Gus burst into terrified tears, and the Bentines were off to Australia.

Prior to sailing I had sweated through several nightmares prompted by my decision to accept the substantial offer I had received. My anxiety manifested in stark pictures of corrugated-iron shacks, an endless procession of unreceptive audiences, and my unhappy family trapped for a year-long contractual period in a country they did not like.

It was not easy to rationalize these grim visions and to dismiss them summarily. I reassured myself that I was being 'guided'. I reasoned that the whole trip was a necessary experience for me in order to re-establish my faith in my own style of comedy and its further development. But it was the nagging doubt that I might be making the wrong decision for the happiness of my family that worried me the most.

It was the new luxury liner's 'shake-down' voyage to the Antipodes, and she had one or two minor problems to solve. One was in the upper deck restaurant, where excessive engine vibration had a tendency to shake all the cutlery on to the deck. Fortunately this drawback did not extend to the main dining saloon below decks, which was rock steady.

We left on a blustery day from Tilbury Docks, glided

slowly down river, and round the North Foreland, passing the Goodwin Sands to starboard, and headed out past Dover into the choppy Channel, giving us a last glimpse of those grubby white cliffs glowing rusty red in the sunset.

The children fell asleep in their bunks as though being aboard a great ship had always been their way of life. In contrast, Nursie told us she was so excited she hardly slept at all.

Clementina and I soon realized that our cabin stewards were part of a substantial gay contingent among the crew. When they learned that my wife was a ballet dancer our popularity increased exponentially. Ballet usually included a high proportion of talented gay dancers, naturally attracted to that graceful art, and Clementina had many friends among them. Our personal stewards adored her, showing their favouritism in many ways such as their daily provision of freshwater baths, a shipboard luxury which they guarded from intruders with grim determination.

Bless the lot of them! They were wonderful with the children, caring and kind. We were invited to the crew's 'horse races', a kind of shipboard Ascot played with huge dice and wooden horses, where the gay stewards, squired by their escorts, paraded up and down the lower deck, wearing make-up, silk blouses, and tight satin pants of every hue.

Clementina had brought her portable sewing machine, and the word soon got round that she was an excellent seamstress. Our cabin stewards asked her to design and run up some of their more unusual garments, thereby ensuring those unlimited freshwater baths and their constant, devoted attention throughout the long voyage.

The last leg of our cruise brought us to Fremantle, the port that serves Perth and Western Australia. My anxiety returned when I saw that the corrugated-iron shacks of my pre-voyage nightmares made up much of the small town that adjoined the harbour.

I was contracted to David N. Martin who had described

himself to me as Australia's leading entreprenure (to rhyme with manure). His office, from which he controlled his Tivoli Circuit of theatres, was based in Melbourne, 2,500 miles away.

He was not present when we landed. Instead, we were welcomed by Edgeley and Dawe, an elderly British double-act who, after touring Australia for many years, had retired to Perth and now owned the local theatre.

They took us to a comfortable bungalow which was to be our home for the next three months and, thankfully, Perth turned out to be one of the loveliest cities in Australia. What was more, the people were friendly and hospitable.

The show opened two weeks later, and the bill was topped by Donald Peers, an enduring middle-aged Welsh singer who had just flown in from Britain. Donald, whose records were very popular at that time, did well with his polished and easy-going style. In contrast, I found that I had to slow down my delivery and broaden my material and style to suit the middle-aged and elderly members of the audience who were Donald Peers's fans.

I knew I was in for a struggle on the opening night when my first gag failed miserably. I used to start my act, 'Good evening, ladies and gentlemen. You all probably think that I'm wearing a false wig and a false beard. Well, you're quite right [taking them both off]. This is what I *really* look like [showing the audience that I looked exactly the same underneath all the false fuzz].'

In Britain this had produced a sure-fire belly laugh. But in Perth it was met with puzzled silence. Not a titter was to be heard. Only a clear nasal voice said, 'Why does he wear a wig and false beard, Ethel? The bloke's got enough hair of his own.'

However, though I seemed to puzzle the older people who made up the bulk of the audience, the youngsters thoroughly enjoyed my act, and responded wholeheartedly. And, thankfully, the local press were kind. Apparently, they were bored stiff by the conventional music-hall acts who came out from Britain for an Australian tour.

I realized that there was quite a difference between the British and the Aussie sense of humour. Possibly because of the climate, the Australian sense of humour seemed to be much drier!

During those three months in Western Australia, the enormous difference between the vast Antipodean continent and the British Isles became increasingly apparent. I adapt rapidly to changing circumstances as an integral part of my survival mechanism in both war and show business, and I quickly became accustomed to the contrasting lifestyle. Clementina also was used to change, having spent much of her childhood being ferried back and forth between Britain and East Africa. She soon adjusted her way of thinking to Australian conditions, but she confessed to me that she found the local social scene difficult. Apart from being disturbed by the heavy drinking that went on at most parties, Clementina was quite taken aback when the very drunk hostess of what was supposed to be a 'society affair', told her, 'Do come again, dear. You've been no bloody trouble at all.'

Our children also settled down to their new life, largely due to Nursie's reassuring presence. Frances Forbes, as always, rode over the surface of life with smiling determination, radiating a complete sense of security. I am sure that Nursie, had she ever learned to swim, would have become a champion surfer. She had that sort of self-confident stability.

After three months in Perth, our next date was Melbourne, which entailed a three-day train journey across the awe-inspiring Nullarbor Plain. Our train was derailed in the middle of the plain. Fortunately nobody was hurt or even shaken. We just left the rails and came to a gentle stop in the desert scrub.

It is only when you find yourself in the middle of nowhere, such as the vast Nullarbor Plain, with rails stretching hundreds of miles in both directions, without a single curve until the lines disappear on the shimmering horizon, that you realize on what titanic scale the Australian landscape has been formed.

While we waited for the relief train to pick us up, about twenty near-naked Aborigines appeared from nowhere and stood leaning on their spears, watching us with polite interest. They were a remarkable group of people, obviously perfectly attuned to their nomadic way of sunscorched life. There did not appear to be a spare ounce of flesh on any of them.

Their attitude changed to wonder when suddenly, out of a searing sky, a thunder cloud appeared and it started to rain. This was an event which the amazed conductor told us had not happened for over a hundred years. This did not surprise me, as I appear to be able to make rain anywhere, anytime, and in all conditions, or so it seems to me after a lifetime of rain-soaked holidays. I am sure that had these desert nomads suspected this ability in me they would never have let me go.

After a short delay we were rescued and continued to Port Pirie, where we changed trains and sat on bum-numbing wooden benches in the carriages which took us to Adelaide. We spent one day there, sleepily huddled together under a blanket on a windswept beach before boarding the train to Melbourne, where we arrived in pouring rain.

We were met by David N. Martin's manager, who triumphantly announced that he had found us 'a genuine Tudor residence in Toorak'.

This turned out to be an oak-beamed Elizabethan-style house all of twenty years old. It was spacious and we soon settled down to enjoy our stay in Australia's well laid out second city. Melbourne's climate is much like Britain's, hot in summer but chilly in the long winter, and often lashed by storms. Here we were to stay for eleven weeks.

David N. Martin, the bald-headed, steel-rim-spectacled accountant turned showman, was already a legend among the performers he had brought out from England. These legends were unflattering, but he treated me fairly, probably because, despite my early troubles in Perth, I was making him good money. The new show got a wonderfully enthusiastic press reception. It starred David Hughes, a young Welsh tenor, and the theatre did great business. In those days Australian theatre critics could make or break a show, so we were fortunate in their approval.

This time my act included the lighthouse scene, where the two aged keepers have been marooned for weeks by storms, and stoically wait for their relief to come. Jack Hylton had leased this sketch from me, and Tony Hancock and Jimmy Edwards were currently playing it in his show *London Laughs* at the Adelphi Theatre.

The whole piece is pure slapstick, starting off with the old keepers carrying a pretty mermaid down from their bedroom and chucking her back into the ocean. As they do so, the head keeper remarks ruminatively, 'There *must* be a way!'

This gives some idea of the intellectual level of the sketch, which is filled with broad sight gags. The running gag throughout is that every time the assistant lighthouse keeper opens the porthole to look out, he gets drenched by a bucketful of water thrown through it, complete with fish. As it was cheaper to buy fresh fish daily rather than have the prop department make up dozens of convincing rubber ones, I never knew what 'fruits of the sea' I was going to get in my face. We wore oilskins so the soaking did not matter. One night a new prop man used frozen fish, which nearly knocked me out and gave me a splendid black eye.

Being basically visual in content, my lighthouse keeper sketch has been played all round the world. It is the nearest thing to a sure-fire certainty that you can get in comedy. Many performers have played it, some without my permission.

I was partnered by a new friend, John Bluthal, a fine Australian character actor with a wide range of dialects. To keep the sketches fresh, we often played them with different accents. One night John, who is Jewish, played his part in Yiddish. This upset our 'entreprenure', who told him sternly, 'I'm not paying you to speak French.'

There are many true stories about David N. Martin (I never did find out what the N stood for). Once, when auditioning an excellent American ventriloquist, Canfield Smith, who used a dummy called Snodgrass, he called out from the stalls, 'Mr Smith, could you hold the dummy closer to the microphone. I can't hear what he's saying.'

On another occasion, when a massive invasion of flying ants caused the Tivoli show in Brisbane to be abandoned, the stage manager sent his boss a telegram, *'Show stopped by Flying Ants.'*

David N. cabled his reply, *'Book them for a further week.'* He was not joking.

Nevertheless, he had a flair for sensing what would be a success with his Australian audiences, even though he had next to no knowledge of show business, having come into it later in life than was usual.

He once asked me to come down to the theatre to give my opinion on a new Australian act that he was auditioning. 'Mike, I'm thinking of including this bloke in our new finale, Australiana.'

'What does he do?'

'He's the fastest apple-wrapper in Tasmania. He wraps a gross of apples in three minutes. It's a world record.'

To the accompaniment of our rehearsal pianist, Vi, a large middle-aged lady who smoked incessantly while playing, a lean, sun-tanned Aussie solemnly wrapped a full gross of apples and boxed them in precisely three minutes. I pointed out to David that while this feat was noteworthy, it would hardly hold the audience's riveted attention for three minutes, even to the spirited accompaniment of the William Tell Overture pounded out by Vi.

'How about the "Ride of the Valkyries"?' asked my determined boss.

I also pointed out that the cost of dozens of fresh apples every few shows would be expensive. Reluctantly,

David N. Martin dropped the idea, and the disappointed apple-wrapper returned to Tasmania.

A similar discovery of David N.'s, the fastest wood-chopper in Australia, managed to make the opening night, encouraged by shouts from his mates in the audience, but that was his first and final performance. The spectacle of that muscular giant wielding his heavy axe in a blur of action and showers of sweat, accompanied by Vi with her rendition of the 'Ride of the Valkyries', was undoubtedly much more exciting than that of the record-breaking apple-wrapper, but his wood-chopping was too danger-ous. On the opening night, a big slice of tree-trunk was projected into the audience, nearly braining a lady in the stalls.

John Bluthal told me about David N.'s publicity stunt with a strong-man performer, Wilfred Briton, who was actually Polish. I had seen this immensely broad-chested, chunky little pocket-sized Hercules at the Kingston Empire. His feats of strength were truly amazing. When Mr Briton came to Australia, David N. decided that he needed some special public feat of strength from Mr Briton to bring people into the theatre. He arranged for him to pull a double-decker Melbourne bus up Elizabeth Street with his teeth.

The press turned up in force, and Wilfred duly made the attempt, which he was confident he could perform, even though the bus was to be pulled uphill. The powerful muscles of his short, thick neck stood out like twisted steel cables as, to his surprise, he had to strain himself to the limit to move the big bus. However, by nearly killing himself, he did succeed in towing the double-decker a few feet up Elizabeth Street before he had to give up, with most of his teeth loosened by the effort. It was only then that the driver admitted laconically, 'I didn't trust yer, mate, on the hill, so I had me brakes on.'

A number of Wilfred Briton's best feats of strength depended on his having firm teeth, and David N. Martin outrageously refused to honour his contract because the poor man was no longer able to do his full act. The head of the Tivoli Circuit had the reputation of being a hard man, but this seemed to be grossly unfair.

Luckily, I had a cast-iron contract but Tommy Trinder had endless rows with David N., even when Tommy was a smash-hit in Australia.

Tommy intensely disliked his Australian producer. Years later, when David N. Martin died suddenly in San Francisco, and his body was brought back to Australia for burial, a friend of Tommy's wrote to him to say that he must have been wrong about the impresario's unpopularity, because over two thousand people had turned up at his funeral.

Tommy replied, 'Give the people what they want and they will always turn up.'

In Melbourne we were joined by Andrew Briger, Mme Legat's nephew. He had been a good friend to us whenever we needed his help and, as he had just lost his mother, I invited him out to Australia and sent him the ticket.

When the show closed in Melbourne, Andrew, who was show-wise from his long experience with his for-midable Aunt Nadine, came with us to Adelaide and helped to manage me during the seven-week season. While we were there, we all fell in love with this elegant city in South Australia, not only because of the warmth of its welcome, but because I was able to enjoy thirteen weeks of blissful holiday, as a contractual break before opening with Mel Tormé in Sydney.

For the Adelaide show we were joined by the Norma Miller Dancers, a wildly energetic team of black danc-ers, led by the redoubtable Norma Miller. This hyper-adrenalated lady was a real trouper, a skeletally thin go-go dancer of sparkling energy and, led by her example, her team really set the stage alight.

Norma had a unique line of impromptu patter. When asked to do a free charity act, something that is not allowed by the American Actors Equity Union, she re-plied, 'Honey, I wouldn't give a crippled crab a crutch.' On another occasion, after we had played to an unusually unreceptive audience, she remarked, 'Mike baby, it's so quiet out there, you could hear a rat piss on cotton.'

Her troupe of ten dancers stoically suffered a series of serious accidents which reduced their numbers, one by one. First, the fire-curtain unexpectedly descended on Stoney, injuring his leg so badly that he was out of the show for many weeks. Next, an ancient gas geyser in the bathroom of their digs blew up while two of the male dancers were having a bath together, scaring them both half to death, and putting them out of the running for a week with shock and burns. Then another member of her troupe had serious trouble with her Achilles tendon, depriving Norma of one more performer.

Her reaction to the last disaster was typical. Gloomily surveying the remnants of her performers, she turned to me and said, 'Shit, man, we're a dancing act, not that fuckin' nursery rhyme!'

While I enjoyed my thirteen-week break at the seaside in Adelaide, the rest of the company went off to Perth, which of course I had already played. We had a marvellous time as a family, exploring the surrounding coast of South Australia, with its great rolling green downland and its yellow, wattle-covered countryside, enjoying the beautiful beaches, which we often had entirely to ourselves, and sampling the excellent wines of the Barrossa Valley.

My final season with the Tivoli Circuit was scheduled for Sydney, in September 1956. Mel Tormé, the star of our show, turned out to be a cheerful charmer, with a fund of stories and a great gift for telling them. He enjoyed what I did and often used to watch me. 'Your sketches are so goddamn different, Mike. Being mainly visual comedy, the action changes every performance. I never know what is going to happen next.'

Neither did I, but, coming from such a dedicated professional, his comments were really appreciated.

Watching this ebullient performer taught me a lot, especially when I saw the way he could charm an audience. With his vibrant, throaty voice and relaxed manner, he seldom kept to scripted lines but ad-libbed his way through his act, which was something I found hard to do (i.e. playing myself rather than a character). This was probably due to a subconscious fear that I might stammer. Mel Tormé helped me change that, and I shall always be grateful to him.

The Sydney season was very successful, and when it was over we started to pack up to go home. I had refused David N.'s offer to play New Zealand, because we were homesick. But, just before we were due to leave, an unexpected phone call changed all our plans.

Eric Pierce, an Englishman, had made a very successful career producing shows for Australian radio, which in those days was the principal entertainment medium down under. He rang me to ask if I would write and perform a series of comedy programmes for a Sydney station. I told him we were going home, but he was so insistent that Clementina felt it would be worthwhile lunching with him.

At that fateful meeting, Eric and his boss, Dave Worrals, a typical down-to-earth Aussie businessman, kept upping the offer until I found it hard to refuse their generous terms. I talked it all over with the family, and we decided to stay.

My radio show *Three's a Crowd* ran for thirty-nine episodes and gave us a substantial 'grub-stake' with which to return home. The series would have run much longer but, by that time, I had proved to myself that I could devise and sustain a successful radio series, and I had exorcised any lingering doubts I might have had about leaving *The Goon Show*.

I performed the radio show with two other actors, both Australian. John Bluthal, with his wide range of accents, was an obvious choice, and we were joined by David Nettheim, another experienced character actor, who specialized in 'English' narrative voices, all very BBC. David also helped me get down my ideas and comedy concepts in a form which the Australian public would understand. 'Remember, Michael, we're an ignorant mob out here,' he would say, only half joking.

Both John and David did a lot of radio, playing in the numerous soap operas which, with sport, were the mainstays of Australian broadcasting. Some of the radio soaps, such as *The Blue Hills*, had been running for years, building up a dedicated radio audience all over Australia by their constant repetition. Little ever happened on 'Dinkie-D' radio serials, most of which were set in the outback, with the characters drinking endless cups of tea, and speaking slowly and laconically between sips. They were a far cry from later television series such as *Neighbours*. When I was there, the modern image of 'The land of Oz' was still unborn.

Three's a Crowd was unlike the usual run of Australian radio comedy, much of which was imported from Britain. For example, I used radio's mind-to-mind potential to the full, but as I did not want to be accused of copying the Goon radio formula, I had to find a contrasting approach.

Aided by our clever eighteen-year-old Australian studio engineer, Stephan Sargent, I developed a whole technique of multi-recorded voices by which the three of us became choirs, parliaments, and large crowds, foreign or domestic. We could even hold multiple conversations with ourselves. The impression given was that I had a cast of thousands. We soon became a success, with a rapidly growing cult-following. David N. Martin became interested and wanted me to do a stage version of *Three's a Crowd* which, of course, would have been impossible.

Suddenly I felt that we had to get back home. Refusing other offers of work, we embarked on the French passenger/cargo ship *Tahitien*, and in July 1957 we set sail from Sydney harbour. We were seen off by a large crowd of our friends, including a tearful Andrew Briger, who wisely had decided to stay down under to find his fortune.

We had enjoyed our stay in Australia. It had opened

up new horizons for me, in both performing and writing original comedy. During our time there as a family we had laughed a lot, the children had been happy, and both of them were well. Nursie had loved it, but felt, 'They're not quite like us', and Clementina still had a few reservations about the social scene. But we all agreed that it had been a marvellous experience.

The *Tahitien*, on its long voyage to Marseilles, stopped at every opportunity to pick up copra, her basic cargo. In search of the coconuts our ship visited Noumea and Espiritu Santo, among other exotic islands of the South Seas. Only two bona fide families were aboard this comfortable ship. They were ourselves and the Miots, a French family with three children, whose father was the Consul in Sydney, returning to France on leave. All told, there were about sixty other passengers on the *Tahitien* and, apart from our small group, the rest of them seemed to play 'musical cabins', seldom spending two consecutive nights in the same quarters. In that way, the voyage was about as archetypally 'French' as you could get. However, none of this extra-marital activity affected our two small families, and we were left to our own devices.

I had decided to make a short documentary film of our voyage back home. I had purchased two excellent movie-cameras but had been unable to obtain the special Wratten filters I needed for the correct exposure of the film. I was told they were obtainable in Noumea, and Clementina and I had gone ashore there to find them. When we had left the ship, an uninterested ship's officer told us we had plenty of time. He lied.

As we sauntered back to the harbour, *Tahitien* blew her siren. This puzzled me until I realized she was leaving. We made a dash for the dock, still some hundreds of yards away. As we arrived on the quay, out of breath and badly shaken, we saw that *Tahitien* was drifting away from the harbour wall.

The port gangway was still down, level with the top of the harbour wall, but a formidable six-foot gap was increasing by the second. We had to jump for it. I leapt first and landed on the gangway, turned and held out my hands for Clementina. At least I could catch her if she fell, or else dive into the swirling waters after her, forgetting that I was not a strong swimmer.

Summoning all her ballet skill, Clementina took a short run and hurled herself across the rapidly widening gap. She flew towards me in a graceful arc and landed flat on her tummy, with her legs dangling over the water. The passengers lining the rail above us cheered, and the children burst into tears. Incredibly, not a single member of the crew was there to give us a hand.

Nursie, fearful for our safety, was comforting the children. We were shaking with shock, and when we had staggered up the gangway, I had a few words to say to the officer of the watch. Being French, he shrugged his shoulders and said it was our fault.

Papa Miot was furious. He felt that the honour of France had been impugned and he insisted that the captain give us a full apology, which he did. You cannot sustain resentment within the close confines of a ship, so we let the matter drop.

The Miots were fun. They had a cheerful teenage son and daughter and a small boy, Pierre. He was a real 'Puck' of a child, as mischievous as the mythical sprite he so closely resembled. Both Fusty and Gus got along famously with this adventurous changeling, and Nursie constantly had to be on the alert to foil the more perilous of Pierre's pranks, especially when they involved our children. She once caught him leading an attempt to swarm up the funnel. We often wonder what happened to Pierre. I am sure it must have been something special.

After ten days at sea we arrived at Tahiti, and stayed for a week. It was a wonderful opportunity to visit that beautiful island, when tourists were still a novelty. When we landed at Papete, most of the crew vanished ashore, where they had girlfriends. Unlike our gay stewards on *Oronsay*, the French crew were macho to a man.

We lived aboard during our stopover in Tahiti, so the crew's defection made shipboard life less than convenient. Only a resentful skeleton crew had been forced to stay to run the ship, which they did badly. We found it more convenient to eat ashore, and spent lazy days sunning ourselves on the black sand of the beaches, riding the 100-year-old giant tortoises, and generally exploring the island. I found the traditional 'pareo', a wide length of colourful cotton cloth draped round the waist, to be most comfortable tropical wear, and I still have my Tahitian straw hat with its sea-shell hatband.

We met Gauguin's son, a fat, middle-aged man, drinking heavily and making his living by being photographed with tourists. His famous father had left him nothing, and he owned none of those marvellous paintings. Otherwise, he would have been a multi-millionaire.

I could not understand why Gauguin had seldom painted the island itself, except as a half-seen background. Instead, he had used his great talent to depict the island people, mainly women.

Intrigued by this, I tried to paint Tahiti. I then understood why Gauguin had concentrated on portraiture rather than on painting the exquisite scenery. In the ever-changing light, the elusive colours kept altering. Working as fast as I could, I still was unable to keep up with that rapid transmutation of tone and hue. From minute to minute, the combination of swirling patterns of light in the sky and the sea magically transformed the whole aspect of the islands. It was a humbling experience.

We had reluctantly sailed from Papete when the ship succumbed to the *grippe tahitienne*, a virulent form of influenza. It quickly worked its way through the ship, affecting passengers and crew alike, leaving the Miots and ourselves to the last. We were through the Panama Canal before we fell victim to the vicious bug.

We were all alarmed by the virulence of *la grippe*. At our next port of call, Guadaloupe, I raced round Pointe-à-Pitre desperately looking for penicillin when the ship's supplies ran out. I found some, and just got back aboard without having to jump for it.

The young ship's doctor, recently qualified and relatively inexperienced, was reluctant to give our children an injection until Nursie stood over him with a determined look in her eyes and threatened to do the job for him.

We arrived in Marseilles flat broke. From the ship, I had asked my bank in London to cable funds to get us back home, but the money had not yet turned up at their Marseilles branch. I had to leave *Tahitien* still owing the ship's ferret-faced purser a tidy sum. He had no option but to let us go but I am sure he did not expect his heavily over-stuffed bill to be paid.

Clementina was worried but, having been broke at various times in my life, I remembered that while you are in residence at a first-class hotel, you can charge everything to your bill. Forthwith, I booked us into the best hotel I could find. As we seemed to be a typical British family on holiday, instead of temporarily being destitute, we were accepted as such. We were now able to eat, get our laundry done, and generally enjoy our stay in comfort. But, until the money arrived at the local bank, we were confined to walking around the town, which was about the only free activity available in Marseilles. Outside our luxurious hotel, we did not even have the price of a fruit drink for the children.

I daily telephoned Lloyds Bank in London from the hotel, and each time my co-operative bank manager assured me that he had already cabled the funds to Marseilles. The last time I phoned, it dawned on me that there could have been *another* franchised bank at which the draft might have arrived. It was situated immediately opposite the one we had visited twice a day without success. Nobody there had told us about the existence of the other branch across the street.

I immediately contacted this other bank and, sure enough, the money had been there all the time. Rich with multiple francs, I returned to the hotel in triumph.

I gave most of it to Clementina, and immediately took a taxi to the harbour. The unpleasant purser was on leave, so I did not have the full satisfaction of seeing him proven wrong, but I paid his cheerful assistant the required sum, and tipped him on the understanding that he would not pass any of his *pourboire* to his sour-faced boss.

The next day I paid off the substantial bill which we had run up, unnecessarily, at the four-star hotel and we caught the night-express to Paris. Two days later, after a calm cross-Channel passage, we arrived back home, exhausted but happy.

Unfortunately, the people to whom our estate agent had let our home for a modest rent, on the express condition that they looked after the house, had not bothered to do so. When she saw the filthy state in which our home had been left, Clementina burst into tears. But my wife is a determined woman and, assisted by Nursie and Fifi, our wonderful daily, she eventually got it back into its original condition. But the walls of our home had to be scraped and scrubbed down in order to remove over two years of accumulated dirt and grease.

Chapter Twenty-six

'I Thought You Were Dead'

Shortly after our arrival back home a BBC producer said, 'I thought you were dead.' It was the sort of greeting I soon came to expect after our two and a half years in Australia. Much had changed, and I had not been part of it. I also encountered a surprising degree of hostility among the press. This puzzled me as my relations with Fleet Street had always been very friendly.

Perhaps someone had been busy while I was away. I was even told that my variety act with the chairback and sink plunger had not been original, but had been done before by someone else. Moreover, according to certain people, I had had no connection with the Goons whatsoever, and had contributed nothing to the success of the show.

Furthermore, my forty-one *Goon Shows*, counting the earlier *Crazy People* versions, had all been wiped out of existence. Officially, *The Goon Show* started immediately after I left. By any standards, that is a plain distortion of the facts. Even my photograph had been neatly excised from the earlier Goon pictures. I still cannot understand why.

Only recently, after I complained in a letter to the Director-General Michael Checkland, have I found my picture replaced in the group pictures of the original Goons, displayed in many BBC buildings. It obviously was going to be a hard battle to re-establish my reputation, which had been difficult enough to do in the first place.

The other Goons had far outstripped me. I wished them well in their good fortune, and they were glad to see me again. Fortunately, Peter Sellers, who had just embarked on his remarkable career in the movies, rang me, 'Lovely to have you back, Mike. Can you write some television shows for me? I've still got six more to do to finish my contract with Rediffusion. Could you please start right away?'

David Nettheim from *Three's a Crowd* had followed me to England and I enlisted his services to help me get the shows down on paper. Within four weeks I had six substantial new scripts to show Peter. He liked the sketches very much, but when we came to record them I found that I had misjudged the market. Peter had already done some TV shows, which were in the same vein as *The Goon Show*, then at the height of its popularity. My shows were written in a different idiom and, although Peter was delighted with them, this was not what the TV critics wanted to see him doing. At that time, Peter could do no wrong in their eyes, and I was slated for daring to try something different.

Yet the shows had many strong comedy sketches. In one of them, Peter, playing the part of an elderly gardener, demonstrated to the viewers how to get rid of snails in their window boxes. He did this by employing psychological warfare, destroying the male snail's confidence in itself with the aid of a dummy female snail. This animated device, which Peter wore on the end of his finger, 'spurns' the male's romantic advances. When the frustrated snail's sexual ego is shattered by these repeated rejections, it bursts into tears and hurls itself to its death off the end of the window box. Peter's final line was, 'He's committed insecticide. I hate my work.' (Exits, sobbing.)

One of Peter's favourites of the many pieces I wrote for him was when he played an old 'actor laddie', an octogenarian film extra, who had been appearing in crowd scenes in films since the First World War. I had enjoyed writing it, and my friend played the part beautifully. In fact, he portrayed the pathetic old 'thespian' so well, and with such sympathy, that the sketch became quite moving, even when he had such lines as, 'Then I struck a bad patch. I was out of work for twelve years.' The interviewer asks the film extra if he has ever worked closely with a great movie star.

'Indeed I did. I worked in three moving-pictures as a stunt man with that charming film star, Mr Victor Mature. My first movie with him was a biblical film. Mr Mature, who was playing the part of Samson, struck me behind the ear with the jawbone of an ass, accidentally fracturing my skull. Then, in my second film with Mr Mature, which was a historical movie, during a sword-fight he ran me through with his sabre, breaking two of my ribs. My last picture with this great star was another biblical epic. In the temple scene, Mr Mature picked me up and threw me into the blazing sacrificial fire. I remember that I got quite badly burnt. Yes, indeed, I am proud to say that Mr Mature *always* asked for me in his motion pictures. I can't think why. I had never done him any harm.'

The recording that Peter Sellers made of this five-minute sketch is still one of my favourite memories of him.

We completed the six shows, each one increasing our viewing figures, but that was it. Peter was contracted to do another film, and once more I was out of work.

Because of the impact of television, audiences in the music-halls had become much reduced. This meant that variety bookings were not plentiful. Fusty was now nine years old and Gus was eight. Nursie was thinking of leaving us to live with her sister Joy, a school teacher in Norfolk. Our dear friend knew that money was tight with us and, much as the thought of leaving us saddened her, she did not want to be a financial burden. Happily, Clementina once again realized that she was pregnant. Nursie agreed to stay on to help her during the pregnancy and to look after the new baby.

By the time our second son arrived in September 1959, my economic situation had improved considerably. The preparations for his birth had been largely stress-free, and Clementina calmly sailed through labour with practised ease. It says much for the theory of pre-natal influence that, from the moment of his birth, Richard, or 'Peski' as we called him, was a happy, self-assured baby, who seemed to take life as it came and shake it by the tail.

The upturn in our family fortunes had been heralded by a phone call from my old friend, Pat Dixon. He, too, was pleased to see me back in Britain, and immediately offered me a thirteen-part radio series. I wrote these shows, with David Nettheim getting them down as they spilled out of me, and added some of the strongest material I had created in Australia, once again using my *Three's a Crowd* technique of multi-recording to give the effect of an enormous cast.

Round the Bend was received well but, being 'non-audience' shows, they had little chance of competing with the all-conquering *Goon Show*, which was punctuated throughout by yells of laughter from its studio audience, which by then was part of a very large cult-following. The few *Goon Shows* which had been recorded *without* a studio audience never had the same success as the shows with one.

As *Round the Bend* progressed, I became more than happy with Pat Dixon's enthusiastic approval. Moreover, the listeners' 'appreciation index' was high, and so I received a commission to write twenty-six more programmes. Everything seemed to be going well until Pat was suddenly taken ill and was rushed off to St George's Hospital. There he was diagnosed as suffering from abdominal cancer. Radical surgery was attempted but it immediately became evident that his condition was inoperable.

I went to visit him and was very moved when he told me how much he had enjoyed working with me. He faced death with exemplary courage, leaving his many friends sadly missing his kindliness, his wise counsel, and his sense of humour, which he never lost, even when he was dying. He was one of the finest friends I have ever known.

After his untimely death, I lost my enthusiasm for continuing with *Round the Bend*, but I had already signed the contract, and Pat Hilliard, the Head of BBC Light Entertainment, phoned me to suggest that this next series should be produced by Charles Chilton who, like himself, was a great admirer of Pat Dixon.

When we first met to talk this over, I instantly liked him. At the end of our meeting, he said, 'Think of these shows as a tribute to the man who used to produce them.' That scored a bull's-eye, and my doubts vanished. We recorded twenty-six more of these radio shows which eventually, for some obscure reason, the BBC also wiped from their archives. Much of the contents of *Round the Bend* would more than hold their own today, largely because the shows were ahead of their time.

In the middle of making the series, David Nettheim left to join Alfred Lunt and Lynn Fontanne in a London theatre season. Another writer, John Law, a young Scottish journalist, joined me to help get my ideas on paper. He was an excellent wordsmith and we made a good team. I thought up the ideas and concepts and John, being a good journalist, put them down succinctly. As I am the world's worst typist, this saved a lot of time, and John's cheerful enthusiasm eased the usual loneliness of creative writing.

Charles suggested that we bring in an actress to give the new series a broader appeal. Until then I had always worked with an all-male cast, probably a hangover from my perennial shyness with women. Any female roles in my scripts had been played by actors caricaturing archetypal women. With an actress in the team, I realized that it was equally easy to write for women.

However, whether written for male or female performers, the basis of all my comedy in the unlimited medium of radio was to dream up unusual side-effects unexpectedly arising from valid situations.

A typical example of my thinking was when I used the authentic atmosphere of a Farnborough airshow, with the addition of a visit by an imaginary Soviet formation aerobatics team, the Red Bears. During their display the Farnborough commentator switches the mid-air instructions given by the Russian leader to his formation via the public address system. So far, there was nothing unusual about that; it is a routine part of any great airshow. My variation on this theme was to have the Soviet flight commander accidentally relayed to a Farnborough telephone box, where a young man is trying to contact his girlfriend, Gladys. The public address system broadcasts the entire conversation to the crowd:

Telephone user: Hello! Is that Paddington 9437? May I speak to Gladys, please?
Russian Leader: Gladys? This is Red Leader. Who are you?
Telephone user: I'm Fred. Who are you?
Russian Leader: I am Colonel Kropinsky, leader of the Red Bears. Where are you, Fred?
Fred: I'm in a Farnborough telephone box, near the railway station. Where are you?
Russian Leader: I'm at thirty thousand feet. You're much too low, Fred. Join the formation immediately.
Fred: Righty ho!
(Sound of button B being pressed, and the Farnborough telephone box taking off to climb to formation altitude.)
Commentator: And what a magnificent spectacle the Red Bears make, as they are joined by the Farnborough telephone box. And there they go into a spectacular formation slow-roll. A most unusual sight!

The skilled BBC sound engineers, who are probably the finest radio technicians in the world, never batted an eyelash at this sort of unusual challenge to their ability to produce evocative special effects. This series tested them to the limit, and they never once failed me.

To vary the character range I suggested using guest artists, and we were fortunate to have Ron Moody and Ronnie Barker with us at different times, both of them at an early stage in their careers. Each brought more funny 'characters' to the show and subsequently both went on to well-deserved fame and fortune.

While doing these radio shows I met Dick Lester, a bright young American director. He had worked with Peter Sellers and Spike Milligan in their short television series *A Show called Fred*, *Son of Fred*, and *The Idiot Weekly*, after which he had been out of work. I invited him to join our small team and, though he was restricted in his range as an actor, Dick made up for it with his enthusiasm and his knowledge of modern music. He suggested using speeded-up voices, together with my multi-recording techniques, to create singing groups. These worked very well. Dick was new to comedy, having gained his experience in the States working in TV serials, but he greatly admired the understated British sense of humour, and he quickly saw that I could produce comedy ideas and concepts in abundance.

After I finished the last *Round the Bend* series, he asked me to team up with him, with the idea of my devising and writing a late-night television series which he would present to the commercial company ABC for production in their Birmingham studios.

I agreed, and we duly succeeded in getting ABC to broadcast the first six TV programmes, *Before Midnight*, in the early autumn of 1958.

These half-hour shows at first were broadcast only to the Midlands, but ABC decided to extend my contract into a new series of thirteen programmes, *After Hours*, scheduled for the same late-night spot, to be transmitted throughout the North of England.

Although we were basically a late-night chat show, *After Hours* included a number of my sketches which I ad-libbed to Dick, who jotted them down roughly. The ridiculously short time between signing the contract and the actual production of these shows precluded a more conventional method of scriptwriting.

I devised them red-hot, with no time for refinement or second thoughts. Any special props we used in them had to be ordered within an hour of finalizing the material. Moreover, rehearsals were minimal. At the most we had forty-eight hours in which to rehearse our small team, which consisted of Dick Emery, Clive Dunn, David Lodge, Joe Gibbons, and Benny Lee. After the first three shows, I joined them.

We even had to use our train journey to Birmingham for rehearsals. These shows were transmitted live, except for small items of pre-filmed material that we managed to squeeze in. We also used short cartoon films which I devised and recorded and which Dick 'inlaid' over live action. It was a minor miracle that we managed to get the shows together. The first time that we played my sketches in costume, and with the props, was on transmission. But they worked.

Among other ideas, I dreamed up a 'traditional' olde English sport which I called 'Drats'. I got the idea from a misprint in a local newspaper, describing a darts match.

Drats, or as it later became known, Nurdling, was a game played in a country pub, where a TV commentator (myself) interviewed a collection of rustic Dratters, each of them carrying a ten-foot-long painted Maypole. Gripping these 'dratting poles' in front of them like a lance, each in turn hurled himself through the pub's open front-door into the pitch-black night with wild cries of 'Queen Elizabeth's bedsocks', 'Duke of Wellington's knee-caps', 'Napoleon Bonaparte's athletic supporter', and other cryptic code-words.

The customers in the pub listened in tense silence while the sound of the dratter disappeared into the distance, the heavy thudding of his booted feet fading away accompanied by successive crashes, splintering wood, sonic booms and breaking glass, as the rustic competitor evidently smashed his way through a series of unseen obstacles, scoring points as he did so. His score was solemnly marked up on a large blackboard by the landlord, Clive Dunn.

One of the competitors in this invisible assault course obviously came to some hideous end. This was denoted by various evocative sound-effects of disaster, ending in a horrific, skidding car-crash.

In the hushed silence that followed the unseen mayhem, the landlord hoarsely announced, 'My Gawd, 'e's *nurdled.*'

This was followed by shocked gasps of dismay from the customers at the bar who had to reinforce themselves with yet another pint of ale.

I combined the 'seen' and the 'unseen' to let the imagination of the audience participate in the comedy in the same way as a story-teller uses the imagination of his listeners.

This was the basis for many of my more extreme ideas, such as the Invisible Flea Circus, in which an unseen flea jumps into a small arena, his progress being denoted by small spurts of sand. The 'flea' apparently rolls a big ball up a steep slope, accompanied by mini-grunts of effort, then climbs the bending rungs of a ladder to the top of a diving platform, where he hops to the end of a miniature diving board, which sags under his weight. Finally, the athletic flea dives off the twanging board and lands in a teacup which is set a foot below the small diving-board. As the flea hits the water with a loud splash, the liquid squirts dramatically upwards.

With the aid of an ingenious model which I designed and Bruce Lacey, an eccentric prop-maker friend of mine, built, the illusion was startlingly real. It even got enthusiastic applause from the studio technicians, our only audience.

I later developed this idea into a whole series of 'invisible' scenarios, the most prophetic of which featured a border raid perpetrated by a gang of invisible Irish leprechauns against a Northern Irish town. This was in 1960, long before there was any sign of the horrific carnage which was later to explode in Northern Ireland. Today, of course, I would not have even considered writing it.

Many times, an event I depicted in a comedy sketch, no matter how unusual or bizarre, occurred soon afterwards, almost exactly as I wrote it, but usually in dramatic circumstances. For example, in *Three's a Crowd*, I featured an incident in which a suicidal horse jumped off the Sydney Harbour Bridge. Two weeks later, a horse bolted and did exactly that, the only time this had happened since the bridge was built. Coincidence? Perhaps, but this sort of thing has happened too often to be governed solely by the laws of chance.

Dick Lester was all for using my wilder notions and, with a small increase in our modest budget, I was able to enlist the skills of the designer, Bob Fuest, and we branched out into some very odd sketches. For instance, I dreamed up a mid-act argument between the members of a two-man head-to-head balancing act. These were played by Dick Emery as the bottom half of the partnership and Benny Lee as the inverted 'top man'. Dick angrily walks off, leaving Benny hanging upside down in mid-air. In this position Benny sang a song, with all the contents of his pockets falling out, apparently upwards.

Destroying Benny Lee in mid-song was a running gag which we used in each show. We shot him with a firing squad, drenched him with rain, made him vanish in thick fog, smothered him with falling leaves, and even blew him up, flying him out of shot on wires. Throughout his many ordeals, Benny remained as good-natured as ever, taking it all in his stride.

To show you how broad my material had become, here is just one of the wilder scenes I devised: I had read in a local paper that a mayor's parlour had been flooded by an unexpected cloudburst while the City aldermen were enjoying an official luncheon. I decided to reproduce this event in our small studio.

With the designer Bob Fuest's help, our technicians built a tank in the studio, twelve feet in diameter, dressing it with a realistic set of a panelled mayor's parlour, and filling it with three feet of water. In the icy cold water, Dick Emery, Joe Gibbons, David Lodge and myself as the mayor and aldermen, wearing traditional robes, sat round a submerged dining table, on which lunch had been laid. This consisted of 'lamb and two veg' and a large, wobbly jelly, all of which were placed under water.

My pre-recorded voice set the scene while the TV camera mixed-through from the photograph of a town hall and panned slowly over the mayor's parlour, only zooming out at the last moment to reveal the flood. This was the first time we had been able to play the sketch with the tank flooded and in full costume, so we had no idea how well it would work.

As the mayor and host of the luncheon, I reached into the water, and took the lid off a large vegetable dish. The contents immediately bobbed up on to the surface. The floating vegetables were scooped up and served on to the plates, which the aldermen held out of the water.

I carved the lamb under water, and served the meat in the same manner. Each time, the filled plates were solemnly replaced on the submerged table and their contents eaten from that position.

At one point, Joe Gibbons asked for a drink. He brought his glass up out of the water and emptied it so that Dick Emery could refill it from a water-jug, which he had produced from below the surface, the whole action being insanely logical.

The jelly was carefully raised from its position under water and spooned on to dessert plates. Finally, the mayor and corporation played whist. I dealt the cards on to the surface of the water, where they floated until we picked up our 'hands'. While we did so, Dick Emery took a nap. He spread a sheet of newspaper over his face and lay down on a small, submerged couch, disappearing completely under water and breathing through a large straw.

Unknown to us, Bob Fuest had brought in three ducks, which swam, quacking, round the set. The whole scene took only five minutes, and we played it dead straight without a glimmer of a smile, chatting away with the sort of banal conversation that a rather pompous mayor and his aldermen might have.

The studio staff laughed out loud, the cameras shook and the whole show was a great success. Many Northern viewers still remember it with affection. The hardest part was trying to keep a straight face while the unrehearsed and unexpected happened all around us.

I was asked by a group of wealthy backers to adapt the sketches into a stage revue. Dick Lester directed the show, which we called *Don't Shoot, We're British*. In all my performing experience there was nothing quite like our opening night in Newcastle in 1960.

There were thirty-three scenes in the show and thirty of them went wrong. The remaining three scenes were cut out as we went along.

One of the 'lime-boys' – the operators of the two powerful spotlights that were to follow the action on stage – had had a row with Dick Lester at the dress rehearsal and had walked out, leaving us with only one spotlight operator, and no lime-plot, i.e. no master plan for the front lighting of the show.

Dick had no alternative but to operate the second 'follow-spot' himself, without ever having done so before. This tied up our director for the opening night so that he was not on hand to sort out the mayhem back-stage. Despite the last-minute addition of even more staff, the over-ambitious scenery, which I had not been allowed to see earlier, threatened to overwhelm the sweating stage management. It was incredible that the show went on at all.

The spotlight missed every one of my entrances so I finally walked on holding a lighted match to give the un-rehearsed operator a clue as to where I was. Astonishingly, the audience enjoyed it all, yelling with laughter when things went wrong. As most of the audience were fans of Goon humour they thought it was all part of the show.

Thank God we had such an experienced cast, which included Dick Emery and Clive Dunn. No matter what happened, the performers carried on as though it was all part of the show. I have never ad-libbed as much as I did that night, and at the end, to my amazement, we got a standing ovation.

The critics in the Newcastle press were more than kind, but Dick Lester told us he was too shaken to continue. After a couple more nights of near-chaos, our director pulled out of the show. This left us with no-one but ourselves to pull the show together and to carry on with the eleven-week tour, which the backers now begged us to do since the takings from the week at Newcastle had been astonishingly good.

Being old pros, we did our best. That first week had been exhausting, but we were sustained by the excitement. The tour continued, with consecutive weeks of long journeys from Scotland to the extreme south of England and back north again. I found the strain becoming unbearable. I was carrying the responsibility for the material in the show and for holding the continuity together, as well as performing in the sketches.

In Blackpool I went down with a bad bout of influenza, and Dick Emery had to act as compère for the rest of the week, something he had never done before, being essentially a character comedian. Dick found it hard to be 'himself', an odd trait in such a good performer, but one that he shared with Peter Sellers, who also dreaded having to play straight.

Our last touring date was Bournemouth. There we were approached by the management of a London theatre who booked us for the West End. We were all game to try our luck in London. However, the vogue was for political satire and we were dismissed as 'end of the pier stuff'. We closed after two weeks. All that effort, worry, exhaustion and unnecessary stress had been for nothing. It seemed that Dick Lester had made a shrewd move in pulling out right at the start, leaving it to the cast and writer to fulfil their professional obligation to try to get it right.

I thanked our small cast for all their efforts with a farewell dinner, and we all set about looking for work. Almost immediately I was fortunate enough to receive two offers. Dennis Norden and Frank Muir had come to see the show. Being imaginative writers themselves, they could see the possibilities for a new kind of television comedy arising from the quasi-documentary approach I used in my work. At the time they were the advisers on comedy to BBC Television, and they persuaded Eric Maschwitz, who was the current Head of BBC Television Light Entertainment, to offer me a pilot show with an option for a possible series.

I also won a part in a British film called *Five Golden Hours*, which was to be shot later in the month, so I was able to do the BBC show first.

Once again, Dick Emery, Clive Dunn, Benny Lee and Frank Thornton (who had joined us for the ill-fated London opening) were working with me. We also had a lot of help from an enthusiastic BBC technical staff and the full co-operation of my new producer, Barry Lupino.

Barry immediately saw the possibilities of my new show, which I called *It's a Square World*. He gave me every opportunity to expand my ideas into an elastic 'documentary' framework. John Law was out of work at the time, so I co-opted my Scottish friend to help me get the show into the new framework. This time we worked to a studio audience, and I used my experience in variety and revue to warm them up before we did the show. The result was recorded on Ampex machines, which were then in their infancy, making editing difficult, so we were virtually doing a live show with all its intrinsic difficulties.

I included a sequence in which we served a full dinner on a fast-moving train. The designer, Richard Henry, made me a wonderful restaurant-car set, with the floor mounted on large, semi-inflated tractor inner-tubes, providing us with marvellous movement. The more we staggered around the rocking, wobbling dining-car trying to serve the meal, the wilder this movement became.

It was pure slapstick in the rich vein of the old silent screen. I believe my idol, Buster Keaton, would have enjoyed working with this kind of action-packed material, and my team of experienced comedians joined me in making the most of it. While the BBC hierarchy studied the result, I dashed off to make *Five Golden Hours* starring Ernie Kovacs, a brilliant American comedian with an expressively lugubrious face. We liked each other from the moment we met.

Ernie Kovacs particularly liked my 'invisible' scenarios, and told me he, too, had devised an 'invisible ant', which he 'kept' in a matchbox, complete with miniature furniture. The upshot of our meeting was a firm offer from this great comedian to join him in the States, to work with him as a writer. I was overjoyed. It looked as though the tide of misfortune had turned for me.

However, on my second day of filming I developed a high fever and a punishing cough. The terrific effort to keep *Don't Shoot, We're British!* from going under had taken its toll. Right in the middle of one of my scenes, an anxious Ernie Kovacs stopped the take with the words, 'Mike, you're on fire!' My fever was so high, I was actually steaming in the heat of a large studio lamp.

The studio had me driven home. Our family doctor examined me and rushed me straight into Bolingbroke Hospital. I had double-pneumonia and was faced with a grim fight to survive. Once again, I was to leave my body and stand on the threshold between life and death.

Chapter Twenty-seven

Squaring the World

The last thing I remembered was the sound of a baby crying in the next ward. I knew it was a little boy. He sounded exactly like my younger son, Peski, who was just a year old. There was overwhelming regret, an almost unbearable grief at the thought of leaving my family. Beyond tears, I wanted desperately to live. Despite the intense pain, I struggled hard to survive. I felt myself fainting, and realized I was dying.

Abruptly, the pain stopped. I felt my body receding from the earth at tremendous speed. Once again, as in 1942 and 1945, I felt that my soul was in pawn while the doctors and nurses fought for my life. This time I was unaware of that ambience of golden light I so clearly remembered from my previous brushes with death. I was suspended in a limbo of sleep, velvet darkness surrounded by absolute peace. I was filled with awe, waiting. I do not know for how long: it could have been eternity or a micro-second. I was beyond time. As in a falling dream, I felt a thump as my heart restarted. I was back in my body. I was very grateful.

It took me two weeks before I could get out of bed. When I did so and sat in an armchair, an agonizing pain shot up my groin. It was worse than the most acute cramp I had ever known. I was alone in the small room with a Lebanese nurse whom I had nicknamed Sheherazade. She immediately recognized the symptoms of acute venous embolism and rushed out for a doctor.

An agonizing minute passed. Then a young houseman appeared, armed with a hypodermic and the requisite drugs. He took one look at my now obscenely swollen leg and administered an intravenous injection of heparin, a powerful anti-coagulant. The consultant arrived. He examined my chest and promptly gave me an injection of pethidine to dull the pain. The small room seemed to be filled with doctors and nurses. I thought, 'Oh, Christ, here we go again!'

Mercifully, while the staff busied themselves trying to contain the blood clots, I slipped into unconsciousness.

Poor Clementina, who was near the end of her pregnancy with our fourth child, and had more than enough to contend with, now had to divide her time between Bolingbroke Hospital and home. Thank God, Nursie was still with us. Our dependable friend relieved Clementina of the responsibilities of the children, while Fifi came in to help with the cooking, both of them trying to allay the worst of her fears.

Our good friends David Lodge and Peter Goodall immediately came to the rescue. Twice daily, they ferried my anxious wife between the hospital and home, a round trip of some ten miles. Other friends phoned constantly for news. Sam and Marty Kershen visited me regularly, complete with chicken soup. Marty called it 'Jewish penicillin'. Sam Kershen, who is not only a close friend but also my accountant, quickly put my mind at rest over our financial position. That helped a lot: a practical example of 'holistic healing' by removing as much domestic worry as possible.

Peter Sellers, Harry Secombe and Ernie Kovacs all sent lavish gifts and phoned regularly to know how I was. Benny Lee visited me at every opportunity. Dick Emery came to see me and cheered me up, even though he was convinced I was dying. Clive Dunn and Barry Lupino also visited me. David Lodge always popped in whenever he drove Clementina over to Bolingbroke.

My brother Tony and his wife Mona brought friends to give me healing. Frank Muir came to tell me that Eric Maschwitz wanted to go ahead with the production of six *Square Worlds* as soon as I was better. I thanked them all. It felt good to have such friends, but it was sad to note the silence of others.

The pain was kept under control with injections of pethidine every five hours, but my left leg was now very swollen and badly discoloured. Finally, Barry Murray, my specialist, told me frankly, 'Unless the condition of your leg improves, I may have to amputate.'

I was so woozy with drugs that I did not care. The pain was even breaking through the cloud nine effect of the injections. Then the miracle occurred. Soon after my specialist left, Florrie Dott, my father's large, motherly Northumbrian housekeeper, came to give me direct healing. I told her what Barry Murray had said. Florrie snorted her dismissal of medical opinion, and said in her broad accent, 'Way, aye, Michael! Whar not goin' to lose whar leg!'

Despite the sickening smell of gas gangrene, which I remembered from the war, Florrie placed her warm hands on either side of my obscenely distended leg. It was just like being under intense infra-red radiation; yet there was no pain. I do not know how long the healing took, because very soon I drifted off into a peaceful sleep. When I woke up, the pain was no longer intense and, after another injection, I slept again.

At seven o'clock the next morning, Barry Murray came in. He was ready to order the pre-med injection, but first he took a final look at my leg. When he saw the extraordinary change in its condition, he showed his surprise. 'What the hell's been going on?'

'A healer has given me treatment.'

My specialist looked at me over his half-moon glasses. He grinned. 'I wouldn't argue with that. I've seen this sort of thing happen before. Not often, especially with your condition. Well done, Michael, you're going to keep your leg. By the way, you'll have to come off pethidine. At this rate, you'll soon be addicted. We'll have to change you to Omnopon and progressively decrease the dosage.'

'I'm a writer, Barry. Can't I have the cold turkey cure? I've read about it. I believe it would be a useful experience.' Looking back on that ill-considered request, I think I must have been insane at the time.

Barry Murray thought so too. 'I don't recommend it. Frankly, Michael, I don't think you'll be able to stand it. Withdrawal symptoms are most unpleasant. I don't think you know what you're letting yourself in for.'

I do not know what perverseness made me do it, but I would never go through that appalling process again, even for a fortune.

Over the next forty-eight hours, I experienced something of the hell that addicted drug users suffer during withdrawal. I refused to give in. I realize that it was sheer, mulish stupidity on my part, but that experience completely altered my attitude towards drug-addicts. Since then I have felt great compassion for them. I also believe that anyone who chooses to take the drug route to 'Nirvana' is tragically misguided.

At the end of the withdrawal symptoms, which Barry Murray told me were mild in comparison with what some poor devils go through, I woke from my first real sleep in two days and nights. Matron came in, all smiles, and told me that Clementina had presented me with a lovely daughter. Suddenly life felt good. But it took over three months before I could walk properly and was fit enough to tackle the first six shows of *It's a Square World*.

Being back at home with my family and my adorable baby daughter Serena, whom we nicknamed 'Suki', did me more good than all the medications and skilled nursing. But I am very grateful to the staff of Bolingbroke Hospital, and especially to my lovely Lebanese nurse who immediately spotted that near-fatal pulmonary embolism.

In 1961, after a four-year search, we found a new home in Esher. Little Tylers was a large, well-proportioned

Surrey farm house built in 1921 by Blair Imrie, a pupil of Edwin Lutyens. It stands in an acre of garden. It was ideal for bringing up a family. We all loved it, and lived there for twenty-seven years.

It's a Square World was destined to run with increasing success for over four years, finally gaining viewing figures of around fourteen to sixteen million and winning for the BBC and me the Grand Prix de la Presse at the 1963 International Television Concours at Montreux, and my Writers' Guild award for the same year.

It was a period of intense effort, requiring total concentration. It was also one of the most creative eras of my life and, as my health improved, I enjoyed its challenge, though sometimes my miraculously retained left leg troubled me. I am delighted that many viewers remember this series with such affection.

Just after *Square World*'s extraordinary success at Montreux, I found myself trapped on *This Is Your Life*, presented by Eamonn Andrews. Pop was delighted by the recognition I was receiving. He told me, 'I realize that, through your comedy, you will be able to open many doors, and use your clairvoyance and prevision to help people in many ways. After all, that is what I trained you for.' A week later, he died in his sleep.

Square World introduced the British public to a new approach to small-screen comedy. My team of character-comedians included my friends Clive Dunn, Dick Emery, Leon Thau, Frank Thornton, Joe Gibbons, Bruce Lacey, my erstwhile prop-maker, and, later, John Bluthal. Once again Benny Lee performed and sang, until we 'destroyed' him in various ingenious ways. The first and second series were produced by Barry Lupino, who gave me every encouragement and assistance, making significant amounts of pre-filming readily available for the show.

Dick Emery's remarkable talents had in the past been so woefully underemployed by television that at one time he had seriously contemplated suicide. At that point, I invited him to join my cast for the ABC *After Hours* series. He soon emerged as an outstanding member of the team and from then on, Dick Emery's luck changed dramatically. Until the day of his death, he told press interviewers how much he owed me for radically changing his sorry circumstances at that time and launching him on his subsequent career. He was one of the very few artists, among a considerable number of performers whom I have helped over the years, who actually acknowledged my efforts: for which kindness I thank him.

Square World had quite a battle to establish itself as a top television series, but right from the start we acquired a cult following, mainly among the young. It looked to me as though we were following the same lines that had governed the growth in popularity of the early *Goon Shows*. But there the similarity ended.

I had no intention of creating archetypal characters who would appear in every one of my shows with appropriate catchphrases, a technique we had avoided using in the early *Goon Shows*, but which later became an integral part of the series after I left.

In one *Goon Show* we even introduced a character who entered and exited accompanied by the sound of a door opening and closing. He muttered one line, 'No coal today!' This was followed immediately by a recording of hysterical laughter and applause.

We played this running-gag several times during that one show and finally tagged the 'No coal today' character's last appearance by Peter asking Harry, 'Who was that?'

Harry replied, 'We don't actually know. But whoever he is, he has the world's finest sound effects record of a door opening and closing, followed by hysterical laughter and applause.'

We included this bit of nonsense because we were sick of that ubiquitous 'entrance/exit' gimmick, which had been started by the wartime *ITMA* show, starring Tommy Handley. It was odd that eventually even *The Goon*

Show reverted to that way of getting easy, conditioned laughs from a studio audience.

I used the *Square World* comedians to the best of their abilities by writing specifically for each one's individual talents. For example, one of my best sketches was *NATO War Games*, which was performed round a three-dimensional model of a battlefield set out on a large table top.

Dick Emery made a marvellous British general, playing him as a pompous, latter-day Montgomery, complete with lisping 'Rs'; the lanky American commander was a fine caricature by Frank Thornton; Clive Dunn, who had learnt his German in a prisoner-of-war camp, accurately portrayed the autocratic German general; and the part of the incomprehensible, excitable Turkish commander-in-chief was performed by that splendid eccentric, Bruce Lacey. I played the multi-lingual British interpreter who not only has to translate every instruction into German and Turkish, but also has to transform the words into colloquial Texan for the benefit of the confused American commander.

The whole sketch played beautifully, progressing logically from the increasing difficulties of translating Dick Emery's simple instructions, which were basically, 'We will carry out the manoeuvres using Mark Five tanks.'

The comedy develops through a series of unfortunate misunderstandings enhanced by the accidental breaking of one of the German general's model tanks by a careless blow from the British general's swagger-cane, and rapidly turns into a complete shambles, with the infuriated Allied commanders engaging each other in a miniature table-top battle, using the models as their weapons.

The climax comes when the Texan general goes berserk and fires a model nuclear missile. The missile rises out of a trap-door in the table top and flies through the collapsing ceiling, presumably soaring out into the stratosphere on its fatal trajectory. This catastrophic action stops the warring commanders cold, eliciting the final, stiff-upper-lip remark from Dick Emery, 'Well, gentlemen, that gives us all about four minutes. Who's for a cup of instant tea?'

The description of this sketch may not strike the reader as being particularly funny, but I assure you that it not only did well with the studio audience but it also worked on-screen, a combination of achievements which does not always occur.

Of course, as *Square World* was a largely experimental series, not every sketch worked so well, but most of the comedy material was very successful, hence the large viewing figures that the series eventually commanded.

John Law's role was to get my ideas, situations, and character dialogue down on paper just as I described them to him as the scenes passed across the inner screen of my mind. Nevertheless, John sometimes came up with an excellent idea of his own, for example when an unemotional, archetypal BBC newscaster of that era is reading out the football results, and suddenly realizes that he might have the winning Pools coupon. He takes it out of his pocket and starts checking his forecast against the actual result, rapidly becoming hysterical until he finds that Fortune has turned against him, and he starts to get his coupon wrong. Broken in spirit, he hastily reverts to his usual unemotional reading of the results.

I enjoyed that piece so much that I played the excitable newscaster and later re-recorded it for one side of a disc, which became very popular and is still being played on radio. It remains as an affectionate memory of my late friend.

I designed many intricate models for *Square World*. These were filled with frenzied miniature action denoting the presence of the tiny invisible participants in such situations as 'The Flea Olympic Games', 'Climbing the Smutterhorn', 'The Battle of Waterloo', 'The Shoot-Out at the K.O. Corral', 'The Roman Invasion of Britain', etc.

These were made to my designs by Jack Kine and his splendid team at the BBC's Visual Aids Department.

When we first started using their talents, Jack's assistants were a small, often neglected outfit, mainly engaged on making models for science programmes. By the time *Square World* had run its four-year course, Jack's department had grown exponentially, and it was very much in demand by everyone, including many other comedy shows. I would often work late into the night helping them put together the more outrageous of my ideas.

These miniature scenarios often went wrong on transmission, and did not perform quite as I had intended, but that only made them funnier. Muttered conversations and muffled curses from the special effects operators who were crowded together under the tables on which the complex models were mounted often became audible to me, and I reacted accordingly, unable to refrain from giggling as I altered my commentary to fit the unexpected changes in the visual action and effects. This gave the animated models an unexpected life of their own, adding a new dimension to the comedy.

The extravagant, pre-filmed endings to most of the shows seem to have remained vividly in viewers' memories, with such episodes as 'Sinking the Houses of Parliament with a Chinese War-Junk', 'The Russian Expedition to Climb Woolwich Rubbish Dump', 'The Search for the Source of the Thames', 'Moby Tom, the Great White Whale' and 'The Great Escape from the BBC, by Tunnel'.

Another popular part of each *Square World* was when I read the News as a typical solemn-faced newscaster. The type of news item I read was the role model for similar material in many subsequent shows such as *That Was the Week That Was*, *The Two Ronnies* and *Not the Nine O'Clock News*.

Writing and making well over fifty of my half-hour *Square Worlds* was a wholetime job, starting on 1 January of each of those four years of intensive effort, and finishing with my last recording each year, which sometimes occurred just before Christmas. Here are some examples of incidents that occurred while we were filming some of my more off-beat end-pieces. The episode 'Moby Tom, the Great White Whale' was about Moby Dick's thirty-foot-long 'younger brother', who swam up the Thames to attack Clive Dunn, a latter-day 'Captain Ahab' Thames Conservancy lock-keeper, complete with a wooden peg-leg. Jack and his team had constructed a marvellous 'Moby Tom', which could proceed equally well in water or on land. This huge rubber whale fitted neatly on to a wooden raft propelled by an outboard motor, but it could be detached from its floating platform and carried by nearly the whole of Jack's devoted team inside it, for use on dry land.

It was wonderfully realistic but the Thames Conservancy Board refused me permission to navigate it in the confined waters of their area of the river, mainly because it was 'insufficiently manoeuvrable' but also, as they pointed out, 'As a vessel, it is not properly fitted with a chemical toilet.' Jack offered to carry out this modification, but the Board remained adamant.

Instead, John Street, the producer who had succeeded Barry Lupino, arranged for us to film the great white whale on the extensive waters of the Welsh Harp.

I remember that it was a bitterly cold day when we launched our marvellous prop and started filming the sequence where Clive Dunn attempts to harpoon 'Moby Tom' from a rubber dinghy. Jack Kine and an assistant were inside the whale, steering it with the outboard motor, operating its mouth and rolling its eyes with great effect. Although both of them were wearing wet-suits, they were chilled to the bone, so I handed Jack, through 'Tom's' big mouth, a bottle of rum as a specific against the extreme cold.

We were two hours filming that scene, and my frozen friends took full advantage of 'Nelson's blood', finishing the bottle of rum between them. The whale now lurched around the Welsh Harp in wild circles, a unique spectacle. We were helpless with laughter, which made the filming harder, and as we finished, Clive, whose dinghy was rammed by the whale, was thrown overboard. It must have been icy but Clive was laughing as much as we were when we hauled him out.

At the end of the scenario, 'Moby Tom' comes out of the river near Chelsea, where we got permission to sail our weird craft, and proceeds to the Kensington Natural History Museum, where his 'Mother', the huge blue whale, comforts her 'Baby'.

Of course, there was no way we could film that touching moment in the museum so we compromised by filming the whale making its way there along the road, supported inside by a large detachment of Jack's long-suffering team. Nobody seemed to take any notice of this phenomenon, even when the thirty-foot white whale waited patiently at the traffic lights. We were even allotted two policemen, who gravely stopped the traffic to let the great mammal through a busy intersection.

'The Russian Expedition to Climb Woolwich Rubbish Dump' required the visiting 'Russian' mountaineering expedition to disembark from Captain Scott's ship, *Discovery*, and proceed along the embankment on skis, while roped together, traversing the zebra crossing and disappearing down the escalator of the underground. Once again, the British public politely ignored this stirring sight, as Frank, Leon, Joe, Andrea (our cheerful stunt-lady), with me leading, trudged up the gangway, and skied along the pavement (with ball-bearings beneath our skis).

Like many of my other ideas, this scenario had been suggested by a chance encounter. While driving to the BBC studios at Ealing, I had noticed a building with the intriguing sign 'Isleworth Explorers Club'. Naturally, I stopped the car and went inside to enquire who would want to explore Isleworth.

The friendly caretaker explained to me that this was the home of a boys' club which sent out youngsters to undertake explorations as a character-building exercise. My imagination started to go into overdrive especially when he told me that the older boys had gone to Russia to climb a mountain there and, in return, the Russians had sent an expedition to do the same sort of thing in Britain.

Isleworth is flat as a board, so I transposed the Russian operation to Woolwich, where the highest point is the towering rubbish dump, which we eventually climbed with the permission of the Woolwich gas works. I can still remember the smell, and nearly being engulfed by a 'rubbishlanche', which was arranged to thunder down upon us and which got a bit out of hand. We had to have showers at the gas works, where we were entertained most hospitably to a welcome lunch.

Perhaps the most ambitious scenario that I dreamed up was 'The Sinking of the Houses of Parliament'. I was with my family on the Thames in my small estuary-cruiser *Bumbly Seven* when I noticed a striking all-teak Chinese junk moored beside a bungalow. I came alongside and asked the owner for permission to come aboard. He turned out to be an actor who was 'resting' and proudly showed me over the beautiful vessel, a marvel of Chinese woodcraft with an intricately carved interior.

I sensed immediately that I could use such a vessel with great effect in *Square World*, and I asked the owner if I could hire it for this purpose. He replied, 'Only if you use me as an actor when you film my ship.'

A week later, I was filming down in Limehouse. A young Chinese doctor who was watching the proceedings asked me if I could help him with his protest against the Greater London Council's declared intent to move London's Chinatown from Limehouse to a new site in Gerrard Street. I asked him what he intended to do about it. He grinned as he told me, 'I would like to sail my grandfather's old war-junk up the Thames to Westminster Reach and bombard the Houses of Parliament with cannon fire.'

I thought, what a splendid idea! When I returned to the Television Centre, I told John Law what I had in mind, and that I had found a real Chinese junk. John would not believe me until I showed him some pictures of the vessel. Our producer, John Street, was enthusiastic and set about getting the requisite formalities underway.

One morning a few weeks later, my resolute team of comedians, dressed as eighteenth-century Chinese warriors, boarded the junk and set sail in Westminster Reach opposite the Houses of Parliament. The ever-resourceful Jack Kine had armed the fierce-looking crew with Chinese cannons in the shape of Dogs of Fo and loaded them with pyrotechnics.

With Clive Dunn dressed as Fu Manchu in full mandarin robes, plus his warriors, Frank, Joe, Leon, *et al.*, and with our actor-owner friend at the tiller, for two hours we bombarded the Houses of Parliament with polystyrene cannon balls. Yet during that time, nobody walking over Westminster and Lambeth bridges, at either end of this scene, took a blind bit of notice.

Of course, we had been given full permission for our vessel to manoeuvre in this particular reach of the river and to let off various sound effects so the Metropolitan River Police could not interfere with us, but they watched the proceedings from their motor launch.

At the end of filming, the police launch roared out from underneath Westminster Bridge and a police sergeant shouted over his hailer the immortal words, 'Do any of you gentlemen speak English?'

In the final scenes we showed the House of Commons sinking, with bowler-hatted MPs hurriedly abandoning that stately edifice. Previously I had shown them discussing the vital issue of whether there should be purchase tax on British-made raspberry-blowers. Over the last, static shot of the cheering crew on the war-junk, we rolled the caption, 'You have been watching a party political broadcast on behalf of the British people'.

Compared with subsequent media attacks on the Conservative Government in power at the time, it all seemed harmless enough. Therefore, the reason the Director-General of the time, Sir Hugh Carleton Greene, himself gave the order to cancel the particular *Square World* which featured this episode seems to have been a personal one. As I had devised and filmed the piece many weeks before the announcement of the General Election, I could not possibly have known, or even guessed, when this event would be held. I was as surprised as everyone else at the odd coincidence.

But I did appreciate that my scenario might conceivably upset some pompous politician, therefore I bowed to the BBC's decision to postpone the episode until the election was over. It was the press who were tickled by this decision and they played it for maximum effect. And there the matter should have ended, but Sir Hugh Carleton Greene evidently wanted blood. He wrote an article in the *Sunday Telegraph* in which he accused me of demeaning the great institution of Britain's Parliament.

In a phone call to Keneth Adam, the Assistant to the Director-General, I objected to the wholly inaccurate angling of this article, and pointed out that Sir Hugh Carleton Greene was lying when he wrote that he had seen the episode himself since the film was still in pieces and therefore unviewable. Keneth Adam became extremely angry and demanded that I apologize.

I flatly refused to do so. I stuck to my point and told him that unless I received an immediate apology in writing, I would place the whole matter in the hands of the press. That shook him, and it must have sealed my fate as far as the inflexibly autocratic BBC hierarchy were concerned. Of course, with hindsight, I can see that I should have given that story to the press and let them sort out for themselves what was going on. Nevertheless, I got my apology.

I believe the reason I had incurred the wrath of the Director-General was because I had refused to follow a directive given to me by a VIP in the BBC to use *It's a Square World* specifically as a satirical political weapon against the Tory Government.

I pointed out that if I agreed to carry out such a biased directive, I would be betraying my wartime comrades-in-arms in at least one of the main principles which we had fought for, and for which many of my friends had died, i.e. freedom of speech.

From the moment I took my stand against that immoral directive, I was given the cold shoulder, even when *It's a Square World* won the Grand Prix de La Presse in 1963 at the Montreux International Television Festival.

This was the first-ever comedy award to be won by the BBC at this world-renowned television festival, and it should have been the cause for some sort of congratulations from the high brass. Instead, I felt it was with brusque and obvious reluctance that I was invited up to Keneth Adam's office and given a glass of warm champagne, with the cursory words, 'Apparently, Bentine, you have won some kind of award at Montreux.' That was the sole 'congratulatory' statement to me.

A number of people in the know told me that my show was also the hot favourite to win the coveted Golden Rose as well as the Grand Prix de la Press. They also told me a strong protest had been made by the Russian judge on that television jury. He objected to my show receiving the Golden Rose and vetoed the sketch in which I had featured Khrushchev pounding his desk to the tune of 'Black Eyes'.

This incident occurred in a pre-filmed episode in which I had turned the United Nations Assembly into a huge international *Juke Box Jury*. It was a piece that apparently had also upset Sir Hugh Carleton Greene. What was even more bizarre was that a Russian judge should have been included, for the first time ever and at the last moment, on this particular Montreux Festival jury when the Russians did not even have an entry in the festival.

As I have explained, I finished each series of *Square World* with a piece of comedy film. My first series finished with Jack Hawkins, who was well known for his roles as heroic Royal Navy captains, ordering the abandoning of the BBC Television Centre, after it had been hit by torpedoes from a German U-boat (during my interview with him about his film *The Cruel Sea*).

In the course of subsequent film endings, I destroyed the personnel at the BBC TV Centre with a giant man-eating orchid. I next set alight to the famous round building, which to me looked a bit like a defensively circled wagon-train, using fire-arrows shot by a band of marauding Apache Indians led by their chief (Dick Emery).

Finally, an absent-minded Dr Who (beautifully played by Clive Dunn) ignited a giant space-rocket in the studio and projected the whole TV Centre into outer space. As the BBC orbited the earth, it was accompanied by a straight-faced commentary by Patrick Moore, the television astronomer. In his own ad-libbed words, 'There are rumours that there is a form of intelligent life inhabiting this new and spectacular object in the night sky, but I, personally, do not believe this to be so.'

It was not too surprising that when a gang of stocking-masked criminals drove up to the BBC accounts department at the Television Centre, rushed inside, knocked out the cashiers, and nicked a payroll of some £10,000, the BBC security guards, so the story goes, made no effort to intervene and, as the gangsters drove off in their stolen Jaguar with the loot, shouted after them, 'When is the programme going to be on, Mr Bentine?'

Despite all the drawbacks, I really enjoyed devising and making *It's a Square World*. Apparently millions of viewers enjoyed watching the results. Which, of course, made the whole thing worthwhile.

Chapter Twenty-eight

My Inca Genes

My Amazon adventure started with the sudden death of my eldest cousin, Pedro, in spring 1966. When I heard the news my still small voice told me to go to Peru.

I had long wanted to introduce Clementina to my Peruvian family *en masse*. There were then fifty-six of them, apart from a few Bentins in Germany, the result of my Uncle Arturo's first marriage to Margarita Weiss in 1910. Over the years, a number of my family had met Clementina on visits to England, and they all had become close friends, especially my 'niece' Rosa Montori, daughter of my cousin Rosita and John Tudela.

My wife is used to my making on the spot decisions and she is, in her own words, 'always ready to go a couple of hundred miles to see a nut cracked'. So Clementina agreed that we should visit Peru and meet the rest of the family before tragedy could strike again. My wife is very family-minded and keeps up massive correspondence with our many relations scattered all over the world. I cabled Rosa that we were coming.

Nursie as usual took charge on the home front, and we left Heathrow within the week. The children were as thrilled about it as we were, especially Gus, who longed for a Jagua blow-pipe from the Peruvian *selva* (rainforests).

During my first flight to Peru, I often wondered what my father's thoughts must have been as he made that long-dreamed-of flight back to his homeland in 1951. He had not believed the first news of the Wright brothers' classic hop of under two hundred yards in 1904, and had put it down to yankee propaganda. Yet, only forty-seven years later, he had flown back to Peru in a four-engined Boeing Stratocruiser.

We arrived at Jorge Chavez Airport at two in the morning. The apron of the airport is normally unavailable to anyone except passengers, aircrew and airport staff, but because the Bentins owned Aviaçion Faucett, fourteen people had been allowed to wait on the tarmac to embrace us. We kissed and hugged them all, including the one on the end of the line who turned out to be the Customs officer. Being Peruvian, he hugged and kissed me back.

Accompanied by the affectionate Customs official, we were whisked through airport formalities and driven by Antonio's chauffeur to the country club in Mira Flores where he lived. We were convoyed there by cars containing the rest of my welcoming cousins, 'nephews' and 'nieces' sounding horns joyously in a triumphant procession.

My family, especially *en masse*, tend to speak at the same time as everyone else, part in Spanish and part in English. I am used to it, and adjust accordingly, but Clementina was somewhat confused. She told me she was not sure which one was speaking or whose question to answer.

Cousin Antonio, that most considerate of men, gently but firmly shooed them all away and sent us both to bed to sleep it off. We did not wake up till noon, to be greeted by a family lunch at which twenty more cousins turned up to welcome us to Peru.

Another Peruvian trait, which is pretty well standard throughout South America, is for everyone to greet everyone else as though they had been apart for years, even when they were together the night before. My family is no exception. Because Clementina has spent many years with that marvellously mad Russian ballet family, the Legats

374

and the Brigers, she soon settled into this affectionate pattern.

Many times, both before and after the Second World War, it was suggested by one or other of my Peruvian cousins that my brother and I should make our homes in Peru. Cousin Antonio, knowing my passion for flight, wanted me to join him in Aviaçion Faucett to learn airline management, the more so after the war because of my four years' experience with the Royal Air Force. I wanted very much to go to Peru, and would have accepted gladly but I felt I first had to prove myself in my chosen profession, which happened to be show business. By the time I had done so, I had become so involved with comedy that I let slip the many opportunities offered by my Peruvian family.

Those few weeks in Peru flashed past in a hectic whirl of activity. There was so much that every member of my family wanted to show us. It seemed to Clementina that every day she met yet another Bentin. At one family party, thrown for us by my cousins, Luis and Luisa, all of the many Bentins present were labelled with their names, except the thirteen Bentin-Humbert children, who were simply numbered 1–13.

At this party we met Angelica, my father's nurse. She was then over ninety, a much-loved member of the family, whom Grandfather Bentin had brought down from the sierras when she was only seven years old. We noticed that everyone, on arrival, made a special point of kissing her with great affection. This remarkable lady had one of the most striking faces I have ever seen. I longed to draw her portrait, but I was told that Angelica would not have liked it, believing that I would have been 'capturing her soul'.

To my delight, Angelica clearly remembered my father as 'Adancito'. She even knew the names and relationships of all the British Bentins. As Angelica sat there, surrounded by the children, she made *picarones* for us. These are a kind of small pretzel-shaped doughnut, made out of sweetened batter, cooked in boiling-hot oil, and dipped in cane sugar, a great favourite with the children, including me.

My cousins were enchanted with Clementina, even my female relations who, like all South Americans, tend to be very wary of other women, especially pretty foreign ones. Jealousy is a Peruvian trait. My wife, being blonde, slim, and lovely, contrasted vividly with their brunette Latin voluptuousness. Although the male Bentins buzzed around her, their wives still clasped Clementina warmly to their ample bosoms. I was surprised that the typical Peruvian female reserve had melted away like Lima's morning mist. When Antonio noticed this interesting phenomenon, he nicknamed my wife 'Neblinita' meaning 'Little Morning Mist'. Clementina was an outstanding hit.

One slight embarrassment was that, owing to Pedro's recent death, all the Bentin family wore black, while we gringos steadfastly wore cheerful fabrics and light-coloured suits. I explained to each member of my family that this was a deliberate choice on my part because of my firm conviction that a good soul such as my beloved cousin Pedro must have passed over into the happiest of realms, where he was surrounded by all the loving members of his family who had preceded him. Therefore I believed that this was a time for celebration of his happiness not mourning for our grief.

One or two of the more hidebound members of the family felt some resentment at our lack of conformity, but even this mood soon passed and the rest of my cousins, 'nephews' and 'nieces' took the hint and changed from their sombre clothes into something more cheerful in honour of Pedro, whom we all loved so much. Rosa Montori remarked, 'Thank God! Until you crazy gringos came and cheered us all up, we looked like a lot of crows.'

It was decided that we should visit Cuzco, Machu Picchu, Pisac and the whole Alto Plano. We went with Mimi Bentin, Cousin José's daughter, whom we knew from her schooling in England. She had been delegated to act as our guide and interpreter.

Flying into Cuzco airport, 10,000 feet above sea-level, in cloudy conditions can be an unnerving experience. On this occasion, as a member of the Bentin family, I was allowed to sit in the co-pilot's seat, and I flew the Douglas DC-6b for part of the journey.

On the way, Captain Sanvitti told me about phenomena that both he and another senior Faucett pilot, Captain Kling, had witnessed at different times while flying over the plain of Nasca, which is world famous for its strange ground markings. He explained to me, 'Flying in Peru, as in most of South America, is mostly over rough country, mountainous regions, and jungle. Therefore radio contact at regular intervals is all-important, as radar coverage is only possible near airports. Standard Operating Procedure is to send regular progress reports *en route*. These go out about every fifteen minutes. When flying between Lima and Arequipa, Lima Radio passes the aircraft over to Arequipa Radio at Nasca, and from then on we use the Arequipa Range, for our regular position reports.

'The idea behind this SOP is that if there is a May Day emergency-call or an aircraft misses its routine radio check, search planes will know approximately where to look for it. While *en route* for Arequipa, my radio went off the air and naturally Lima and Arequipa operators got worried. They both thought we were down.'

The pilot hesitated before continuing, 'The reason we couldn't transmit was because we were being buzzed by a flying saucer.' Captain Sanvitti looked quizzically at me. 'I'm telling you this, Señor Bentin, because your cousin Antonio said you would be interested and that you wouldn't think I was crazy.'

I was fascinated. 'I assure you, Captain Sanvitti, I have no doubts whatsoever about your sanity, or my wife and I wouldn't be flying with you.'

The experienced Faucett captain smiled wryly, 'Neither my friend, Captain Kling, who had a similar experience, nor I, like to talk about such things. After all, we both want to go on flying long enough to collect our pensions. It is not a good thing for a pilot to gain the reputation of seeing things. But I don't mind filling *you* in on the details of our sightings of these Ovnis, as we call them. Your term for them is UFO, is it not?'

I nodded excitedly, 'Please go on, Skipper.'

'We were flying over the Nasca ground markings on a clear night with unlimited visibility when my attention was called by the second pilot to a flashing light on our starboard bow. It was pulsing, varying in colour between red, blue and green. The varying bright light was certainly not coming from another aircraft or a helicopter. The position of the light was wrong for either of them.

'I was reluctant to report the encounter to Lima or Arequipa. I thought that the sighting might be caused by lightning. In the dry air above the Nasca desert there are a lot of strange electrical phenomena. But I had never seen anything like that.' He paused. 'However, as it was time to contact Lima, I sent a positional check and a sighting report. Or rather I tried to do so. The radio was dead. We tried repeatedly to make contact, but all we got was either dead air or unusually loud static, drowning out everything. Nothing was getting through to either Lima or Arequipa.

'All the while, the flashing light kept pace with us and even flew round us a number of times, always keeping at a safe distance as though it was looking us over. The odd thing was that although our radio-set seemed to be out of commission, our four piston-engines were not affected in any way, so whatever was causing the severe electrical interference didn't affect the spark-plugs.

'Meanwhile the cabin staff were busy reassuring the passengers, who had seen the unusual phenomenon and were becoming alarmed. They took a lot of calming down. We must have been out of radio contact with both Lima and Arequipa radio-watches for over fifteen minutes beyond our normal reporting time.

'Naturally, both airports were very relieved when we eventually came back on air. Captain Kling, who is a very able pilot, with many thousands of hours flight time, had an almost identical experience over the same region twenty-four hours later. The only difference was that he was *en route from* Arequipa to Lima.'

'Could it have been St Elmo's fire?' I suggested.

'Not a chance. Both Kling and I have seen that sort of classic electrical disturbance before, but this phenomenon was nothing like it.'

I told Captain Sanvitti about the experiences of my Lancaster crews after two separate heavy raids on the German coast at Peenemunde. The crews had reported being pursued by lights which manoeuvred round the Lancasters at high speed without attacking them. Allowing for the obvious differences between war and peace, his own experience seemed to be an exact parallel. The pulsating light had made no hostile moves but had appeared to be inspecting his aircraft.

Later, when I flew to Iquitos with Captain Kling, he confirmed Sanvitti's story. The same thing had happened at more or less the same position over the Nasca desert the night after Sanvitti and his crew had seen the strange light. He had no explanation either. Kling, who was German, just told me the facts without indicating what he thought might have caused the phenomena. Neither of these two fine pilots had the slightest doubt that they had encountered something completely outside their long experience of aerial phenomena.

Cuzco airport in those days had none of the modern landing aids that have made today's mountain flying so much safer. We landed through cloud by taking a sighting on a prominent mountain peak before sliding into the 'clag' and then, at an exact air speed and by using a large stop-watch, Captain Sanvitti made two steep turns which, when we broke through the cloud-base, brought us precisely on to our final approach, two miles from the end of the runway.

Obviously, I was not flying the DC-6b at that time. I just stared mesmerized at my set of blind-flying instruments while the skilled pilot performed this feat of airmanship. It did not appear to worry him one bit. However, I prayed a lot.

In accordance with Antonio's precise instructions, we spent the first twenty-four hours in Cuzco as effortlessly as possible. This did not prevent me from getting the savage mountain sickness caused by the greatly reduced oxygen at that height. It felt like the worst migraine I had ever experienced. I lay on my bed like an animal in pain and breathed oxygen from the cylinder that Antonio thoughtfully had provided. Once it was over, I felt fine. I recommend anyone making that trip to the Alto Plano to follow instructions to the letter.

We had an excellent guide around Cuzco in Theresa, Faucett's local representative, a large, ebullient lady who spoke Spanish and English with equal rapidity. She had been born in Lima and had moved to Cuzco to cure her asthma which is prevalent in Peru, especially in the coastal regions. Mimi had not been to Cuzco before and was just as excited as we were about the whole trip. At that altitude, I was all for taking it easy, but Clementina wanted to see everything.

The ancient Inca city is a marvellous place. Its many Spanish colonial buildings which make up the principal architecture of Cuzco are typical of the heritage left by the Conquistadors who had ruled there after 1533. Fortunately, the massive, accurately cut, hard-stone walls built by the Inca master masons are also perfectly preserved. We were never in doubt as to who originally had built this 'city of the clouds'.

Sacsayhuaman, pronounced 'sexy woman', is a titanic stone fortress above Cuzco which dominates the entrance to the Urubamba, the sacred valley of the Incas. A third of a mile long, the towering granite ramparts, constructed of colossal megaliths, rise in three separate tiers high above the frowning hill top, dwarfing the sprawling city below. It is a stupendous achievement, to my mind as impressive as the Egyptian pyramids, considering that the Incas had no knowledge of the wheel and possessed no hard-metal tools other than bronze.

The hundreds of gigantic blocks, each of which weighs in excess of three hundred tons, have been so accurately cut, and engineered with such precision by these master masons, that it is not possible to run a knife-blade between their perfectly chamfered facets. I know, because I have often tried.

Machu Picchu, which is only a couple of hours by train down the valley from Cuzco, is the so-called Lost City of the Incas, a stone town with no obvious fortifications, invisible from the jungle-covered valley floor. It clings in terraces to the steep face of one side of a high saddle of rock, the other side being a sheer precipice overhanging the Urubamba river, a seething torrent of white water well over a thousand feet below. I defy anybody not to be impressed by its lonely magnificence and not to marvel at the precise masonic skills with which it was built.

As I sat beside the Intihuatana, the massive stone gnomon or astronomical/sun-clock on top of Machu Picchu at the edge of the precipice, my mind ranged over all that my Inca ancestors had achieved, from their gigantic megalithic architecture to their surprising skills in medicine and surgery, involving successful trepannations of fractured skulls, the use of anaesthetics (cocaine) and complex antiseptic techniques using boiled dressings of llama wool and plant extracts.

Yet despite all their experienced armies and their many undoubted skills, in one year, 1532, the Incas were conquered and decimated by my other ancestors, the ruthless invading Spanish Conquistadors.

Only here, in Machu Picchu, did the Spanish Conquistadors fail to conquer. The reason was simple. They never found the legendary city. Its invisibility from the Urubamba valley below kept it safe. Archaeologists are divided in their opinions as to whether Machu Picchu was inhabited at the time of the conquest. Whoever is right, this mysterious city remained inviolate until it was discovered in 1911 by Hiram Bingham, the American Rotarian from Chicago who loved adventure.

We stayed on long after the other visitors had left and watched the sun set. It was spectacular, as Inti, the sun-god of the Incas, disappeared behind the western peaks in a quivering ball of blood-red fire. It was easy to understand why the Incas had chosen this isolated place for the building of their hidden city. Machu Picchu was not a fortress, it was a temple.

While we watched we ate wild strawberries, which grow plentifully at the summit of the mountain city. As the short twilight closed in, and before the snakes came out of the undergrowth, we reluctantly trudged along the short trail to the visitors' hotel. On the way, I told Clementina and Mimi I had experienced an eerie feeling of *déjà vu* when I had walked along the narrow cat-walk which tops the spacious Court of Sacred Games.

This enclosed pitch, about four times the size of a tennis court, is sited in the centre of the hidden city. The flat, sandy surface, covered by a short fuzz of mountain grass, is enclosed by high walls rising in terraces, where spectators once sat to witness the sacred sport. Archaeologists believe that a ritual game, using a murderously hard gutta-percha ball, was played by apprentice priests. Vase paintings on Inca jugs and drinking vessels show various versions of this arcane game. They depict Incan athletes wearing close-fitting headdresses, presumably for protection, competing in a savage version of volley-ball.

By the fierce expressions on the players' faces, they are trying desperately hard to project a solid-looking ball, about the size of a large grapefruit, towards a stone ring which juts out from the centre of one wall of the court. According to the paintings, the use of the participants' hands was prohibited. The scowling players are shown striking the ball only with their forearms, thighs and feet, which have protective bindings wrapped round them.

Earlier in the day, from the vantage point of the Inca's Walk above the stone stadium I had visualized this deadly sport in progress. It was only a brief glimpse of the past, but the clairvoyant vision was vivid and disturbing.

My imagination was fired by this magical place, by Cuzco and particularly by Sacsayhuaman. When we returned to Lima, I talked with several scholars at the archaeological museum. They confirmed the details of what I had visualized as I stood on the Inca's Walk.

We had only a few more days in Lima, and our time was filled with voluble family parties as each segment of the Bentin clan vied with the other in their overwhelming hospitality. Antonio was determined that we should see Nasca. He particularly wanted us to meet his friend, Maria Reiche, the German scholar who had become the recognized authority on those mysterious ground markings. She had devoted her life to interpreting the meaning and purpose of the Nasca lines. Sadly, Dr Reiche was not well at the time and Antonio felt that without her presence and phenomenal insight, such a visit would be incomplete. Instead, he flew us to Arequipa, the city in the southern sierras of Peru which has the reputation of being the most shaken by earthquakes in the world.

As a consolation prize for missing out on meeting the eminent Dr Reiche, *en route* to Arequipa Antonio asked Captain Sanvitti, who once again was our pilot, to circle the ground markings on the Nasca plain. One obvious advantage of flying on the Bentin family airline was that we could enjoy an orbital tour of Nasca even on a scheduled flight. The other passengers were equally surprised and delighted by this bonus as the full effect of these gigantic figures, laid out on the desolate Nascan plain with such geometric precision, is evident only from the air.

Antonio wanted us to see Arequipa for a number of reasons. This colonial city was built on its original Inca site in the shadow of three great volcanoes, all of which are intermittently active. My cousin was fascinated by the Arequipaenos themselves. They live under the constant

383

threat of erupting volcanoes and are often shaken by earthquakes, yet they would not want to live anywhere else. They are famous for their sudden changes of mood which are not entirely due to the daily quivering of the ground beneath their feet but are mainly because of the periodic release of sulphurous fumes from the active volcanoes, which can have a physiological effect. When my cousin first described this environment to me, I could not understand why anyone would want to live there, until I saw the city itself, and its breathtaking surroundings. To understand the magic of Arequipa you have to go there. We were just as enthralled with the place as my cousin.

On our return to Lima, we were plunged once more into a whirl of family activity. The whole family seemed determined to outdo each other in the warmth of their hospitality and every hour, except that of the blessed siesta, seemed to be filled with intense social activity, ranging from deafening family lunches to exciting sessions at the race-track and lazy afternoons watching the parades of the *caballos de paso*, the beautiful *walking* Arab horses for which Peru is justly famous.

One of the proud owners, seeing my polite interest, mistook me for a horseman and courteously offered me a ride. Horses and I have a mutual agreement. I do not bother them and they leave me alone. However, this time my polite refusals were swept aside as the owner handed me the reins. The Bentin family honour appeared to be involved. It was inconceivable to this Peruvian horse-owner that a Bentin was not a keen horseman.

The horse looked harmless enough and, after all, it only walked. So I duly mounted the well-trained animal before Clementina could come over and stop this insanity. In an instant, I was away, the horse pacing away like a clockwork toy.

From the start, I made a basic mistake. Not realizing that riders of these highly bred animals use a long stirrup, straight legs, and no knee pressure, I rode 'English-fashion', with my thighs and knees tightly gripping the barrel-body of my mount. It was the only way I knew how to ride and stay on.

The *caballo* snorted its outrage at this indignity and walked even faster. I clung on more tightly with my legs. This nearly drove the animal insane and its legs almost disappeared in a desperate attempt to walk still quicker. It paced itself forward in a sweating blur of action. Thinking I was doing the right thing which, in my book, was to stay in the saddle, I clutched harder with my rapidly tiring knees. By now my leg muscles were nearly in spasm.

Clementina and Rosa watched this performance with growing alarm, especially my wife, who was familiar with my attitude towards horsemanship. Rosa had naturally presumed that I could ride as well as my father.

'Oh God, he's going to be killed!' Clementina's fears were nearly confirmed when the *caballo* decided to rid himself of his offensive rider. Abruptly the small horse swerved at right angles, broke into a semi-gallop and made straight for the low-arched entrance to its stable, obviously intending to swipe me off its sweating back.

Luckily, I had suffered a similar manoeuvre in my youth when a filthy-tempered hack used a low branch as its unseating device. I hung on tight, bowed low over the *caballo*'s neck and prayed. We whizzed under the low arch with a couple of feet to spare and came to a dead stop inside the stable yard, the poor beast trembling with shock, indignation and fury that it had failed to kill me.

I dismounted gingerly, sweating even more than the horse, and gently patted its foaming neck till it had calmed down sufficiently to whinny its protest at such treatment. I was leading it out of the stable yard when my alarmed relations and the owner rushed in. Clementina could not believe I was still alive.

I politely offered the reins to the shocked owner. 'I'm sorry about that. What a beautiful animal. It was my fault, I must have done something wrong.'

The red-faced owner took the reins from me, speechless with disbelief. In slightly less than three minutes, I had ruined years of dedicated training. The valuable *caballo de paso* was now just another horse.

On another family occasion, we visited my cousin Miguel Mujica's gold museum in a subterranean vault. It is as near burglar-proof as possible. It is now owned by the Peruvian government, having been bequeathed to the state in perpetuity by Miguel Mujica. As he explained to me, years later, 'If I hadn't done so, the Marxist military government would have taken it away from me anyway. This way, they have had to account for every bit of it to the Peruvian people. They can't salt away any part of it for themselves.'

By amassing his incredible collection of ancient Peruvian gold and silver artifacts, he rendered his country a great service. Had he not done so, unscrupulous grave-robbers would have sold these irreplaceable artifacts to foreign collectors instead. Miguel is a unique person in a greedy world.

We were shown round the museum by its creator and curator, together with Linda Bird Johnson, the tall daughter of the former President of the United States. She was a quiet, modest young woman, the antithesis of what one would have expected with such an extrovert Texan father. We liked her very much.

I was particularly interested in Miguel's collection of Incan 'feathered cloaks', beautiful shoulder-coverings and headdresses made entirely out of feathers from rare, exotic birds. Their subtle colours have not faded over the centuries, and they are preserved in all their natural beauty. Clementina and I were entranced by them.

Of course, the gold artifacts are stunning. Their intricate craftsmanship is both highly stylized and singularly unsophisticated and is most cunningly wrought. I was proud to think that I might possess even a fraction of those Inca craftsmen's genes in my own mixed-up blood-line.

At one point in the tour, Miguel paused in front of a large show-case. He seemed reluctant to reveal what was inside it, using his big frame as a shield, and trying to hurry us along.

Miss Johnson gently chided him, 'Come now, what is it that you do not want us to see?'

'It is *nothing*! There are other far more interesting things I would like to show you.'

Linda Bird Johnson was not to be thwarted. She stepped forward and gently but firmly eased my large cousin to one side. When she saw what Miguel had been concealing, she gasped, 'My God! What *is* that?'

She was referring to a beautiful miniature gold Huaco, a marvellously made piece of Inca erotica in the form of a water vessel. It was cast in the shape of a fat little Inca with a proud smile on his chubby face, holding in both hands his magnificent golden erection, which is as long as he is tall. Obviously, he is very happy.

I could not resist answering the American girl's startled question. 'Miss Johnson, whatever it is ... It is either *early* Inca ... or late Texan!'

The President's daughter gave a loud neigh of laughter. From then on, we all enjoyed Miguel's extraordinary collection of imaginative erotica. It is quite amazing what the artistic mind can create when the imagination is turned in that direction.

Of all the events laid on by my family to honour Clementina and make her welcome, it was Antonio's safari which topped them all. He arranged for us to go to Iquitos, the capital of the Peruvian *selva*. After the frenzied social round in Lima, the rapid transition to the peaceful isolation and primeval beauty of the *selvas* was like arriving in another world.

Iquitos was everything I had imagined an Amazonian town would be. It exactly fitted the image that novelists have used in their torrid tales of jungle adventure. The colonial buildings facing the waterfront are covered in marvellous old picture-tiles imported by the Spanish and Portuguese vice-regal hierarchy who administered the Amazon basin after the conquests of Peru, Ecuador and Brazil.

Just as in the vast rainforests of the Brazilian Amazonas, the *selvas* of Peru and Ecuador shelter the remnants of ancient Indian tribes such as the Jaguas, Jivaros and Aucas. All these tribal entities have been debased to a certain extent by their unscrupulous exploitation and brutal treatment at the hands of many European entrepreneurs and adventurers, most of whom came to the jungle only to rape it.

That first visit to Peru taught me a lot of things. The first lesson I learned was that I was far more British in character than I had ever dreamed. The acute poverty that separated the wealthy *mestizo* Peruvian citizens from the tragic descendants of the Incas was a hard fact to digest.

My own family were acutely aware of the debt we owed to the Inca side of our family and treated modern Peruvian Indians with trust and affection, without being paternalistic. But there were plenty of other 'Old' Spanish families who thought of them in the same way as many United States citizens regard the descendants of the indigenous North American Indians.

That was a nasty shock. More than ever, I wanted to do something constructive to help Peru as a nation. Potentially Peru is Midas-rich in everything that is valued highly. Its mountains contain enormous quantities of gold, silver, copper, vanadium, nickel, wolfram, tin, and even uranium, platinum and other rare ores, while the vast resources of the Amazon rainforests have scarcely been tapped.

With careful husbandry, the perfect hot-house conditions of the *selvas* could feed the entire earth, without leaching that incredibly productive soil which, in the upland jungles of Peru, has lain mainly untouched since prehistoric times. There is no need to burn off the jungle before cultivation. Thousands of machetes in skilled hands will do the job far better and with no irreversible damage. Furthermore, only the borders of the three great tributaries of the Amazon – the Marañon, Napo and Ucayali – need be cultivated, with plenty of untouched land lying fallow between the areas under agricultural control.

Since 1938, successive Peruvian governments have supported pilot schemes for the colonization of the *selvas*, developing farms such as the one at Nazareth, which I have visited, almost at the head-waters of the great Marañon river. Yet no Western conglomerate has taken the slightest interest in the outstanding success of this revolutionary scheme. The great potential for cheap food-production in the east-Peruvian *selvas* still lies untouched, while hundreds of millions starve worldwide. It does not make sense.

Part of the answer lies in another source of great wealth which lies below the eastern *selvas* of Peru. There are vast, almost untapped subterranean lakes of high-grade oil, tightly compressed by the pressure from the colossal land-mass of the Andes and therefore easy to drill for and pump.

I asked a cynical old American oil engineer who had brought in a number of very successful wells in this jungle area why this extensive source of wealth had been found years ago but only recently exploited in a comparatively minor way.

He told me, 'The international price of oil is quite low enough without depressing it still further.'

That was the second lesson I learnt in Peru: '*Big business controls the world!*' Poverty does not concern people who *really* hold the reins of power. Only when it suits *their* interests will these international cartels move in and bring temporary prosperity to some poor Third World nation such as Peru.

The people of the *selvas* also suffer from too much interference by the 'do-gooders' – not the dedicated medical teams who do invaluable work among the Indian tribes scattered along the banks of the great tributaries but the know-alls, the self-proclaimed international experts who arrive in Iquitos to give the long-suffering military in charge of the whole area the 'benefit of their ignorance'.

While I was in the *selvas*, the Commanding General, José 'Pepe' Benavides, graphically described to me a demonstration of a 'jungle-flattening' machine which some misguided American organization had brought to Iquitos at great expense. 'It consisted of a heavy steel platform, fitted with large mechanical flat feet and driven by a number of powerful diesel motors. The idea behind this weird and futuristic device was to crush the dense jungle undergrowth into a mass of mulched humus by stamping it flat.' The General chuckled at the memory. 'We were given a lecture on the capabilities of this wonderful machine by an enthusiastic American engineer, and the engines were started up. The noise was deafening as the massive platform slowly churned its way forward, its big mechanical feet stamping up and down. It certainly worked. The trouble was, it worked too damned well!'

I was enthralled by the mental picture the General's words had conjured up. 'How do you mean, Pepe?'

He laughed, 'The goddamn thing not only successfully flattened the undergrowth with its pounding; it also broke right through the jungle floor. Before the engineers could shut down the engines, the whole machine had beaten itself deep into the soft ground. It took them days to dig it out. We were all hysterical. The gringos didn't like that. One of them shouted, "OK, amigos, if you're so goddamn smart, what's your solution for clearing this fucking jungle?" '

The General grinned mischievously. 'I couldn't resist it. I shouted back, "How about five hundred stainless-steel machetes that will keep a sharp edge? My soldiers will clear the jungle for you in no time!" '

I got to know Pepe Benavides well and admire him for his courage and honesty.

From Iquitos we travelled in two fast metal motor-boats to meet the Jaguas. We belted around the confluence of the Napo and the Amazon for about two hours at a steady thirty knots, with a welcome wind in our faces. Finally we stopped weaving in and out of the reed islands and entered a world of clogging water-weeds, stopping repeatedly to clear fouled propellers, chopping off the rope-like tentacles of the thick succulents with machetes.

The last narrowing waterway petered out and we landed at the Jagua village. About fifty members of the tribe were waiting for us, wearing their long grass skirts and accompanied by their bare-breasted women and small round-bellied children. All the men were armed with *cerbatanas*, their long, hollow, reed blow-pipes, the seven-foot barrels of which are tightly bound with dried grass and narrow strips of tree bark. It is a weapon which the Jaguas can use with great accuracy at ranges exceeding fifty yards, but in the lush jungle they can get much closer to their prey. The ammunition consists of thin eight-inch slivers of bamboo. The blunt end of the dart is wrapped with raw cotton to make an air-tight fit in the bore of the pipe and the razor-sharp business-end is tipped with deadly *curare*, a plant poison.

It all looked very authentic until we realized that we had seen some of these 'warriors' before, working as wharf-labourers on the Iquitos docks, when they had been sporting hardhats, old T-shirts and well-worn jeans. Nevertheless, they were genuine Jaguas, a tribe of warrior-hunters who were proudly self-sufficient before the Europeans got to them. The fierce panther of the *selvas* is named 'jaguar' after these tribesman, with their once-legendary reputation for deadly ferocity.

The small tribe was friendly but reserved, understandably somewhat embarrassed by having to put on a performance for the visiting tourists. Evidently they had a financial arrangement with the guide, but they accepted the ceremonial gift of a carton of cigarettes with their natural courtesy. In return, they let us photograph them, then they showed us their remarkable prowess with the *cerbatana*.

With pin-point accuracy they all blew their bamboo darts into an empty cigarette packet pinned to a softwood tree some twenty yards away. I was fascinated by their marksmanship and seeing this, one of them offered me his long blow-pipe. He showed me how to load the bamboo dart and demonstrated the correct blowing technique by filling his cheeks to bursting before forcefully expelling the air into the wooden valve at the mouth-end. The others stood back to watch the gringo make a fool of himself.

I had used an aluminium version of the *cerbatana* since the age of ten, when Antonio brought me one on his second visit to Folkestone. I suppose using any weapon is like riding a bicycle; once you have learnt how to do it, you never forget. I took a deep breath, blowing out my cheeks like a horn-player, instinctively allowed for the flat trajectory and blasted the bamboo dart across the narrow clearing, hitting the lowest part of the cigarette packet. The watching Jaguas gave a howl of approval and I bowed to my family's applause.

It was a very satisfying moment, and I managed to put two more darts into the same target. After that, the Jaguas relaxed, full of genuine friendliness, and we all had a fine old time. Wisely, no hard liquor was allowed, but we drank numerous toasts to each other in the Jagua home-brewed beer and an ice-cold case of my family's good Crystal lager. However, I felt sad that my Jagua friends had lost so much of their culture to the crass commercialism of the modern world. But to survive, they had no alternative.

A factor in what was to turn into a dedicated project for me was a clairvoyant vision I had while we were at anchor in a particularly beautiful part of the river. Suddenly, as I gazed dreamily across a mile-wide stretch of water, I clearly saw a large hovercraft pass across my line of vision. It was so real and so solid that I automatically grabbed my binoculars to get a closer look. As I did so, it vanished.

I told Clementina what I had seen. My remarkable wife did not turn a hair. 'It would be the ideal place to use a hovercraft,' she said.

Just before coming to Peru I had written a script for a film commissioned by the *Daily Mail* about British inventions and products that could become world bestsellers *if* they were properly promoted. Underselling our wares is a national trait. The famous newspaper wanted to reverse the trend.

One of the most interesting British products in the script was the Westland hovercraft, the revolutionary invention by Sir Christopher Cockerell, taken up and built by the Westland Aircraft Company. Two examples of this marvellous machine were used on the regular run between Southsea and the Isle of Wight. It was one of these Westland-Sikorski SRN6 forty-eight-foot hovercraft that I had visualized with such clarity crossing that remote stretch of the Amazon.

When we returned to Lima, I was told that President Beleaunde Terry would like to meet me. He had been approached by Miguel Cruchagga, a clever young architect married to Cecelia Bentin, Luis's daughter. Miguel had been a pupil of President Beleaunde Terry when he was Professor of Social Architecture at the University of Lima. Miguel was also the President's nephew.

President Beleaunde turned out to be as shy as I was, and although the first few minutes were stiff with formality, once the introductions were over and Miguel had discreetly left us Clementina and I soon relaxed, especially when the President got going on his favourite topic, which was the development of the *selvas*.

This handsome, middle-aged man was a visionary. Like most great architects he had a dream. His idea was for Peruvians to reconquer their own land, not in military terms but by rebuilding the social entity that the Incas had created where coast, mountains and *selvas* all became one, interconnected by a complex series of roads.

I found myself becoming mesmerized by his enthusiastic discourse. Carried away by his vision of the future, I asked, 'How can I help you, sir?'

The President smiled and leaned forward, 'There is a special favour I wish to ask you, Señor Bentin. I am very interested in a recent British invention which I believe could be of inestimable value to my plans for the development of the *selvas*. I understand that you call it the hovercraft. Can you possibly help me to get this remarkable machine to Peru?'

For a moment I was stunned. Then I protested, 'Your Excellency, I am a comedian not an engineer. Naturally, I know one or two people to whom I could pass on your request. But I have no influence in these matters. My business is show business.'

The President chuckled, 'I am fully aware of that, Señor Bentin. Both Miguel and Don Antonio have told me a lot about you. Apparently some of your father's scientific expertise and much of his enthusiasm and love for Peru have been passed on to you. Your Peruvian family is very proud of you.'

'If you think I can help Peru in this way,' I said, 'I certainly will try. But I will need some sort of official assurance to back me up when I go to see Westland-Sikorski. By the strangest chance I know them and have written about the hovercraft.'

President Beleaunde showed his surprise. 'I had no idea that was the case. Well, Señor Bentin, it seems as though fate has brought us together.' He stood up. 'Now, let us have a photograph taken as a souvenir of our meeting.'

As we drove out of the presidential palace, Clementina was aghast. 'What have you got yourself involved with now?'

Chapter Twenty-nine

Hot Pies and Mooshy Peas

We were given one final family party at which the entire Bentin clan came to see us off, and we were on our way home. With all the love, kindness and overwhelming generosity that had been lavished on us in Peru, and for which I can never thank my family enough, 'home' was still England.

Back at Heathrow, the young Customs officer asked me to open my valises. He started to rummage about inside the first one. I warned him, 'Do take care! There are blow-pipe darts inside that bamboo quiver.'

'I've often wondered what they look like,' he said, taking one of the long bamboo slivers out of its case. 'Sharp, aren't they? What's the dark stain on the tip?'

'*Curare*. It kills by paralysing the heart muscles.'

'Interesting,' he remarked as he gingerly replaced the dart in the quiver. He did not seem overkeen to examine the rest of my kit.

Shortly afterwards I appeared on an Eamonn Andrews TV show. Eamonn, who was well aware of my Peruvian interests, asked me to show some of the unique film that my friend, Father Pelosi, a Franciscan missionary, had taken of the Jivaro and Auca tribes in the region.

One reel showed a large jungle clearing where two groups of Jivaros were firing long, razor-sharp bamboo arrows at each other in a savage test of manhood. These agile young warriors were able to avoid being hit until one of them got an arrow in his side and fell to the ground, writhing in agony. The studio audience yelled with laughter and applauded wildly. Eamonn and I were astounded at the reaction. After the show, a middle-aged man came up to me, still chuckling to himself. 'Michael, I really must congratulate you on that super bit of fun. How you think 'em up, I do not know. But of course, bein' a Goon fan, I twigged right away you were sendin' us up. I'm a Londoner. I know Wimbledon Common when I see it.'

Our welcome home had been rapturous. I remember thinking how fortunate we were to be such a happy family and to have such good friends. Almost immediately I was plunged into a whirlpool of professional engagements, starting with a resident twelve weeks summer season at Weymouth with my stage show *It's a Square World*.

This would have been better attended, had it not been the hottest summer since 1947. The entertainments manager said, 'Pray for rain!' I did not follow his advice, but he was right; directly it rained the theatre was packed. It was gratifying that the audiences, large or small, obviously enjoyed the show. The cast were friends, or became so, and we all did our best. It was a worthwhile experience, and I broke even at the end of it. I also had the bonus of having my family with me, which was a rare treat for me when working away from home.

There was another perk, which seemed to me to be prophetic. Westland-Sikorski had a factory nearby, at Yeovil. I was able to visit them and explain what President Beleaunde Terry had asked me to do. Among those I talked to was the chief salesman, Tony Gawade, who was clever, persuasive and a great believer in the future of the hovercraft. Like me, he could see the enormous potential in this marvellous craft, especially in such an ideal testing ground as the Upper Amazon. When I had finished my 'pitch', he asked me, 'Can you get me an interview with the President? I have been trying to get to see him for a long time but I always seem to get bogged down in Peruvian bureaucracy.'

396

'I'll telephone my cousin Antonio tonight.'

I don't think the management entirely believed me. However, shortly afterwards Tony Gawade phoned me to say he was flying to Peru for talks with the President.

When he returned I hurried down to Yeovil to lunch with him. 'The President was charming. He is a big enthusiast over the future use of hovercraft in the Amazon area as you are, Michael. Thank you, and your family, very much indeed for all the help. Now, how can we repay you?'

I was embarrassed. I explained that none of us expected anything out of this project other than the satisfaction of having helped the *selva* people of Peru. Then, suddenly, the still small voice gave me the answer. 'Why not assign me the film rights? I could make a film about the venture. That will cost Westland nothing, and act as a record of the project.'

Tony nodded his agreement. We shook hands, and I gave him a hug. Tony laughed. 'I'm never going to get used to that, coming from an Englishman.'

I made a preliminary approach to the BBC about filming the Amazon project, and was given warm encouragement. I completed my summer season, had a short breather while we moved back to Little Tylers, and then started on my winter plans to play the circuit of working men's clubs which had sprung up all around the north of England. Dreams of opening up the *selva* had to take second place to earning a living in show business.

I was uncertain whether my brand of visual humour would be popular up north. Previously, I had presented a twelve-minute music-hall act, full of action and props. Now I would have to hold the same kind of audience for over an hour. At the pace I usually worked, I felt this would probably kill me.

However, Alfie Ravel, who had been with me at Weymouth working in my sketches and managing the show, was certain that I would go over well in the clubs.

Jack Kine had made me a portable version of my

397

original 'Invisible Flea Circus' illusion, which I had developed into many other action models during the making of *Square World*. It was a marvellous mechanical prop, providing me with a strong finish to my new hour-long act, and topping just about everything I had done before. I first used this version of my 'Flea' act at Weymouth, where it had been an instant success.

I also included the 'Slobodian Medical Examination' in my new act. I played the Slobodian medical officer and Alfie was the patient. The whole piece was intended to run five minutes at the most but proved so strong that I built it up into a ten-minute routine of sustained laughter. As it is entirely visual and the words are Slobodian, i.e. gibberish, the sketch seemed to work well everywhere I played it, from Glasgow to Hong Kong.

I will never forget that first week playing two northern working men's clubs a night. When I drove us up the M1 motorway the weather was vile, with heavy rain. We stopped for a lunch break about half way, and I nearly lost my nerve. I told Alfie, 'I've got the jitters. I don't think I can go through with it.'

Alfie was a wily old pro. Without batting an eyelid, he said, 'Then don't do it! Just turn the car round and drive back home. It's a free country. But they'll sue you for sure.'

I laughed and we finished the journey.

The first club was in Burnley and the second in Rotherham. This meant driving between them in the endless rain. The management had laid on a car and a driver, and we loaded the props aboard as soon as we had finished each show.

To my surprise, the Burnley club, which was in a converted cinema, was full. The warm-hearted (if they liked you) northern audience was generous with its welcome, and I started my act with 'Impressions of People You've Never Heard Of', a routine that finishes with some 'Impersonations with an Inner Tube'. It hit the right note, and from then on it was a joy to work with such a receptive audience. In Alfie's words, 'There wasn't a dry seat in the house.'

To my amazement, at the end of the act, which because of continuous laughter had taken well over an hour to perform, the club was suddenly filled with flying cardboard beer-mats, all aimed at the stage by the cheering audience. Afterwards, the beaming club-owner explained, 'That means they luv yer.'

Thank God it was not a Greek club. When they like you, the Greeks throw plates!

There was no time to be lost, as quite a few miles separated us from the second club in Rotherham. We packed up the props and off we went, our driver chuckling to himself, 'Bloody 'ell, B., what about the flea circus? By gum lad, yer paralysed 'em.' He turned half-round in his seat. 'Yer know what they say about Burnley?'

Alfie and I said the words with the driver, 'If yer please 'em 'ere, yer can please 'em *anywhere*.'

'Oh, yer've heard about Burnley then?'

Individually, we had listened to those words in every town and city we had played. We even heard them in Hong Kong, where Alfie and I became hysterical when the Chinese driver made the same boast.

Alfie Ravel, who had been in the business for over forty years, taught me a lot. His advice was sound, 'Relax, Michael, and "lie back" on the audience. Let *them* do the work.'

I have never been one to walk off the street and go straight on to the stage. I need time to settle my mind before I face an audience, just as much as I need time to unwind afterwards. That is why I call myself 'the reluctant jester'.

Alfie made me slow down, as I often tended to be too quick for the audience. I have always had a good sense of timing for comedy but I was inclined to speed up my delivery as I went along. Alfie called it 'The Gallopade'.

We worked together for five years, playing everything from clubs to concerts, pantomimes, summer seasons, the

London Palladium (my sixth season there but Alfie's first), and three overseas tours. They were five tough years for me, although they did not seem to worry Alfie. It was a great time for improving my comedy-craftsmanship, and I took full advantage of it.

While I was touring the clubs, I telephoned Tony Gawade and he told me that his company was all for the hovercraft project, but that it would take some months to set it up. He promised to keep me informed.

The club owners were so pleased with the reception I was getting that many more bookings came in. One of these venues was called the Paradise Club. It was situated above a garage in Guiseley, a small Yorkshire town not far from Leeds. It was in a long dimly lit room packed with small tables. I remember that each table had a small lamp glowing inside a coconut shell.

I was 'doubling' the Paradise with a much larger club, the Fiesta, outside Leeds. As usual, I had to drive in the pouring rain to and from each venue, but the warmth of the Yorkshire audiences made up for everything. On the last night at Guiseley, the act was going particularly well. I noticed a small man sitting close to a much younger woman at a front table, both of them a bit tipsy. By the rapt expression on his face, the small chap was having a wonderful time. I put this down to the success of my act.

A large woman stormed into the club, spotted the couple sitting at the front table and, with a loud shriek, bore down on them. 'What the bloody 'ell do you think you're up to, George?' she yelled. Then she realized what had been going on underneath the table-cloth. She screamed, 'Put *that* down, you bloody bitch! That's mine. It's not yours to play with.'

The small man was paralysed with terror. The young woman yelled some obscenity back at the older woman and threw her drink in her face. Speechless, the older woman whirled up her handbag and belted her rival, knocking her clean off her chair. Judging by the force of the blow, there must have been a brick in the bag.

The battered girl rose from the floor and hurled herself at the woman, grabbing her opponent's hair in both hands. In an instant, the two of them were hard at it with their fists, clawing each other with their long nails and kicking like bucking mules. Trying to part them would have been suicide so I did the next best thing. I gave a spirited commentary on the fight, while the club bouncers tried to separate them. Both women promptly turned on the big men and attacked them in unison. In the mêlée, tables went over, sending glass and cutlery flying through the air while the Saturday-night audience, who were well oiled, cheered hysterically.

Slowly, the burly club manager, with the aid of his sweating muscle-men, dragged the women screaming up the aisle. The small man followed them, drunkenly apologizing to everyone. When they had gone, I asked the audience to give three hearty cheers for the winner, if any. It was pandemonium, with the audience yelling, 'Encore!'

One couple came up to me after the show and said, 'It was bloody marvellous. That cast of comedians must cost you a pretty penny. Mind you, they're worth it. It's the most original act we've ever seen. We're going to tell all our friends. When are you coming back again, Michael?'

'Never,' I said.

Of course, it was not always as rowdy in the clubs. Most nights, the northern customers were the friendliest and the most enthusiastic audiences in Britain. They really know how to enjoy themselves 'oop north'.

Sometimes drunks could be a problem, but I learned how to deal with them, especially when they were hecklers who fancied themselves as comics. The cockney comedian Tommy Trinder taught me how to handle them. 'The secret is never lose your temper. Your best move is to laugh and then ask the heckler to repeat what he or she has just said. Act as though you did not quite catch it. They nearly always fall into that trap. The second time, of course, it does not sound nearly as funny. By then, you've had time to think what to say. An experienced comedian can deal with any heckler. In fact, Mike, most of my bloody act depends on ad-libbing.'

I have given thousands of performances in many journeys around the world and I have never come across two audiences who reacted in exactly the same way. If you tell a hundred people a sad story, you usually get a similar kind of reaction. But tell the same hundred people a funny story, and you will get a hundred different reactions, according to their individual sense of humour.

One club audience was thoroughly enjoying my act, when the club manager yelled out, 'Hot pies and mooshy peas!'

As one, the audience left their seats to get their pies and peas. There was absolutely nothing I could do about it. I had an inspiration and shouted, 'Get me some, too!'

'Well done, Michael, you're learning, son,' called Alfie from the wings.

When I told those stories to Peter Sellers, who by then had become an international star, he said fervently, 'Rather than go through that sort of performance, I'd commit suicide.' What's more, he meant it.

One infuriated club owner, trying to calm a particularly rowdy audience, threatened them with the words, 'If you don't shut oop, I'll put the bloody comic on again.'

I still do a one-man act with my *From the Ridiculous to the Paranormal* show, which runs well over two hours. Nowadays, I can manage to summon up enough energy for only two shows in a week. It is *that* exhausting. I shall continue to perform while I am able to do so, and while there are people who still get a laugh out of my comedy efforts. I also happen to like people, and I love to see them enjoy themselves.

Unfortunately, I also tend to trust people too much. That was why I got a rude shock when I finally got the go-ahead from Tony Gawade and immediately telephoned my contact at the BBC. Without any preamble, his words were, as closely as I can remember them, 'Hello, Michael.

Now don't start thinking that we have pinched your idea, but we have got the hovercraft people under contract, and we are taking it on our own expedition down the Orinoco. After all, there is no copyright in an idea.'

I was speechless, then the still small voice took control. I drew in a deep breath and spoke calmly, with an icy clarity so that there could be no misunderstanding, 'You can take the Westland-Sikorski hovercraft down the Orinoco, up the Amazon, or wherever the hell in South America you like. But if you shoot and show one foot of film of your expedition using one of *their* machines, I'll sue both you and the BBC. For your information, the exclusive film rights were given to me.'

I heard a gasp at the other end as I put down the phone. I immediately rang Tony Gawade. He was as shocked as I was. 'Tony, will you confirm in writing our verbal agreement about my having the film rights for the hovercraft in South America?'

Without hesitation, he answered, 'That is the very least I can do. Of course, we will back you to the hilt.'

Tony Gawade was as good as his word. Within forty-eight hours, the written confirmation of my exclusive rights to film the Westland-Sikorski hovercraft in South America was in my hands. And that, I thought, was that.

Chapter Thirty

Hovering up the Amazon

Apparently someone at the BBC rang Tony Gawade soon after I had put the phone down. Tony told him exactly what he had told me.

The hovercraft was essential to both projects. My own aim was to focus world attention on the importance of the *selvas* of the Upper Amazon as an area where food could be produced without interfering with the natural functions of the rainforest or leaching its invaluable soil, and thus bring prosperity to Peru.

I had asked for the film rights on the spur of the moment, and at the urgent instruction of the still small voice. It would satisfy the apparent need of Westland-Sikorski to express their gratitude for our efforts in introducing the hovercraft to Peru, and it would cost them nothing.

The situation was at an impasse. The BBC had an exclusive contract with the operators of the hovercraft machines but had not reckoned on my owning the film rights. Without those rights the project was worthless to the BBC. Our problem was that the machines were now tied up and not available for our project. The approach came from the operators of the hovercraft.

By this time it was winter and I was playing in pantomime at Bromley in Kent. I was laid up with a savage bout of influenza at a local hotel, and unable to perform on stage for several days.

Clementina was looking after me at the hotel, as neither of us wanted me to give the vicious virus to the family at home. My wife warned me to take great care with these representatives. I am glad she did, because their offer to release the hovercraft for the Peruvian expedition was contingent on stringent conditions.

The first was that I must hand over *all* film rights, but when I protested that the President was entitled to have a record of the effectiveness of the hovercraft in Peruvian *selva* conditions, they agreed reluctantly that I should be allowed to film it, providing that I did not show the film publicly for longer than a *four-minute* extract.

Clementina pointed out that the exclusive film rights were worth a lot of money, but the last thing I wanted was to be involved in a 'financial arrangement'. She said, 'You'll just have to make the best of it. You must go in the expedition to Peru to make certain that it is the first project and that Peru gets a fair deal; and you must film it to prove your point. The BBC can go on their expedition up the Orinoco afterwards. One other thing, you will have to pay out quite enough money to film the expedition without having to pay for the return air fare to Peru and your expenses while you are there. They must pick up the tab for that. The film rights are worth a great deal more to them than your expenses. Believe me, the BBC will do very well out of all this.'

Of course Clementina was right. And that is how we left it. The letter I received makes interesting reading. It is about the most one-sided document I have ever seen. I had to sign it and send it back but at least the copy I kept is proof of the shenanigans that had gone on.

As soon as the pantomime was over, I left for Peru. When I arrived in Iquitos, I was met by Tony Gawade and my friend General Pepe Benavides who, to my delight, was to accompany us on the expedition.

The British media campaign to promote the 'Last Great Journey in the World', up the Brazilian Orinoco, which would follow our Peruvian expedition, had continued to build back home. The BBC was especially active in its self-promotion. When I phoned Clementina, she told me that any resemblance between what was being printed and broadcast and the truth was purely coincidental. In particular she thought that Arthur Helliwell was writing about the Brazilian project in the *People* as though everyone would face near-certain death on the coming expedition up the Orinoco.

Our objective and, indeed, our whole attitude was the exact opposite. In order to encourage future interest in the ecologically safe development of the Upper Amazonas, our expedition was being undertaken to demonstrate to the world that the hovercraft was able to overcome all the potential dangers and difficulties of any journey up the great rivers of the Amazonas.

We emphasized that it was only travellers in small boats, dug-out canoes and rafts who were at risk in the whirlpools, back-eddies and, above all, the rapids – the feared white waters. Our contention was that the SRN6 hovercraft could radically alter these inherent dangers in the Amazonas, providing safe transportation and rapid communication in all weathers for the benefit of everyone.

One chilly pre-dawn, we left the seaplane base at Iquitos, where the hovercraft had been made ready, and, packed with equipment and full of high hopes, we headed down the ramp and on to the dark waters of the great river.

The hovercraft's chief pilot was Don Ellis. A fellow Folkestonian, staunch and determined, Don was a top ex-Royal Navy test pilot with many thousands of flying-hours behind him, and an expert on hovercraft, which he had been testing for the military in Saudi Arabia. What a contrast the Peruvian rainforest must have been for him!

This bright skipper, sturdy, handsome and sandy-bearded, with his quiet sense of humour in the face of any difficulty, epitomized everything I have always liked and admired about the British. He reminded me of the popular image of Sir Francis Drake with his aura of dependability and quiet assurance. I would have followed Don and Pepe Benavides cheerfully to hell and back.

Besides Don, there were two other pilots, Captain Stuart Syrad representing the Royal Marines, and Lieutenant-Commander Grahame Clarke of the Royal Navy. Pedro Larranaga, our liaison officer, was a tall, cool and distinguished member of an old Peruvian diplomatic family. It tickled his sense of the ridiculous that an Anglo-Peruvian gringo clown should be part of this venture. He asked me, 'Miguel, what are you going to do next, after we finish this crazy expedition?'

I consulted my pocket-diary. 'My next engagement, Pedro, is in cabaret, at the El Latino club, South Shields.' To this day, he refuses to believe me.

We had a river-pilot with us, a tough, inscrutable Peruvian sailor from the Amazon region, who knew the intricate pattern of this mass of waterways as a spider knows its web. At first he shut his eyes every time Don Ellis took us at full speed over a jutting point of scrub-covered land. Later, every time this happened he would grin at me, showing his gold tooth, and mutter, '*Olé!*' He was also our interpreter with the rainforest Indians.

Johnnie Hollingsworth was our resourceful chief-engineer. He had a cheerful assistant who was a devoted Goon fan. One thing that puzzled Pepe and his team was our crews' constant reference to the Goons, and the Goon voices which they used from time to time, especially with me.

As usual, I had assumed the jester's cap and bells, and kept the tone of the proceedings as light as possible. To me that was all part of the job. It certainly worked well. Humour is a useful tool to keep up morale especially when, because of the lack of air-conditioning aboard, the interior temperature topped 110 degrees Fahrenheit. The warm, super-saturated air of the jungle virtually soaked us to the skin. I do not remember a single dawn during that whole trip when I did not put on a damp khaki shirt, which I had washed the night before and hung up to 'dry' through the night.

Oddly enough, none of us went down with pneumonia or the dreaded Atahualpa's revenge. In a fluvial society, such as that of the tribal groups living along the banks of the Amazon tributaries, gastro-enteritis is endemic, a too-often fatal disease. The further downstream a tribe is situated, the more amoebic detritus there is in their water supply.

On that trip, I suffered only a twenty-four-hour bout of 'jungle fever', which taught me to stick to Crystal lager rather than water, however many 'purifying' tablets I had added to it. My ever-thoughtful cousin Antonio had provided Pepe with some cases of our excellent family brew, and he had stowed these in ice-boxes so that we all could enjoy that luxury. There is nothing I ever tasted that was half as good as a bottle of my family's ice-cold Crystal lager on that historic journey up the Marañon. I deliberately use the term 'historic' because, on that initial 450-mile leg of the hovercraft's epic journey, according to the *Guinness Book of Records* we established several new world records. On the return journey over the same distance we clocked up a few more. At least I had helped to gain *that* satisfaction jointly for Peru and Britain.

Hour after hour, we roared along that wide river between the endless rows of tall trees and dense jungle undergrowth. How you look at the *selvas* depends on your individual point of view. For me, they will always be a panorama of immense beauty. To one American oil engineer, who had been there too long, 'Once you've seen one fucking tree, you've seen 'em all!'

There certainly were millions of trees, and a noisy hovercraft may not have been the best vantage-point from which to appreciate such natural beauty and peace. But we all felt a sense of awe engendered by the sheer scale of that remarkable environment. When you consider that the entire Amazonas could contain Europe, the Mediterranean and a large part of the Sahara, a sense of wonder at the size of it all is understandable.

The General's first objective was to visit Teniente Pinglo, a military base which must be one of the most remote forts on the earth. Set on top of a steep bluff, it dominates the confluence of the Rio Marañon with the Rio Santiago, commanding the mist-shrouded western entrance to the fearsome rapids of the Pongo de Manseriche.

Anyone travelling up or down the Marañon has to pass under its guns. Far more important, from my point of view, was the fact that this small military camp contained the only medical facilities for many thousands of square miles of jungle. God knows how many lives have been saved by the dedicated teams of successive medical officers who run the tiny hospital.

We arrived at Barranca, at the lower end of the Manseriche rapids, and coasted in to the small quay which fronts this tiny river port. A helicopter was waiting for us, its rotor blades slowly turning. Don Ellis, Tony Gawade and the General, accompanied by our spare pilots, Stuart Syrad and Grahame Clarke, climbed aboard, and the chopper immediately took off to fly them along the whole course of the infamous Pongo.

For fifteen miles, this seething maelstrom rushes between high stone cliffs, topped by jungle and part-covered by lush undergrowth, which somehow clings precariously to the steep precipices on either side. The Manseriche's hurtling progress is further impeded by giant rocks jutting menacingly out of the white foam. Some of these great boulders have been worn smooth by the scouring action of the rapids, while others, recently fallen from the cliff face, are still murderously jagged. The Manseriche is a fearsome place which has claimed thousands of lives. The following day, the hovercraft would have to conquer it.

When the chopper returned, the scouting party looked thoughtful but they were confident that the machine would succeed in riding over the raging narrows. Despite my protests, I was not allowed to accompany them on the hovercraft's first attempt to breach the Pongo de Manseriche. Tony explained that, as I was a supernumerary member of the hovercraft crew, I was not covered by their insurance. I sighed resignedly and accepted the condition but, as a consolation prize, I was given the opportunity to fly chase in the chopper. That trip turned out to be much hairier than being aboard the hovercraft.

The pilot, John Waddington, a very experienced airman, flew me. We followed closely in the wake of the hovercraft. I was using an Arriflex 16-mm professional film camera as well as I could, and I spent most of that fifteen-mile flight scared witless, with one eye shut and the other glued to the viewfinder. It was just as well that my view of this dramatic event was restricted, because we roared along a scant twenty feet above the rushing torrent and, in places, the tips of our rotor blades were only a few yards from the rock walls of the Manseriche.

When we landed, and my heart had stopped pounding, I was dismayed to find that, owing to the amount of 'G' we had been pulling to avoid the cliffs in tight turns during our twisting progress along the serpentine Pongo, the film had jammed solid inside the camera. I had not succeeded in recording a single foot of film of that whole exciting chase. I do not know who was the most disappointed, the pilot or myself, but we both swore picturesquely and at considerable length before we burst out laughing. 'I'm not bloody well doing that again,' said John firmly.

Our arrival at Teniente Pinglo was a triumph for the General. He could not have made more impact if he had stepped out of a flying saucer. Which brings me to an interesting point. Twice on the way up river, when we stopped to refuel at our special fuel dumps in small waterside settlements, the Indians who lived there were not in the least surprised to see the hovercraft. There was no wonder in their eyes at their first sight of this large oval craft that had bellowed its way up river to their settlement. They accepted us at our face value and quietly got on with helping the engineers to refuel the machine.

Intrigued by their dismissive attitude, I asked them, through our interpreter, what they thought of our machine. Their answer shook me. 'It's just like the other flying saucers we have seen. Yours is much noisier, for we heard you coming a long way off, but otherwise it is much the same as all the others.'

They certainly were not confusing us with the small seaplanes which are often used in these waters by the military and also by medical missionaries. High-flying jets they also knew from their daily flights above them en route to Iquitos and Brazil. Helicopters were equally familiar to them. I still do not know what to make of it.

That night the camp-commandant had laid on a formal dinner-party at the camp mess. It was a very special effort, and the wives of the officers and NCOs who were billeted there had produced miracles of Peruvian cooking. The whole fort was *en fête*. Pepe told me, 'Boredom is their biggest enemy. I try to keep them as busy as possible. We lay on trips to Iquitos for them all, by helicopter and seaplane. We have to. It would take forever by boat. The wives are under special stress. This visit will do them all good. I'm going to make you work hard tonight, Miguelito.'

By ten o'clock, the wives had retired gracefully. As with all servicemen, the object of a party is release, to blow off steam. In this case, officers and NCOs were all together and the open windows were lined with soldiers who were just as welcome, and were provided with more than sufficient Crystal lager.

I have appeared in many strange places, and performed to some very unusual audiences in my life, with varying degrees of success, but I am sure I never worked to a more appreciative audience than those few hundred Peruvian officers, NCOs and Amazon-Indian soldiers who packed into or surrounded that large wooden hut in the middle of the Peruvian *selvas*.

Somehow, through a mixture of Aymara coming from our interpreter, my bad Castilian Spanish, Pedro Larranaga's excellent translation and much graphic pantomime, I kept my audience in hysterics for upwards of an hour. At the end of it, the jungle night rang with their appreciation and I was in tears. It was not just the effect of the drink. We were all in the highest of spirits and filled with relief that the hovercraft had worked so well.

For me, it was the justification of all the trials and aggravations which had plagued me from the start of the enterprise back in Britain. I wish my contact at the BBC could have seen it. He might have learned something from it. But somehow I doubt it.

We had succeeded in establishing the viability of the hovercraft as a safe, all-weather form of transport for passengers and/or freight in the Amazonas. We now set out to prove it again by breaking more records on our return journey to Iquitos. Before doing so, Tony, at the request of Mobil Oil, demonstrated the machine to the drillers manning the oil-rigs up the Rio Santiago. They were impressed and wrote glowing reports on its capabilities. The result was that the Bell Aeroplane Company in the USA, which had the sole rights to manufacture Sir Christopher Cockerell's revolutionary machine in America, built many more.

The Americans used them in Vietnam and subsequently equipped the US Navy's amphibious assault ships with the machines. The Soviet Union created a large number of much bigger Hovercraftskys for their invasion fleet, which was based at Murmansk.

Westland-Sikorski sold none in Peru, but they did manage to sell a machine to the off-shore oil-rigs in Venezuela. That, to the best of my knowledge, was the disappointing outcome of the hovercraft project in South America. Why?

I believe the answer is simple. By the time they had finished sensationalizing the 'Brazilian project', the *People* newspaper and the BBC had laid so much emphasis on the 'perils of the Amazonas' and the gallantry of the crew of the hovercraft in overcoming these great odds that the *practical* aspect of the whole expedition became obscured.

They made no mention of our successful and safe record navigation of over eight hundred miles of the Marañon to Nazareth and the same distance back to Iquitos, passing without incident through the most dangerous rapids in that area of Peru.

Consequently, some prospective buyers were put off from acquiring the hovercraft because they had formed the impression that it was still in a stage of 'experimental development'.

The trouble is that the loud-voiced Cassandras prophesying disaster through the media receive more attention than do the voices of more positive people who know what they are doing.

Before I left for England the General took me aside. 'Miguelito, you have proved your point and fulfilled your dream. Now, try and tell the rest of the disbelieving world what a wonderful place the jungle is. There are two things I must ask you. Can you help our problem with leprosy? And can you raise some money to buy badly needed medical supplies with which my young medical officers can fight the region's widespread gastro-enteritis? It is killing 30 per cent of the children in the *selvas*!'

Pepe's sincerity would have melted the stoniest heart. I am a pushover for such a sincere appeal. As Clementina told me, on my return home, 'Darling, you do get yourself involved!'

At Heathrow the Customs officer said, 'There's a crazy rumour going round that you've been up the Amazon on some sort of expedition. The things people believe these days. I told 'em straight: not even Michael Bentine's mad enough to pull a stunt like that.'

I expect he remembered *Square World* and the piece where I lead an 'expedition' to find the source of the Thames, which turns out to be a dripping tap in a field near Oxford. You cannot blame him for not taking me seriously. It was my own fault for dreaming up all those off-beat comedy ideas.

At the first opportunity I went to see the picture editor of the *News of the World* to offer him my photographs of the expedition. My aim was to put the money received from the exclusive sale into a fund to provide the medicine Pepe Benavides had requested. John Jowett, the picture editor, examined my stack of pictures. 'Tell you what, Michael, I can offer you nine hundred pounds for the exclusive, and I will guarantee front-page exposure for the story. That should help a bit. Who do I make the cheque payable to?'

That nice man was as good as his word, and the following Sunday the story, complete with my photograph of the hovercraft emerging from the mouth of the Rio Santiago in the Upper Amazonas, appeared on the front page of the *News of the World*, together with a straightforward report of what we had done. Moreover, it was bought by a top American magazine and published round the world.

I had finally established that the Peruvian expedition was a viable first for both Peru and Britain, and as a result the Peruvian army doctors would have nearly a thousand pounds' worth of medicine for the children of the *selvas*.

A further piece of good news came when the Central Office of Information phoned me and asked me to lend them a copy of the film I had taken of the Peruvian expedition so as to copy it for their records.

I told them, 'I am not a professional cameraman and I had quite a lot of trouble with the film negatives, which were affected by the extreme humidity in the jungle. Thankfully, a friend who is a first-class film editor took my film and had it specially printed so that it was colour-compensated. But why don't you use the film from the BBC coverage of the Orinoco expedition? That is bound to have been well made.'

'Mr Bentine, it is simply not of the same interest to us. We want a record of the first Anglo-Peruvian hovercraft expedition, the original South American trip up the Amazon and the Marañon. That is the historic film we need. The one you were involved in.'

Truth won out in the end. When I told them, Tony Gawade and Don Ellis were particularly delighted.

Chapter Thirty-one

Nightmare

When my son Gus did not return home on the night of Saturday 28 August 1971, and no phone call had been received from him, as was his usual considerate practice, we all became very concerned.

When he left on that fateful morning, he had said he was going sailing. It turned out that he had decided to go flying with his friend Andy Slade instead. Apparently, this was a spur-of-the-moment decision.

Among the many calls I made to find out where he had gone, I telephoned Lasham airfield. This was because Andy Slade's sister Janet had telephoned to ask if her brother was with Gus, and if we knew where they were. She said, 'Andrew mentioned something about going to Lasham to fly as a glider-towing pilot.'

When I rang the gliding club and asked about Gus, one of the members told me, 'He hasn't been here today.'

Further worried phone calls throughout Sunday evening elicited no further information. The chief flying instructor was away on a flight to the continent. I could not get hold of his deputy.

It was not until the Monday morning that an anxious young assistant flying instructor admitted that one of their aircraft was missing. 'We've only just found out that it isn't here.'

I was stunned. I could hardly believe his words. 'Surely, you must know at the end of each flying day how many of your aircraft have landed? For Christ's sake, how many aircraft have you got?'

'Four,' the young man choked on the word. 'One is missing. We think your son was in it with his friend Andy Slade who was the pilot.'

'When did it take off?'

To my amazement he replied, 'Saturday, around lunchtime.'

Nearly forty-eight hours had passed before the alarm had been raised. In the RAF, an aircraft would be reported missing a few minutes after it was presumed to have run out of fuel.

So started a tragic time for all my family, and one of the most dreadful phases of my life. Had not my mind been 'open', I would never have learned the truth behind my son's death. As it is, the horror of it still haunts me in nightmares.

During the course of the following years my long investigation received great help from members of Special Branch and from Colonel Airey Neave, one of my wartime mentors. The first thing I found was that, owing to the appalling permissive state of private flying at that time, a pilot was not required to inform an airfield before take-off of the destination of his flight or to give its estimated time of arrival. In the case of my son and his friend, nobody knew where they had gone or even if they had taken off. They had no idea when their fuel tanks would be dry or where to look for the wreckage if they had crashed.

Furthermore, within days of starting my investigations I received two anonymous phone calls to my unlisted home number. These were short messages and to the point. The first voice said, 'If you don't stop asking questions, you and your family will suffer.'

The second caller warned me, 'If you don't stop your investigation, you're dead.'

I carefully considered the situation and then called Scotland Yard. I told an inspector that I had received threatening phone calls from persons unknown regarding my enquiries into my son's disappearance, and that this made it clear to me that I was beginning to uncover something extremely sinister. I told him that I believed this new development was not a cover-up of the flying club's stupidity, nor was it intended to conceal the general lack of control over private flying. 'I suggest to you that this whole ghastly business is an indirect result of the *criminal* misuse of private aircraft. Knowing my son and his friend the pilot, I am certain that neither of them would be involved in anything of that nature, but I feel there is something very sinister going on. Those two threatening phone calls confirmed my suspicions. I badly need help, and probably protection as well, as I fully intend to continue my investigations. Will you help me?'

Special Branch immediately sent me one of their best men, a young detective sergeant. He arrived at our house within twenty minutes.

I owed it to my family, and especially to my missing son and his friend, to find out the truth, even though we still officially did not know that they were dead. That tragic fact became a media field-day when their bodies were found inside the wreckage of the plane in the woods near Petersfield over *nine weeks* later.

The more my investigations uncovered, the more I could see that Britain was totally without a security roof, certainly as far as private flying was concerned. For one thing, a criminal record did not preclude a person from gaining, or retaining, a private pilot's licence. Smuggling on a large scale using private planes was flourishing, and enormous illegal profits were being made.

The arrival of the bright young Special Branch officer gave me reassurance. I soon found out he had an excellent sense of humour, and that further encouraged me. When I told him of my suspicions, he did not try to minimize them. On the contrary, he agreed with me that the situation, especially where national security was concerned, was grim. He added that his department would help me in every way it could.

'How many of you Special Branch specialists in air security can we count on? We're going to need a lot of men.'

He grinned, 'I *am* air security Great Britain. There's only me.'

I was completely at a loss. 'During my time in RAF Intelligence we had thousands of security specialists readily available.'

The detective sergeant was frank, 'In peacetime we have been drastically cut down and we are badly undermanned. In the present situation, drugs, illegal immigrants and even dogs belonging to wealthy people who want to get round the strict quarantine laws are being brought in by air. In addition, hi-tech instrumentation, including a complete jet-engine, as well as the rich proceeds from many large-scale robberies are being flown illicitly out of the country.'

He paused to let all this sink in. Then he added, 'There is also a large trade in illegal arms, explosives and ammunition which are being flown into Britain and Northern Ireland. These weapons, presumably, come from Libya and other countries which support international terrorism.'

From then on we investigated as a team. Even my Special Branch colleague was astounded by the ease with which private aircraft could leave and return to our country, seemingly without any control whatsoever.

There were virtually hundreds of disused wartime airfields where private aircraft, single or multi-engined, could be landed, day or night, and a significant number of these were in fact being operated clandestinely. By day all that was needed was a few 'smudge-pots' to indicate the position of the field with smoke. By night, a torch flashing signals and the headlamps of a couple of cars would prove sufficient to guide an aircraft to a safe landing.

Nobody seemed to complain or even notice what was going on, and the authorities were swamped by the sheer volume of air traffic coming into and going out of the country, much of it illegally. I was deeply disturbed, and spent many sleepless nights worrying about it.

Thankfully, right from the start it was obvious that my son and Andy Slade were innocent victims of these permissive circumstances. They were in no way involved in the criminal misuse of private aircraft.

According to the skilled evidence of the Farnborough medical expert, both Gus and Andy had been killed instantly, or nearly so, upon impact. In one way, this was a mercy, because it is unlikely that either of them would have suffered. Furthermore, had they survived, badly injured, nobody at Lasham would have known where to look for them nor did anyone there even start to look for them until nearly two days had passed. I cannot start to convey to you the sort of horrific images this conjured up in my mind. But I still had to try to root out the truth. That was the least I could do.

Understandably, my family was in a state of shock but somehow they were managing to cope with their grief, Nursie being an outstanding comfort.

The press did not help. The sensational aspects of the whole grisly business seemed to be their sole concern. We had no peace from them, especially from the investigatory efforts of the sleazier side of journalism. Their behaviour was appalling.

Here then, is a summation of what I found out. Anybody and anything could be transported in and out of Great Britain at that time, seemingly without any effective control. In fact, 104 KGB operatives were forced to leave Britain at the time of our investigations. I do not believe that was entirely a coincidence.

I made a special visit to Northern France and, during the course of it, found a significant number of private grass-strip airfields between Calais and Le Havre. These airstrips showed unmistakable signs of traffic-wear, commensurate with the operation of heavily loaded single and twin-engined aircraft. This indicated a two-way transportation system in operation which, as it was not channelled through commercial airports, strongly suggested clandestine activities.

Fanciful conjecture in the mind of a distraught parent of a dead son? I do not think so. Neither did my contacts in France, some of them from old wartime associations. The officer in the Police de l'Air, whom they introduced to me, certainly did not seem to think so either.

It may well have been purely coincidental, but from the moment Labour was elected in 1974 any official assistance I was receiving from Special Branch and the police immediately ceased, not without sincere regrets and sympathy on the part of my new-found friends.

But I still had an ace up my sleeve, a loyal friend of many years' standing, an aeronautical engineer with a great deal of experience in the light-aircraft industry. He was an expert gliding-instructor as well. Because of his qualifications and his impartiality, he was welcome wherever he went, and he was so upset by what had been going on that he volunteered to help me. I can never thank him enough for all his efforts.

My engineering friend confirmed that air-smuggling, including hi-tech espionage, was completely out of control. Moreover, certain persons in positions of authority evidently were allowing it to happen.

When I was completely certain of my ground, which was after my investigation had spanned three miserable years, I wrote a full report of my findings, and those of my colleagues, and sent it via a mutual friend to Colonel Airey Neave.

What made this dreadful period of my life harder for me was that I still had to earn a living by writing and performing comedy. This was very difficult, especially in the first year after the crash, because audiences were reluctant to laugh at anyone whom they now saw in a tragic light. However, being a hardened old pro and a former Goon, I was able to overcome their embarrassment.

Johnnie Downes, a BBC producer who specialized in children's TV shows, asked me if I would like to do a series of programmes with him. The Revd Fred Secombe, Harry's brother and an old friend of mine, had also suggested that I should go back to writing for children's TV, 'You're full of resentment and hate, Michael. That is quite understandable, but it's not good for you and it's not like you. Why not do some children's shows? The children will help you forget the hate burning inside you.'

I wrote and performed, with Johnnie producing and directing, thirteen shows called *Michael Ben 'T' ine Time*. Children loved the shows and we got excellent viewing figures. Had not the BBC management kept me waiting for so long before offering me a further contract, I might have continued to write the shows for the Corporation.

However, when I received a firm offer from Thames Television, I went with the commercial channel instead. The new show, *Michael Bentine's Potty Time*, ran joyously for over seven years, and enjoyed enviable viewing figures. Since then *Potty Time* has played around the world – in Australia, New Zealand, the Near, Middle, and Far East, East Africa, and in many other countries. The main exceptions are the US and Canada, but who knows? The Potties might yet play there as well.

From my point of view, keeping so busy with the Potties helped to keep me sane during that awful time.

I had headed my report to Airey Neave 'Blue print for a Take-over'. Some twenty-six pages long, it revealed the probable methods by which Britain could be taken over and used as a satellite by Soviet Russia. I do not know who else read it besides Neave and some of his close friends in Westminster but at least I had finished my part of the job. I had done everything I could to expose the truth about the crash which had killed my son and Andy Slade, and in doing so I had stumbled on a number of alarming facts concerning the national security of our country. I had also nearly wrecked my health and, according to my doctor, had given myself chronic asthma owing to the unremitting strain.

Parts of the overall picture of treachery and betrayal

of Britain have since emerged, and I remember a conversation with Harry Chapman Pincher, an acknowledged expert on Intelligence matters. He agreed with me on many points. In fact, we were able to give each other corroboratory evidence of a number of aspects of the incredible situation.

Now, at last, things look as though they might be beginning to break, for Her Majesty's present government will, I hope, tell the truth about many aspects of the last forty or so years, in which Britain, unarguably, has been infiltrated and betrayed by a number of Soviet agents.

Many people have asked me if I experienced any assistance from paranormal sources during this tragic and difficult period of my life. I had warned my son twelve weeks before he and his friend were killed that if he flew with Andy Slade they both would die in a plane crash. I had also pointed out that this had nothing to do with Andy's ability as a pilot which, I am sure, was more than adequate, but that it would be the outcome of their flying together. It would be 'a crossroads in time'.

'After all,' I told him, 'I am not warning you against scuba-diving with Andy, only against flying with him.' In one dreadful flash of subjective clairvoyance on a sunny day at home I had 'seen' the crash.

Then, after the crash, I was alone in the garden, desolate with grief, and sensed my son's presence. I saw nothing but my heart leapt with joy. I felt him beside me, his hand touching my shoulder. His voice sounded clearly inside my head, 'I'm terribly sorry, Daddy! It wasn't Andy's fault. The bloody machine went wrong in the air.'

I sensed his overwhelming shock and grief and tried to comfort him. The bond between us was absolute. For a long moment, Gus and I were together. Then, like a loving whisper, he was gone. A flood of tears washed away my grief, and for the first time in two days I felt at peace.

His words were hardly the most spiritual of messages. They were the sort of apology a son might make for damaging the family car, which is why I found them so convincing. They were the words Gus would have chosen. Moreover, I had been thinking that whatever had happened *was* Andy Slade's fault, mainly because of the grim warning of impending disaster that I had passed on to Gus.

As I have explained, the wreckage of the Piper Cub with their bodies inside was not found until nine weeks later. Therefore, when I sensed my son's presence in the garden, I had no way of knowing that he was dead. Only my 'still small voice' told me so.

It took the Accidents Investigation Branch over eleven months to publish their findings after a thorough examination of the wreckage reassembled in a hangar at the Royal Aeronautical Establishment at Farnborough. Their report notes that there was a fatigue crack in the cabin heater/engine exhaust system, but concludes that the evidence was insufficient to determine whether the crack resulted in the presence of toxic fumes in the aircraft cabin. The cause of the accident, the report states, was that 'the aircraft, which was not equipped for instrument flying, went into cloud when taking action to avoid power cables while flying low in poor visibility and subsequently went out of control'.

However, the report recommended that 'consideration be given to the development of a reliable carbon-monoxide detector for aircraft cabins'.

Self-delusion or not, that momentary 'contact' with Gus gave me great comfort at a time when I desperately needed it. For me, it remains a remarkable and uplifting experience.

From that moment on, I accepted that whatever had happened in the air was primarily *not* Andy's fault. As the pilot of the aircraft, the train of events leading up to the accident developed beyond his competent control. The Accident Investigation Branch also told me that the pilot had managed to switch off the ignition just before impact. Andy Slade was doing everything he possibly could to avoid a fatal crash.

I had another nightmarish premonition two days prior to Airey Neave's murder in 1979. I had been plagued by a nagging phrase, 'Blood Sacrifice'. The words had been quite distinct and had occurred four or five times a night. I had been especially worried by them because our younger daughter, Suki, was in the process of flying out to join an aunt and uncle in Africa at the time. Happily, she had arrived safely, and I spoke to her by telephone.

I had told Clementina about my disturbing clairaudient experience then, almost immediately after I had finished speaking to Suki, the phone rang. My wife answered it. She was white-faced with shock as she came into the sitting-room to tell me who was on the phone.

'It's a friend of yours from Scotland Yard. He says that Airey Neave has been blown up by a bomb.'

I spoke to my friend at the Yard. He said, 'I'm sorry to be the bearer of such bad tidings, Michael. But I know you had great respect for him, and I thought you should be informed of his death.'

I thanked him and hung up. Then I sat down with Clementina, and we both said prayers for Airey Neave's soul, and for the comfort of his bereaved family. God knows, we both knew enough about that sort of tragic experience!

As we finished praying, we both distinctly heard a loud rap, apparently coming from *inside* a wooden coffee table, a favourite piece of mine. It was an unmistakable sound and was *not* caused by the long-seasoned wood drying out. I recognized it as being exactly the same sound as I had heard during telekinetic phenomena which had occurred while I was training with my father.

At the same time, I distinctly heard the phrase, 'And all the trumpets sounded for him on the other side.' I told Clementina.

The next time I heard those words was a few days later, at Colonel Neave's memorial service. Coincidence? Possibly, but I do not think so.

As to the meaning of the words 'Blood Sacrifice', all I

can say is that, after this cowardly act of wanton murder, the somewhat ineffectual government of that time was replaced by a Conservative government under Margaret Thatcher. Is it possible that the sacrifice of Airey Neave's life influenced the British electorate's choice at that crucial time? Frankly, I do not know. It remains one of the many unsolved mysteries of that horrific era of my life.

I am certain that on each of those grim occasions, I sensed the same sort of awful warning as I had 'received' during the war, when I positively knew which members of my aircrews would die that night.

I pray that none of my readers ever suffers from such appalling experiences.

Chapter Thirty-two

The Balance Sheet

People's reactions to the tragedy of Gus's death were startlingly individual. Often it was the friends we knew least well who were the most comforting and helpful. Surprisingly, some others, whom we had thought of as close friends, completely shunned us.

Gus's funeral was another ordeal, made far worse by the press, despite the care with which we had concealed the venue for our son's cremation, to which only immediate family and a few close friends had been invited.

In our desperate need for privacy, we resorted to using the name 'Albert Hall' for Gus, a pseudonym he had used in some of his youthful escapades. It is hard to forget how the sleazier side of the media behaved: because of the circumstances surrounding the accident, its ghoulish news value had lasted weeks longer than the media's usual nine-day period of exploitation.

Together with the Slades, we held a joint memorial service for our dead sons, conducted by two parsons. We asked Harry Secombe's brother, the Revd Fred Secombe, to speak on Gus's behalf. Our friend paid him a moving and comforting tribute, after which I felt we had fulfilled our part of the required formalities. But I still wanted to pay a personal tribute to my son.

My opportunity came a few weeks later when Peter Roddis, a bright young entrepreneur of musical events, was approached to produce a charity concert for the

Royal Philharmonic Orchestra. Their manager told him that he wanted the concert to be in the style of the late Gerard Hoffnung, whose marvellously funny musical evenings were greatly missed. Peter asked me to devise it.

At first I was reluctant, as comedy was the last thing on my mind, but when he told me the event was to take place at the Albert Hall, Gus's favourite concert hall, I realized that here was the ideal opportunity for paying my personal tribute to him. I started free-scanning for possibilities, and immediately a whole host of ridiculous ideas marched across the 'inner screen' of my mind.

My family agreed that, as the event was to be a combination of classical music and visual comedy, it would be the kind of tribute that Gus would most appreciate. (Until then, our only memorial to him had been a plantation of cedar trees on the slopes of Mount Lebanon in the Holy Land.) The proviso I made to Peter Roddis was that the media must not know the real reason behind my role in this Royal Philharmonic concert.

As I was to compère the event, and even conduct part of it, I called the concert, 'Mike, Phil and Albert'. I still have a video tape of the concert made by Thames Television and directed by Chris Palmer.

By five o'clock on the day itself the box office had sold tickets for under a thousand people, a very small audience for the Albert Hall. But an hour before the start thousands of young people converged on the main entrance. When the concert began, the building was packed with an audience buzzing with anticipation.

We started the evening conventionally enough with a fanfare from four trumpeters dressed in heralds' uniforms from the Army's college of music. As they marched on, I explained to the audience that owing to the sweeping cuts in Britain's defence budget, the Army's college of music had been forced to pawn their instruments. 'Therefore, the fanfare will be played with the mouthpieces only.'

The four trumpeters, in unison, blew a one-minute amplified raspberry. I had gambled everything on that shock opening, and it paid off handsomely.

Next came Mozart's posthorn piece, with a slight difference, which I announced, 'Tonight, we are indeed fortunate to have, from Slobodia, Master Zygismund Popoudopulos, the youngest posthorn soloist in the world.'

The unseen infant prodigy was wheeled on in a hooded pram by his English nurse, accompanied by two uniformed guards, whom I explained were members of the Slobodian secret police. This was in case the young musician, or his British nanny, should attempt to defect.

With the pram turned sideways-on to the audience, one of the guards apparently popped the long posthorn into the unseen soloist's mouth, and the concerto began.

The actual horn solo was played off-stage. During the player's pauses the nurse gave the invisible infant his bottle. In the longest pause, she reached inside the pram and changed the unseen baby, finishing with a liberal dusting of talcum powder. At the conclusion of the piece, the nurse put the baby over her shoulder, and burped him to thunderous applause. By this time, even the diehard Albert Hall regulars, who initially had been confused by the turn of events, decided to relax and enjoy the fun.

The Musical Olympic Games came next. I explained that music had been an integral part of the original Olympic Games over two thousand years before. We kicked off with the glockenspiel slalom, using specially modified xylophones, fitted at one end with racing handlebars. The players used runners' foot-blocks for the Le Mans start. Playing Saint-Saëns's 'Carnival des Animaux', two two-man teams (pusher and player), from France and Japan, raced round the concert platform. The Japanese soloist, an ex-kamikaze pilot and digitsu (finger-fighting) master, used his specially hardened fingers to strike the notes instead of employing traditional xylophone mallets. By saving this extra weight, the Japanese team, with highly questionable race tactics, won in a photo-finish.

The second event was a roller-skating violin duet, performed by an excellent skating act from Germany. To the

'Skaters' Waltz', they whirled round the concert platform to loud applause, with the lady 'violinist's' legs clasped perilously behind her male partner's neck.

At the end of the act, the orchestra held up numbered cards in the manner of judges at the Olympic figure-skating finals. Afterwards, I learnt that the lady skater was over four months pregnant.

We concluded the first half of the concert with 'The Ride of the Valkyries'. In view of the maritime tradition that ships' musicians played while their vessel was sinking, I announced that the Musicians' Union had recently introduced new and stringent safety precautions for the protection of shipboard musicians. I finished with the words, 'Ladies and gentlemen of the Royal Philharmonic Orchestra, your life-jackets are under your seats.'

Suitably equipped, the orchestra gave a spirited performance of Wagner's music during which the stage lighting changed. Suddenly, a thunderstorm, complete with jagged lightning, burst over the platform. Sailors in oil-skins hung lifebuoys on the conductor's podium, together with port and starboard lights and large rubber life-rafts which inflated automatically. One smaller raft had to be foot-pumped, and the conductor turned towards it to set the tempo of the pumping.

The conning-tower of a German submarine, marked 'Berlin Philharmonic F U 2', now rose dramatically from a deep well at the side of the platform. The *Kapitan* emerged from the hatch and opened fire on the SS *Royal Phil*, scoring immediate, explosive hits on the brass, woodwind and percussion sections. Amid a whooping ship's siren the cry rang out, 'Abandon the Royal Albert Hall! Women musicians and child prodigies first!'

The large life-rafts were launched into the arena and the crew scrambled aboard as the U-boat crash-dived out of sight.

In the interval, an elaborate garden scene, complete with pergolas, hedges and plants, was set up at the front of the platform. When the audience returned to their seats, I told them that this was a facsimile of Queen Victoria's favourite garden retreat, where she and Prince Albert often sang duets together.

At this point, a young boxer, stripped for action, hurried down the stairs at the side of the stage, accompanied by his trainer who exhorted him to 'finish off Basher Bates in round three'.

I interrupted, 'You're *early*. Boxing is next week.'

As they exited, I introduced 'A Potpourri of English Garden Songs'. A Victorian octet, conducted by Benjamin Disraeli, played the introduction to Percy Grainger's 'Country Gardens', and Prince Albert made an impressive entrance through the garden gate. As he finished his song, he was joined by Queen Victoria, a diminutive coloratura. She first appeared behind the hedge, singing a duet with an unseen flautist. This culminated in a cascade of sparkling arpeggios, in unison with a large white dove, which was trilling away on the top of the gated pergola. As the duet reached its climax, an aged gardener, played by me, blasted the singing dove off its perch with a shotgun.

There was a roar of laughter as Prince Albert immediately segued into 'Come into the Garden, Maud', but Her Majesty was unable to accept his invitation as the garden gate had jammed shut. Without missing a note, Prince Albert nobly struggled with it until he pulled the gate right off its hinges.

The Queen entered the garden and sang 'Cherry Ripe' while watering a dwarf cherry tree, which grew exponentially as she did so. Still holding the half-full container, she joined Albert in a duet. As they turned inwards for close harmony, the royal watering-can swung across Albert's tight trousers, soaking him thoroughly.

Undaunted, the royal duettists followed this with 'The Last Rose of Summer'. Unseen by them, the gardener pushed on a barrowload of 'steaming manure', and stood in the background, spreading muck on the flower beds.

The audience yelled with delight when the royals thought the fumes were emanating from the last rose of summer, and hurriedly passed it between them. A continuous gale of laughter punctuated their stately minuet as they sang Handel's 'Where'er You Walk', and Albert led Victoria over the lawn sprinkler, just as the gardener turned it on, filling the imperial crinoline with swirling spray as the startled Queen reached her highest notes.

The audience was hysterical by the end of Ivor Novello's 'We'll Gather Lilacs in the Spring Again'. During this duet the gardener clipped the overgrown hedge, accidentally removing the heads of the newly gathered lilacs in Albert's hand. He then chopped off the back of Victoria's crinoline as Her Majesty swayed back against the hedge in Albert's arms. This exposed her 'Can-Can' knickers when the royal couple waltzed round the garden until they were run over by an out-of-control, steam-driven lawn-mower.

I conducted the orchestra for Johann Strauss's exhilarating 'Thunder and Lightning Polka'. This was the result of private rehearsals with my friend Dennis Holloway, for many years assistant musical director at Covent Garden. As I could read the percussion part of the score, and could count, the Phil and I started and finished together.

We closed the concert with Tchaikovsky's '1812' Overture, accompanied by the usual explosive effects, and the staff at the Albert Hall, who had been swept up in the general euphoria, voted it the most memorable musical finale ever performed there. Tubular bells fired volleys of blanks, tympani turned into exploding mines, a double-bass was riddled with bullet holes and was rushed off on a stretcher by roller-skating Florence Nightingales. Smoke-trailing mutes were shot out of tubas like mortars, or were launched from telescopic-sighted trombones; while, in the closing bars, clouds of dust drifted down from the ceiling when double-charged thunderflashes were fired by the over-enthusiastic stage staff.

At the end, a blizzard raged, covering the whole orchestra who never stopped playing. The audience went wild. They stood up, shouting and applauding for a full three minutes while we applauded back. I felt Gus standing beside me, and heard the deep chuckle I knew so well.

The point I am trying to make is that, utterly ridiculous though this concert might seem, by a determined effort of will I had made something positive from a tragedy. Together with my friends, I had also given a lot of pleasure to a large number of people, not least to Gus's favourite Royal Philharmonic Orchestra. The fact that people still tell me how much they enjoyed that wild and wonderful evening confirms my belief that this was the best memorial I could have given my son.

Turning the physical loss of someone you dearly love into some sort of benefit for others is something that I also managed to do after my two elder daughters, Elaine and Marylla (Fusty) died of cancer in hospital in 1984 and 1987 respectively. After each of their untimely deaths, by putting grief aside, and concentrating on making positive efforts on their behalf, I was able to help both the Royal Marsden Hospital in Chelsea and the Royal Surrey Hospital, Guildford, whose splendid nursing staffs had been so kind and so caring. I was able to assist the Marsden in getting their new CAT scanner for the early detection of cancer, and I managed to provide television sets and microwave cookers for the nursing staff at the Royal Guildford. In both cases, I considered these to be gifts from my late daughters.

The physical loss of someone you love is inevitably a sorrowful time. It would be unnatural not to grieve. But my own experiences have shown me that the sooner the survivors can release the pressures of their mental pain the better.

Among animals such as whales, elephants, dolphins or members of any other highly intelligent species, you have only to witness the piteous grief at the loss of a mate or offspring to realize that this is Nature's way of dealing with the appalling shock. The same sense of loss that humans feel in similar circumstances sweeps over the surviving animal, and the pitiable evidence of its anguish indicates that it is releasing part of the awful pressure of its grief. But the animal's will to survive quickly reasserts itself and it returns its attention to the perpetuation of its species.

In contrast, the human race has loaded society with complex rituals, full of grim funerary pomp and circumstance. These depressing rites have become a highly profitable business with costly embalming skills, over-crowded cemeteries, and expensive funeral furnishings attended by synthetic professional solemnity. Most of it is completely out of tune with Nature, and often burdens the bereaved with heavy debts.

This is a very delicate area, and I do not wish to offend anyone's beliefs, but I sometimes feel that the natural and necessary process of grief is often needlessly prolonged, and even worsened, by the gloom of ostentatious funerals.

I have laid much emphasis on Gus's death, and have seemingly attached far less importance to the subsequent deaths of my two elder daughters. This is certainly not because I love them one whit less than Gus, but because I feel that I should make the strongest protest against the appalling stress generated by the sensation-seeking media which was particularly evident in my son's case.

I believe that there should be definitive legislation to curb such criminal invasion of privacy. This Bill should be designed to protect those who are undergoing the agony of grief. The media, including television and radio, showed us no mercy whatsoever in the pursuit of sensation for the sake of swelling newspaper circulation or increasing viewing, or listening figures.

A stringent professional code of ethics exists for practitioners of advertising, so why should there not be one for the conduct of the media towards the general public?

After the deaths of both my daughters, thankfully, we were not quite so badly molested as we had been with Gus's passing. During the years of their long illnesses and great suffering, which both girls bore with extraordinary

434

and exemplary courage, they made us all feel very proud of them.

Only by being totally positive, and by giving them all the loving strength that we were capable of, were we able to be of any help. A negative attitude would have made their situation even worse.

In Elaine's case, such holistic absent healing as she received helped her psychologically, but the extensive surgery she endured in France seemed to me to have been cruel and absolutely pointless at that stage of her terminal condition. A second surgeon was so upset by it that he advised my son-in-law to take Elaine back home to die in peace, rather than let her be subjected to further surgery.

Because Fusty was accustomed to holistic healing, she received greater benefit from direct and indirect healing. In spite of this, she relapsed when the cancer spread. Her original radical surgery had not given her more than five years' respite from the relentless onslaught of cancer.

Bravery alone cannot beat terminal conditions such as these, but I am convinced that a positive attitude can often help to bring about a long-lasting remission. A number of oncologists have told me that stress figures prominently in cancer, causing pronounced acceleration in the growth of malignant tumours. The same specialists emphasized that every effort should be made, by relatives and friends of the patient, to alleviate stress factors.

During these intense periods of grief, I was fortunately able to undertake various positive projects, to continue to provide for the rest of my family and to help them to set up their own homes. In the twenty years since Gus's death I have watched my surviving children, Richard and Serena (Peski and Suki), grow into the kind of adults I hoped they would become, affectionate and kind, with strong personalities and inventive minds, both of them experts in the art of communication. Despite all the traumas that we have been through together as a family, I can honestly say that I feel very lucky indeed to have had such a wife and children.

435

Now we have grandchildren and great grandchildren. Marie-Laurence, Elaine's daughter, is married to Pierre Sinet and is the mother of William and twins Arthur and Nicholas. Elliot is the son of Richard and his wife Rebecca, who is expecting 'Harry'. All of them are lively, loving and wholly delightful. What more can a man ask?

The last twenty years have been a busy time for me professionally. While still investigating Gus's death, I presented *Golden Silents*, a BBC series of twenty-six half-hour television programmes reviewing and analysing the work of the great comedians of the silent screen. These were Keaton, Chaplin, Laurel and Hardy, Langdon, the Keystone Kops, and a host of lesser-known masters of mime and inventive slapstick comedy.

I was delighted that this series, which played all over the world in many languages, showed my deep respect for Keaton's undoubted comedy genius and helped to restore him to his rightful place as one of the top exponents of silent screen comedy.

I will never forget a night in 1973 when I presented Keaton's masterpiece, *The General*, to a packed Variety Club audience in St Helier, Jersey. My friend, Florence de Jong, the silent-movie accompanist, played piano throughout the screening. At the end of that marvellous film, the entire audience stood up and cheered for four minutes in a long-overdue tribute to the true genius of Buster Keaton. Afterwards, I sensed that the wheel had come full circle. *The General* was one of my clearest memories of early childhood, and Buster Keaton had been the main inspiration behind my decision to become a comedian in 1946.

Since then, among many performances all over the world, I have given one-man shows to Middle Eastern sheikhs and international oil-men in Doha, Dubai, Sharjah, Bahrain and Oman; I have performed before kings, queens, princes and presidents, prisoners in gaols, patients in hospitals and children everywhere.

I helped present the first and second twenty-four-hour telethons in New Zealand for sixteen hours at a stretch, from which we raised the equivalent of over a million pounds sterling for various charities, from a population of only three million people. When I returned to Britain and enthusiastically promulgated the idea of telethons to the BBC's Director General, at that time Sir Charles Curran, I was told bluntly that telethons would never work in Britain. Circumstances have proved me right.

Throughout 1990, I was proud to be asked to give my services to the Royal Air Force Benevolent Fund's fiftieth commemorative year tribute to the Battle of Britain. During this 'maximum effort', I gave many broadcasts, TV interviews, compèred an auction and fronted RAF band concerts, ending up in Hong Kong with a cabaret show before the packed audience in a large hangar situated only 500 yards from the main runway at Kai Tak Airport.

All this helped the fund-raisers to gather in over twenty million pounds to assure the continuity of the RAF's splendid work of looking after its servicemen and -women and their dependants. I believe this to have been the best memorial tribute I could have given to all my wartime comrades-in-arms who lost their lives or were disabled in our fight against tyranny.

For the past five years I have been touring Britain with my one-man show, *From the Ridiculous to the Paranormal*. These shows are a fascinating experience for me, especially at the end of my performance, when I invite the audience to join me in a question-and-answer session. Once people lose their shyness and tell me about their own encounters with the paranormal, the evening seems to take on a magical dimension.

Since 1975 I have written thirteen books, two of which, to my surprise, have been bestsellers. I devised and scripted, designed and pre-recorded over one thousand character voices in presenting over seventy *Potty Time* puppet shows, a very complex process which became the most enjoyable experience of my forty-six years in show business.

In those same years, I have used original comedy to present high-tech plastics, to demonstrate fork-lift trucks at international exhibition centres, and to front business conferences on frozen foods, computers, pharmaceuticals, automotive products, fashion shows, toy fairs, advertising campaigns, and many other contrastingly different events.

I have also lectured on the paranormal at universities and demonstrated ecologically safe techniques for developing the Upper Amazon tributaries into the world's largest emergency food-producing area. This project is intended to benefit millions of people in Third World countries who are faced with starvation owing to drought, flooding and other natural disasters, a huge global problem which faces us today and will increase in the future.

I have listed all these activities because they show that by adopting a positive attitude to the deaths of my three elder children, I have been able to utilize the extensive training in the creative art of visualization that I received from my father and other wise mentors. This enabled me to harness my imagination to a wide spectrum of practical endeavours for the benefit of many others as well as for myself. I am deeply grateful for this, as it has given me a sense of purpose and fulfilment and has helped to fill some of the vacuum that the physical loss of my much-loved children has left in my life.

I have been privileged to have been given many opportunities to witness and even to become involved in some of the extraordinary events played out on this planet during my part of the twentieth century. The fact that I have usually met these events in head-on collision is largely due to my temperament and my upbringing.

One thing is certain: in order to survive harrowing collisions with world events I have forced myself to see them from the viewpoint of a jester, however reluctant I happen to be at the time.

I agree with Kipling: a person needs to be able to

> ... meet with Triumph and Disaster
> And treat those two impostors just the same.

It is not a bad way to deal with the shock of the unexpected events of a lifetime. I still keep my cap and bells handy. I never know when I may need them.

Index

443